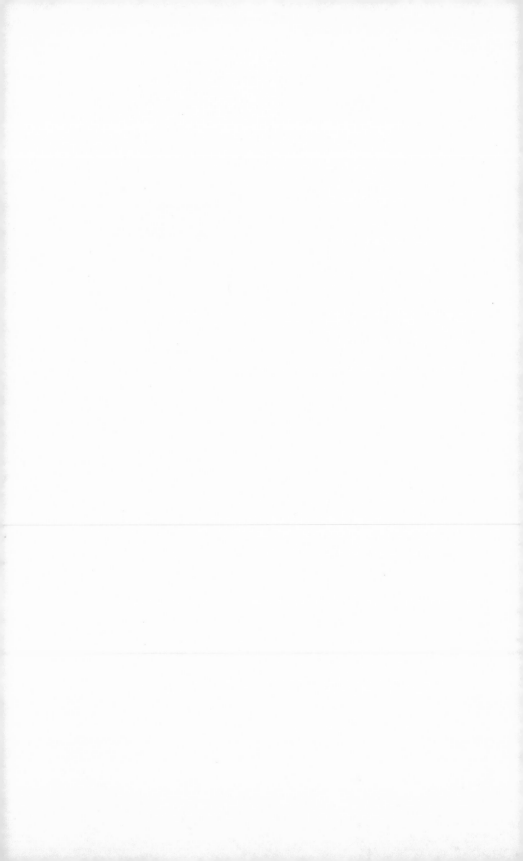

Afghanistan

Afghanistan

A Military History from the Ancient Empires to the Great Game

Ali Ahmad Jalali

 University Press of Kansas

Published by the University Press of Kansas (Lawrence, Kansas 66045), which was organized by the Kansas Board of Regents and is operated and funded by Emporia State University, Fort Hays State University, Kansas State University, Pittsburg State University, the University of Kansas, and Wichita State University.

Library of Congress Cataloging-in-Publication Data

Names: Jalali, Ali Ahmad, author.
Title: Afghanistan : a military history from the Ancient empires to the great game /
   Ali Ahmad Jalali.
Description: Lawrence, Kansas : University Press of Kansas, 2021. |
   Includes bibliographical references and index.
Identifiers: LCCN 2021003586
   ISBN 9780700632633 (cloth)
   ISBN 9780700632640 (ebook)
Subjects: LCSH: Afghanistan—History, Military.
Classification: LCC DS357.2 .J35 2021 | DDC 958.1—dc23
LC record available at https://lccn.loc.gov/2021003586.

British Library Cataloguing-in-Publication Data is available.

Printed in the United States of America

10 9 8 7 6 5 4 3 2 1

Contents

List of Maps

Foreword

Ali Ahmad Jalali is a professional soldier and politician as well as a noted scholar with an exceptionally acute analytical mind to complement his deep understanding of Afghanistan's military and political history. Already the author of accomplished works on his country—including *A Military History of Afghanistan: From the Great Game to the Global War on Terror,* the chronological sequel to this book—his *Afghanistan: A Military History from the Ancient Empires to the Great Game* is magisterial in its scope and scholarship yet highly readable to academic and lay historian alike. It is an absorbing account of a country that evokes emotion in most of us, whether because of a romantic understanding of the Great Game or as a result of more recent conflicts that have frequently dominated our television screens. Professor Jalali sheds fresh light on the Mujahedin's role in a war that contributed directly to the collapse of the Soviet Union and the rise of the Taliban before finally examining the well-intentioned but often rather clumsy attempts to ensure the Taliban do not reassert their rule in Kabul after the post-9/11 invasion.

Wars and warriors, armies and clannish fighters, foreign invasion and popular resistance all figure prominently in the long history of the land occupied by modern Afghanistan. The distinctive geography of the country has shaped its history, which is in most part a military history.

As a crossroad of conquests, Afghanistan's past is largely instilled with accounts of military developments and warfare as various armies from different areas using a multitude of different arms and tactics descended on and invaded the country. From the Persians and Greeks in antiquity to the Mongols and Turks in the medieval period to the British, Soviets, and Americans in modern times, outsiders have led military conquest into the mountains and plains of Afghanistan, leaving their indelible marks on this ancient land located at the confluence of four geographic zones.

Afghanistan is a survey of the geographic, social, and political foundations of wars as well as the social impacts of internal and external conflicts on the evolution of military organization, strategy and tactics, and arms and armed men in this multiethnic nation. The book encompasses an immense panorama of wars, conflicts, and battles spanning the full length of Afghanistan's extraordinary history from the first millenium to the Durrani Empire.

The book examines the nature and conduct of military action by different armies, with varying arms and equipment at different stages of history, offering insights into the politics and statecraft of each age, which was often decided by military exigencies. Political history has until very recent times been a narrative of military strength, hegemony, and dynamism. Yet history has witnessed powerful armies handicapped by nonmilitary factors such as terrain and hostile populations as well as their own faulty strategies and flawed tactics, let alone the impact of unanticipated adversaries. Since much of Afghanistan's history is the story of wars, battles, generals, and the common soldier, this work undoubtedly sheds much light on the tumultuous and dynamic history of the country as a whole.

No work has hitherto chronicled the vast and rich accounts of Afghanistan's military history in the comprehensive manner achieved in this work by author Jalali. A series of books and professional studies focusing on separate wars and battles have been published in the past, particularly on Anglo-Afghan wars in the nineteenth century by British authors. Recently, all published historical studies on Afghanistan either lack professional military focus or look at single wars and conflicts.

This work provides general readers of military history, as well as scholars and professionals, with the definitive history of warfare in Afghanistan. Broad in scope and based on authoritative primary sources, the book covers ancient conquerors and modern invasions with equal rigor. With its all-encompassing illustrative details and analytical features, this book deserves to become a *locus classicus* in the annals of Afghanistan's military history and of military history more generally.

David Richards
General the Lord Richards of Herstmonceux GCB, CBE, DSO

Preface and Acknowledgments

This volume is a prequel to my previously published *A Military History of Afghanistan: From the Great Game to the Global War on Terror* (2017) and covers the military history of Afghanistan over twenty-five hundred years—from the ancient empires up until the Great Game in the nineteenth century. It is a forerunner to the modern history of the land, which is basically shaped by its pre-modern military experience and influenced by different waves of military invasions from the outside—often as distant as Greece, Rome, or deep Eurasian steppes and Mongolia. The many military incursions into Afghanistan from the Assyrians, Persians, and Greeks in antiquity to the Mongols and Turks of the medieval period have left their unique and indelible mark on this ancient land and shaped the modern history of the country. In these pages we will look at events distant in time but with deep influence on current life.

Although there has been a lot of interest in studying the region's modern history which has been widely published, there is no comprehensive work published on the centuries-old military experience of the region up to the Europeans' colonialism epitomized by the romanticism of the Great Game. Armies commanded by Cyrus the Great, Alexander the Great, the Muslim conquerors, Chinggis Khan, Tamerlane and Babur and their feats in Afghanistan campaigns have greatly enriched the military history of the region and of the world in general. It was at the apex of this period when the Afghans founded their modern state and a vast empire under Ahmad Shah Durrani, which shaped the environment for the Great Game in the nineteenth century.

This work on the military history of Afghanistan from the ancient empires to the Great Game is the culmination of my research and work on the military history of Afghanistan that began over four decades ago. This has been both a labor of love as well as what I perceive, and hope will be a critical work at a time when the country has been the focal point for the international war on terrorism and accompanying military efforts.

Based overwhelmingly on primary and modern sources for each period, it is a full account of Afghanistan's military history from ancient times to the modern wars. The motivation for writing this book is to make accessible to researchers, scholars, educators, and policy makers as well as for the general public, a work that will help to explain and elucidate the many factors for the country's turbulent past and more recent problems within the context of its military and political dynamics. It is targeted toward the trained specialist as well as the lay reader.

In completing this task, I am grateful to many whose support and assistance was indispensable. I would like to thank those individual Afghans who throughout the years added significantly to my own knowledge and experience of Afghan military history. By sharing their personal stories and experiences during the course of my military career in the Afghan army in the 1960s and 1970s, while serving in the anti-Soviet resistance of the 1980s, during my stint as a cabinet minister of the post-Taliban Afghan government and afterward, they have enriched this work. While this list of individuals is too long to mention, they know who they are, and I thank them wholeheartedly.

I am deeply grateful to my long-time colleague, co-author in previous works, and friend, Dr. Lester Grau for painstakingly reading the manuscript and offering valuable comments and editorial suggestions. I am also greatly indebted to US Army Reserve officer Dr. Charles Bartles for his remarkable assistance with the battle maps. Chuck was extremely generous with his time and effort to improve my original sketches into high quality professional maps that are published in the book. This could not be done without his help.

Finally, it was the love and support of my family that sustained my energy and allowed me to finish this massive work in a timely manner. I am especially grateful to my wife and partner of forty-five years, Homaira, for her patience and endless encouragement even when she had to endure long hours of being alone while I was engaged in this work. I would like to thank my children, Wais and Bahar, for their love and enthusiastic support of my career. Finally, I dedicate this work to the new generation of my family, my grandchildren—Sophia, Dean, Noah, Alexandra, and Roxana Bahar Jalali.

Afghanistan

Introduction

This book looks at events distant in time but with deep influence on current life. A study of ancient and medieval military history of Afghanistan in a wider regional context is both interesting and edifying to better understanding of military developments in modern times.

In the past twenty-five hundred years, the history of the lands encompassing today's Afghanistan is tortuously linked to the history of West, Central, and South Asia. Afghanistan's identity as a state is based less on geography and more on history. The country and its geographic peripheries have been absorbed into larger military confrontation in the wider region. Throughout its long history, the country has served as the buffer between expanding empires or as the collision space between competing regional powers. Major armies crisscrossed the mountainous country from north to south and from west to east. The many military incursions into Afghanistan by the Assyrians, Persians, and Greeks in antiquity to the Mongols and Turks of the medieval period have left their unique and indelible mark on this ancient land and shaped the modern history of the country.

The territory of today's Afghanistan overlaps the boundaries of all these regions and is thus part of each one. It represents one of the definite geopolitical fault lines in the world and is constantly exposed to the dynamics of changing geopolitics in the region. Afghanistan has had open borders with the regional states that rose to power in the course of history in Central Asia, Persia, and India. This placed Afghanistan between all these three regions. This peripheral status has been characterized by two unique attributes in the past. On the one hand, it often turned Afghanistan into the battlefield of competing regional powers that clashed on their geographic edges. On the other hand, this outlying position contributed to weaker control by the imperial centers and helped the land to become independent as their central influence declined. Furthermore, the people of modern Afghanistan were not passive spectators but often fought the invaders and took advantage of their unique location to invade adjacent lands in Central Asia, India, and Persia that resulted in the establishment of vast empires centered in today's territory of Afghanistan.

Consequently, the history of Afghanistan is strongly influenced by the dynamics of its peripheral status between major regional centers of power and the impact of its location on the geopolitical fault line astride West, Central, and South Asia. The history of Afghanistan in general and its military history particularly should be studied in this context. Given the varying geohistorical features of these regions, strategic opportunities opened to Afghanistan, and its vulnerabilities to outside powers have been of a varying, divergent, and changing nature. Historically, Afghanistan has been vulnerable to invasions from the north and impervious to attacks from the east. The situation forced Afghanistan to defend in the north and take advantage of its favored geographic position in the east to overrun areas in the Indian subcontinent. To the west, the military situation changed by shifts in the balance of power within the greater Iranian plateau.

These trends are exemplified during military exploits throughout history. In the sixth to fourth centuries BC, Afghanistan was on the northeastern periphery of the Persian Empire under the Achaemenids. During this period the center usually kept an unsteady control over the eastern satrapies (areas overseen by a satrap, or provincial governor), particularly when the imperial armies were preoccupied in the west or elsewhere.[1] Alexander the Great is said to have encountered no Achaemenid-appointed satraps in the Hindu Kush and Gandhara Valley on his way to conquer India.[2] Less than eighty years after the death of Alexander in 323 BC, and the vast empire he had built was quickly unraveled, Afghanistan territory became the bone of contention between competing powers of the Maurya Empire of India and the Seleucid Empire of Syria. But the remoteness of the land from the imperial centers of gravity facilitated the independence movement in Afghanistan, and in 250 BC it emerged as the center of the Greco-Bactrian Empire, the limits of which eventually stretched from Central Asia to northern India. The Greco-Bactrians were succeeded by the Kushan Empire (first–third centuries AD) and later the Ephthalite Empire (fifth–sixth centuries) that ruled over a vast area from Central Asia to northern India. These Afghanistan-centered states were inevitably drawn into regional competition for power with the Sassanids of Persia and the Western Turks in Central Asia.

During the Islamic era, Afghanistan evolved into one of the main centers of the Muslim world and a cradle of Islamic civilizations. Using Islam as the religion of power, local dynasties (Saffarids, Samanids, Ghaznavids, and Ghorids) expanded their power into Central Asia and India in the tenth–twelfth centuries and Islamized many non-Muslim areas in the region. The Mongol and Turk invasions in the thirteenth–fifteenth centuries forced Afghanistan once again into a peripheral state, first between the Chaghatay khanate of Central Asia and the Ilkhanids of Iran, and later between the Mughal Empire of India, the Safavids of Iran, and the Uzbek khanate of Central Asia. In the second half of the eighteenth century, Ahmad Shah Durrani, the founder of modern Afghanistan, restored the centrality of regional power to Afghanistan by establishing control of government over the entire present-day Afghanistan, Pakistan, and parts of eastern Iran and stretched the rule of the empire to northern India as far as Delhi. But in the nineteenth century, the Afghan Empire came under threat first by the Persians in the west and the Sikhs in the east and later by the European imperial powers. The "Great Game" competition between the British and Russian Empires over control of Central Asia turned Afghanistan first into a battleground and then into a "buffer state" to block military clashes between imperial Russia and British India. Afghanistan played that role but was forced to fight both powers as the twentieth century wore on.

Over the past three millenniums, Central Asia, the Middle East, and South Asia have been the vortex of numerous military conquests that facilitated exchange of military culture and technology in Asia and also influenced military developments far beyond this region. The unceasing competition for supremacy by the dominant powers in the region not only led to constant clashes among the rival armies but also resulted in the exchange of military culture. Consequently, different warring states and armies learned from their experiences and adapted the best practices demonstrated by various militaries on the battlefield. From the heavy infantry of the Macedonians to the fast-moving, lightly armed nomadic mounted archers, a wide variety of military skills were demonstrated in centuries-long confrontations.

The experience covered all forms of military science, including force structure, battle formations, weapons and equipment, and combat tactics. The process disseminated the Grecian culture of heavy infantry (the *phalanx*) to the east as far as India, as well as the employment of heavily armed cavalry (the *cataphract*) from Asia to Rome.

One of the major areas of military cultural exchange was the balance between the light and heavy forces that was so aptly configured in Alexander's army. The Greco-Persian Wars since the fifth century BC and Alexander's victories proved that lightly armed troops could not stop heavy and well-trained infantry such as the Greek hoplites and phalanx. Such forces could be met only with heavily armed and highly professional cavalry causing disorder in the massed ranks and then by attacking them at vulnerable points with arrows and missiles, capable of piercing armor, and lances, effective against shields. This lesson was learned and implemented by the Parthians in the second and first centuries BC in fighting the Seleucids Greeks in Persia. They also learned from the armament, tactics, and strategy of the Romans.

Meanwhile, similar cross-adaption of weapons and war machines took place across the region. The Macedonians' introduction and use of siege engines such as catapults and siege towers were initially alien to Parthians, but they adapted to their use as they expanded to the west and faced the Romans. The Romans, too, subsequently improved the quality and technology of siege equipment and introduced and improved heavily armed cavalry. The reputed skills of the Scythian archers captured the attention of many armies, and Scythian mounted archers were widely employed as mercenaries.

In Afghanistan, like everywhere else, people have their distinctive assumptions, perceptions, and preferences that may underpin their way of war. But they transform over time and are subject to ideological, economic, political, and environmental changes. Although for the past thirteen centuries Islam has been an important ideological and cultural element in the Afghans' approaches to warfare, its implementation has been strongly influenced by political and social conditions.

Mapping the military culture of the people living in modern Afghanistan and their different approaches to war at different stages of history requires a review of the state's relationship to society; the social, political, and economic drivers that motivated state armies, tribal levies, and community militias to fight; and the factors that shaped their modes of war. A review of the evolution of the military institutions and their role in politics and social development is essential to this study.

The nature of the military forces that emerged and operated on the Afghanistan political scene throughout history has been conditioned by the makeup of the state-society relationship and the dynamics of projecting power within a changing environment. Imperial and dynastic rulers often administered major urban areas and highways through direct control and maintained nominal sovereignty in marginal areas. These included hard-to-reach places and remote tribal societies where they left the local leaders in control. Society remained segmented and immobilized. The lack of integration made the communities, particularly in tribal areas, semi-independent, mostly relying on their own resources and their own traditional institutions. This included local military forces that were mobilized during intertribal conflicts or foreign threats. The tribal militias also could be mustered in support of or against the central government during domestic disturbances. This nation-in-arms status provided for the rise of local and tribal leaders and nonstate armed groups when the central government collapsed or the state army disintegrated in the face of foreign invasion or dynastic upheavals.

Thus, there were varied military institutions created and nurtured by dynasties, empires, tribes, and communities to achieve their distinctive goals and secure their interests. From very ancient times state armies existed, as did public military forces in areas not fully governed by the state. The state army was the instrument of dynastic power, whereas the public military was part of political and social institutions of tribes and other communities that had to depend on their own resources for local security, which was rarely provided by the sovereign prince. The tribal levies and local militia were also essential for supporting local interests in a volatile and competing environment.

As a result of these patterns, few state armies in premodern Afghanistan successfully monopolized the use of force. Generally, the state army was not the only military institution within a social system imbued with military pluralism. The rulers usually relied on a smaller standing army of well-trained and loyal soldiers intricately linked to them in addition to larger contingents provided by satraps, local governors, and tribal leaders. These contingents gathered when needed to fight rival powers, conquer other lands, and crush domestic rebellions. Meanwhile, a cycle of constant rise and fall of ruling dynasties and the dominance of an unstable security environment reinforced a state of localism in political, social, and military life. While state armies focused on dynastic interests, nonstate local groups and factions with paramilitary capacity emerged to secure local interests and sometimes acted independently as sources of local resistance.

The "armed nation" concept dominated the Avestan age in Bactria when the nation at the same time was the army, obliging every able-bodied male adult to serve when needed. This concept was drastically transformed during the imperial period into a system of state armies supplemented by local militias and professional mercenaries. The Achaemenid army's core element consisted of regular Persian and Median troops that were augmented by the contingents contributed by subject nations and hired Greek mercenaries. This system was emulated by successive empires and dynasties including the Parthian (247 BC–224 AD) and Sassanid (224–651 AD). As the Parthian Empire was less centralized, it maintained a small standing army consisting of Parthian skilled warriors, the backbone of which consisted of the Iranians themselves. The imperial military structure was conditioned by the feudal system in which regional tribal lords and garrison commanders would join the imperial army with their designated-size levies at the appointed place when the need arose. The Sassanids built a well-trained standing army by restoring the Achaemenid military organizations and retaining Parthian heavy cavalry (*cataphract*). The military system gradually developed in parallel to the Roman model, making both militaries mostly identical by the sixth century. However, the Sassanid imperial army extensively employed, as allies or mercenaries, troops from warlike tribes who fought under their own chiefs.

The nomadic hordes that descended in successive waves from the Eurasian steppes on the sedentary areas in the south between the second century BC and fifth century AD were not an exception. Their unified military machine, based on tribal solidarity, failed to survive the dynastic power struggle and decentralization of the military forces as they established the Kushan, Saka, and Ephthalite Empires in wider regions in Central and South Asia.

The dynasties that rose to power in Afghanistan and adjacent areas during the Islamic period (seventh–thirteenth centuries AD) either grew up from local principalities (Saffarids, Samanids, and Ghorids) or developed from the military dominance of Turkic people of Central Asia (Ghaznavids, Seljuqs, and Khwarazmids). In both cases the dynasties reigned and expanded in a highly impulsive and competing environment. Under such conditions, survival necessitated constant growth, and growth required keeping and sustaining formidable military forces that were expensive. The rulers could neither afford to maintain large regular armies nor rely too much on the loyalty of tribal contingents provided by feudal lords and subject governors. Consequently, all dynasties kept a mixed force of a standing army closely attached to the ruler plus a larger irregular army composed of different tribal militias mobilized during the war.

The core of the Muslim dynasties' army in the middle ages was the slave force (*ghulaman, Kashagan, mamalik*), which played important roles in securing the throne and fighting wars. The significance of the corps of slaves was its close attachment to the king through personal bonds. The slaves were displaced people with no roots or local connections. Their lives were very much dependent on the fate of the rulers they were serving. Most of them were of Turkic origin, hired or brought at a young age from Central Asia and raised to serve and trained to fight. They were a counterbalance to the tribal-based contingents whose loyalty was not always trusted. This system of slave armies was institutionalized throughout the Islamic world from North Africa to India. According to Nizam ul-Mulk, the Abbasid caliph al-Mu'tasim (833–851) had 70,000 Turkic slaves in his army, many of whom reached the high command rank of amir.

While all these military forces served dynastic interests, they hardly touched the local communities in a positive way. Dynastic wars and foreign conquests meant higher taxes for the citizenry as well as providing supplies for the army, which often lived off the land. The state was usually unable or unwilling to create a wide network of institutions with the broader participation of different segments of the population. This lack of participation in the state made the social communities at the subnational level semi-independent of the state and mostly reliant on their own resources and their own traditional institutions. This gave a self-governing and self-sufficient character to social communities. The basic unit of social structure was the *qawm*, which literally means "tribe" but is a more kaleidoscopic term referring to any form of solidarity group or what the Arab philosopher of the fourteenth century, Ibn Khaldun, called *assabiyya*, or instinctive social cohesiveness. The *qawm* affiliation in Afghanistan has existed for centuries as the basic subnational identity based on kinship, residence, and sometimes occupation. It includes tribal clans, locality-based groups, ethnic subgroups, religious sects, or any other grouping united by a community of interests, beliefs, kinship, and place of living.

In general, Afghanistan's military history is shaped mostly by three unique features: a distinct geography unsuitable for large invading armies and difficult to sustain logistically; the decentralized sociopolitical order of self-relying local communities; and the multiplicity of military institutions within a social system imbued with military pluralism. Under such a sociopolitical setup, few state armies in the past successfully monopolized the use of force. The state military establishment was involved mainly in protecting the state, while local community militias and the people at large defended their lands and social values against foreign and internal incursions. This created a potential to wage thousands of wars in villages and towns when needed.

Gaining a reasonably clear picture of military events that took place centuries and millenniums ago is not easy. The task is challenging particularly when it pertains to the number of troops in wars and other military actions. Many contemporary sources are either biased or lacked access to reliable sources or are often inclined to inflate numbers of troops in a war, especially those of the enemy, for propagandist purposes. Muslim chroniclers of the thirteenth century reported that Chinggis Khan led an army of 600,000 to 700,000 troops to invade Central Asia and Khorasan in 1219–1223,[3] whereas the population of the Mongols at the time hardly exceeded one million. In the eighteenth century, at the battle of Panipat (1761), Ahmad Shah Durrani put the number of enemy troops at more than a million.[4] Given the demography, logistics, and topography of the battlefield, such figures are extremely inflated. The real numbers may have been ten times lower than the reported ones.

Finally, the premodern armies often lived off the land as they lacked supply lines, and therefore their movement was dictated by local logistics considerations. Armies larger than 30,000 faced enormous logistical challenges. The larger the size of the army, the wider were the impediments in its operation. Applying the usual yardsticks, in arid lands an army of 30,000 troops with one-third cavalry plus one-third followers would need 120 tons of grain and 55 tons of forage daily. To carry such a daily load would require nearly 1,000 pack animals. The tonnage of the baggage needed for long periods of operation by such an army could have become exponential. Furthermore, a large army would need to take a significantly longer time in movement by stages, where a normal daily rate of march could hardly exceed 10–12 miles. To approximate the real numbers of troops, their rate of daily advance and operation requires a close look at the demographical, logistics, and topography considerations as well as the economy of the theater of operation. This is the challenge in verifying what really happened in the distant past.

1   A Geographic Overview

Geography is a defining factor in Afghanistan's military history. The country's location and its topography had a profound impact on the course of events and the nature of military movements in and around the land occupied by today's Afghanistan. Geography also influenced social and cultural developments in the country, with important political consequences. Located at the confluence of four main regions in Asia, Afghanistan has been entwined in unrelenting wars and conflicts throughout its turbulent history. Outside conquerors advancing their imperial ambitions, competing regional powers clashing on their geographic edges, and violent reactions by indigenous highlanders to outside incursions kept the people living in Afghanistan in a constant struggle for survival. At times, Afghanistan itself became the hub of powerful empires with easy access to neighboring regions for military conquests.

In Afghanistan, as elsewhere, the geography has not been merely a static space where the time-bound history was played out. The mutability and vicissitudes of history altered the stark reality of geography while the geography, for its part, adjusted the course of history. Political, social, and cultural shifts transfigured the geographic landscape while the geopolitics of regional powers and forces from beyond the region often accentuated the impact of geography on history. Ancient conquerors, whether they came from the north—such as Aryans (second millennium BC), Kushans (first century AD), Ephthalites (fifth century), Turks and Mongols (tenth–fifteenth centuries)—or ventured from the west—such as Achaemenids (sixth–fifth centuries BC), Alexander the Great (330–327 BC), and Arabs (seventh–ninth centuries)—all used Afghanistan as the gateway to India. Before the discovery and use of sea routes to India, the subcontinent was well protected in the north by the Himalayan Massif and in the south by the Arabian Sea. Access to the region was limited mostly to major mountain valleys and passes in the west that passed through the hilly terrain of Afghanistan.

In the fifteenth century, with the discovery and use by European pow-

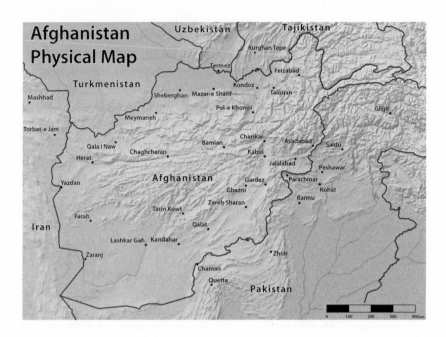

ers of the sea routes, the gates of India, in the word of Thomas Holdich, became "Watergates," and the way to India was by way of the sea.[1] Sea transport diminished the attraction of previously well-beaten land routes that brought to the subcontinent Aryans from the north and conquerors from the west. Later, with the rise of the so-called gunpowder empires in the region, the Mughal Empire in India looked at Afghanistan as India's gateway to the outside world. Abul Fazl-i-'Allami (1551–1602), the leading court chronicler of the Mughal emperor Jalaluddin Akbar (1542–1605), wrote that "Kabul and Kandahar are considered two gates of India. The former provides access to Central Asia and the latter to Iran. . . . Both facilitate links to the outside world."[2]

Centuries later, during the ferocious strategic competition among the European powers in Central Asia, British-controlled India was threatened by Napoleonic France and Tsarist Russia. The rush to rediscover the land routes to India through Afghanistan intensified. Once again, geography exerted strong influence on the course of history by defining its consequences. This time, Afghanistan became the forward line of defense for the British Indian territories. Facing the potential threats from the west, the geography of land-gates to India dictated the deployment of British military forces on the Indian subcontinent. The Khyber Pass gate in the northeast of Afghanistan and the Bolan Pass gate in the south were the two major highways leading to the British dominions in India. During most of the British rule in India, the territorial military forces were deployed along two major strategic axes: the Bengal army was based along the northern axis to include the key locations of Calcutta, Allahabad, Delhi, Lahore, and Peshawar facing the Khyber Gate; and the Bombay army deployed on the southern axis along the line of Madras, Bombay, Sind, Bolan, and Quetta facing the Bolan Gate. The latter axis could also be reinforced through sea routes from the port of Karachi.

The geographic influence in Afghanistan has internal and external dimensions. Internally, the topographic nature of the land exerts political, military, and social influences. The country's physical structure comprises rugged mountains in the center and plains in the north and southwest. The northern plains gradually slope down toward the Amu Darya River and merge into the plains of Turkmenistan, while the western and southwestern plateaus and deserts join those of Iran. The northern and western plains that cover ancient Bactria are the most fertile regions and are well populated. In the south, population centers are spread mostly along basins of the Kabul and Helmand Rivers.

The climate of the Hindu Kush influences the political, social, and economic development of the land. Communities are isolated by geography and climate. The average annual precipitation is 313mm (12 inches)—one-third of the world average. Scarcity of water has forced people to live where water is available, spreading people over widely separated small areas. The distance and remoteness of habitable areas limit contacts between people and force local communities to become self-reliant. The impulse of self-reliance drives societies to limit themselves to a sustenance economy, with little prospect for surplus production to be marketed elsewhere. The situation is visible particularly in mountainous areas where people have been pushed into the inaccessible folds of the Hindu Kush by conquering armies who dominated the lowlands. The social, economic, and political history of the highlanders is significantly shaped by geography. Many remote valleys, from Nejrao to Upper Laghman, Nuristan, and Panjsher and from Keran-o-Munjan to Farkhar, are museums of unique ethnicities that have retained many of their original customs and traditions. The lack of access roads, poor communication, and severe climate have isolated these areas from the neighboring provinces and from one another. While the impregnability of the mountainous country has dissuaded or frustrated outside military incursions, the number of competing communities and parochial social attitudes have impeded mass mobilization of the people for common causes. This has been exploited constantly by outside powers to dominate the difficult territory. Many conquerors faced fierce resistance from local people who used the harsh physical nature of their homeland to their advantage. However, the invaders exploited the social and political differences in the area. Negotiations and political deals became a more effective means of dominance than weaponry. In 327 BC, Alexander the Great fought, negotiated peace, and even recruited combatants during his military operations in the area.[3]

The immense Hindu Kush mountain chain played a pivotal role in shaping the region's history. Its influence parallels the effect of the Alps in Central Europe. Both massifs have often defined political and cultural frontiers between communities living on opposite sides of the highlands. The Hindu Kush marks a cultural watershed between northern and southern expanses in the region, with the north having closer cultural affinities with Central Asia and the south with the Indian subcontinent and Iran. This is like one of the great cultural frontiers of Europe between the cultural sphere of the Mediterranean and the transalpine cultures to the north drawn by the eastern Alps. Both chains are identified with great conquerors who successfully led massive armies across the rugged mountain passes. The feat of Alexander the Great, who crossed the Hindu Kush in the cold weather of early spring of 329 BC, has been exalted by military historians much like Hannibal's passage through the Alps in the late fall of 218 BC.

The Hindu Kush as a geographical feature has exerted exceptional sway over events in Central and South Asia. The intertwined mountain ridges channeled military columns and commercial caravans through distinct tracts and corridors. The restrictions affected all kinds of traffic moving from west to east and from north to south and produced two distinctive patterns. In the first pattern, large movements from the west heading east were forced to branch off to the north and south of the central massif. The northern branches were directed toward northern Afghanistan (ancient Bactria) and the trans-Oxus region. The southern branch moved through Sistan and Kandahar to Sind and southern India or through Kabul and the Khyber Pass to northern India. The two divergent axes occasionally converged and linked up at the north–south passes of the Hindu Kush.

The second pattern involved north–south movements that were restricted to a network of mountain passes across the Hindu Kush. In spite of the hurdles associated with rugged terrain and harsh climate during most of the year, the barriers failed to deter armies, trade caravans, migrants, refugees, religious proselytizers, and other travelers from moving back and forth between the north and south. The centuries-old links between Central Asia and South Asia, grounded in political, social, and economic interaction, have been too strong and deep to be blocked by the terrain. Few powers survived in this geographic location unless they controlled the Hindu Kush passes. Cultural and political ties between the peoples of South Asia and Central Asia trace back to ancient times. The two-way exchange of ideas and military conquests resulted in mutual cultural and political influence. The changing correlation of political and military forces and the dynamics of geopolitical conditions also shaped the long history of interaction between the two regions. In general terms, while southward incursions were mostly of a military nature—typified in raids by the mounted warriors of the steppes including the Scythians, Kushans, Ephthalites, Turks, and Mongols—the northward influence was predominantly of a cultural nature such as the spread of Zoroastrianism, Buddhism, Manichaeism, and Islam.

The territory of today's Afghanistan straddles the geographic boundaries of three main regions. It encompasses the converging space and dividing verges of Central Asia, the Middle East, and South Asia with historical connections to China. Its identity as a state is based less on geography and more on history. Throughout its long history, the country has served as the buffer between expanding empires or the collision space between competing regional powers.

Afghanistan contains the key strategic lands of the ancient Ariana, an extensive geographic area between Persia and the Indian subcontinent. "Ariana" means the "land of Aryans" and has its roots in Zoroastrianism's Avesta. It is also believed that the designation is the Greek name for greater Iran, which covered a far wider expanse than today's Iran—the name adopted for Persia by the Pahlavi dynasty in 1935. The limits of Ariana are not exactly defined by ancient geographers. Ariana is not mentioned by the Greek historian Herodotus (484–425 BC) or the geographer Ptolemy (90–168 AD). But the Greek geographer Eratosthenes (276–194 BC), known for being the inventor of the first map of the world based on the available geographic knowledge of his time, identifies a large territory named Ariana, which he placed between Mesopotamia and India. He defined the Indus River as the eastern border of Ariana while it was bounded to the north by what he called the Tauros Mountains.[4] The southern border of Eratosthenes's Ariana was formed by the sea while its western limits included the lands between Carmania and the Caspian Sea.[5] But Eratosthenes noted that the name "Ariana" was extended to a certain part of Persia and Media as well as to the Bactria and Soghdiana to the north who speak roughly the same language.[6]

Later, the prominent Greek geographer Strabo (64 BC–24 AD) and Roman author Pliny (23–78 AD) defined the boundaries of Ariana with certain clarity.[7] Strabo describes its eastern boundary as the Indus River and its southern boundary as the Indian Ocean from the mouth of the Indus to the Persian Gulf. The western limit of Ariana is identified in two different ways: In one case it is marked by a line drawn between the Caspian Sea to Carmania (Kerman); and in another case the boundary is described as a line separating Parthia from Media and Carmania from Persia that includes the whole of Yazd and Kerman but excludes Fars.[8] The northern boundary is the Paropamisus Mountains (Hindu Kush), which is the continuation of the massif that forms the northern limit of India. However, Strabo includes some of the eastern Persians, the Bactrians, and Soghdians as part of the people of Ariana living in the north of the mountains apparently because of the affinity of their language. Therefore, Ariana is said to have comprised the provinces of Parthia (the country between Herat and the Caspian), Aria (Herat), Carmania (Kerman), Bactria (Balkh), Margiana (Murgab-Merv), Hyrcania (Gorgan), Drangiana (Sistan), Gedrosia (Makran), Arachosia (greater Kandahar), and Paropamisus Mountain (Hindu Kush).[9] This includes the eastern extremities of the Iranian plateau, the entire modern-day Afghanistan, east and south of Iran, Tajikistan, parts of Uzbekistan, Turkmenistan, and northwestern Pakistan.

During the Islamic period, Afghanistan was the essential part of Khorasan, a variously defined area located east and northeast of the Kevir Desert in eastern Iran covering northern Afghanistan and parts of Central Asia. The space has been differently defined in terms of geography, administrative divisions, and cultural affinities of the people living there. Geographically, Khorasan covered the area bounded by the Oxus River to the north, the Kevir Desert in central-eastern Persia to the west, and the Hindu Kush Mountains to the south. It was an area with four main provincial centers: Balkh, Merv, Herat, and Nishapur. Administratively, Khorasan boundaries surpassed its geographic space and extended to the north to Transoxiana between the Oxus and Jaxartes Rivers, with Samarkand and Bukhara its major cities; and to the south to the area south of Hindu Kush encompassing Sistan, Zabulistan, and Kabulistan,

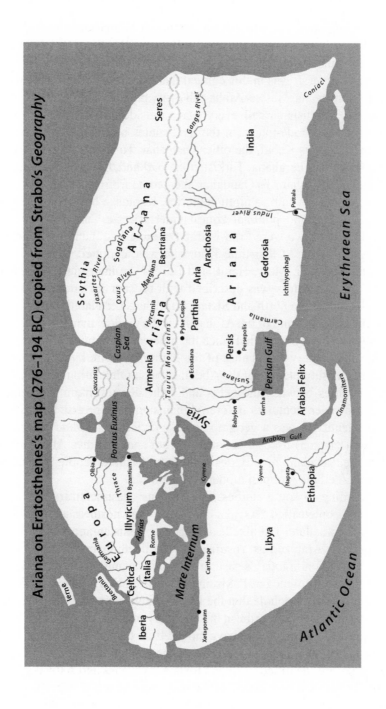

Ariana on Eratosthenes's map (276–194 BC) copied from Strabo's *Geography*

which geographically was considered the Indian borderland.[10] Culturally, Khorasan covered even a much larger area where the inhabitants shared distinctive cultural affinities and extended from eastern Persia to the Indus River. It was in this context that Babur wrote in the early sixteenth century that "just as Arabs call every place outside Arab (Arabia) *Ajam*, so Hindustanis call every place outside Hindustan, Khorasan. There are two trade-marts on the land routes between Hindustan and Khorasan; one is Kabul, the other Qandahar. To Kabul caravans come from Kashghar, Ferghana, Turkistan, Samarkand, Bukhara, Balkh, Hissar, and Badakhshan. To Qandahar, they come from Khorasan."[11]

During the seventh to ninth centuries, Khorasan became one of the three strategic and political zones under Islamic Caliphate domination. The other two were Eraq-i-Arab ("Arabic Iraq") and Eraq-i-Ajam ("Persian Iraq"). At that time Khorasan was identified with four key centers: Nishapur, Merv, Herat, and Balkh.[12] In later times the extent of Khorasan territory was described with broader parameters to cover Transoxiana in the north and Sistan, Kandahar, and Kabul in the south.

Afghanistan ("land of the Afghans") is the modern name of the country internationally identified since the nineteenth century following the eighteenth-century foundation of the Durrani Empire by Ahmad Shah Abdali, a Pashtun leader of the Abdali tribal confederation, who unified the territories between the Oxus and Indus Rivers into a multiethnic state. However, centuries before Afghanistan became a state with political identity, it was a geographic designation of the land where the Afghan (Pashtun) tribes were settled from ancient times. Historically, the name "Afghan" mainly designated the Pashtun people, which are the largest ethnic group in modern Afghanistan.

According to some studies, the Afghans (Pashtuns) are identified with the people called "Asvaka" in Sanskrit, also known as Ashvakan. The name was later Latinized as Assacenii, Assaceni, or Aspasioi (*yusapzai*, later Arabized as Yusufzai?), who lived during Alexander the Great's invasion in today's eastern Afghanistan and the current Khyber Pashtunkhwa Province of Pakistan.[13] They are linked to the Kambojas. Modern studies conclude that the Kambojas were an Avestan-speaking eastern Iranian militant tribe at the boundary of the Indo-Aryans and the Iranians, and they appear to have moved from the Iranian into the Indo-Aryan sphere over time. In reference to the equestrian nature of their society, they are identified in Indian texts Ashvayanas and Ashvakayanas from the Sanskrit root word *ashva*, meaning "horse."[14] Pactyan is one of the nations Herodotus lists as in the army of Xerxes (r. 486–465 BC) along with the infantry and cavalry of Bactria, Aria, Arachosia, and Gandhara.[15] Some studies associate the Herodotus "Pactyans" with the Pashtuns.

Afghans as a distinct people were mentioned as Abagan and Apakan in the third-century inscription of the Naqsh-i-Rustam Temple in Shiraz, Iran, engraved during the rule of the Sassanid emperors Shahpur I (242–272) and Shahpur III (309–379).[16] In a sixth-century study titled *Brhat-Samhita*, written by the Indian astronomer Varaha Mihira, Avagana (Afghana) as a people and as a land are recorded in several passages.[17] A century later, the Chinese pilgrim Hieun-Tsang, who traveled in South and Central Asia in the years 629–645, indicated that, on his return journey from India, after crossing the Indus in the modern Sind Province, he traveled northwest across the mountainous territory to what he called "A-Po-Kan" (Afghan), and from there he traveled northwest to Tsao-Ka-Pa (Arachosia) or Tsao-Li (Zawoli?) with its capital named Ho-Si-Na (Ghazna). It seems the territory had encompassed the Gomal Valley and the Afghan Paktia and Paktika Provinces extending to Ghazni (Ho-Si-Na), Zabul, and Kandahar. Then he turned north to the Kabul Valley and traveled across the Hindu Kush through the Khawak Pass to Andarab.[18] Further, in a description of the countries in the region, Hieun-Tsang records a mountainous principality of "In-Po-Kien" or "A-Po-Kien" located about 200 *li* (about 100 kilometers) southeast of Badasthana (here meaning Badakhshan).[19]

The tenth-century anonymous Muslim author of *Hudud al-'Alam* speaks, in several passages, of a people called "Afghans" who lived near Gardez and in the Nangrahar area.[20] Abu Rayhan al-Biruni (973–1048), an eleventh-century Muslim scholar and polymath, referred to the Afghans as people of various tribes living on the western frontier mountains of the Indus River,[21] while the fourteenth-century Moroccan traveler Ibn Battuta, who visited the region in 1333, wrote that Afghans are living even in Kabul and "they hold mountains and defiles and possess considerable strength and are mostly highwaymen. Their principle mountain is called Koh Suleiman (Suleiman Mountain)."[22]

"Afghanistan" as a geographic name is cited in Islamic sources at least since the fourteenth century.[23] This area has been defined as the territories between the Indus River and the Hindu Kush Mountains, with its center at the Suleiman Mountains in the southeast of modern Afghanistan. In the sixteenth century, Babur, founder of the Mughal Empire in India, and his descendants referred to the traditional ethnic Pashtun territories between the Hindu Kush Mountains and the Indus

River. In the nineteenth century, Afghanistan rulers adopted the name "Afghanistan" for the entire Afghan Empire after it was used in various treaties between British India and the Qajarid dynasty of Persia. Afghanistan as the official name of the state was internationally recognized before it was commonly used in all parts of the country. According to the nineteenth-century British author Henry Bellew, Afghanistan was understood as a land bounded on the east by the Indus River from Gilgit to the Indian Sea, on the south by the Arabian Sea, on the west by the Persian Kerman and Khorasan, and on the north by the Oxus River (Amu Darya). "The name Afghanistan, as applied to the region thus defined," he wrote, "is not commonly known, or so used by the people of the country itself, either in whole or in part. It is the name given to the whole region in a general way by its neighbors and by foreigners from the appellation of the dominant people inhabiting the country and appears to have originated with the Persians in modern times only."[24] Actually, the recognition of Afghanistan as the name of the state is rooted in the unification of the territories between the Oxus and Indus under the Durrani Empire in the middle of the eighteenth century.

2 The Early History of Afghanistan

Migrations, Displacements, and the Struggle
for Domination

There is little accurate knowledge about the early
history of the people living in today's Afghanistan. There are stories
mentioned by Sassanid histories and later Islamic-era sources that describe early dynasties that ruled thousands of years ago in Balkh over
a vast area covering northern and southern Afghanistan and beyond.
These dynasties are mostly wrapped in myths and legends and some
factual history. What is known can be traced to the oral traditions related
to Avestan figures in northeastern Iran. Some studies of early regional
history are referenced in religious scriptures of the Indo-Iranian people
who migrated in successive waves from their original abode between
the Aral and Caspian Seas to the Iranian plateau and to other lands in
the early second millennium BC. Some initial waves of these migrating Arians or Aryans moved south through Herat and across the Hindu
Kush Mountains to the valleys of the Helmand and Kabul Rivers. Under
the pressure of following migrants, they moved farther east through the
Bolan, Khyber, Kurram, Gomal, and Kunar Valleys and settled in the
Indus basin, Punjab, and farther east in northern India. The saga of these
eastward migrants, identified as "Aryans," is detailed in the Vedic scriptures, which are a collection of religious teachings and hymns written
over several centuries covering the period of migration from the Hindu
Kush and Helmand regions down to the Ganges plains.[1]

The subsequent waves of Iranian people apparently moved in two
streams, spreading over the lands east and west of the Carmanian Desert. The eastern stream settled in Soghdiana, Bactria (Bakhtar–Balkh),
Carmania (Kerman), Margiana (Murghab-Merv), and Aria (Herat) and
drove their Aryan kinsmen into India. The western Iranians, whose foremost tribe was the Persians, headed west of the central Iranian desert followed by the Medes, from whom the Indo-Germanic settlers in
Phrygia and Armenia are said to have been offshoots.[2]

The Iranians who settled in Bactria,[3] a land between the Hindu Kush
Mountains and the Oxus River, became the most powerful people in
the region and established the East Iranian civilization that lasted for

hundreds of years. With its fertile soil and well-watered land, the region prospered and extended its influence on both sides of the Hindu Kush and across the Oxus River to Soghdiana. Bounded mostly by natural barriers of mountains in the east and south and the Kevir Desert in the west, Bactria was a distinctive geographic body and often an independent political entity for more than a thousand years. Its crossroads location between West, Central, and South Asia made it a major trade center of the Old World. As Thomas Holdich notes, from the ancient times and an unknown beginning Bactria and Babylon must have been the two great commercial centers of Asia.[4]

At the time their Persian and Median kinsmen in the western extremities of the Iranian plateau were influenced and constrained by their powerful neighbors, the eastern Iranian people centered in Bactria were drawn into constant wars with the invading Turanian nomads attacking from the Central Asian steppes. The exploits of this period of history and the feats of larger-than-life heroes of an epic age are manifested in the Avestan texts and reflected in the epic narratives of Firdausi's epic poem *Shah-Nama* (Book of Kings, compiled in the tenth century) and other traditions. It was here that Avesta, the primary collection of the sacred texts of Zoroastrianism, originated. The phrase "Avestan people" refers to the peoples linked to the Zoroastrian religion and culture settled in eastern Iran. As Wilhelm Geiger suggests, the country in which the civilization of the Avesta people arose was eastern Iran. It is a civilization of great antiquity and dates back at least to a time before the Median and Persian kings.[5] In spite of the reference to Ragha (Rey, near Tehran) in the Avesta, he writes that the greater part of Media, all of Atropatene (today's Azerbaijan and Kurdistan), Susiana, and Persia were outside the pale of the Avesta people.[6] The territories inhabited by the Avesta people are identified as the "land of the Aryans," whose inhabitants shared a common race, language, and descent. The name corresponds with Strabo's "Ariana" that embraces the eastern provinces, which was the original home of the Iranian race, as well as modern Iran. Strabo called Bactria "the pride of Ariana."[7]

This pre-Islamic history of Afghanistan is derived from traditional stories, Avestan narratives, and historical accounts that are related in the voluminous epic of Firdausi's tenth-century *Shah-Nama*. The *Shah-Nama* consists of about 60,000 couplets and is based mainly on the *Khwday-Namag* (Book of Kings), which was a late Sassanid period compilation of the history of the kings and heroes of Iran from mythical times to the sixth century. The accounts of *Shah-Nama* are partly

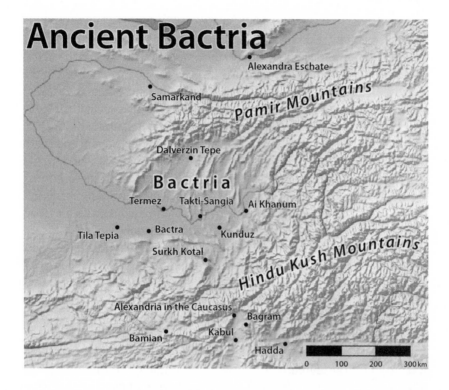

grounded in Avestan narratives, where the earliest history of kings, heroes, and their opponents are outlined and entwined with religious codes. The "Book of Kings" is the traditional history of greater Iran, with stories of four ancient dynasties including the Pishdadid mythological world kings. It continues with the Kayanid kings' heroic period from ancient times to Darius III (who was defeated by Alexander the Great) and the two historical dynasties: the Arsacids (or Parthian) kings, and the Sassanid dynasty to the Muslim Arab conquest. These Avestan-based stories have also been narrated in Arabic and Persian at various lengths in the Islamic era.

The early military history of the land known to classic writers as ancient Ariana is linked to three sets of constant struggle between rival forces: the struggle between migrating hordes and the natives; the war of settled communities against the nomads; and the strife between the religious followers and the unbelievers.

Clashes between invading immigrants and natives who were displaced by the newcomers continued over hundreds of years. The natives did not give up their lands without a struggle. The newcomers came with a higher civilization, a reformed religion, and ambitions for conquest. Continuous conflict between immigrant Aryans and the indigenous people in India known as "Dasa" and "Dasyus" is recorded in the Vedic sources. As the Aryans settled in the new lands, the natives were either subjugated or driven to the mountains and other inaccessible areas.[8] In Vedic collections, there are many hymns addressed to Indra, the material deity of the conquering Hindus, asking for help against the dark aborigines—the Dasyu or Dasa. "Indra protects his A'rya worshiper in wars. He who protects him on countless occasions protects him in all wars. He subdues for the benefit of [Aryan] men, the races who do not perform sacrifices. He flays the enemy of his dark skin, kills him, and reduces him to ashes. He burns those who are harmful and cruel."[9]

The Iranians, including the Medes and Persians, who moved west had to deal with the natives in West Asia and for nearly three centuries after arriving in the region fell under the domination of the Assyrian Empire (911–609 BC), based in nearby Mesopotamia. At the end of the seventh century BC, with the decline of Assyrians, Iranians began to dominate the Iranian plateau to its western borders and beyond.

The war between immigrants and natives was a racial and cultural war. Aryans considered non-Aryans to be primitive and evil, even as souls degenerated into demons; they fought them under the leadership of mythical heroic figures glorified in the lengthy epic poem *Shah-Nama*. The colonizing struggles were presumably waged in very ancient times when the first immigration of Aryan tribes took place and invading hordes subjugated the primitive inhabitants of the Iranian highlands. The Avesta and native legends assign those events to the reign of Jamshed (Yama), the first king of the mythical Paradhata (Peshdadi dynasty) who built his capital city in Balkh. In these legends, the struggle is defined as the war of civilized people against what is termed *daivas* (demons), and therefore the war was presumably bloody, definitive, and decisive. The invasion of Varna in northeastern parts of the country (today's Tabaristan) by the Iranians pushed the non-Aryan inhabitants into the almost inaccessible mountains of Alburz. In Avestan texts, these natives are described as the "wicked people of Varna" and are closely associated with another group of aborigines, the "demons of Mazandaran," who survived in the swampy forests on the coast district between the Caspian Sea and Alburz.[10]

The second set of conflicts was waged by the settled societies against invading Scythian nomads who were descending from the depths of their Central Asian steppes across the Jaxartes River (Syr Darya) onto villages and towns of Bactria and Soghdiana before swiftly returning to their barely accessible northern plains.

The Indo-European nomadic tribes that still wandered over the steppes as migratory herdsmen were engaged in conflicts with the Soghdians, Persians, Medes, and Bactrians, who had taken to cultivating the land and established settled communities. From very ancient times, the lowlands between the Aral and Caspian Seas, as well as the plains on the northern shores of the Black Sea, were inhabited by various tribes of nomads that wandered the vast steppes pursuing a pastoral life. "Scythian" is the name used by the Greeks to classify these various peoples throughout classical antiquity, in the same way the Iranians lumped together people of various languages and different bloods into the vague and general expression "Turanian." In these wars, racial differences and national contrasts were not the main source of conflict between the inhabitants of the Iranian plateau, including Bactria and the Scythians of ultra-Jaxartes. It was the economic separation and religious schisms that pitted the nomadic Scythians against the sedentary Iranians.

The third set of conflicts was linked to religious differences. The early Aryans worshiped the elements. Fire, air, water, sky, the plant and drink Soma, and soil were revered as sacred and often linked to certain deities. Later, religious beliefs developed in different ways as people moved further apart and cultures separated and evolved. Among the Aryans in the east, the conflict was between people of faith and unbelievers, as reflected in this Vedic hymn: "O Indra! Rishis still extol thy ancient deed of prowess. Thou hast destroyed many marauders to put an end to the war; thou hast stormed the towns of enemies who worship no gods; thou hast bent the weapons of enemies who worship no gods."[11]

The appearance of the Iranian prophet Zarathushtra Spitama (Greek: Zoroaster) in Bactria, most likely in the middle of the second millennium BC, ushered in a major religious reform that led to the emergence of a new religion: Zoroastrianism. In the Avesta, the primary collection of the sacred texts of Zoroastrianism, the central idea of the faith is described as the existence of a dualism in nature where evil is the work of Ahriman and good is the work of Ahura Mazda. As evident from the scriptures, very marked social and religious differences existed among the different peoples. The separation of people into believers and nonbelievers begins in the Gathas, the oldest section of Avesta, and continues throughout the whole of the Avestan collections, which discuss the adherents of the Zoroastrian religion and their opponents. The religious and the economic schisms in the population of old Iran were also linked to the contrast between the settled populations and the nomads, where Zoroastrian doctrine thrived among the settled populations who first accepted it, while the nomadic tribes mostly declined to submit to its binding and restraining laws.

In such a pugnacious environment, the peace of settled communities was constantly under threat from within and without. The situation that lasted many centuries could be described as a state of "no peace" rather than as a state of war. Like all inhabitants of borderlands, the people living in the Eastern Iranian Plateau were continually at war and had to be constantly watchful and ready to take military action against various threats. The geographic isolation of farming communities restrained collective action against common enemies. The settlement of the people in agriculturally suitable valleys and well-watered plains, which were isolated by topographical barriers, resulted in the development of a patchy network of self-reliant communities of clans and tribes, villages, and territorial nations. Territorial association of the tribes provided them with a regional identification that was eventually supported and hardened by the local distinctiveness of the communities within a larger nation of Aryans bonded together by race, culture, and geography. It was a feudal society where the king wielded absolute power by divine right, while a powerful aristocracy enjoyed power locally through allegiance to the king. In general, it was a patriarchal system in which political and military authority was exercised by the heads of family, clan, tribe, and province.

Under the prevailing sociopolitical conditions, local communities relied on their innate military capacity to respond to enemy attacks within their space. But wars and conflicts were not always local. The Aryans undertook regular campaigns against their shared enemies under the king's banner to conquer new lands or to retaliate against enemies' pillaging incursions. Furthermore, internal conflicts among clans and tribes were not uncommon. The situation kept the population's martial spirit alive—the "armed nation" was the norm for the state, while valor, gallantry, and heroism were the traits for individuals. The nature of the military establishment was intricately linked to the societal structure and geographic distribution of clans and tribes. Its structure was consistent with the constitution of the state itself. The family, clan, and tribe and their territorial domains constituted a network of military and political units. In moments of danger and in waging wars, each unit provided fighters from among their able-bodied adult males to form the collective military force. The ties of kinship within these units made them the most cohesive teams in fighting the enemy. They fielded what the Avesta refers to as the "troops of heroes" who fought for their religion and their land: "Give strength and victory, give herds that create prosperity, give a troop of heroes, able and eloquent, victorious and unconquered, who may overpower the opponents, who may subdue the enemies, who may bless the people and protect their race."[12]

The armies of Vedic Aryans in India were modeled in the same way. The heads of village (Vis-pati), clan (Gramma-pati), and tribe (Gutra-pati) would mobilize their respective members to form the king's army for wars commanded in the field by the army commander (Sena-pati).[13] Local political and military power was centered in the tribal councils. A notable feature of the polity was the institution of two political-military decision-making units, the Sabha and the Samiti. The Sabha was at the village, clan, and tribe levels and consisted of the body of elders, and the Samiti was the assembly of the people.

The feudal system accentuated the power and role of local leaders who not only provided the bulk of the king's army against his enemies but also wielded much power and virtual independence within their distinct geographic domains. For example, the house of Saam (to which Zal and Rostam, the iconic Iranian heroes, belong) ruled in Zabulistan and Sistan. Saam was repeatedly called upon to save the king and the country from imminent disasters facing them. Key figures in Ferdousi's *Shah-Nama*, such as Rostam, Tus, Zal, Saam, the Mehrab king of Kabul, Goodarz, Garshasp, and others were like vassals and knights of the monarch with distinctive local identity and self-governing authority. Despite the absolute power enjoyed by the kings, there have been occasions when the nobles voiced their objections to a king's decision or conduct. For instance, Rostam angrily protested against Kavus, who had reproved his arriving late at the capital when he had been summoned to the court. According to the *Shah-Nama*, when Rostam of Sistan fell out with King Gushtasp, who had sent his son Esfandyar to arrest him, Rostam bragged of his local "Zabuli" and "Kabuli" identity in defiance of the "Iranian" army. The *Shah-Nama* quotes him: "If you want war and blood shed, let me bring the Zabuli horsemen armed with Kabuli daggers, you too bring the 'Iranians' and see the test of the merit against the worthless."[14]

The volatile situation caused by continued conflicts stimulated the development of military forces and their weapons in an evolutionary process that took hundreds of years. The warfare developed from early primitive duels by single combatants in which physical strength and the individual skills and ability of warriors were the decisive factors. According to traditions, in such battles the warriors made frequent use of lassos (*kamand*) and clubs (*gorz*), two ancient and primitive weapons. But as the Indo-Iranians moved to new lands and faced new enemies, their ways of war improved with the use of horses and battle chariots that enhanced operational mobility and battlefield maneuver and shock action.

The Indo-Iranian tribes, with their cultural links to Central Asia, where the horse was first domesticated and then spread around the world, were accustomed to breeding and using horses in war and peace from ancient times. Many geographic names in greater Iran and the Indus basin bear the appellation of Iranian terms "Aspa" and "Sanskrit Asva," which mean "horse." Other examples are Zar-aspa (golden horse), Aria-aspa (Aryans horse), Hazar-asp (thousands of horses), Bever-Asp (owner of ten thousand horses), and so on. But before the Iron Age, the use of horses on the battlefield was largely related to the employment of war chariots. As early as the second millennium BC, the chariot was adopted by the settled Indo-Iranians both as a military technology and as an object of ceremony. Massive use of cavalry came at a later age, as it formed the third oldest combat arm after the infantry and chariotry. The power of mobility provided by chariots was offset by the difficulty of raising large forces and by the inability of horses to carry heavy armor. This led the equestrian nomads of the Central Asian and Iranian steppes to adopt innovations in cavalry techniques.

In both Avestan and Vedic texts, the chariot warriors are described as a distinct section of the army. Their role in battle was like the feat of Homeric heroes. "The expert charioteer stands on his chariot he drives his horses whosesoever will. The reins restrain the horses from behind. Sing their glory. . . . The horses raise the dust with their hoofs, and career over the field with their chariots with loud neighing. They do not retreat but trample the marauding enemies under their hoofs."[15]

As was fashionable in other ancient armies, each Aryan chariot fighter was accompanied by a charioteer who held an equally honorable status as the combatant himself. The chariot warriors usually challenged the enemy chariot fighter in single combat and rarely took part in the general melee. However, with the development of military tactics, the massive charge by chariot warriors in the battlefield became normal practice until the use of chariots in war became obsolete in the third century BC.

The most powerful asset of the chariot warriors was their steeds, for whose strength and vigor they prayed. "Famous through chariots" is a term of praise bestowed upon the horse. The princes are called "possessors of snorting steeds and rumbling chariots," and the wheels of the chariot seem to have been regarded among the Iranians (as is known to have been the case among the Indians) as the symbol of world-conquering power.[16] And it is said of Zarathushtra that he first of all made the wheel roll over the demons and wicked sons of men and that his empire embraced Aryans and non-Aryans.[17]

The Aryans were skilled warriors. Faced with an existential enemy threat, their weapons were more offensive in nature than defensive. However, the use of bronze armor was also known, especially by those who fought on chariots. In their exposed position, they stood more in need of protection than did other combatants. Only people of rank who belonged to the military nobility fought from chariots. The rest of the nation fought on foot around them. Cavalry were present to a certain extent. The Vedic Aryans' most effective weapons were the bow for long-range impact and the spear for short-range encounters. In both Vedic and Avestan texts, the bow, the horse, and the chariot are exalted. Rigveda calls the bow the "conqueror of the battle": "We will win the cattle with the bow; we will win with the bow; we will conquer the fierce and proud enemy with the bow. May the bow foil the design of the enemy. We will spread our conquest on all sides with the bow."[18]

But for the Avestan people, the spear played the most important role. The spear is named first in the Avestan enumeration of weapons. It is followed by the sword, the club, the bow with quiver and arrows, and finally the sling and the sling stones. It is assumed that, because of the nature of threats, the open-plain terrain of India was more suitable for long-range weapons, while in the closed terrain of Ariana the weapons of close encounter were more needed and more effective.[19]

What can be gleaned from a collection of Sassanid and later sources and traditions is that from the second millennium BC the current territory of Afghanistan was part of a powerful confederacy in eastern Iran, of which Bactra (Balkh) was the center. It was dominated by an influential aristocracy that enjoyed local autonomy in different provinces around the Hindu Kush. The first recorded invasion from the west was an Assyrian incursion into Bactria sometime before the rise of the Achaemenids. The legendary war of Ninus and Semiramis is originated by Ctesias, a Greek historian of the fifth century BC who served as physician in the court of the Achaemenid king Artaxerxes Memnon (r. 404–359/58 BC).

Ctesias accompanied the king in 401 BC on his expedition against his rebellious brother Cyrus the Younger, at which time he made a journey to Bactria.[20] Ctesias's account, quoted by Diodorus Siculus (90–30 BC), says that Ninus, king of Assyria, led his army of two million (!!) to invade Bactria. The Bactrian ruler Oxyartes confronted the invader with indomitable courage but was forced to retreat into the capital Bactra (Balkh) and was besieged by the Assyrians. The city successfully resisted, and when Ninus lost hope of its capture, Smiramis—who had joined her husband, Menon, an officer in the Assyrian army—proposed a plan of attack by which the city was taken. Her contribution to the heroic act was praised and rewarded by Ninus, and she became queen and successor.

The veracity of the story has been disputed by some who argue that the Assyrians never invaded Bactria, although they had subjugated the Medes and Persians in western Iran.[21] Others speculate that the conquest of Ninus may have some connection with the legend of the invasion of Bactria by the mythological figure Zahhak (Azhi Dahaka in Avesta) who defeated Jamshed (Yama) in Balkh and enslaved the people.[22] In the legend, detailed in the *Shah-Nama* and other Persian and Arabic sources, Zahhak is described as an evil figure of Arabian or Abyssinian origin and "foe of *Ahura Mazda*." According to the legend, Zahhak was destroyed by Feridun (Traetaona in Avesta), who according to some traditions was the grandson of Jamshed and to others was eight generations removed. Since in modern studies Zahhak is thought to have come from Assyria and Babylon,[23] his Assyrian connection is more probable. Furthermore, the recovery of the independence of Bactria and the reestablishment of the capital at Balkh by Kai-Khosrow (Kavi Husravah in Avesta), as related by the traditional sources, are probably the same events that Ctesias recorded about Bactria in connection with the Ninus story. His accounts indicate that Bactrians became independent after the decline of the Assyrian Empire and continued as an independent state until the rise of Achaemenids under Cyrus.[24]

In the seventh century BC, the decline of the Neo-Assyrian Empire (934–609 BC) opened the way for the western Iranian people to break away from the Assyrian yoke and form a united Median-Persian kingdom. With the eventual fall of Nineveh, two new nations—Median and Babylon—became the dominant powers in West Asia. Subsequently, as Babylon expanded toward the Levant and Egypt, the Medians swept across Asia Minor and brought Lidia under its sway. About a century later, both the Lydian and Babylonian Kingdoms were incorporated into a new imperial expanse: the Achaemenid Empire. Cyrus the Great (r. 559–530 BC), the leader of the Achaemenid house of the Persians, overthrew the Median Confederation and eventually ruled over significant portions of the ancient world, which around 500 BC stretched from the Indus Valley in the east to the northeastern border of Greece. With the rise of the Achaemenids, the eastern Iranians could no longer maintain their independence and isolation from the west. Soon after the fall of Babylon, Cyrus led his armies to the east, where Bactria and other provinces south of Hindu Kush were annexed into the new empire. Consolidation of Achaemenid control over the lands west of the Indus River was achieved mostly during the rule of Darius I (r. 522–486 BC).

The vast size of the Achaemenid Empire and its enormous cultural and geographic diversity made central control extremely difficult. Darius adapted an administrative reform to enhance central authority. The reform included the development of a wide road network across the empire and the introduction of a uniform monetary system along with making Aramaic the official language of the empire. Darius also divided the empire into provinces and placed satraps with local power to govern them. Each satrap paid a fixed sum of taxes to the imperial treasury.[25] The annual tribute paid to the Achaemenid emperor by different satrapies is listed in a series of carvings from the early sixth century BC, at the ruins of the Apadana Palace at Persepolis. Such control measures were effective under powerful rulers. However, the delegation of power to local governments would eventually weaken central authority, causing the center to exert much effort to quell local rebellions, particularly in remote provinces such as Bactria and other satrapies around the Hindu Kush and in the Indus Valley. When Alexander the Great invaded Persia in 334 BC, he was faced by Darius III, a ruler who presided over a divided dominion, with disastrous consequences for the Achaemenids.

The territory of modern Afghanistan was part of seven satrapies of the Achaemenid Empire: Bactria (Balkh); Margiana (Murghab District in Afghanistan and Marv in Turkmenistan); Aria (Herat); Drangiana (southern and southwestern Afghanistan); Arachosia (Kandahar, Lashkargah, and Quetta); Sattagydia (Ghazni); and Gandhara (Kabul, Nangrahar, and Peshawar). The main Achaemenid city in the north of Afghanistan was Bactra or Baktra (present-day Balkh). Bactria, the cradle of ancient Iranian civilization, figured prominently in the center-periphery relationship throughout the Achaemenid period for several reasons.

First, Bactria was the ancient settlement and presumed birthplace

Extent of the Achaemenid Empire

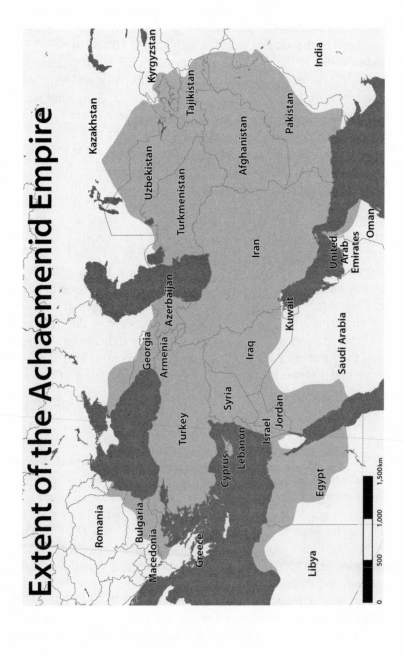

of Zoroastrianism. This was the principal faith practiced in Iran from Achaemenid times until the advent of Islam and was held in high regard spiritually and historically. This was one of the reasons that Cyrus started the tradition of appointing a prince of the blood as satrap of Bactria to act as the king's viceroy. The tradition was followed by his successors.

Second, the distance of eastern provinces from the center of the empire in western Iran, along with the focus of imperial expansion into West Asia, Europe, and Egypt, allowed Bactria to drift away from the center. For example, when Cambyses II (r. 529–522 BC), the successor of Cyrus, was engaged for too long in Egyptian conquest, the influence of the center weakened in the east and his brothers rose against him. Meanwhile, with the growth of the Magi (Magus) influence in Bactria, similar to the Brahmans' sway in India, the Zoroastrian priests aspired to become the power behind the throne. The king's brother Smerdis (Persian: Bardyia), the satrap of Bactria, was tempted to set himself up as an independent ruler. Even when he died, the Magis, taking advantage of the prolonged absence of Cambyses, put one of their own members on the throne pretending he was the dead prince.[26] The imposter, who ruled for more than a year, fueled a royal feud and the appearance of new pretenders from Babylon to Armenia. Cambyses then died under suspicious circumstances. It took Darius two years to overthrow the Magi usurper in Bactria and to restore peace and the authority of the empire. A similar situation is recorded after the death of Xerxes when his successor Artaxerxes (465–424 BC) had to quell the rebellion in Bactria after two pitched battles. With the decline of the center influence in the fourth century BC, the eastern satraps drifted away from imperial control.

Third, Bactria was the frontline province facing constant raids by Scythian nomads from across the Jaxartes. Cyrus the Great launched a major campaign to contain the threat and built a great frontier fortress known as "Cyropolis" to the Greeks. But Cyrus was killed during his second expedition against the nomads across the Jaxartes in a battle with Massagetae nomads. Herodotus has romanticized the disputed story in much detail. His account reports that Cyrus led his army against the Massagetae hordes, ruled by their queen, Tomyris. Tomyris, who allegedly rejected Cyrus's offer for marriage, tried to dissuade Cyrus from waging war against her nation, and when Cyrus did not concur she offered to pull back from the river so that Cyrus could cross unchallenged and pick up the fight with her forces beyond the river. Cyrus agreed and crossed the river with no interference from the enemy. The Achaemenid king then fought and defeated an advanced army of Tomyris's, during which her son was taken prisoner. The young man could not tolerate captivity and killed himself as soon as he got the chance. The subsequent encounter between the belligerents was very bloody. The main body of the nomadic queen's forces defeated the Persian army, and Cyrus was killed on the battlefield.[27] Cyrus's successors continued to face the threat from the north. On one hand, the situation raised the importance of Bactria and Margiana as the main defense lines of the empire; on the other, it offered a good opportunity for the defenders to hone their military skills and develop fighting experience.

Finally, Bactria, as well as the satrapies south of Hindu Kush, offered access routes to the Indus basin. In 512 BC, an important expedition set out from Bactria to the Indus Valley. The purpose of the expedition was a survey of the Indus River and adjacent areas for trade and cultural exchanges.[28] The expedition traveled to Caspatyros (Peshawar) and the land of the Pactyke (Pashtuns?) and sailed down the river to its delta and continued westward to the Red Sea, ending the voyage after thirteen months by landing at the site of modern Port Suez. Taking advantage of the survey, Darius subdued the upper and lower Indus basin and expanded relations with India. Bactria established road links to the Indus Valley across the Hindu Kush, which extended the influence of Bactria to the south of the Hindu Kush and promoted the development of trading centers.

The Achaemenid army, which initially was a multiethnic militia, developed into a formidable force as the empire expanded for more than two centuries. In addition to trained regular troops of Median and Persian infantry and cavalry, the subject nations contributed contingents of military forces to participate in imperial conquests, manning local garrisons, and protecting the borders. Hired mercenaries from within and from outside the empire also constituted a major element of the armed forces. The *spada* (standing army) consisted of charioteers, cavalry (*asabara* or *asavaran*), camel riders (*ushabara*), and mounted and foot spearmen and bowmen.[29] Among the full-time regular soldiers, the "immortals" (*hang-i-javedan*) held a special status. "Immortals" is the Greeks' term for the elite of the Persian army. They were handpicked for bravery and so rewarded. Their name comes from the fact that their number never fell below 10,000, as the division was always kept up to full strength and retired or fallen soldiers were always replaced. In this way, their strength was always 10,000 men, never more or less.[30] Entry to the ranks of the Immortals was restricted to those with Persian, Mede, or Elamite ancestry.[31]

Satraps provided allied contingents that supplied their own equipment and fought in their own style. Herodotus lists the contingents of different nations in the army of Xerxes (r. 486–465 BC), including the infantry and cavalry of Bactria, Aria, Arachosia, and Gandhara.[32] He wrote:

> The Bactrians served [in the expedition] wearing about their heads nearly. The Aryans [Herat] were equipped with Median bows, and in other respects like the Bactrians. The Parthians and Chorasmians and Soghdians and Gandaryans and Dadicans serves with the same equipment as the Bactrians. The Sarangians [Sistan] were conspicuous among the rest by wearing dyed garments; and they had boots reaching up to their knee, and Median bows and spears. The Pactyans [Pashtuns?] were wearers of skin coats and had native bows and daggers.

Like other earlier and later eastern armies, the Achaemenid army was organized on a decimal basis. The troops were grouped in tens (*datha*), hundreds (*sata*), thousands (*hazara*), and ten thousand (*baivara*). An officer commanding ten men was titled *Dathapatis*. The leaders of a hundred, a thousand, and ten thousand troops were called *Satapatis*, *Hazarapatis*, and *Baivarapatis*, respectively. The king acted as the commander in chief of the imperial armies in most battles and campaigns but at times delegated command to one or more generals of prominence and of high birth. The satraps usually commanded the contingents from their own satrapy or were promoted to command forces of mixed nationalities. The king appointed the generals and named commanders of thousands and ten thousand, while the leaders of ten men or a hundred were named by the commander of ten thousand.[33]

From the early days of the empire, the Persians enlisted Greek mercenary units, who received free boarding and lodging. By the time of Alexander's invasion of Persia, the Greek mercenaries were fully integrated into the Persian army. The hiring of Greek mercenaries was a general practice in the fourth century BC, as the fighting power of Greek hoplites and their efficiency was well recognized. Ionian Greeks supported Darius's invasion of Scythian territory in 512 BC, although they revolted against Persian rule in 499 BC and fought and lost a war lasting six years to retain their independence. Nevertheless, they still served in the Persian army in 490 BC, fighting side by side with the Persians at the Battle of Marathon. Marathon was a battle that could have meant the end of independence for the rest of Greece. In 479 BC, 13,000 pro-Persian Greeks hoplites and 5,000 cavalry fought for the Persians at the Battle of Plataea.[34]

War chariots were still used throughout the Achaemenid period in different roles. However, their effectiveness gradually declined in the fourth century BC. Similarly, the use of camels in combat waned, although the beasts still played a major role in the baggage train and supply services. In 480 BC, the Arabs supplied archers mounted on camels to Xerxes's army, with each animal carrying a pair of archers. As seen in reports on the Battle of Gaugamela, camel riders and combat chariots as well as elephants were used in the battle.

The logistical services were provided by a network of supply stations set up along major roads that replenished the field baggage trains that accompanied military forces during expeditions. Military campaigns were normally initiated in spring; rivers were crossed by building bridges or by using rafts and inflated animal skins. Battles were fought exclusively in daytime, normally being started with the bowmen and slingers discharging a barrage of fire to disrupt the enemy forces. The initial barrage would be followed by heavily armed infantry and cavalry flank attacks to crush the enemy ranks.

The soldiers used both offensive and defensive weapons. A foot soldier carried a short sword, a lance with a wooden shaft and metal point, a quiver full of arrows with bronze or iron points, and a bow curved at the ends, which were decorated with animals' heads. Their wickerwork shields were either small and oval-shaped or big and rectangular. A felt hood constituted their headgear, although the use of helmets was not uncommon. Elite units also wore coats of mail to cover their chests.

Herodotus describes the order of march of Xerxes's army when he moved out of Sardis on his Greek expedition in 480 BC. According to his account, Xerxes's chariot was followed by

> spearmen, the best and most noble of the Persians, a thousand in number, holding their spear-points in the customary way; and after them another thousand horsemen chosen out from Persians; and after the horsemen ten thousand had upon their spears pomegranates of gold instead of the spikes at the but-end; and these enclosed the others round while the remaining nine thousand were within these and had silver

pomegranates. And those also had golden pomegranates that had their spear points turned toward the earth, while those who followed next after Xerxes had golden apples. Then to follow the ten thousand there were appointed a body of ten thousand Persian cavalry; and after the cavalry there was an interval of as much as two furlongs. Then the rest of the host came marching without distinction.[35]

By the time Alexander the Great invaded Persia in 334 BC, the might of the Achaemenid Empire under Darius III had long declined from its zenith under Darius I and his successor, Xerxes. The regression caused gradual decay in the morale and professional prowess of an imperial army that increasingly depended on hired mercenaries. Xenophon considered the Persian soldiers of later times far softer than those who had fought under Cyrus the Great. "In the time of Cyrus," he wrote, the Persian soldiers "clung to Persian self-restraint," but over time they became soft and more interested in luxury and the easy life. He asserted that Cyrus trained fighters to close with an enemy and awarded them accordingly. "The generals of today," he wrote, "flatter themselves that untrained men will serve quite as well as trained. Now none of them will take the field without Hellenes to help them. . . . The Persians of today are less religious, less dutiful to their kindred, less just toward other men, and less valiant in war."[36] Furthermore, the waning influence of the center weakened its authority in remote provinces such as Bactria, which itself had turned into a semi-independent kingdom. Bessus, the satrap of Bactria, and his allies south of Hindu Kush were hardly inclined to have much respect for the weakened Darius. They saw him as a puppet in the hands of conspirators who had raised him to an undeserved dignity without the ability to rule the empire. This was believed to be the reason that only 1,000 Bactrian cavalry took part in the great Battle of Gaugamela in support of Darius against Alexander.[37]

3   The Passage of Alexander the Great, 330–323 BC

More than twenty-three centuries since he passed through the lands encompassing today's Afghanistan, the name of Alexander the Great survives in local legends romanticizing his life and extraordinary exploits. The conqueror is exalted particularly in local folklore, as he is erroneously identified as the Quranic super-character Dhul-Qarnayn.[1] Even today one may come across a Pashto folk song that symbolizes the pomp and glory of Alexander (locally called "Sikander") as the display of utmost splendor.[2] But in Afghanistan's history, Alexander is one of many ancient conquerors who invaded the land and faced fierce resistance from the natives, who fought for their homes and their way of life. Alexander left behind destroyed villages and burned fields; he is remembered as a great victor, not a grand builder.

The story of Alexander, as told and retold by ancient Greek and Roman writers, is a fascinating drama depicting one of the most extraordinary feats ever achieved by any military leader. The glare of spears, the shimmer of phalanx armor, and the miraculous charges of the Companion cavalry rounding the enemy flanks highlight the tale of Greek columns fighting the so-called barbarians. In fact, however, the Macedonian army—Alexander's army—measured glory in terms of enemy casualties, and everything great and grand is linked to the name Alexander. Yet there is not much recorded about administrative and organizational achievements, excepting those made in support of outright military conquest.

Alexander's invasion of the lands occupied by today's Afghanistan came as the continuation of the Macedonian conquest of the Persian Empire. However, once the Macedonian armies defeated the Achaemenid imperial military machine and continued their conquest into Afghanistan and Central Asia, the nature of warfare changed drastically. Alexander crushed the military might of the Persian Empire in three monumental battles: Granicus (April 334 BC), Issus (November 333 BC), and Gaugamela (October 331 BC). But as Alexander led his army into

Central Asia, his conventional military power became engaged in numerous native wars in the most difficult terrain and confronted a climate inhospitable to outside intruders. As Benjamin Wheeler notes, whereas Alexander had overrun Syria, Persia, Media, and Parthia, a domain a thousand miles wide, in a single year (July 331–July 330 BC), it took him more than two years (April 329–May 327 BC) to win submission of a district of 350 square miles.[3]

At Issus and Gaugamela, the Persian soldiers were fighting a king's war, whereas in Hindu Kush, Bactria, and Soghdiana the local people were fighting for their homes, for their religion, and for traditions against foreign aggression. The area was the very center of the Iranian religion and the cradle of Zoroaster's teachings. This was the toughest resistance Alexander had encountered since entering Asia. The people he faced were devotedly attached to their homes and were untainted by the luxury and easy lifestyle of their kinsmen in the west. The Macedonian phalanx and Greek hoplites found themselves caught up fighting in local villages and towns. There were no major armies to engage in pitched battles; instead there was widespread guerrilla activity and fortified defenses in mountainous fortresses and strongholds. The Macedonian military was not ready for this type of warfare and had to make structural and tactical adjustments in dealing with the native forces.

The Macedonian Army of Conquest and Correlation of Forces

The backbone of the invading army was the Macedonian heavy infantry, known as "foot Companions," which was organized on a territorial basis in six brigades of about 1,500 troops each. These brigades were commanded by Alexander's six experienced generals: Perdicas, Coenus, Craterus, Amyntas, Meleager, and Philip. These brigades operated together in phalanx formation. The army's right flank in battle was protected by an elite corps of "Guards" composed of a royal battalion (*agema*) of 1,000 men plus two other units of the same size. Alexander often used these troops along with cavalry and light armed troops on rapid marches and other mobile action such as pursuing Darius in 330 in Parthia and moving in rapid march from the vicinity of Khujand in Central Asia two years later to face the native leader Spitamenes, who had massacred a Macedonian contingent near Maracanda (Samarkand).

Other infantry contingents included 7,000 heavy troops contributed by the Corinthian League, 5,000 Greek mercenaries, 7,000 Thracian and Illyrian light troops armed with javelins, and two units of archers from Crete and Macedonia. The 1,000-strong Agrarian unit was an outstanding unit among the light troops. Along with the archers and the Guards, they took part in reconnaissance and skirmishes as well as fighting in set battles.

The Macedonian "Royal Companions" were the elite cavalry units in Alexander's army. The 1,800-strong troopers were organized in eight squadrons (*ilai*) under the command of Philotas. Among them, the "Royal Squadron" was Alexander's personal bodyguard and spearheaded the cavalry charge in major battles. The Companions were deployed immediately to the right of the Guards protecting the right flank of the phalanx, which was lined up in the center. The left side of the phalanx was covered by the 1,800-strong Thessalian cavalry under command of the veteran general Parmenion (father of Philotas) and often held off enemy charges while the right flank, usually led by Alexander, delivered the decisive blow against the enemy's left in a flanking maneuver. More than 1,500 cavalry troops were provided by the Greek allies and hired as mercenaries.

A special force of light Macedonian infantry, the *hypaspists*, was a corps equipped with linen corselets, lighter shields, and longer swords than those carried by the hoplites. The hypaspists were swifter in attack than the heavy brigades and more heavily armed than the light troops. This new kind of corps was very useful on the battlefield in Macedonia: the soldier of the phalanx was too heavily armed to protect the person of the king, and the light armed soldier was neither of high status nor capable enough.[4]

The combination of heavy and light forces ensured battlefield flexibility. Anchored in the stability provided by the heavy infantry, the agile forces maneuvered to challenge the enemy lines. Such a setup counterbalanced the numerical superiority of enemy forces and helped Alexander win pitched battles against the Persians. But what also helped Alexander was the weakness of the Persians. As Hans Delbruck notes: "Even after their defeat at Gaugamela the Persians could have defended themselves in the manner of the Parthians, but all the large cities—Babylon, Susa, Persepolis, Ecbatana—opened their gates to the Macedonians without any opposition."[5] The Macedonian force posture, however, faced trying situations when dealing with nonconventional ways of warfare in Bactria, Soghdiana, and Indian borderlands.

The Logistics

Two remarkable features of Alexander's military campaign in the east were the ability to keep the army up to required strength, and the ability to maintain the logistic system along a lengthy line of communication. Alexander continued to recruit troops from Greece as well as from the conquered lands as his force advanced. Gaps in the ranks were constantly filled, and the fighting strength of the forces was maintained at required levels. Despite the need to station troops in garrisons along the way, Alexander fielded around 40,000 infantry and 7,000 cavalry at the Gaugamela in October 331 BC.[6] The army ranks were filled by mercenaries from Greece and through the enlistment of similar fighters in Persia. Although strength figures of armies of the ancient world are always open to question, Alexander's host must have been exceptionally large. Curtius, for instance, gave the army a total of 120,000 at the start of the Indian campaign.[7]

The Macedonian forces in their Asian campaign lived off the land. Their logistic system was based on local procurement of supplies and a network of bases established along the line of communication. Following his father Phillip's reforms, Alexander kept his army lean and mobile to limit the number of baggage trains accompanying the long marches, particularly through territories offering insufficient provisions. During his conquest of Asia, he had to pass through arid lands and rugged mountains that often required carrying several days' provisions with the army by a large train of pack animals. Additional large columns also included servants, support staff, traders, wives and women, siege trains, and engineers. The combatants and followers as well as the cavalry horses and pack and draught animals all needed food, water, and fodder to the tune of hundreds of tons per day. For example, according to one analysis, after the army crossed the Hellespont, 1,121 pack animals were required to carry only one day's requirement of grain for Alexander's 48,100 soldiers, 6,100 cavalry horses, and 16,000 followers. The number would go higher to 1,553 when daily forage is added and up to 8,542 pack animals when the daily water requirement is also included. Furthermore, there would be 1,300 baggage animals to carry other supplies such as tents, blankets, fuel, and hammocks.[8] In arid lands, the Macedonian army usually carried larger provisions of stocks. In the 325-mile march from Kandahar to Kabul, the Macedonian army carried a fourteen-day grain supply.[9] To reduce the size of the baggage train, Alexander limited the number of servants to one for every ten foot soldiers and one for every cavalryman. With an infantry-to-cavalry ratio of roughly six to one, this would indicate an overall ratio of one servant for every four combatants. Both Philip's and Alexander's troops carried their own arms, armor, utensils, and some provisions while marching.[10]

However, the pace of movement was mostly dependent on the status of the local economy and the availability of a sufficient amount of supplies. Marching with a large train of supplies would slow the pace of movement. Therefore, Alexander preferred to maintain a lean and mobile army free of the hindrance of heavy baggage. In 330 BC, as the army started moving toward Bactria, the columns could scarcely get moving under the weight of its spoils and extravagant impedimenta. Then, according to Alexander chronicler Curtius, the king ordered that all wagons be destroyed to enhance the speed of the marching columns.[11] Plutarch recorded a similar event on the eve of Alexander's expedition to India when he noticed that his soldiers were so burdened with booty that it hindered their marching; he ordered that the wagons be set on fire, including his own, to restore high mobility to the columns.[12] In order to keep the line of communication open, he built a network of colonies and forts along the route and at key points. These not only facilitated security and provided a place to drop off sick and wounded soldiers but also helped the efficiency of the logistics system.

The rate of Alexander's daily march during his Asian conquest is an interesting question. Obviously, the rate varied according to the composition of the army, its size, the experience of the marchers, the terrain conditions, and the weight of baggage trains. While the speed of the whole army on march was reported to be between 11 and 19.5 miles per day, smaller, lighter detachments could march up to 45 miles.[13] Some authors believe that Alexander's army marched 36 miles per day when it was pursuing the retiring Darius in 330 BC. This may have been the case on specific occasions. For example, in Parthia, Alexander covered 45 miles in one day and night to catch up with the fleeing Bactrian satrap Bessus, who had Darius under his control. Months later in Aria (Herat), Alexander marched 75 miles in two days to punish the rebellious Satibarzanes.

However, such speed was the exception, not the rule. In 329 BC, Alexander crossed the 47-mile Hindu Kush pass of Khawak in seventeen days, meaning an average of 2.7 miles per day, which is about the hourly speed of foot marches in normal conditions. In urgent cases, Alexander's leading light forces may have achieved a high speed, but when he was moving with a large and composite column his speed was restrained by logistics and other impediments. Hannibal's average speed was 10 miles per day, which compares with the speed of Elizabeth I's armies of 15 miles per day for both horsemen and foot soldiers.[14] Alexander's speed over long distances could not be more than this. For a medieval army of conscripts with a long supply train moving off the main roads, 12 miles per day is quite fast. Large armies with lots of wagons often strayed into single-digit marching speeds. And to be clear: marching speeds are highly variable based on terrain and the rest. In 1839, during the first Anglo-Afghan war, the British Army of the Indus, with some 30,000 combat troops and tens of thousands of service providers and camp followers, covered about 1,200 miles in about ten months with an average daily march of 11.5 miles.[15] The length of the marching column and the size of baggage trains were also key factors in defining the speed of march. A 30,000-man corps of the German army a century ago was known to be 14 miles long,[16] which may take nearly six hours more for the column to close in.

It would be difficult for Macedonia to wage war with the Persian Empire, which was fifty times larger than Greece. Comparison of the troop strength and armaments between the opposing sides was even less in Macedonia's favor when Philip died and the Macedonian treasury was exhausted. Alexander spent 800 talents (about $800,000) to equip his army. This left him with no more than 70 talents ($70,000) to begin the war with Asia.[17] According to Plutarch, the Macedonian king had no more than 70 talents to pay the soldiers and had no more than thirty days' provisions for the conquest.[18] But the lack of money did not hamper Alexander as he eyed the great treasuries of the Achaemenid Great King and the Persian satraps that would fall into the hands of his victorious army. After the Battle of Gaugamela, the Persian treasures seized in Babylon and the Persian camp amounted to 180,000 talents ($180 million).[19] Further, the conquered areas were totally pillaged along the invasion route. At just one location in Persia, the invaders seized 30,000 sheep.[20] Later, in the war with the Aspasians (inhabitants of today's Kunar and Bajaur), Alexander seized 230,000 oxen, from which he selected the best and sent them to Macedonia for use in agriculture.[21]

On the Way to Bactria

The Battle of Gaugamela dealt a decisive blow to the military might of the Persians. Alexander began the final pursuit of Darius, who intended

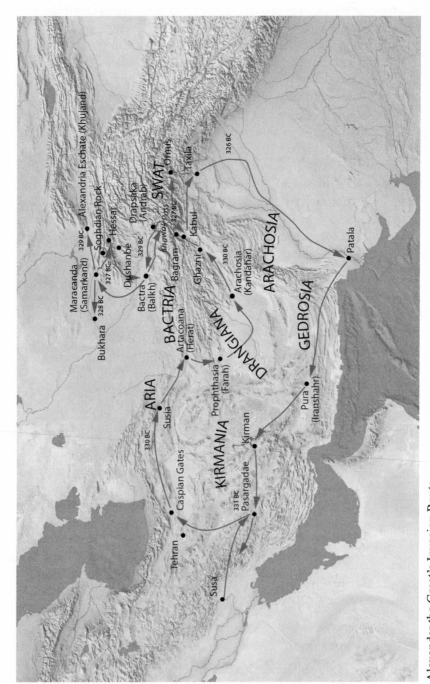

Alexander the Great's Invasion Route

to move to the eastern extremities of his empire and face the Macedonian invaders on more difficult terrain. However, the area around the Hindu Kush Mountains, particularly in Bactria and Soghdiana, were no longer under the control of Persepolis. The most powerful regional leader was Bessus, the viceroy of Bactria. He, in alliance with the governors of Aria (Satibarzanes) and Drangiana and Arachosia (Barsaentes), intended to defend their countries against the invasion. They had provided military contingents and fought gallantly with Darius in his battles with Alexander, but they were not impressed by the mild and weak Persian king, who they saw as a puppet in the hands of court conspirators who had elevated him to an undeserved position.

It was for this reason that, when Darius was on the run, Nabarzanes, the general of the regal guards, suggested that Darius abdicate in favor of Bessus. "I realize that the opinion I shall express will not sound good to you at first," he said.

> The doctors use harsh remedies to cure more serious ailments. . . . We have the gods against us in this war and fortune had not ceased from her relentless hounding of the Persians. What we need is a fresh start with fresh omens. Temporarily transfer your authority and your command to another who can carry the title of king only until the enemy quits Asia and who can then, victorious, return your kingdom to you. . . . So if Bactria, the safest heaven for us is our goal, let us appoint Bessus, the Satrap of the area, as temporary king.[22]

Predictably, Darius not only objected to the proposition but also labeled it as treason. But Darius was losing control. His small force was being thinned by daily desertions, while most of those who remained were the contingents of the still unconquered territories—Bactria, Arachosia, and Drangiana—under the orders of their respective satraps.

Should Alexander trap the forces of the satraps, Bessus and his colleagues intended to make their peace with Alexander by surrendering Darius. However, if they had time to reach Bactria and Soghdiana, they resolved to organize a dynamic resistance under their own joint command for the defense of their lands. Their lands were inhabited by the most warlike population of the empire. The Bactrians had maintained their military prowess and the will to resist foreign incursions from their constant war with the Scythians. Furthermore, they were untouched by the corruption of the Persian court due to their distance from the center. They did not believe that Darius would recover from his defeat and make another stand in the east. Fighting Alexander in the east was a possible option, but it would not succeed under the command of Darius, who had twice fled from the battlefield, betraying both his friends and his empire. For the resolute and energetic Bactrians, unless they were prepared to submit immediately to the invader, there was no choice but to depose Darius.[23]

Learning that Bessus and his allies intended to rid themselves of Darius, Alexander hastened to overtake their retreating columns. Taking a shortcut through a waterless desert while covering 45 miles in one day and night, Alexander neared the columns. Seeing that Alexander was so close, Bessus killed Darius and disappeared in the desert, heading to Bactria beyond Alexander's immediate reach.

Many of Alexander's soldiers thought that the death of Darius marked the end of the conquest of Persia. But for Alexander the job was not finished: The eastern half of the empire was untouched by his expedition; the defiant satraps of the east were not defeated or subdued; and Bessus, a distant cousin of Darius, proclaimed himself king and assumed the name of Artaxerxes V. Also, Alexander had far greater ambitions than conquering Persia. He aspired to surpass the feats of ancient conquerors such as Cyrus the Great and legendary heroes and divinities like Hercules and Dionysus. Alexander also dreamed of reaching the notional "eastern Ocean" beyond India.[24] So when a rumor spread throughout the camp that the expedition had reached its end and their king had decided on an immediate return to Macedonia, Alexander took immediate action to dispel any such notion. He addressed his soldiers in a passionate speech urging them to follow him in still greater conquests.[25]

These words were received with great enthusiasm by the soldiers, who told him "to lead them wherever he wished."[26] In the next seven years (330–323 BC), until the end of his life, Alexander would go on to conquer the eastern half of the Achaemenid Empire and various independent tribes beyond its limits. He never again saw his homeland or many of his acquisitions in the west. The conqueror embarked on waging a different war that had little to do with Grecian vital interests. While the Macedonian conquest in Asia Minor and the western half of the Persian Empire (March 334 to March 330 BC) were of significant importance to the strategic standing and security interests of the Hellenistic world, Alexander's conquest in the east had scarcely affected Grecian cities in any way. The long marches of the Macedonian phalanx and Greek hoplites to the heights of the Hindu Kush and the banks of the Oxus, Jaxartes, and Indus Rivers; the laborious transport of bulky siege engines along rugged mountain paths; and the endurance of severe cold and extreme heat in the Asian highlands and deserts by the Macedonian soldiers went down in the annals of military history as the most celebrated of any soldiering exploits. This segment of the campaign contributed to the personal aggrandizement of Alexander as the great conqueror of the known world, but it added little to his power over the Greeks. Neither did it go beyond a military occupation of the conquered lands during Alexander's lifetime.

Alexander's military campaign in the east can be classified into three distinctive phases:

1. The passage to Bactria through a circuitous route to secure the flanks of the expeditionary force and maintain a strategic line of communication.
2. The conquest and pacification of Bactria and Soghdiana and securing the Scythian frontier on the Jaxartes.
3. The mountain war in the highlands west of the Indus River as part of the intended conquest of India.

The Passage to Bactria

In the first phase, the main effort was directed toward a rapid and secure advance to the power base of Bessus and his Central Asian allies in the Oxus and Jaxartes regions. During this phase, the Macedonian army rarely subdued areas beyond the marching route. The pace of the movement was subject to logistical imperatives and the need to build security posts along the route.

After a brief preparation and regrouping of the army in Zadracarta (modern Asterabad), Alexander set out on his long march to Bactria in the late summer of 330 BC. He took the main caravan route that ran through Susia, Aria (Herat), and Merv to Bactria. The distance between the Caspian Gates and Aria, according to Strabo, was approximately 730 miles,[27] which should have been covered in nearly two months, reaching there in September 330 BC. As Alexander arrived in Susia, Satibarzanes, the satrap of Aria and a confederate of Bessus, visited Alexander and pretended submission to buy time. Alexander confirmed him in his office, and Anaxippus, one of the Companions, accompanied him on his return with an escort of about 40 mounted javelin throwers. Greek writers place Susia at about 39 miles from the capital of Aria, Artacoana, which is about the distance of a place called Zuzan from Herat. Other modern sources place Susia at the ruins of Tus, which is about 296 miles northwest of Herat.

But while the Macedonian army was toiling toward Bactria in the early autumn of 330 BC, Satibarzanes revolted in Aria (Herat) and massacred the Macedonian escort headed by Anaxippus. Arrian wrote that Satibarzanes was arming the Arians (Heratis) and concentrating them at Artacoana, the capital. The location of Artacoana is believed to have been close to the current city of Herat on the River Arius (Harirud).[28] The Greeks described it as a city situated on a plain of exceptional fertility at a nexus where the main roads from north to south and from east to west crossed each other.[29] No other location other than the modern Herat can match such a description. Furthermore, the location of Artacoana in the vicinity of modern Herat is also confirmed by the course of Alexander's movement and his subsequent march to the capital of Drangiana (modern Farah) in the south. Satibarzanes's design was to wait until Alexander was sufficiently distant and then join Bessus and Barsaentes (the satrap of Drangiana and Arachosia) with the force under his command to attack the Macedonian army from the rear and flanks and thus cut its line of communication. Had the plan succeeded, the Macedonian army would have been trapped in a serious situation on difficult terrain and in an unfriendly environment. Alexander could not afford to let that happen. As soon as he received the news of the troubles in Aria, he immediately changed his plan: he turned in his tracks, left Craterus in command of the army, and took a fast-moving detachment of lightly armed foot and cavalry[30] and marched with all speed against Satibarzanes and the Arians, reaching Artacoana after covering some 75 miles in two days.

The fast approach of Alexander took Satibarzanes by surprise, and he fled with 2,000 horsemen to Bactria. Some of the nationalists who stayed behind were hunted down by the Greeks; some were killed, and others were sold into slavery. Curtius wrote that Alexander set out in pursuit of Satibarzanes but soon found out that the Arian (Herati) nationalist was too far away to be overtaken, so he returned to Artacoana. The city's defenders and unarmed population took up positions on a nearby mountain ridge, which they fortified by cutting trees and building other obstacles. The ridge was most likely located to the east of the city, probably in the mountainous parts of the modern Karokh area west of Obeh. Greek historians describe it as a rising precipice on the east with a sloping side on the west. The mountain, two and thirty stadia in circumference (about 3 miles), had at its summit a verdant plateau. Alexander on his return detached Craterus to besiege Artacoana and directed his men to move against the ridge defended by the Arians. However, as the Macedonians struggled forward, the task proved to be more difficult than expected. Alexander was not sure what action to take, as going forward was difficult and going back was dangerous. "In a quandary as he was, chance provided him with a scheme when his reasoning could not."[31] A strong wind rose from the west, and in their efforts to make way over the rocks, the soldiers had cut large quantities of wood, which had dried out in the heat. Alexander ordered more trees to be piled on to fuel a fire, and the heap of logs soon rose to the height of the mountain position of the Arians. Then the Greeks lit the wood on all sides; helped by the wind, it swiftly engulfed the defenders' positions in flames. Attempting to escape the inferno, many Arians died, and those who could escape were cut down by Alexander's soldiers, who had blocked their escape routes. A few, severely scorched, were taken prisoners.

Alexander returned and joined Craterus, who had besieged Artacoana. He ordered the siege towers to advance and batter the city walls. Unable to withstand the bombardment and discouraged by the massacre of their compatriots on the mountain, the reduced garrison at Artacoana surrendered to the victor. According to Greek writers, Alexander declared an amnesty, not only raising the siege but also restoring all the property of the inhabitants. He built a new city in the vicinity and named it "Alexandria Aria," which is believed to be the origins of the modern city of Herat. Persian sources indicate that Alexander destroyed the ancient city of Herat before building a new one to which he moved the inhabitants of Herat.[32] Alexander appointed Arsaces as the governor of Aria.

The experience in Aria changed Alexander's advance route to Bactria. Instead of resuming his advance to Bactria along the northern route, Alexander intended to move south. Barsaentes, the satrap of southern provinces and a confederate of Bessus, was defying the Greeks. Concerned about the potential resistance in the south and true to his invariable habit of leaving no unbeaten enemy on the flanks of his march, Alexander decided to take a circuitous route to Bactria through Drangiana (Sistan), Arachosia (Kandahar), Ortospana (Kabul), and the Paropamisus Mountains (Hindu Kush) to Bactra (Balkh). The length of this route was three times greater than the northern route to Bactria. The direct route from Aria to Bactra was estimated at 418 miles, while the ancient course of the southern circuitous route was more than 1,200 miles. What made the southern direction a preferred option was the military situation in the south and the need to explore suitable routes to India, where Alexander intended to expand his Asian conquest after dealing with the Bactrians as well as the Scythian nomads in Central Asia. As Alexander moved south toward Drangiana (or Zarangiana), he was joined by reinforcements of fresh troops from Greece, including 500 cavalry under Zoilus, 3,000 foot from Illyria sent by Antipater, 2,600 foot and 300 cavalry from Lydia, and 130 Thessalian cavalry.

Alexander covered the estimated 183 miles from Aria to Prophthasia (the capital of Drangiana) in less than two weeks during October. Prophthasia is probably the modern city of Farah. Horace Wilson places it farther west at Peshawaran, which is 180 miles south of Herat on the northern bank of the Helmand Lake. Drangiana at that time was considerably more extensive than the modern Sistan. Unable to face the large Macedonian army, Barsaentes fled the province to the Indus Valley in an apparent attempt to trade space for time. It took Alexander nearly four years to catch up to him on the banks of Hydaspes (Jhelum) just before the battle with Porus (May 326 BC). Barsaentes and his local allies were arrested by the Indians and handed over to Alexander to win the Macedonian king's favors.[33] Barsaentes, the Arachosian nationalist who was blamed for the "Arachosian revolt," was finally executed.

And then a plot against Alexander's life was unveiled in the capital of Drangiana. Philotas, one of his senior generals, was implicated in the conspiracy. Philotas was the commander of the Companions, the corps of Macedonian cavalry that also provided bodyguards and attendants to the king. He was tried and executed after confessing under torture. The tragedy did not end there but resulted in the murder of Philotas's father, the renowned Macedonian general Parmenion. Parmenion had been a right-hand man to both Philip and Alexander. He was now seventy years old and therefore no longer viable for field command during the invasion of the eastern satrapies. He commanded the great depot and treasure at Ecbatana (Hamadan). He was murdered there on Alexander's orders. One of the immediate results of the tragedy was Alexander's decision to split the Companions corps into two separate divisions and appoint Hephaestion and Cleitus in command of one division each. He thought it was not safe to put such a large body of cavalry under a single person.

Alexander advanced from Prophthasia to Ariaspes on the Helmand River (probably the site of the ruins of Ram Rud). Prophthasia was on a major road that had been traversed by military forces in the past. According to Greek writers, the inhabitants of this place were *euergetai*, or benefactors, a Greek designation for the help they extended to Cyrus when he had been in great difficulties while passing through this area.

For this reason, Alexander treated them well and let them maintain their freedom. Ariaspes and the rest of the locations along the Etymander (Helmand) had been a very fertile area from ancient times. Native traditions and Avestan legends speak of the prosperity of the region from the epic period of the Kiani dynasties. Today the length of the Helmand Valley is dotted with ruins of ancient villages and townships that stretch for hundreds of miles. Availability of water along the valley allowed armies to follow the riverbanks all the way to the junction of the Helmand and Arghandab Rivers at Bust and then along the Arghandab stream to Kandahar. This was a much longer but more suitable route for military movements than the shorter northern road connecting Farah to Zamindawar and Kandahar.

Four days after Alexander entered Ariaspes, he received the news that Satibarzanes, with 2,000 cavalry, had entered Aria (Herat) and that the Arians had again risen in revolt against the Greeks.[34] Concerned about the threat to his line of communication, Alexander ordered two Companion officers, Erigyius and Caranus, along with the Persian officer Artabazus and 6,000 Greek infantry and 600 cavalry to quell the revolt. He also ordered Pharatapbernes, the satrap of Parthia, to assist in dealing with the Arians. The battle in Herat was a unique confrontation. Overwhelmed by hatred of the enemy and determined to end the conflict with a personal feat, Satibarzanes dared the Greek commander to settle the matter with a one-on-one fight. Erigyius accepted the challenge. Satibarzanes entered the fray helmetless. The brisk duel culminated in hand-to-hand combat, during which Erigyius's spear hit the Arian nationalist in the neck, killing him. This ended the battle as the Arian army fled and the Greeks reestablished control over Aria.[35]

Alexander halted for about two months in Ariaspes, probably awaiting the arrival of reinforcements from Ecbatana, and then moved along the Helmand (Etymander) banks to Arachosia (Kandahar area). Ptolemy describes the province of Arachosia as bounded on the north by the Paropamisus Mountains (Hindu Kush), on the east by India, on the west by Drangiana (Sistan), and on the south by Gedrosia (Makran–Baluchistan).[36] The capital of the province was recorded as Arachotes, from which the Arabic name al-Rokhaj is derived and is later described as the major city in the area during the Islamic period. Arab geographer Ibn-i Hauqal (d. 988 AD) specifies the distance from Sistan's capital, Dushk, to Bust as nine stages and from Bust to al-Rokhaj another four stages. This places al-Rokhaj some 390 kilometers from Sistan, matching the location of modern Kandahar. It was here that Alexander built another city, named "Alexandria Arachosia," and made it his main base of operations in southern Afghanistan. The Macedonian army spent the winter (330–329 BC) there while subduing the province. In Kandahar, the Macedonian army reunited and prepared to continue the march to what the Greeks called the Indian Caucasus (the Hindu Kush Massif), which they had to cross to reach Bactria. The army, which was in the past under the late Parmenion's command, joined Alexander. It included 6,000 Macedonians, 200 noblemen, and 5,000 Greeks including 600 cavalry. Alexander appointed Menon as the governor of Arachosia and garrisoned the city with 4,000 infantry and 600 cavalry.[37]

In early spring of 329 BC, Alexander moved his army northeast to Kabul and passed through rugged territory with severe weather. The inhabitants endured the snow and a harsh environment. Although the Greeks managed to subdue the inhabitants after much difficulty, Alexander's men suffered severely from exhaustion and lack of supplies. Many died, and many others were stricken with frostbite and snow blindness.[38] Arrian describes the place as the land of neighboring Indian tribes, but the geography and the sequence of the march to Kabul undoubtedly indicate that it was the rugged country around Ghazni where the western heights of the Suleiman Mountains meet the eastern offshoots of the Hindu Kush and create a mountainous corridor between Kandahar and Kabul. Now the army was passing through the area in early spring, when the weather in Ghazni is not usually severe. However, there have been exceptions. In the local folklore of Ghazni, one story tells how the city was twice destroyed by snowstorms during the first days after Nawroz—the first day of spring.

The army felt relief and found sustenance as it descended into the fertile and lush valley of Kabul and its northern extension of Kohdaman at the foot of the Hindu Kush. Ptolemy lists the cities of the region as Ortospana[39] and Kabura, which corresponds to the city of Kabul, and he calls the inhabitants "Kabuliti." Other townships in the area are identified as Irgurda (Arghandeh), Lukarna (Logar), and Bagarda (Wardak).[40] Strabo says that Alexander spent the winter among the Paropamisadae, in whose country the towns were numerous and supplies of every kind, except oil, abundant.[41] Alexander did not halt long in Kabul and moved north to Kapisa at the foot of the Hindu Kush Massif. He established his camp near the modern city of Charikar at the bottom of the Khwaja Sayaran hill, most likely at the Opian high ground. Here he planned the construction of a military fort known as "Alexandria ad Caucasum" (Alexandria by the Caucasus) to secure the opening of the Panjsher, Shutul, and Ghorband Rivers that stream out southward from the Hindu Kush. Arrian calls the mountain range "the Indian Caucasus," as the Greeks knew the entire northern chain from Herat to northeastern Afghanistan and beyond as the Caucasus. Curtius claims that the chain in fact splits Asia in two.[42] The Greeks adopted local names that differed from place to place for the same mountains. Accordingly, "the Paropamisus" was commonly used to denote all the mountains west of the Indus River and north of the Kabul River all the way to Herat.

The location of Alexandria on the Caucasus is disputed. Some place it in Bagram, about 25 miles from Kabul; others place it as far west as Bamian. Alexander supposedly crossed the Hindu Kush Mountains through Khawak Pass at the head of Panjsher Valley. This meant that he should have built his military fort close to the confluence of the Panjsher and Ghorband Rivers that dominate three routes going east to India, north to Bactria, and west to Arachosia. Recent archeological studies in Afghanistan suggest that Alexandria by the Caucasus was located at the current town of Jabal-Saraj. These studies also indicate that Nicaea, another city built or repaired at the same time, was located at Bagram on the banks of the Panjsher River. It is likely that Nicaea was the "other city" described as a place a day's journey from Alexandria.[43] Alexander reportedly built two other military posts in the area that were located at a day's journey from Alexandria. They were Cartana at the foot of the Hindu Kush Mountains and Cadrusi inside Panjsher Valley.

In the spring of 329 BC, when the Hindu Kush became passable, Alexander began his most stupendous march across the precipitous gorges and along the snowy paths of the mountain. Before leaving, he settled 7,000 among the older Macedonians and other retired soldiers. According to Donald Engels, studies of the known time spent crossing the 47-mile Khawak Pass, over the Hindu Kush, which was seventeen days, help determine numbers for the Macedonian army. Assuming that a double-file of 10,000 soldiers, as well as about 4,000 cavalry horses in single-file, each occupy a stretch of 12 miles, the time the army took to clear the pass means there were 64,000 troops, 10,000 cavalry horses, and 36,000 noncombatant followers.[44] The lengthy Macedonian columns took those seventeen days to cross the mountains even while they suffered from severe weather and lack of supplies. "Grain shortages had brought the troops to the verge of starvation. . . . The men survived on freshwater fish and herbs, and when even those means of sustenance had run out, they were given orders to slaughter the pack animals. They managed to stay alive on the meat from these until they reached the Bactrians."[45]

The first city the forces reached after crossing the Hindu Kush was Drapsaka (modern Andarab, located in the fertile valley of the same name). This has long been a major caravan staging point for travelers coming across the mountains through Khawak Pass. It remained a major highway between north and south before motor vehicles became available in the country. Even today, the stage houses remain at the edge of the Andarab Valley. After a rest in Andarab and regrouping of his forces, Alexander was ready to move to Bactra and deal with Bessus. This concluded the first phase of Alexander's military campaign in the east. Its goal was to open and secure his strategic line of communication to Bactria and to support his further advances to the northern limits of his conquest at the banks of the Jaxartes River.

The Conquest of Bactria and Soghdiana

The second phase was the conquest of Bactria and Soghdiana, as well as building a sustainable defensive line against the constant threat of Scythian raids across the Jaxartes. In this phase the Macedonian army faced three challenges:

1. Defeating Bessus, who had declared himself the successor of Darius as the Great King of Iran.
2. Pacification of the turbulent area across Bactria and Soghdiana.
3. Containing the persistent threat of incursions by nomadic hordes from the Central Asian steppes.

Bessus failed to make use of the time he had to make necessary preparations to confront Alexander. Although after the death of Darius most leaders in the east looked to him as the king who could stand up against the European invaders, Bessus failed to act as an effective leader. He had expected that the invading army would march on to India from its conquered lands in the south. However, during the previous five years, Alexander had never left a defying enemy on his flanks. Once the Greeks' intention to cross the mountain was known, Bessus had a good chance to block the invasion using the difficult terrain of the Hindu Kush. From a base in the Andarab Valley, he could put up an effective defense and possibly inflict heavy losses on the invaders. He had criticized Darius for "negligence that had increased the enemy's reputation" and a failure to face the enemy on favorable terrain or behind many rivers that created formidable obstacles to an invading army. And yet, Bessus ignored his own advice given to the late Darius.[46]

Bessus was terrified by the speed of Alexander's approach and was confused about how to respond to the enemy now at his doorstep. At a council of war in Bactra (Balkh), he tried to boost the morale of his men by understating the power of the Macedonians and playing up the influence of himself and his allies in Bactria and Soghdiana. The plan he proposed to his friends was based more on wishful thinking than the reality of the situation. The 8,000-horse Bactrian cavalry under his command were no match for an enemy force seven times greater. He decided to withdraw into Soghdiana and use the Oxus River as a barrier against the enemy until strong reinforcements could join his force from neighboring tribes, including the Choarasmis, Dahae, the Sacae (Sakas), the Indians, and the Scythians living across the Jaxartes. While his courtiers praised the plan, one of his councilors, Cobares, offered a soberer assessment. He cautioned King Bessus (Artaxerxes V) that a ruler who had a great burden on his shoulders should think and act realistically and in moderation. He said the king needed careful planning, not impulsive action. He laced his argument with a famous local proverb: "A frightful dog barks more fiercely than it bites and that it is the deepest rivers that flow with least noise."[47] Cobares then proposed a plan that angered Bessus. He suggested that, because he could not defeat the enemy by force, it would be wiser to make peace and accept the suzerainty of Alexander to maintain his own position and save his lands from the wrath of the victor. To this, Bessus—a proud Bactrian king— reacted so furiously that he could hardly be restrained by his friends from murdering Cobares, who managed to escape and join Alexander.

Bessus faced an odd situation. His long hesitation in facing the enemy and the speed of the enemy approach caused his army to lose confidence in him, and they began to desert. The beleaguered Bactrian king ordered his people to lay waste to the area in the path of the advancing enemy and then fled with some of his followers across the Oxus to Nautaka (modern Karshi in Uzbekistan), a town near Maracanda (Samarkand), the capital of Soghdiana. He missed another opportunity to put up a fight on the Oxus, at a place that was unfavorable for the enemy. It seems surprising that Bessus did not avail himself of this opportunity to resist Alexander's crossing, particularly since the Oxus is difficult to cross by fording. Even if he hoped to stop the enemy by devastating the area and burning the boats along the Oxus, these measures could only hinder the advancing Greek columns but not stop them unless the obstacles were covered by an active defense. Most of the Bactrian cavalry abandoned Bessus when he fled across the river.

Chasing Bessus

After a long stay in Andarab, Alexander marched through the Samangan plain and, without much trouble, seized control of Aornus (Tashqurghan) and Bactra (Balkh), the chief city of Bactria.[48] To check the advance of the invading army, Bessus stripped and laid waste to eastern Bactria up to the foot of the mountains. This slowed the advance of Alexander significantly in his pursuit of Bessus across the Oxus River. Having named Artabazus satrap of Bactria, and placing Archelaus with a garrison in Aornus, Alexander marched northward toward the Oxus River, the boundary between Bactria and Soghdiana. After a weary march of two or three days through the hot desert, Alexander reached the banks of the Oxus and found that Bessus had burned all the boats and crossing craft. Greek writers say that Alexander crossed the river in five days on skin-tents stuffed with straw. It is likely that he crossed at Kilif, a traditional crossing point located on the shortest distance between Bactra (Balkh) and Maracanda (Samarkand), which was Alexander's next destination. Arrian wrote that the width of the river at the crossing point was about 1,200 meters.[49] The description of the Oxus at that location fits closely with Arrian's account. It is deep and rapid there, with the hill fortress of Kilif on the right bank and the Dev Kala and rocky hills on the left forcing the river into a narrower channel that has kept a course unchanged through the ages.[50] Many other armies in later times crossed the Oxus at Kilif, where the banks contract to about two-thirds of a mile and the speed of the water is slower. In 1832, Alexander Burnes crossed the river in 15 minutes at Khwaja Saleh, 33 miles lower, by ferry drawn by swimming horses. He estimated the width of the river as 800 yards and its depth from 7 to 20 feet.[51] Kilif now rests on the Afghanistan-Turkmenistan border.

Bessus lacked loyal support north of the Oxus. His Soghdian allies had no intention of sacrificing their country for this royal pretender. Alexander's advance over the Oxus caused panic among the local leaders. The confederate forces of Bessus, including those under Spitamenes and Datapherenes, lost hope that King Bessus would lead them to victory against Alexander. To buy time, Bessus's associates decided to betray him and hand him over to Alexander, hoping thereby to pacify the invader and put an end to further conquest in their region. They were mistaken to expect that Alexander's only object was to capture Bessus, after which he would then withdraw from Soghdiana and accept the Oxus as the northern boundary of his dominion. Spitamenes and company sent a message to the Macedonian king offering to surrender their ally Bessus. Alexander immediately sent Ptolemy with 6,000 men to secure Bessus, whom they found in a walled village, deserted by his Soghdian friends. The spiteful way Alexander treated his royal prisoner leaves an unanswered question: Was his extremely brutal punishment of Bessus based on utter hate, or was he sending a strong message to others who may have been contemplating resistance? In any case, Alexander mistreated Bessus, who was a king at least to the Bactrians, cruelly and in contravention of local expectations on how a king and a soldier should treat his captured enemy. At Alexander's order, Bessus was publicly humiliated by placing him naked and fettered on the roadside as the victorious army marched past. Later he was scourged and sent in chains to Bactra, where he was mutilated before being transported to Ecbatana (Hamadan) and executed. Destiny caught up with Bessus as he fell victim to the same kind of conspiracy that he had concocted against Darius more than a year before.

Unmoved by the appeasement attempt by the Soghdian leaders who handed over Bessus, Alexander continued his campaign and did not slow his march. He intended to annex Soghdiana and fix the northern limit of his empire at the Jaxartes. The Greeks called this river the Tanais (the ancient name of River Don), imagining that it was the same river that flows into the Meiotic Lake (Sea of Azov) and thus was the boundary between Asia and Europe. This mistaken interpretation well served the morale of homesick Macedonians by giving them the impression that they were not extremely far away from Europe. Strabo felt that the designation was part of a stratagem to claim that Alexander had conquered all of Asia.[52] Having seized and garrisoned Maracanda (Samarkand), the army pushed on northeastward to the river Jaxartes and pillaged and burned the neighboring villages there.

Local Resistance

The local forces, led by their national leaders, resorted to two modes of resistance: defensive battle behind the walls of their fortified villages and cities; and guerrilla warfare. Most of the villages and towns in the area were traditionally protected by walls and defensive works. The local population had recognized the strategic value of fortified towns as they had faced relentless raids by nomadic hordes from the steppes to the north. In many cases, these forts were almost impregnable to frontal assaults and could exhaust the fighting resources of invaders such as Alexander the Great. Strabo offers a detailed account of the area's strongholds.[53]

In his march across Soghdiana, Alexander left garrisons in various towns that initially experienced no resistance, although detached bodies of the natives hovered on his flanks. But as the Greeks showed intentions to colonize the area, the mood of the people changed, and a national resistance movement began to take shape. The uprising was also fueled by religious feelings as the invaders showed hostility toward Zoroastrianism, the dominant religion of Bactria and Soghdiana. Alexander banned the local burial customs; his army ransacked libraries and temples and destroyed or desecrated the Avesta books. The Greek writers are quiet about the persecution of the Iranian religion, but Persian sources are vocal about it and speak of the conqueror as the "*Gazeshte Alexander*," which means "Alexander the accursed."[54]

On the Jaxartes, at the northeastern confines of Soghdiana, Alexander planned to found a new city to protect against incursions from the Scythian nomads on the other side of the river. The Jaxartes, which streams out of the chilly vale of Fergana and flows through the steppes, was a geographic feature of the highest importance. The Fergana Valley is the entrance to the line of communication between southwestern Asia and China through the pass over the Tianshan Mountains, descending on the other side into the lands of Kashghar. Here Alexander, with strategic insight, resolved to fix the limit of his empire, and on the banks of the river he founded a new city, Alexandria Eschate (Alexandria the Ultimate). This city stood at the modern location of Khujand in today's Tajikistan.

But his plan was interrupted when he received the news of an uprising led by Spitamenes and supported by the Bactrian leader Oxyartes and other nationalists. The rebellion began with 7,000 Bactrian cavalry and spread like a brushfire across Soghdiana and Bactria. Losing his temper because of these events, Alexander resorted to harshness and brutality. He did not have to worry about public opinion in his treatment of the hostile natives, whom the Greek considered to be barbarians. The invaders began to employ pacification by force during which entire cities were razed to the ground and their inhabitants sold into slavery. Whole regions were depopulated and recolonized with a new population imported from the more tractable lands to the west. The pacification strategy, which bordered on virtual genocide, was accompanied by the foundation of more than a dozen cities in Bactria and Soghdiana.

The Macedonians now faced a different kind of warfare, however.

The enemy refused decisive engagements and instead exploited the strengths of their local fighting tactics. Using hit-and-run guerrilla tactics, they avoided pitched battles with the Macedonian heavy armor but kept the Macedonians on the move and off balance by dispersing their forces across the entire theater of war. The resistance leaders never concentrated their forces in numbers sufficient for Alexander to pin them down and destroy them. Instead they launched swift raids on isolated garrisons, baggage and supply convoys, and vulnerable detachments. The guerrillas often ambushed and harassed Macedonian columns sent out to rescue beleaguered outposts.

In 329 BC, Alexander made important changes to the organization of his Companion cavalry. The eight squadrons (*ilai*) of cavalry were expanded into at least eight regiments (*hipparchiat*), each consisting of two, or perhaps more, squadrons. Some of these squadrons probably included or consisted of the excellent Iranian cavalry. In addition to the Companions, Alexander made use of Iranian cavalry and mounted javelin men. At the battle near the Hydaspes River in 326 BC, his army also included a body of Dahae mounted archers, as well as horsemen from Bactria, Soghdiana, Arachosia, and the Paropamisus (the Hindu Kush region).

As the uprising spread, natives from seven cities in Ferghana and its vicinity overpowered the Macedonian garrisons and put them to the sword. In Maracanda, the principal fortress of the region, the Macedonians were besieged in their citadel and could hardly hold their own. To the northeast, across the Jaxartes, the Sacae (Sakas), threatened by the construction of a major Greek fortress on the river, gathered in force for a showdown on the far bank while a body of Massagetae troops joined Spitamenes and other Scythian tribes assembled to drive out the intruder. It was a dangerous moment for Alexander.

Ferghana Insurgency

From his camp on the Jaxartes (Syr Darya), 250 kilometers northeast of Samarkand, Alexander launched a major military sweep to reduce the rebel cities in the Ferghana Valley. Cyropolis, a frontier town founded by Cyrus the Great in 530 BC, was at the center of seven rebellious settlements. Cyropolis stood at the location of modern Istaravshan in Tajikistan, formerly known as Urateppe. Alexander first recovered the fortresses along the Jaxartes and personally moved against Gaza (Nau)[55] and sent Craterus to Cyropolis.[56] Using heavy bombardment by siege engines, Alexander scaled and burned five of the fortresses in two days and sent cavalry to cordon off two other settlements. Their inhabitants were massacred as they tried to escape the onslaught. By order of Alexander, all males in these towns were killed. The women and children were sold into slavery, and the army carried off anything else of value. Alexander then moved against the largest city, Cyropolis, 40 kilometers from Khujand—the location of Alexandria Eschate. Cyropolis was protected by much higher walls than the other fortresses and defended by a resolute population. Several attempts to reduce the defenses by siege engines and scaling failed. Then Alexander discovered a dried-up stream that gave access to the town. As the Macedonians kept the defenders' attention focused with their siege engines, Alexander led a raid into the city through the dry watercourse under the wall and surprised the enemy. After recovering from the surprise attack, the defenders launched a fierce counterattack, during which Alexander was wounded by a stone in the head and neck, Craterus was wounded by an arrow, and many other officers were injured. The defenders, however, lost the outer fortress, and they moved to the citadel and continued to fight. Cyropolis natives resisted fiercely, and so did the nearby fortress of a people known as the Memaceni, who made a stand at the ancient citadel of Mug-Teppe, which stood on a high mound 50 kilometers south of the river. According to Curtius, no other city garrison mounted stronger resistance to the siege.[57]

Finally, under the pressure of Macedonian encirclement and lack of water, the defenders surrendered. According to Arrian, out of 15,000 natives, about 8,000 were killed. The fall of Cyropolis was followed by the capitulation of the seventh town. The remnants of the inhabitants of all these places were led in chains to help populate the new Alexandria.

Having quelled the revolt of the Soghdian nationalists, Alexander now faced two other military challenges on the two sides of the Jaxartes. On the west, Spitamenes had besieged the Greek garrison in Maracanda, while on the east Scythian nomads (Sakas) were threatening the construction of the new Alexandria.

A River-Crossing Battle

As the walls of Alexandria Eschate rose, defiant, noisy, jeering Scythians lined the far bank of the river. Their threat became so serious that Alexander decided to cross the river and attack the nomads. The operation was a carefully planned "assault river crossing" in the modern

Battle of Jaxartes

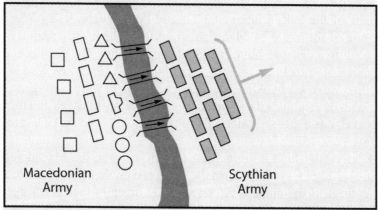

Macedonian Army

Scythian Army

Phase 1: Crossing of the Jaxartes

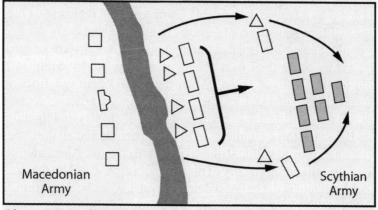

Macedonian Army

Scythian Army

Phase 2: Encirclement

| Macedonian Cavalry | Macedonian Phalanx | Macedonian Archers | Macedonian Slingers | Macedonian Catapults | Scythian Horsemen |

Legend

sense. The Jaxartes at the crossing point was wider than a bowshot, which meant that the Macedonians could board their hurriedly prepared boats and rafts in safety but that they would enter the Sakas' range of fire halfway across the river. Alexander took two measures to secure the crossing operation. First, he arranged for the crossing to take place in one massive wave so that the mounted enemy archers across the river would be faced with more targets than they could engage. Second, he ordered his longer-range artillery (catapults) to cover the crossing boats. As one of the Saka leaders was hit and killed immediately after the opening of the battle by Macedonian artillery, the enemy retired from the bank to a distance out of range of the catapults. The Greeks seized the moment to cross the river by using boats and rafts of inflated skins. The first wave led by Alexander consisted of light forces, slingers, and archers who established a screen to keep the enemy in check and protect the cavalry as it crossed safely. The phalanx soldiers were the last to get across.

After establishing a bridgehead on the far bank, the Macedonians' main challenge was to pin down the Sakas and prevent them from breaking contact. If the nomads retreated to the depth of their territory, Alexander would never have been able to pursue them across the steppes. Alexander wanted to maintain contact and provoke a battle. Therefore, he ordered an advance detachment, composed of a regiment of mercenaries and four squadrons of lancers, to advance and draw the enemy into battle. Seeing the isolated enemy unit, the Sakas were tempted to engage it by using their overwhelming cavalry, but by doing so they would become a fixed target. When the Macedonian spearmen were surrounded and attacked by the Sakas' mounted archers, Alexander launched the main attack. A combined force of cavalry and light forces under Balacrus (three regiments of the Companions and all the mounted javelin men) moved within striking range and charged. Alexander, at the head of the remaining cavalry of his own squadron, attacked the flank of the encircled enemy. The Macedonian cavalry with the support of light forces broke the enemy lines, and in the ensuing clashes the Scythians retreated after suffering heavy losses. Alexander pursued them to a point beyond which his forces could not risk getting caught up in a drawn-out battle in enemy territory with uncertain results. Curtius suggests that the enemy was pursued up to a line he calls the "boundary-stone of Father Bacchus," which must have been a key terrain feature such as a pass over the Moghul-tau Mountains, about a day's march from Khujand. Most likely, the pursuit of the fugitives into the eastern Ferghana Valley marked the limit of Alexander's progress northward. The rapid pursuit of the nomads in the severe heat exhausted the Greek troops, who were suffering from thirst. Alexander fell sick with dysentery from drinking contaminated water and could not pursue the enemy any further. He was seriously ill and was carried to his camp.

The Deadly Ambush in Maracanda

After his victory, Alexander received news of the massacre of his troops at Maracanda by Spitamenes. Alexander sent a Macedonian expeditionary column, composed of 3,000 infantry and 800 cavalry, to raise the siege of Maracanda and neutralize the native forces under Spitamenes. But as the relieving force approached Maracanda, Spitamenes moved away from the city and laid an ambush for the enemy column marching in pursuit of the fugitives. Alexander's forces were entrapped during the ambush, on the banks of the Polytimetus River (Zarafshan River), and were killed almost to a man.[58] Learning of this new disaster, Alexander hurried to Maracanda with cavalry and light troops, covering more than 170 miles in three days in a forced march, which seems almost impossible in the heat of a Soghdian summer for foot soldiers, some of whom were hoplites wearing their bronze helmets and carrying their shields and clad in mail. Alerted by Alexander's approach, Spitamenes, having no intention of entering a decisive engagement with the enemy, swiftly disappeared in the limitless desert far out of reach of the Macedonian forces. Angered and frustrated by his failure to catch the evasive Soghdian chieftain, Alexander exacted his vengeance by ravaging the fertile and densely populated valley of Zarafshan, mercilessly putting to the sword the inhabitants of all the towns that he took along the river down to the vicinity of Ziadin and Kermineh. He pushed his way farther downriver, passed Bokhara, and advanced as far as Karakul, beyond which the river disappears in the sands.[59] But he never caught Spitamenes, who disappeared like the wind into the limitless desert.

The year 329 BC was difficult for both sides. The natives paid a high price for resisting the invader. Tens of thousands of fighters and inhabitants in Bactria and Soghdiana were massacred, and dozens of sites and towns were leveled by the Macedonian soldiers, who desperately aspired for a clear victory that they failed to achieve. Alexander found no enemy capable of meeting him in pitched battle, and yet native chieftains spearheaded by Spitamenes continued to resist, forcing the invaders to crisscross the area. It required another year and more to put down the rebellion. Meanwhile, Alexander and his light and heavy forces underwent the greatest fatigues and hardships during their marches through the rugged terrain, rocky strongholds, and boiling deserts with inadequate supplies. In the autumn of 329 BC, Alexander recrossed the Oxus and moved to Zariaspa (Bactra) to rest there through the extreme winter season. As he had garrisoned many cities in the area, available combat forces were dwindling, and he needed reinforcements. In Zariaspa, he received an army of Greek mercenaries under Asander and Nearchus and another army from Syria headed by Asclepiodorus, the viceroy of Syria, and his deputy Menes.[60] Curtius says that the reinforcements were more than 19,000 strong.[61] In Zariaspa, Alexander put Bessus on trial, accusing him of betraying Darius—the foe Alexander had set out to fight and whose empire he had sought to destroy. Alexander condemned and humiliated Bessus by ordering his nose and ears to be cut off and then be taken to Ecbatana to be put to death. Arrian called the punishment excessive and believed the mutilation of the body was barbaric.

Renewed Uprising

In early 328 BC, news of a renewed uprising in Soghdiana reached Alexander while Spitamenes and Bactrian nationalists were preparing to launch new attacks on the Greeks in Bactria. Many natives had taken refuge in their strongholds and refused to submit to Alexander's viceroys. Alexander returned to the Oxus River with the intention of launching a wide military operation in Soghdiana. He left four of his generals—Polysperchon, Attalus, Gorgias, and Meleager—in Bactra to guard the area and defeat those who had already rebelled. Then he divided the army he had remaining with him into five divisions. The first division was put under command of Hephaestion, the second under Ptolemy, the confidential bodyguard. The command of the third division was assigned to Perdicas, while Coenus and Artabazus were given command of the fourth division. Alexander himself took the fifth division and marched toward Maracanda. The other divisions advanced in separate columns, and during the spring and summer of 328 BC they fanned out across the area, pacifying the rebellious local settlements. Moving through Karakul, Bukhara, Kermineh, and Kata-Kurgan to Maracanda, Alexander put down all resistance and in the meantime established six military towns spaced out within short distances of each other.[62] Curtius writes that two of these towns were south of Margiana (Merv) at locations near Sarakhs and Maruchaq; four cities were located farther east near today's northern Afghan cities of Maimana, Andkhoy, Sheberghan, and Sari-Pul.

While Alexander was busy in Soghdiana, Spitamenes, supported by 600 Massagetae horsemen, resurfaced in Bactria and made a surprise attack on a Greek garrison, killing the soldiers and taking their commander prisoner. Emboldened by his success, Spitamenes marched a few days later to Zariaspa (Bactra) and ravaged the area. Taken by surprise, the small Macedonian garrison sallied out against the enemy and, despite some initial headway, fell into an ambush set by Spitamenes that caused the deaths of scores of Macedonian horsemen. Macedonian general Aristonicus was killed while another general, Peithone, was wounded and taken prisoner. Responding to Spitamenes's incursion into Bactria, Craterus hastened, by forced marches, to intercept the resistance leader. Avoiding a pitched battle with the Macedonians, Spitamenes and his Scythian allies vanished swiftly into the desert. Craterus failed to reach the retreating main body but clashed only with its 1,000 Massagetae horsemen rearguard, who themselves, after losing 150 of their own, escaped into the desert.

At the end of the operations, Macedonian columns reunited at Maracanda. Meanwhile, Alexander relieved the aging Artabazus of the viceroyalty of Bactria at his own request and appointed Amyntas as his successor. He also put Coenus in command of a sizable force, including his and Meleager's divisions, 400 Companion cavalry, all the horse archers, and all the local Bactrians, Soghdians, and others who were under command of Amyntas. This task force was ordered to winter in Soghdiana to protect the country and to deal with possible incursions by Spitamenes. However, Coenus faced difficulty in holding his own against the indomitable Spitamenes, who had assembled a body of 3,000 Scythian horsemen at Bagai, west of Bukhara. Coenus planned to invade Soghdiana. Bagai was located at today's Ustuk, which in more modern times was a frontier fortress of Bukhara, 28 miles below Charjui in Turkmenistan on the opposite side of the Oxus. The hostile forces finally met. Coenus was victorious, and Spitamenes, who fled into the desert with his Scythian horsemen, fell victim to their treachery. They cut off his head and sent it as a peace offering to Alexander. Curtius writes that Spitamenes was murdered by his estranged wife, who plotted his demise while he was camped following his last fight with the Greeks.[63]

During the pause in Maracanda in the autumn of 328 BC, Alexander murdered his close friend Cleitus the Black, who had saved his life in the Battle of Granicus. During a drinking brawl, Alexander became agitated by Cleitus's criticism of the king's increasingly arrogant manners. As the year was ending, Alexander sent his army into winter quarters while he camped in Nautaka for the winter of 328–327 BC. This place has been generally identified with Karshi, the fertile area south of Samarkand.

The Soghdian Rock

Early in the spring of 327 BC, Alexander left Nautaka and marched eastward for a final campaign in the hills of Paraetacene (modern Tajikistan), which was the heart of native opposition in the east, a region that in the twentieth century became the hotbed of the Basmachi uprising against Soviet rule in Central Asia. It is the mountainous country between the upper courses of the Oxus and the Jaxartes (Syr Darya) Rivers, including the hilly district now known as Hissar southwest of Tajikistan's capital, Dushanbe. First, Alexander moved to capture the famous Soghdian Rock fortress, which Curtius calls the "Rock of Arimazes." According to Arrian, the stronghold rose vertically on every side, and the snow-covered surroundings added to its unassailability.[64] The defenders, who had provisioned the fort for a long siege, challenged the confused Greeks, suggesting that they could reach the place only if they could bring soldiers with wings to "fly." Alexander took up the challenge and ordered a group of 300 handpicked alpinists with rock-climbing experience to ascend the steepest face under the cover of darkness. Using iron tent pegs, the Macedonians struggled all night until they reached the top of the rock by dawn, losing 30 comrades who fell during the climb. Alarmed by the unexpected appearance of enemy soldiers at the rock near the fort who were waving cotton cloths to signify their "wings," the natives accepted Alexander's call for surrender with no retribution from the Greeks. It was here that Prince Oxyartes of Bactria had placed the members of his family for safety, including his daughter Roxana (or Roshanak), whose beauty and charms, according to Greek chroniclers, so fascinated Alexander that he fell in love with her, married her, and made her his queen in spite of many warnings from his friends.[65] Some may suspect that the marriage was merely a matter of policy, but as Agnes Savill notes, it was hard to believe that "a man who cared so much for Homer and the Greek drama, which depicted so many noble women, would have entered into loveless marriage at this stage of his career."[66]

The sequence of events and the geography suggest that the fort must have been located somewhere in the mountainous track straddling the current boundary between Uzbekistan and Tajikistan. Some have identified it with the steep crags that line one side of the narrow gorge near Darband called the Iron Gate (Temir Darvoza), which forms the only direct approach from Bokhara and Samarkand (Uzbekistan) to Hissar (Tajikistan), or a point about five miles to its northeast.[67]

From the Soghdian Rock, Alexander continued his march eastward, where the army's advance was halted by another astounding mountain fortress no less formidable than the Soghdian Rock. It is called by Arrian the "Rock of Chorienes" and by Curtius the "Rock of Sysimithres." Its location is believed to be the narrow pass at the Wakhsh River, which is located on the road between Hissar and Badakhshan.[68] It was said to be more than 3,000 meters high and more than seven miles in circumference, rising vertically on all sides. There was only a narrow path that made any ascent, even in single-file, exceedingly difficult. Furthermore, the fortress was defended all round by a deep ravine that prohibited any assault unless the ravine was filled up so that the assault could be made by siege engines from level ground. Alexander was reluctant to turn away from the challenge and decided to capture the fort at any cost. Using the pine trees that were plentiful in the area, Alexander lowered his soldiers into the ravine to work from the bottom upward, building bridge-like structures to enable the troops to get to the base of the fortress across level ground. This enormous work was carried out by the entire army working day and night in three shifts. Failing to dislodge the Greeks from the work by firing missiles from the fort and impressed by the determination and perseverance of Alexander to reduce the fort, the ruler, Chorienes, sent messages of peace, which were finalized through the mediation of Oxyartes.

Then, in the summer of 327 BC, Alexander returned to Bactra to make preparations for an invasion of India. Meanwhile, he dispatched Craterus with 600 of the Companion cavalry and several thousand infantry against Katanes and Austanes, the two defiant local chieftains in the Paraetacene region. In the close battle that ensued, Craterus defeated the natives; Katanes fell in the action, and Austanes was captured. In Bactra, another plot was discovered, this time involving Alexander's pages and his personal historian, Callisthenes. The plot was partly inspired by the increasing arrogance of the king's behavior. Conceited by his military exploits, Alexander increasingly saw himself as being above men. One of the pages, Hermolaos, who had been subjected to some degrading punishment, conspired against the king, who narrowly escaped assassination. When the plot was discovered, the conspirators and their teacher Callisthenes were tried, tortured, and put to death.

The Invasion of India

Alexander made his final preparation for the invasion of India—the third phase of his Asian conquest. Up to this point, Alexander had conquered all the territories of the Persian Empire except its eastern satrapy located west of the Indus. For the Greeks of the time, India was an ill-defined land wrapped in myths and legends. From a distance, it looked to them like a new world of indefinite extent and abounding in wonders and riches. Alexander aspired to surpass the feats of ancient conquerors such as Cyrus the Great and even those of legendary heroes and divinities such as Hercules and Dionysus. He also dreamed of reaching the notional "eastern Ocean" beyond India. So even without any other inducement, he must have eagerly desired to explore and subdue it. However, what the chroniclers called the Macedonian conqueror's "Indian conquest" was in fact only a dash to Punjab through the rugged country west of the Indus.

In the summer of 327 BC, after leaving 3,500 cavalry and 10,000 infantry troops under Amyntas in Bactria,[69] Alexander set out on his Indian conquest at the head of 120,000 foot and 15,000 horse which included at least 70,000 Asiatic troops.[70] He crossed the Hindu Kush through Khawak Pass in ten days and camped at the city of Alexandria ad Caucasus, which he had founded south of the pass more than two years prior. There, after dismissing the ruler of the city for mismanagement, he appointed Nikanor, one of the Companions, to take charge of the city and appointed Tyriaspes satrap of the land of the Paropamisadae and the rest of the country as far as the Kophen River (Kabul River). Furthermore, Alexander populated Alexandria with fresh settlers from the surrounding district and left those soldiers in the city who were unfit for further service.

From Alexandria Caucasus, the Macedonian army moved southeast through Kohdaman to the Kophen (Kabul) Valley, marched eastward, and entered into an assembly area at the confluence of the Alishing and Alingar Rivers, which join the Kophen River in the proximity of Mindrawar in Laghman. Alexander had invited all the chieftains of the satrapy of Gandhara, located in parts of modern-day eastern Afghanistan and northern Pakistan, to come before him and submit to his authority. Ambhi, the ruler of Taxila, whose kingdom extended from the Indus to the Jhelum, complied. But the chieftains of some hill clans, including the Aspasioi and Assakenoi sections of the Kambojas, refused. Modern studies conclude that the Kambojas were an Avestan-speaking eastern Iranian militant tribe at the boundary of the Indo-Aryans and the Iranians and appear to have moved from the Iranian into the Indo-Aryan sphere over time. In reference to the equestrian nature of their society, they are identified in Indian texts Ashvayanas and Ashvakayanas from the Sanskrit root word *ashva*, meaning "horse."[71]

The direct route to the Indus was the traditional road along the Kophen River through Khyber Pass and Peshawar Valley to Taxila, the capital of Upper Punjab. Although in the days before the invention of firearms the passage of troops through defiles such as Khyber Pass was simple and safer from immediate attack, it was strategically risky unless the people living on the flanks acquiesced or were defeated. Since the hill tribes north of the main route refused to submit to Alexander's authority, the flank of the army was exposed. Therefore, Alexander decided to use a two-pronged approach in his advance to Taxila. He divided his army into two columns. He ordered Hephaestion and Perdicas with a strong division—including the brigades of Gorgias, Cleitus, and Meleager, half of the Companion Cavalry, and the whole of the mercenary cavalry, accompanied by the Indian chiefs—to march along the main road down the valley of the Kophen to Peukelaotis (modern Charsadda) and then to the Indus. He instructed them either to seize by force whatever places lay on their route or to accept their submission if they capitulated and, when they came to the Indus, to make whatever preparations were necessary for the transport of the army across that river.

Meanwhile, Alexander took the second division, consisting of the hypaspists light infantry, all the Companion Cavalry except what was sent with Hephaestion, the brigades of infantry called the "foot companions,"[72] the archers, the Agrianians,[73] and the horse lancers. With this division of light forces, Alexander headed northeast along a circuitous route into the hilly country encompassing the modern regions of Laghman and Kunar in Afghanistan and the Bajaur, Dir, Swat, and Yousafzai regions leading to the Indus River. Here lay the territories of three warlike tribes: the Aspasians (Laghman, Kunar, and Bajaur), Gauraians (Panjkora), and Assakenians (Swat and Buner). The Aspasioi were related to the Assakenoi and were a western branch. Both peoples were admired by the Greeks for their fighting ability. Alexander personally directed operations against these clans, who stubbornly resisted from their mountain strongholds and fought the Macedonians fiercely. Even their women took up arms and fought alongside their husbands, preferring in the words of Diodorus (XVII.84.1) "a glorious death which they would have disdained to exchange for a life with dishonor."[74] Alexander was entering a different phase of the invasion, one marked by fierce mountain warfare in the highlands west of the Indus River, as he proceeded toward the intended conquest of India.

The geography and the terrain features suggest that Alexander followed the route across the junction of the Alishing and Alingar Rivers, identified as the Khoes River by the classical writers. While Macedonian infantry moved at a leisurely pace, Alexander led a column of light forces, including the whole of his cavalry and 800 mounted Macedonian foot soldiers, in a rapid march to intercept the native Aspasian hordes that were moving to take up their mountain defenses or bunching up in their strongly fortified cities. When Alexander proceeded to attack the first city, he faced strong resistance and was wounded in the shoulder by a dart. His most trusted general, Ptolemy, was also injured at the same location. Unable to capture the city by a frontal assault, Alexander encamped nearby on the side where he thought the wall was weakest. The next day at first light, the Macedonians attacked the outer of the two walls protecting the city. The outer wall was crudely constructed and was taken without much difficulty. But the inner wall was much stronger, and the attackers encountered strong resistance. Macedonians tried to scale the bulwark, and as the defenders could no longer stand their ground, they resorted to their traditional tactic of storming out of the gates and rushing to their mountain havens. Some of them perished during the flight, but many others managed to escape into the hills, which lay at no great distance from the city. Alexander put to the sword those who were taken prisoner and razed the city to the ground.

From this point on, until Alexander's descent on the banks of the Indus, two patterns of warfare dominated the armed struggle between the conquering forces and the native mountaineers. The natives often traded space for time, whereas the invaders simply killed their way to victory. In the face of an overwhelming enemy force, the natives would break contact and rush to sanctuaries in their rugged mountains, barely accessible to the attackers. This traditional way of war in the mountains of Afghanistan has been sustained for centuries and was common practice during foreign invasions in the nineteenth and twentieth centuries. Meanwhile, Alexander often punished resistance by mass killing and scorched-earth actions—a policy the Macedonian king practiced earlier not only in Bactria and Soghdiana but also in his home country (as with the punishment of Thebes in 334 BC).[75]

Then Alexander marched forward probably across the Gambiri plain north of the Kabul River toward the modern areas of Shega and Khewa. He reached another city which Arrian calls "Andaka" and Curtius calls

"Akadera." The geography and the sequence of Alexander's movement suggest that it was probably located in the hills north of the Khewa and near Dara-i Noor. The Macedonians captured that town with no resistance and garrisoned it with their own troops. Alexander left Craterus there with part of the infantry troops to reduce other cities in the vicinity and to establish Macedonian control over the surrounding district. Taking with him the light infantry (hypaspists, the archers, and the Agrianians), two infantry brigades, the cavalry guard, about four squadrons of the other Companion Cavalry, and half of the mounted archers, Alexander advanced to the Euaspla River (Kunar River)[76] and crossed it somewhere near today's Kama Bridge and moved up the Kunar Valley, where he faced stiff resistance from warlike tribes at several places.

News of Alexander's approach preceded him. At one location, which Arrian identifies as the city of the Aspasians chief (probably an area between today's Tsawkai and Narang), the inhabitants set fire to their own city and fled to the mountains. The invaders followed them as far as the terrain permitted and slaughtered many. At one point during the pursuit, when their chief was killed in a hand-to-hand fight with the Macedonian general Ptolemy, the natives launched a counterattack from the high ground to recover the body of their chief. Seeing the natives' attack, Alexander reinforced his forward troops, checked the advance of the enemy, and pushed them back into the mountains.

Alexander's next objective was the center of the Aspasians. According to Arrian, he crossed the mountains and came to a city at their base named Arigaion. Following the description of the classical writers, it seems that Alexander crossed the Kunar watershed at Nawa Pass into Bajaur and marched to the city of Arigaion, which was not far from today's Nawagai. The natives burned down the city and took to the hills. Here, Craterus, with his staff and the troops under his command, rejoined Alexander after having fully carried out all the orders given by the king. As the city seemed to occupy a very advantageous site, Alexander instructed Craterus to fortify it strongly and to people it with as many local natives who consented to making it their home together with any soldiers found unfit for further service. He then marched to a place where he discovered that most of the inhabitants of the region had taken refuge, and upon reaching a certain mountain he encamped at its base. But during a foraging and reconnaissance mission in the area, Ptolemy detected a massive concentration of natives on a mountain whose campfires were far more numerous than those of Alexander's camp.

Hearing this news, Alexander left a part of his army where it was encamped in proximity to the mountain[77] and took with him an adequate and fast-moving strike force to deal with the enemy concentration. When he reached the enemy's location, he divided his forces into three parts. The first division, including two infantry brigades (more than 5,000 men), was put under the command of Leonnatos, an officer of the bodyguard. The second division consisted of two infantry brigades, part of the hypaspists, two units of archers, half of the cavalry, and the Agrianians (more than 10,000 men) and was led by Ptolemy. The third division, including the rest of the troops, was led by Alexander personally. As the Macedonian army advanced against the position occupied by the main body of the enemy, the native forces came down from the high ground into the plain below, and a sharp fight ensued. According to Arrian, the conflict was fierce not only because of the difficult nature of the ground but also because the natives were "of a different mettle from the other barbarians there and were by far the stoutest warriors in that neighborhood." Still, the three-pronged attack broke the lines of the native forces and pushed them back into the confines of their mountain sanctuaries. In an apparent exaggeration, Greek historians claim that some 40,000 natives were taken prisoner and more than 230,000 oxen were captured in the area. Alexander identified the best oxen for beauty and size, planning to send them to Macedonia to be employed in agriculture. This indicates the efficiency of Alexander's line of communication, which now stretched more than 2,500 miles across difficult terrain.

With these military operations, the conquest of the Aspasians' territory was considered complete, and Alexander marched to invade the country of the Assakenians, the people fighting from horseback, who were reported to have under arms and ready for battle an army of 20,000 cavalry and more than 30,000 infantry plus 30 elephants.[78] The Assakenians' area encompassed the Swat and Buner regions, which today is dominated by the Pashtun Yousafzai tribe. Since Craterus had now completed fortifying the Arigaion city, which he had been instructed to fill with colonists, he rejoined Alexander with the heavily armed troops and the siege engines that were needed to take towns. Alexander himself proceeded to attack the Assakenians, taking with him the Companion Cavalry, the horse archers, the brigades of Coenus and Polysperchon, and the thousand Agrianians and archers. He passed through the country of the Gauraians, where he had to cross the Gouraios, the river named after that country. This river is clearly today's Panjkora River below its confluence with the Swat River. The passage across the river was difficult on account of its depth and swiftness and because the stones on the bed were so smooth and round that men stepping on them were apt to slip. When the natives saw Alexander approaching, they dispersed to their several cities, which they resolved to defend to the end. The ruins seen today on mounds across the hilly country of Swat indicate that the Assakenians built their towns on elevated ground for better defense.

The greatest city in the Assakenians' region was named Massaga, which was most likely situated on the main road that runs from Panjkora through Talash and Katgala Pass to the fertile plain of Lower Swat. Although the exact location of Massaga is not known, it is estimated that it stood north of the Malakand Pass near Chakdara in the lower Dir District where the Panjkora River joins the Swat River. The ancient route from Kunar Valley in Afghanistan through the Nawa Pass and Katgala Pass crosses the Swat River at Chakdara.[79] The narratives of Alexander's chroniclers suggest that this was the road taken by Alexander in 327 BC. Sir Olaf Caroe identified the Katgala Pass at the west end of the Talash Valley with Massaga,[80] which was the capital of the Assakenians' chief. Wilson conjectures that it was located at Mahagram.[81]

As the Macedonian army approached the walls of Massaga, the natives, supported by a body of 7,000 mercenaries brought from a land in the east—identified as Indian mercenaries by the Greeks—sallied out in a massive charge against the Macedonians while they were preparing to encamp. In an effort to draw the attackers to an area suitable for the invading army, Alexander feigned retreat and ordered the Macedonians to fall back to a little hill nearly a mile distant from where he had intended to encamp. The move encouraged the natives to pursue what looked like a fleeing enemy force and therefore charged at a run without any observance of order. But when the attackers moved closer and became engaged in a close-quarters fight with the Greeks, they gave way and fled back to the city, leaving about 200 dead on the battlefield. As Alexander brought up the phalanx against the fortification, he was wounded in the ankle by an arrow shot from the rampart.

Four days of siege warfare ensued, during which the invaders made extensive use of siege engines. During the first three days, they battered down part of the wall and made several attempts to force their way through the breach but failed in the face of strong resistance. Then Alexander ordered the use of gangways launched from wooden towers to cross the walls. This was attempted by the same men who had enabled him to capture Tyre in a similar fashion. The defenders repelled these efforts, and the Macedonians suffered heavy losses when the gangway launched from a wooden tower broke down under the weight of the great throng that was eagerly pushing. Macedonians fell along with the gangway. On the fourth day, the fight took a sharp turn. The Assakenians, who fought with great vigor if their chief was alive, suddenly lost heart when their leader was killed by a missile launched from a siege engine. The uninterrupted siege had already inflicted heavy casualties on the natives.[82] On the fourth day, as Alexander launched another gangway on a different tower against the wall, the defenders sent a herald to make peace. Given the difficulties of reducing the city, Alexander happily agreed with the understanding that any mercenaries would take service in his army's ranks.

With this agreement, the mercenaries left the city and encamped by themselves on a small hill that faced the camp of the Macedonians at nine miles. But as they had no wish to take up arms against their own countrymen, they resolved to leave by night and move off with all speed to their homes. When Alexander was informed of this, he surrounded the hill that same night with all his troops and, having thereby intercepted the mercenaries during their flight, cut them to pieces. Then Alexander turned back on the city and attacked it. Taken by surprise, the defenders formed themselves into a circle with their women and children in the center and offered a desperate resistance in which the women took an active part. Finally, the brave defenders were overpowered by the superior numbers and, in the words of ancient Greek historians, "met a glorious death which they would have disdained to exchange for a life without honor."[83] The fort of Massaga could be reduced only after several days of bloody fighting in which Alexander himself was wounded seriously in the ankle. When the chieftain of Massaga fell in the battle, the command of the army went to his elderly mother, Cleophis,[84] who also stood determined to defend her land to the last extreme. The example of Cleophis drew all the local women into the fight.[85] Greek writers denounce Alexander's brutal treatment of fighters who surrendered. Diodorus (XVII.84.1) wrote:

> When many were thus wounded and not a few killed, the women, taking the arms of the fallen, fought side by side with the men for the imminence of the danger and the great interests at stake forced them to do violence to their nature, and to take an active part in the defense. Accordingly some who had supplied themselves with arms did their best to cover their husbands with their shields, while others who were without arms did much to impede the enemy by flinging themselves upon them and catching hold of their shields. The defenders, however, after fighting

desperately, along with their wives, were at last overpowered by superior numbers, and met a glorious death which they would have disdained to exchange for a life with dishonor.[86]

Plutarch reproaches his slaughter of them as a foul blot on Alexander's military fame. The attack upon the city after it had capitulated on terms admits of no justification. In fact, Alexander took the defenseless city by storm and captured the mother and daughter of the chief of the Assakenians.[87]

Alexander expected that the fall of Massaga would lead to capitulation of two nearby city-fortresses, Ora and Bazira, which stood on the high ground along his intended route to the Indus through the Malakand Pass. The site of Bazira is identified with Rustam (formerly known as Bazar) and stands midway between Swat and the Indus River; Ora is considered to be today's Bazar.[88] But Sir Aurel Stein's field research indicates that Bazira was located at modern-day Bir-Kot. The same research suggests that Ora stood at the current location of Odegram.[89]

While Alexander was besieging Massaga, he sent detachments to reduce the fortresses of Bazira and Ora. Waiting for reinforcements and the arrival of the king, the Macedonian detachments took up defensive positions to contain the city-fortresses. Emboldened by the enemy's inactivity, the defenders at both cities sallied out from the fortresses but were repulsed and driven back within the walls of their cities. Then Alexander decided to contain Bazira and move first against Ora, which was larger and seemed to be on the verge of receiving reinforcements. The siege of Ora did not cost Alexander much effort, for he captured the place with the first assault and seized all the elephants that had been left inside. The fall of Ora broke the will of resistance in Bazira; as with the inhabitants of all the other cities in the area, the population left their cities and fled across the Shang-La Pass to Aornus, a rock citadel on the Indus.

The Battle of Aornus

Aornus was a hard-to-reach mountain stronghold on the Indus River north of the confluence of the Kabul and Indus Rivers. Aornus in Old Indian is identified as "Avarana," meaning "the hiding place." It is said to have had a circuit of about 200 stadia (about 12 miles) and at its lowest elevation a height of 11 stadia (more than 7,000 feet). The rock was washed on its southern face by the Indus, which at this point was very

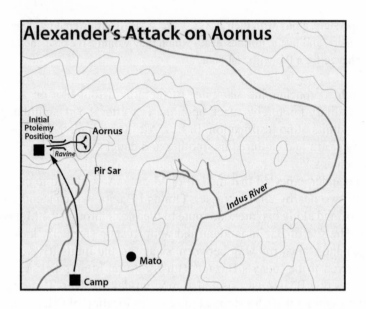

deep, surrounded by rugged crags and precipitous rocks inaccessible from that side. On its other sides the mount was enclosed by ravines, cliffs, and swamps, making it difficult for the most determined assailants to negotiate the barriers. Only a single path provided access to the summit. The fortress was well supplied with water, which gushed out from a copious spring, and contained arable land for cultivation and therefore could not be starved into submission. Aornus was long believed to be the great mountain now known as Mahaban, but in 1926 the site was satisfactorily identified with the modern mountain Pir-Sar in Swat, Pakistan, by Sir Aurel Stein and has been confirmed since by archaeologists.[90] It offered the last threat to Alexander's supply line, which was vulnerable as it stretched over the heights of the Hindu Kush to Persia and Central Asia.

Alexander, upon learning of these particulars, was seized with an ardent desire to capture this mountain bastion. His desire to capture the stronghold (also known as the Rock) was based on military exigencies and motivated by a legend that the demigod Heracles, whom he claimed as an ancestor, had failed to conquer this impregnable site. However, Arrian believes that Heracles did not penetrate so far east and opines that the legend of Heracles was mentioned to make the story of its capture all the more wonderful.[91] Further, a local myth told that a Hindu god, probably Krishna, had been unable to capture the Rock.

Meanwhile, the division under Hephaestion and Perdicas, which had marched to the Indus River on the main route through the Peshawar Valley, had secured Peukelaotis, the center of the region, which was located at today's Charsadda, 17 miles northwest of Peshawar. The column also pacified the surrounding territory and moved to the Indus, where it began preparing a bridge to span the river in accordance with Alexander's orders. Having decided to move against Aornus, Alexander garrisoned the strongholds of Massaga, Bazira, and Ora in the hills of Swat and Buner to control the districts around them and then marched, probably through Shah-kot, to the Indus plain. He appointed Nikanor, one of the Companions, satrap of the territory on the west side of the Indus, then marched toward that river and received the submission of a city that lay not far from the Indus. He garrisoned the city with Macedonian soldiers under the command of Philippos, then reduced other towns situated near the Indus. He was accompanied on this occasion by Kophaios and Assagetes, the local chiefs. Alexander then moved to Embolima, located at today's ruins of Amb, near Aornus, and set up a supply depot under the command of Craterus to support the operations against Aornus in case the assault failed and the siege extended into a blockade.

Helped by neighboring tribesmen, who led him to the best point of access into the stronghold, Alexander spent two days in careful and thorough reconnaissance of the position. He sent the guides with Ptolemy, accompanied by the Agrianians and the other lightly armed troops and selected hypaspists, to the objective. He directed him to secure a position and hold it with a strong guard and then to signal to him when he had occupied it. Ptolemy, who followed a route that proved rough and difficult to traverse, succeeded in securing a suitable foothold on the western spur of the mountain, where he entrenched his men without being detected by the defenders, who were on the eastern summit. Then, as directed, Ptolemy sent a signal to Alexander by raising a beacon, hoping the flame would be seen by him. Alexander did see the signal and the next day moved forward with his army, only to be blocked by the Aornus defenders in difficult terrain. Having checked the advance of Alexander, the natives fell in full force on Ptolemy's position, making strenuous efforts to destroy the enemy's entrenchments. Through a fierce fight, Ptolemy maintained his position, and when night fell the natives began to withdraw.

That night, Alexander sent Ptolemy a letter instructing him that, when the king's forces assailed the rock, Ptolemy should move out from his position and charge the enemy on the mountain, so that the defenders would be faced with attack from the front and rear simultaneously. The next morning at daybreak, Alexander moved from his camp, led his army along the same route followed by Ptolemy, but soon came under fierce attack from the besieged defenders. The Macedonians had to climb and fight not as a unit but as individuals struggling to find the terrain to reassemble. They gained the summit of the pass between the eastern and western summits early in the afternoon after much pain and toil. They then linked up with Ptolemy's men. Now the army held advantaged ground from which they could assault the mountain citadel. But the nature of the terrain would not allow a frontal attack. The mass of the mountain rose abruptly in the form of a steep cone. A deep ravine separated the Macedonians from the defenders' position; the gap needed to be filled and bridged.

The deep ravine kept Alexander and his catapults from ascending the vulnerable north side leading to the fort. Alexander decided to use the timber from the adjoining forest to form a pathway beginning at the top of the hill on which his camp was pitched. Then he would build an earthwork mound to bridge the ravine and bring the siege engines within reach. Alexander's forces seized a low hill connected to the nearest tip of Pir-Sar but were initially repelled by boulders rolled down from above. This led to three days of drumbeat celebrations by the defenders—a celebratory form that the local tribes practice even today.

Within four days, Alexander's force built a great mound from which they could effectively shoot arrows and hurl missiles from siege engines at the defenders. The Macedonians continued to lengthen the pathway, further increasing the effectiveness of Macedonian archers, slingers, and siege engines. The defenders knew that the rising pathway would soon reach their position. They decided to abandon the position and sent peace envoys, whose job was to gain time to withdraw safely from the fortress at night.

When the besieged began evacuating the Rock at night and attempted to escape, Alexander detected their movement and, with 700 handpicked men, scaled up the cliff at the moment the garrison began to retire and slew many during their retreat. Some defenders were so terrified that they threw themselves down the precipices to their deaths. Alexander built a fort on top of the hard-fought terrain and gave command of its garrison to Sisikottos (or Sashigupta), who had defected to him from Bessus's army in Bactria. Alexander then set out from the Rock and reinvaded the land of the Assakenians, who had risen in revolt again. He occupied a town named Dyrta, which probably lay to the north of

Aornus. The inhabitants of the city and the surrounding district had abandoned their homes and taken refuge in the hills across the Indus River.

After reducing Aornus and quelling a renewed revolt of Assakenians in Swat, Alexander crossed the Indus on a bridge probably constructed of boats at Ohind or Und, 16 miles above Attock.[92] Helped by Ambhi, the king of Taxila, Alexander stepped onto Indian soil, which no European invader had ever before touched. Taxila, now miles of ruins northwest of Rawalpindi in Pakistan, was one of the greatest cities in the east and was renowned as the center of Hindu learning in northern India. Taxila's rulers quickly submitted to the Macedonian invader, hoping that Alexander would back them against their enemies in neighboring states. Taxila was then at war with the mountainous kingdom of Abhisara (the tract of the lower and middle hills between the Jhelum and Chenab Rivers) and a more powerful state governed by a king (whom the Greeks called "Porus") who governed the land in the modern districts of Jhelum, Gujarat, and Shahpur.

This concluded Alexander's military conquest of ancient Ariana, a country between Persia and the Indus River. During the campaign, the keys to the Macedonians' military victory were not only their superior organization and better-disciplined army but also how that military machine was used in a cohesive way and led effectively against the native forces. The natives were highly inspired by their passion to defend their homelands and were favored by operating in a hospitable (for them) military environment, but they failed to create a unified front against the invaders. For their part, the invaders were disadvantaged by fighting in a foreign land while facing a resolute enemy on unfavorable terrain. Furthermore, Macedonian military operations were constrained by a lengthy line of communication and the challenge of replenishing the army's ranks as it moved forward. However, the failure of the natives to act together in a coordinated fashion was their most dangerous military disadvantage. Despite offering stubborn resistance against the enemy, the natives' actions were fragmented, piecemeal, and defensive, thereby ceding the initiative to the Greeks to choose the time and place of launching the attack. Meanwhile, the natives' unimaginative way of warfare and their tendency to fight from behind the walls of their fortresses gave the Greeks freedom of action and allowed them to shift forces freely between isolated objectives and to sequence their strikes for maximum impact. What was the primary reason for the tactical and operational disarray among the natives? The answer is probably that tribal confederation and local integration in the region were severely damaged because of the previous Achaemenid conquest and its divisive imperial policies to administer far-reaching corners of their empire.

Having conquered the Persian Empire, Alexander set out to invade India. He marched into Punjab to fight and win the Battle of Hydaspes (Jhelum) in 326 BC against King Porus. Alexander was greatly impressed by Porus's bravery in battle and made an alliance with him and appointed him as satrap of his own kingdom. He even added some land to Porus's kingdom that he did not own before. But the kingdom of Porus was just the gateway to much greater powers in the east along the Ganges River, including the powerful Nanda Empire of Magadha (northeastern India) and the Gangaridai Empire of Bengal. Fearing the prospects of facing other powerful Indian armies and exhausted by years of campaigning, Alexander's army mutinied at the Hyphasis (Beas) River, refusing to march farther east. Thus, that river marks the easternmost extent of Alexander's conquests.

Alexander, faced with a rebellious army, abandoned his ambition to conquer farther eastward and turned south, conquering more Indian tribes along the way. He sent much of his army to Carmania (modern southern Iran) with his general Craterus, and commissioned a fleet under his admiral Nearchus to explore the Persian Gulf shore. Alexander led the rest of his forces back to Persia by the southern route through the Gedrosian Desert (Baluchistan and Makran). The return journey was beset by a series of disasters, including the harsh climate of the Gedrosian Desert, the scarcity of supplies, losses caused by lack of water, and the sudden flooding of streams. Some ancient sources claim that three out of four soldiers perished in Gedrosia, which must be an exaggeration.[93] Alexander finally arrived in Babylon in the spring of 323 BC. A few months later, on June 10 or 11, he died just before his thirty-third birthday.

In contrast to the classical chroniclers of Alexander, most modern writers look at the history of Alexander more critically. They acknowledge his extraordinary military leadership and soldierly creativeness but deny him credit for being a builder. Alexander dismantled what he encountered and built nothing sustainable in its place. He replaced the mild albeit ineffective government of the Achaemenids with the tyranny of a foreign military autocracy that presided over the disintegration of the conquered lands into a battlefield of rival factions.[94] In the romanticized accounts of the classical chroniclers of the Macedonian king, there is a conspicuous absence of planning to build and sustain his new order. Alexander "was of all things an idealist and they who have not read that in the story of his life may as well not have read it at all."[95] The only system of government Alexander had time to organize was that of military occupation, wherein the military commandant of each district was the satrap, who ruled locally in the name of the conqueror. The system worked as long as Alexander was alive (which was not a long time). But upon his death, the controlling power based on the prestige of the conqueror's name and character quickly vanished. As A. B. Bosworth writes: "Alexander's most sympathetic chronicler in ancient times [Arrian] describes his reign as more or less continuous fighting, at times verging on massacre for its own sake, and his emphasis is certainly correct. Alexander spent much of his time killing and arguably, killing was what he did best."[96] This statement is best exemplified by the massacres in the cities along the Jaxartes and the Zarafshan Valley in Central Asia (329 BC), as well as in the mass killing at Massaga (327 BC). The real measure of Alexander's achievement is summarized by Benjamin Wheeler: "If a man's life-work is to be judged only by what he erects into formal organization, then we must pronounce the career of Alexander a failure, and more than a failure. . . . The story of Alexander has become a story of death. He died himself before his time. With his life he brought the Old Greece to its end; with his death the state he had founded."[97]

4   Disintegration of Greek Power in the East and the Rise of New Empires

Greco-Bactrians, Sakas, Kushans, and
Ephthalites, 323 BC–642 AD

The sudden death of Alexander with no apparent and legitimate successor plunged his dominions into a lengthy state of turmoil as his generals fought each other in a fierce struggle for power. The imperial regime created over more than a decade of conquest was about to melt away almost as quickly as it had materialized. Alexander's dream to integrate the conquered lands into a great Greco-Asiatic state was turning into a nightmare.

According to classical writers, Alexander nominated Perdicas as his successor by passing his signet to him. Perdicas was a bodyguard and leader of the Companion cavalry.[1] However, Perdicas favored naming Roxana's unborn baby as the successor, with himself and other close aides of Alexander acting as guardians. Meanwhile, some other generals supported Alexander's half-brother Philip Arrhidaeus (Philip III) to succeed him. Eventually an arrangement was made to name Alexander's half-brother and Roxana's baby son, Alexander IV, as joint kings, albeit in name only, but this did not last long. Dissension and rivalry soon led to a power struggle that involved the satrapies as the power bases of the contenders for power. After Perdicas was assassinated in 321 BC, Macedonian unity collapsed, and forty years of warfare among the ambitious successors ensued before the Hellenistic world settled into four stable power blocks: the Ptolemaic Kingdom of Egypt, the Seleucid Empire in the east centered in Syria, the Kingdom of Pergamon in Asia Minor, and Macedonia. In the turmoil, both Alexander IV and Philip III were murdered.

The Wars of Alexander's Successors in the west reverberated in the east, with calls for secession and independence. The eastern empire included all the countries between the Caspian Sea and the Sutlej River, encompassing what is today eastern Iran, Afghanistan, and the Punjab. This area was exposed to Hellenistic influence by Greek settlements and Greek government. But soon after the death of Alexander, de-Hellenization broke out in these regions. It started in the easternmost corners of the empire. During the wars of succession, the natives of the Punjab seized the opportunity to revolt by murdering the local governors appointed by Alexander and declaring themselves free. A prominent rebel leader known as Chandragupta succeeded in unifying fragmented nations into a major empire, the Maurya Empire, which stretched from the Indus to the Ganges River and beyond. Seleucus Nicatar, who ruled over the Asian territories of the Macedonian dominions from Syria, launched an expedition in 305 BC across the Indus, only to realize that Chandragupta was too powerful and militarily too strong to be brought back into the Hellenic world. They signed a peace treaty in which Seleucus ceded to Chandragupta lands on the west bank of the Indus River that included southern Afghanistan up to the foot of the Hindu Kush Mountains. In return, Seleucus received five hundred elephants.[2]

Farther west, more than fifty years later, Bactria proclaimed independence from the Seleucid Empire of Syria. After the assassination of Seleucus in 281 BC, an intense power struggle ensued between Syria and Egypt. Bactria seized this obvious opportunity to throw off the yoke, which in reality had become nominal. In 250 BC, Diodotus, the Greek satrap of Bactria, revolted, thereby setting the example for others. His Parthian vassal Andragoros followed suit, and two new kingdoms that developed into great empires were born.

In the words of Justin: "Diodotus, the governor of the thousand cities of Bactria revolted and proclaimed himself king; all the other people of the orient followed his example and seceded from the Macedonians."[3] The Greeks in Bactria who had integrated into the Bactrian nation through intermarriage and cultural accommodation "grew so powerful on account of the fertility of the country that they became masters, not only of Ariana, but also of India and more tribes were subdued by them than by Alexander."[4] Shortly afterward, Arsaces, an Iranian by race and a native of Bactra, fled to Parthia because his rival Diodotus had prevailed in his native city. Arsaces followed the Bactrian example. He defeated and killed the former satrap and self-proclaimed king of Parthia, Andragoros, and founded the Parthian dynasty that expanded into a vast empire in West Asia and lasted about five hundred years.

The invasion of Syria by Ptolemy of Egypt weakened the Seleucids' control in the east; consequently, the Parthian king Tiridates (d. 211 BC) not only annexed all of Parthia but also concluded an alliance with King Diodotus II of Bactria to prevent a Seleucid attempt at reconquest of the region. The alliance with Bactria helped the Parthian Kingdom win

The Greco-Bactrian Kingdom

Scythia

Sogdiana

Alexandria
Eschate
Ferghana

Greco-Bactrian
Kingdom
Ai-Khanoum

Tapuria
Bactra
(capital)
Traxiane
Alexandria
in the Caucasus

Parthia
Demetrias
Alexandria
Aria
in Arachosia
Arachosia

Maurya

Gedrosia

0   500   1,000   1,500 km

a decisive victory over the powerful Seleucid monarch in 237 BC and launched the Parthian Empire on its path to greatness, rivaling not only Bactria and Syria but Rome itself.

From this time on, for more than a thousand years the military history of Afghanistan features three major trends:

1. The development of military actions in two opposite directions by dynasties centered in the western and eastern segments of the Iranian plateau. In classic terms, these segments represented the Bactrian-Ariana space in the east and the Persis-Median space in the west.
2. Continuous threats of invasion from the Central Asian steppes across the Jaxartes and Oxus Rivers, pushing weakened dynasties to the south astride the Hindu Kush Mountains and farther to the east.

3. A persistent strategic leaning by powers based in the Hindu Kush area to expand to the east and conquer India, which was easily accessible and seen as a rich land but poorly protected.

Military Actions in Opposing Directions

Dynastic competition and power struggles among the states centered in the eastern and western parts of greater Iran were the hallmark of military interaction among the neighboring states. From ancient times, great empires, with shifting centers, straddled the current boundaries between Iran and Afghanistan. Dynastic borders and identities were carved mostly in the minds of ruling powers that controlled the area rather than in the hearts of the people who lived there.[5]

In the third century BC, there was no love lost between the Bactrians and the neighboring state of Parthia. In Bactria, the state was predominantly Greek, and the natives, at least initially, had little voice if any in the government. But in Parthia, the national feeling was mostly anti-Hellenic. Sandwiched between the Greek rulers of Bactria and Syria, the Parthians dreaded both, perhaps Bactria the most. Therefore, the two neighbors were often in fierce competition for influence in their adjoining territories, causing intermittent clashes on the edges of their dominions. However, these inward encounters were mostly defensive in nature as opposed to their outward power projection in opposite directions.

The growth of Parthia coincided with the decline of the Greeks in Syria and the rise of Rome in the west. Similarly, the expansion of Bactria came on the heels of the downfall of the Maurya Empire in India. Gradual expansion of Parthia westward and the advance of Rome eastward at the expense of Hellas brought the two empires in contact, resulting in several clashes. Consequently, during the early first century BC, Rome became the dominant power of the west while Parthia was the major power in West Asia. Farther to the east, from the late third century BC, the Bactrian Kingdom sought its expansion in the east rather than in the west. The decline of Hellenism on the two sides of the Greco-Bactrian state motivated the Bactrian rulers to reestablish their influence in the east as the opportunity presented itself.

To the north, Euthydemus, the third Greco-Bactrian king, extended his rule over Soghdiana and Ferghana, and from the frontier posts along the Jaxartes River he projected power as far as Kashghar and Urumqi in

East Turkistan, leading to the first known contacts between China and the west around 220 BC. In the words of Strabo, the Greco-Bactrians extended up to the Chinese territories.[6]

Meanwhile, the Seleucid Empire repeatedly attempted to bring in line the breakaway kingdoms in the east. Having lost some influence in the west, the Syrians could hardly afford the loss of Bactria—"the glory of Iran," as it was popularly called. In 208–204 BC, Antiochus III led a great army to repel Parthian intrusions into Media and reconquer Bactria. The campaign, described vividly by Polybius,[7] resulted in pushing the Parthians out of Media and a major encounter with Bactrian army under Euthydemus on the banks of Arius (Harirud) River near Herat. Although the Syrian monarch was able to besiege the Bactrians in their capital of Bactra (Balkh), he apparently failed to break the resistance of the besieged during a two-year blockade. The long absence of Antiochus in Bactria brought the threat of rebellions in the west. Thus, after concluding a defensive treaty with Euthydemus and a peace deal with the Maurya ruler of India, he returned to Syria. As the deal with the Indians was unfavorable to Bactria, Euthydemus decided to regain the territories in the east that had been ceded to Chandragupta by Seleucus Nicatar nearly a century before. The breakup of the Maurya Empire after the death of Asoka (232 BC) created favorable conditions for the success of the project.

Demetrius, the son of Euthydemus, invaded India in 180 BC. The Bactrian king and two of his generals, the Kabul-born Menander I and Apollodotus, completed the conquest by 175 BC through a two-pronged advance to the north and south of the Rajput Desert (also known as the Thar Desert). This established the Indo-Greek Kingdom in northern India that lasted for almost two centuries until around 10 AD. The Buddhist faith flourished under the Indo-Greek kings, foremost among them Menander I. It was also a period of great cultural syncretism, exemplified by the development of Greco-Buddhism. But the extended conquest of India exhausted the resources of the Greco-Bactrian Empire and severed the strategic links between the new gains in India with the homeland base. Back in Bactria, Eucratides, an ally of the Seleucids, overthrew the Euthydemid dynasty and established his own rule around 170 BC. Attempts by the Indian branch of the Euthydemids to regain Bactria failed, and Eucratides campaigned extensively in northwestern India and ruled over a vast territory, possibly as far as the Jhelum River in Punjab. In the end, however, he was repulsed by the Indo-Greek king Menander I, who managed to create a huge unified territory.

But the Bactrian state could no longer hold together as it was attacked and defeated by the Parthian king Mithridates I in 150 BC. Eucratides returned from India to face him but was killed in the encounter. As Justin writes: "The Bactrians, involved in various wars, lost not only their rule but also their freedom, as, exhausted by their wars against the Soghdians, the Arachotes (Kandahar), the Dranges (Sistan), the Arians (Herat) and the Indians, they were finally crushed, as if drawn of all their blood, by an enemy weaker than them, the Parthians."[8] Although Mithridates was the real power in Bactria, for a while he left Bactria apparently because of his expansion drive in the west and the threat of the Sakas. In any case, the Greco-Bactrian king Heliocles finally recovered Bactria, Soghdiana, and presumably Merv, while Mithridates is found in possession of Sistan, Arachosia, and Gedrosia.

About ten years later, Bactria and Parthia both were invaded by successive waves of migrating Saka nomadic hordes from Central Asia. Sakas (or Sakae) were considered part of the Scythian nomads of Iranian stock. Being driven from their habitat in the Ili Valley (in today's Kazakhstan) and around Lake Issyk Kul (in modern Kyrgyzstan) by the Yueh-Chi nomads, another ancient Indo-European people of the steppes, they descended on the southern lands across the Oxus and overran Bactria and Parthia. It is widely believed that the destruction of the Greco-Bactrian city of Ai-Khanoum, dated to around 140 BC, happened during the massive drive of the nomad hordes to Bactria. Recent archeological excavations dug out the ruins of Ai-Khanoum at the confluence of the Kokcha and Amu Rivers in northeastern Afghanistan. The cultural artifacts discovered at Tillā Tape (Golden Hill) archaeological site in northern Afghanistan near Sheberghan are believed to belong to this period of Afghanistan history. Surveyed in 1979 by a Soviet-Afghan mission, the hoard is a collection of about 20,000 gold ornaments that were found in six graves (five women and one man). This extremely rich jewelry find dates to around the first century BC and represents the culture of the nomadic invaders. The stash has been put on public display in recent years in several American and European cities.

The Sakas' invasion of Parthia seriously challenged the authority of the empire. Two successive Parthian kings fell in the war as they fought the overwhelming hordes. The succeeding monarch, Mithridates II (123 BC–88 BC), defeated the invading hordes in 115 BC and drove them out of his territories into neighboring Afghanistan, where they established themselves in the fertile land of Sistan and Arachosia (Kandahar). Sistan (or

Sakistan—the Land of Sakas) still retains the name identified with the Sakas.

The Sakas' invasion drove the last Greco-Bactrian king, Heliocles, south to Kapisa (Bagram) in 135 BC. He was driven farther east as the Sakas settled south of the Hindu Kush. This ended the last influence of the Greeks in the area. The fall of the Greek dominion east of the Hindu Kush coincided with the establishment of the Roman Empire under Augustus and the overthrow of the Hellenistic kingdom of Egypt. As they were buried in history, the Greek dynasties of Bactria and northern India played an important role in connecting western civilization with the east.

In keeping up with the traditions of power projection from the Hindu Kush to the east, the Sakas began their invasion of India in 119 BC, with their hordes reaching Taxila by 77 BC.[9] Following the direct routes from Ghazni and Arachosia, the Sakas streamed out from the Kurram, Tochi, and Gomal Valleys into the Indus basin from where they advanced and conquered Kathiawar and Cutch in the south and Taxila in the east. By 70 BC, their king, Maues, ruled over a kingdom that stretched from Kabul and Kapisa to Gandhara and down to Punjab.

Successive Invasions from the North

Meanwhile, the southward movement of migrating hordes continued across the Oxus, pouring new waves of nomads into Bactria and beyond. In around 120 BC, the Yueh-Chi nomads who had been driven from the Tarim basin to Central Asia (Kazakhstan and Uzbekistan) began heading south and filling the power vacuum created by the overextension of the Greco-Bactrian armies into India. The newcomers displaced their Scythian cousins (the Saka tribes) and pushed them eastward into India, where they came to be identified as Indo-Scythians. In early first century AD, the Kushans (Guishuang), one of five branches of the Yueh-Chi confederation, rose to power and, under Kujula Kadphises, established the Kushan Kingdom in the territories of ancient Bactria that expanded to Kabul and Kapisa. During the first and early second centuries AD, the Kushans, who are identified as the Tocharian, an Indo-European nomadic people, expanded across the northern parts of the Indian subcontinent. The Kushan emperor Kanishka (127–152 AD) made a great name for his military, political, and spiritual achievements and ruled an empire extending from Turfan in the Tarim basin to Pataliputra on the Gangetic plain with its capital at Mathura. The Kushans' capitals at different times were Bagram in Afghanistan, Peshawar and Taxila in today's Pakistan, and Pataliputra in India.

The rise of the Kushan Empire in the east coincided with Roman pressure on the Parthians in the west, facilitating the expansion of Kushans toward the west, including Aria (Herat), Sakistan (Sistan), and Arachosia (Kandahar). Sandwiched between the Kushans in the east and the Romans in the west, the Parthian dynasty in Persia steadily shrank in size, setting in motion the decline of the Arsacid Empire. The fall of Parthian power was completed a century later with the rise of the Sassanid dynasty. Ardasher I, the grandson of Sassan from Estakhr in Fars, overpowered Artabanus, the last Arsacid monarch, and was crowned as king in 226 AD. Under Ardasher's son Shahpur I, the Sassanids launched a major campaign to destroy the Kushan Empire, which, in collusion with Rome, was a persistent threat to Persia over the previous two centuries. This led to the fragmentation of the Kushans into semi-independent kingdoms in the third and fourth centuries AD. The Sassanid Empire moved as far as the Indus River, while the fragmented Kushan principalities in the Punjab and on the Gangetic plains remained under local Kushan rulers for a while before they were absorbed mostly into the Gupta Empire (320–550 AD). The Kushani areas under the Sassanid suzerainty west of the Indus, known as Kushanshahr, were considered key territories with strategic significance and were always ruled by a leading Sassanian noble or prince titled "Kushanshah." The arrangement was like the Achaemenids' administrative policy of appointing a member of the royalty as the satrap of Bactria more than six centuries before.

In the first half of the fifth century AD, the Kidarites—the last dynasty to regard themselves as the inheritors of the Kushans—rose to power in northern Afghanistan and from there expanded their rule to the south and east, overrunning Peshawar and part of northern India. In the north, they conquered Soghdiana in 440 AD before being cut from their Bactrian nomadic roots by the rise of the Ephthalites in the 450s. Many small Kidarite kingdoms survived in northwest India up to the conquest by the Ephthalites during the last quarter of the fifth century. Meanwhile, in the second half of the fourth century, the Sassanids' authority in the east was challenged by a new wave of Indo-European nomadic movements from the north, leading to the establishment of the Ephthalites Kingdom in Afghanistan and its eventual expansion into India.

The Ephthalites (or Hephthalites), also known as the White Huns (apparently with no connections with European Huns), were an Iranian-speaking nomadic confederation in Central Asia.[10] They appeared at the end of the fourth century in modern Kazakhstan and Uzbekistan and invaded Bactria, forcing the Kushans under their ruler, Kidara, south-eastward into Gandhara, where their cousins had long ruled under Sassanian suźerainty. Kidara wrenched control of Gandhara and adjacent regions from the last Sassanian Kushanshah and assumed the same title. The dynasty ruled for nearly a century before being overthrown by the Ephthalites during their invasion of India.

Back in Bactria, the Ephthalites completed the occupation of the area north of the Hindu Kush. The Aiythal or Yaftal branch gained a dominant position among the tribes, and its leader, Ephthalito, was crowned king. The Ephthalites branched out from Bactria and raided the territories of the Sassanids in the west and conquered the countries to the south and southeast, including the Kabul Valley and Gandhara. Although their first invasion of Persia in 427 was repulsed by the Sassanid king Bahram V, the tide turned a century later and the Sassanids became a tributary of the Ephthalite Empire, which lasted well into the sixth century.[11] In the east, the Ephthalites overcame Kidarites in 455 and extended their rule into India. In a series of bloody drives, King Toramans and his son Mihiragula overran the Punjab and destroyed the Hindu Gupta Empire in northern and central India. Then, with their capital at Sagala (modern Sialkot), the Ephthalites became the masters of the subcontinent, with lasting social and political consequences.

The Ephthalites' deep involvement in India weakened their influence in the west and made their northern borders vulnerable to nomadic raids. In the middle of the sixth century, the Western Turks vanquished a rival horde called the Juan-juan and made an alliance with Khosrow Anushirvan, king of Persia, grandson of Firoz, who had been killed by the Ephthalites in 484 AD. They agreed to overthrow the Ephthalites' rule in Central Asia and Afghanistan. The Sassanid monarch welcomed the opportunity to deal finally with a power that had humbled Persia for several generations. The combined forces of the Turks and the Sassanids attacked and defeated the Ephthalite Kingdom in a decisive battle in Soghdiana in 568 AD. For a short time, the Persians held Balkh and other portions of the Ephthalites' territory, but the gradual weakening of Sassanid power soon enabled the Turks to extend their authority toward the south as far as Kapisa. Meanwhile, Ephthalite rule was sustained in India for many more years. At the turn of the seventh century, the territory of modern Afghanistan and part of Central Asia had degenerated into local kingdoms under nominal control of the Sassanids or the Western Turks.

Countering Threats from the Northern Steppes

The outward projections of power from the two ends of the Iranian plateau to the west and east were intricately linked to the successive nomadic invasions from the north. Persistent threats of invasion from the Central Asian steppes pushed weakened dynasties to the south across the Hindu Kush Mountains and farther to the east. From early times in history until the eleventh century, nomadic horsemen of the Central Asian steppes constantly threatened the sedentary regions to the south. Cyrus, the founder of the Achaemenid Empire, met his death in a fierce battle with the Massagetae, a tribe from the southern deserts of Khwarazm and Kyzyl Kum in the southernmost portion of the steppe regions of modern-day Kazakhstan and Uzbekistan. Cyrus's campaign against the Central Asian Scythians (529 BC) was followed by Darius's expedition against the turbulent nomadic hordes in southern Russia.[12] In the following centuries, the Greeks and Parthians engaged in lengthy frontier wars with nomadic hordes in Central Asia and the Caucasus.

Alexander in 329 BC found a land of walled towns and open villages and started building a network of walled-in villages and setting up fortified posts at strategic points throughout Bactria and Soghdiana in his struggle with the nomads on the other side of the Jaxartes. His policy was continued by his regional successors, who built an elaborate network of posts from Ferghana to Merv and from Darband to the Black Sea.[13] Antiochus I (d. 261 BC) fortified the oasis of Merv with a 187-mile-long wall.[14]

Faced directly with the threat from nomads, both the Greco-Bactrian and Parthian kings pursued a policy of fortifying the northern frontiers with exceptional zeal. More than two centuries after Alexander, the Chinese explorer Chang-Ch'ien (Zhang Qian) in 128 BC found Bactria and Soghdiana a land of walled towns. He stated the number of walled compounds only in Bactria at more than a million. These large walled villages were meant to protect the population from nomad raids until the troops of the king or satrap could intervene.[15] The epithet "the thousand cities of Bactria" (*mille urbium Bactrianarum*) mentioned by the classical writers[16] is a reflection of the proliferation of walled towns in Bactria. In fact, *Hazar Shahr-e Bakhter* ("the thousand cities of Bactria"), the historical epithet of Bactria,[17] developed from the walled cities and towns in the region.[18] Many of these military colonies became the hubs of future cities. Border security measures included pacification of turbulent areas through cultural influence. The spread of Zoroastrianism and Buddhism contributed to that effort.

During this period, the borders of Central Asia were set by the relationships between the sedentary and nomadic peoples. The turbulent conquests of nomads were transient, whereas the influence of settled peoples, which changed the nomads through integration and assimilation, was slow but enduring. The legacy of the long frontier war left lasting imprints on the region's folklore and generated sensational historical accounts, myths, epics, and legends.

The Islamization of Central Asia through military conquests began a new phase in the region's history. Beginning in the eleventh century, a wave of Central Asian Turks who had adapted the Irano-Islamic culture straddled the historic borders between Iran and Central Asia. They established powerful governments in the region and projected power into the Middle East and India. Between the eleventh and thirteenth centuries, the Ghaznavids, Seljuqs, and Khwarazm-Shahids conquered vast areas that extended from the Punjab in the east to the heart of the Anatolian Peninsula in the west. The southward Turkic push took a dramatic turn in the thirteenth century as Mongol hordes led by Chinggis Khan invaded the region. The early Mongols unsuccessfully attempted to establish the supremacy of nomadic life in the occupied lands. But the conquerors themselves changed as they adopted the way of life of the people they had conquered. Timur's invasion at the end of the fourteenth century marked the peak of steppe riders' encroachments on the sedentary south.

The Exchange of Military Culture

The unceasing competition for supremacy by the dominant powers in West, Central, and South Asia over the centuries led to constant clashes among rival armies but also resulted in the exchange of military culture over a wide region. Consequently, different warring states and armies learned from their experiences and adapted best practices demonstrated by various militaries on the battlefield. From the heavy infantry of the Macedonians to the fast-moving, lightly armed nomadic mounted archers, a variety of military skills were demonstrated in centuries-long confrontations. The experience covered all forms of military science, including force structure, battle formations, weapons and equipment, and combat tactics. The process disseminated the Grecian culture of heavy infantry (*phalanx*) to the east, as far as India, and the employment of heavily armed cavalry (*cataphract*)[19] from Asia to Rome. Meanwhile, similar cross-adaption of weapons and war machines took place across the region. The Macedonians' introduction and use of siege engines such as the catapult and siege towers were initially alien to Parthians, but they adapted to their use as they expanded to the west and faced the Romans. The Romans, too, subsequently improved the quality and technology of siege equipment and pursued the introduction and improvement of heavily armed cavalry. The reputed skills of the Scythian archers captured the attention of many armies, and the Scythian mounted archers were widely employed as mercenaries.

One of the major areas of military cultural exchange was the balance between the light and heavy forces that was so ably configured in Alexander's army. The Greco-Persian wars since the fifth century BC and Alexander's victories proved that lightly armed troops could not stop heavy and well-trained infantry such as the Greek hoplites and phalanx. Such forces could be met only with heavily armed and highly professional cavalry by causing disorder in the massed ranks and then attacking them on vulnerable points with arrows and missiles capable of piercing armor and lances effective against shields. This lesson was learned and implemented by the Parthians in the second and first centuries BC in fighting the Seleucid Greeks in Persia. They also learned from the armaments, tactics, and strategies of the Romans.

However, Alexander the Great, upon his return to Babylon in 323 BC, proceeded to carry out a sweeping military reform, on which his mind must have been working for some time. It included a complete transformation of his father's phalanx and, in fact, of the Hellenic hoplite system. Alexander's experience had taught him that the phalanx was far from being the ideal infantry formation and system. The advantages of its sheer weight and solid strength were more than counterbalanced by its lack of mobility, which he had experienced in fighting the Bactrians and Soghdians. While retaining the old sixteen-man depth, he made only four ranks of Macedonian pikemen. The twelve intervening places—the fourth to the fifteenth ranks—were filled with lightly armed Persians using their native bows and javelins. This new phalanx required new tactics, which opened up the ranks to allow the archers and javelin men to deploy into the intervals and discharge their missiles, and then close up again, in order to advance in a serried mass, each file bristling with three (no longer with five) spearpoints. It was a combination of heavy and light troops working in tactical unity.[20]

Although the natives incorporated into Alexander's army used outside Bactria were armed, trained, and organized after the Macedonian fashion, the native forces in their homelands maintained their traditional structure and tactics for a while.[21] However, the lightly armed native Bactrian and Scythian horsemen learned their vulnerabilities during encounters with the heavy troops of enemies. The Bactrian's mounted soldiers, who during all the Achaemenid period were lightly armed with bow and javelin, failed to check the advance of Antiochus III at the Battle of Arius (Harirud) in 208 BC. Their bows and javelins were not effective in close combat. The defeat at Arius motivated the Bactrian rulers to begin forming and using heavily armored mounted warriors (*cataphract*) to fight the enemy in cooperation with light horsemen.

The way of war conducted by the nomads of Central Asia proved to be effective if they used the hit-and-run tactics during raids on sedentary areas in the south. Their lightly armed mounted archers, who raided settled areas, towns, and villages and then rapidly dashed back into the steppes, saw themselves as invulnerable to enemies, who would not risk pursuing them into the depth of their endless wilderness. Their invincibility to outside incursions is noted by Herodotus:

> The most important thing which they have discovered is their own preservation. For such is their manner of life that no one who invades their country can escape destruction, and if they wish to avoid engaging with an enemy, that enemy cannot by any possibility come to grips with them. For they have neither cities founded nor walls built, but all carry their houses with them and are mounted archers living not by the plough but by cattle and whose dwellings are upon carts, these assuredly are invincible and impossible to approach.[22]

However once these nomads became involved in wars with enemies outside their home turf, they soon realized their own military weaknesses and tried to adapt to new means and different ways of war. When the Yueh-Chi nomads first appeared in Central Asia and Bactria, their way of war was like that practiced by other nomads: mostly depending on light horsemen in large groups using bows to harass the enemy from a distance. However, once they established their state and empire of Kushans in Bactria and adjacent areas, they fielded armored horsemen intended to fight at close range. Furthermore, they began to incorporate foot soldiers and elephants and developed the art of siege warfare.

This combined and coordinated use of light and heavy troops—both cavalry and infantry—became a common feature of the art of war for Asian armies once they embarked on empire-building across the continent. The Sakas, Parthians, and Kushans developed the combined use of lightly armed mobile archers and the armored mounted lancers (*cataphract*) in combat. The light cavalry, armed with bow and a sword, were the "hussars" suitable for skirmishes, hit-and-run tactics, and flank attacks but could not sustain close combat. Still, the cataphract, which had an enormous striking power but lacked high mobility, became the arm of decisive combat at close quarters. Cataphract lancers wore steel helmets and a coat of mail made of rawhide covered with scales of iron or steel and reaching to the knees. This enabled them to withstand heavy blows. Their offensive arms included a long spear of great strength and thickness, as well as a bow and arrows of unusual size. They likewise carried a short sword for close combat. Their horses were, like themselves, protected by armor made of steel or bronze.[23] Starting in the third century, the Romans also formed units of heavy cavalry of the Oriental type, which they called *clibanarii*.

The usual tactical concept was to employ the light horse-archers in a loose, extended order to engage the enemy ranks with a shower of arrows from a distance and thereby soften up the enemy lines for a striking blow by the heavy forces—the *cataphract*. One of the best examples of such tactics is seen in the Battle at Carrhae (now Harran, Turkey) between the Parthian and Roman armies in 53 BC. It was then that the Parthian light and *cataphract* cavalry headed by Surenas demonstrated their superiority over the famous Roman infantry legions commanded by Marcus Crassus, who fell in the battle.[24]

Meanwhile, the Greek, Saka, Kushan, and Ephthalite armies that conquered India adapted the use of war elephants and war chariots, which were still fashionable in the subcontinent. The war elephants appeared on battlefields outside India in early Hellenistic Bactria under the Seleucids. The Bactrian satrap is said to have sent elephants to Antiochus I to reinforce his army during the first Syrian War (275–273 BC). Later, the use of elephants in battle increased after Greco-Bactrians began to conquer India under the Greco-Bactrian king Demetrius and during the rule of Menander in northern India. The *Milindapanha* (Questions of Milinda), which is a Buddhist text from approximately 100 BC,[25] mentions elephants and war chariots, in addition to cavalry and bowmen (infantry), as the main components of Menander's four-branch army.[26] Although the use of war elephants was also recorded in Europe in ancient times, the effectiveness of the beasts in combat has been controversial. Hans Delbruck writes that one cannot find a single corroborated battle in which elephants accomplished something of importance. He asserts that, to the contrary, usually the side that was stronger in elephants was defeated.[27] Obviously, Delbruck refers to the use of war elephants in the west, and his judgment does not apply to the military history of the east. War elephants survived on the battlefield for centuries because they proved to be valuable assets in tactical combat.

As Central Asians learned to supplement their light forces with heavily armed troops, the Romans learned how to complement the ability of their well-drilled infantry columns with mobile auxiliary troops composed of light cavalry and bowmen. Sassanids' failure to do the same contributed to their defeat in the face of light and mobile Arab armies in the seventh century AD. The backbone of the Sassanid army (*sepah*) was its heavy cavalry. The Sassanians did not form lightly armed cavalry but extensively employed—as allies or mercenaries—troops from warlike tribes who fought under their own chiefs, among whom the Sagestanis (Sistani) were described as "the bravest of all." Sassanid battles were usually decided by the shock cavalry of the front line charging the opposite ranks with heavy lances while archers gave support by discharging storms of arrows. Within the Sassanid military, the cavalry was the most influential element, and Sassanid cavalry tactics were adopted by the Romans, Arabs, and Turks.[28] While heavy cavalry proved efficient against Roman armies, it was too slow and regimentalized to act with full force against agile and unpredictable lightly armed cavalry and rapid foot archers. Therefore, the Persians, who in the early seventh century conquered Egypt and Asia Minor, lost decisive battles a generation later when lightly armed Arabs accustomed to skirmishes and desert warfare attacked them.

5   The Arab Conquest and Islamization of Afghanistan, 642–921 AD

The rise of Islam in the early seventh century in the Arabian Peninsula marked a monumental shift in the social and political map of the world. Islam came as a blessing to Arabia as it unified different warring tribes and clans into an empire-building nation. The polity established by the Prophet Mohammad (570–632) saw a rapid expansion under his immediate successors, the Rashidun (Rightly Guided) caliphs and the Umayyad dynasties that followed them. In six years, the whole of Syria and Palestine came under the sway of the Arab armies, followed by the conquest of Persia. This ended the Sassanid Empire after the crushing defeat of the Sassanian king Yazdegerd III (590–651) at Nahavand in 642. About a hundred years after the death of the Prophet, the Muslim conquests incorporated vast areas into the Muslim world, stretching from the Iberian Peninsula in the west to the borders of China and India in the east. "Under the Umayyads," writes Edward Gibbon in *History of the Decline and Fall of the Roman Empire*, "the Arabian empire extended two hundred days' journey from east to west, from the confines of Tartary and India to the shores of the Atlantic."[1]

The fast advance of the Arab armies was fostered by a combination of the ideological force of the new faith and a strategy to harness the martial culture of the Arab tribes into a unified power for conquest beyond the borders of the Arabian Peninsula. Prior to the revelation of Islam, the nomad culture of raiding other tribes for booty (a practice known as *razzia*) was a way of life in the harsh environment of the Arabian desert. *Razzia* entailed raids for plunder and slaves. The raiders would swoop suddenly with great force upon a small group from a hostile tribe and escape with the booty and no loss of life. *Razzia* was also a way of war between two groups who had serious differences with one another.

The spread of Islam and its teachings brought about a fundamental change in the practice of *razzia*. Islam forbade the conduct of *razzia* against fellow Muslims. Meanwhile, the messianic duty of fighting enemies of the Islamic community and the duty to spread the new faith gave new meaning to *razzia* as it sanctified into *ghazwa* (raiding for the purpose of religious warfare).[2] The Prophet Mohammad found it useful to divert this continuous internecine warfare against the enemies of the faith, making it the basis of his war strategy. Consequently the practice of *razzia* and the idea of Islamic community (*umma*), which forbade raiding fellow believers, focused the Islamic state on an outward projection of power.

Tabari (838–923 AD) recorded the speech of one of the Arab leaders, Mughira bin Zurara al-Usaydi, to Yazdegerd III at the time of the conquest of Iraq. The speech reflects how the spirit of Islam transformed the Arab tribes' approach to warfare. He said:

> There was no body more impoverished than we were. . . . Our tradition was to kill one another and raid one another. . . . But then God sent us a well-known man (Mohammad). . . . He was the best among us and at the same time the most truthful and the most tolerant and forgiving. He invited us to embrace his religion. He grew in stature and we became smaller. Everything he said came to pass. God instilled in our hearts belief in him and caused us to follow him. He said those who choose to follow your faith, give those equal rights and protection and those who refuse make them pay poll tax (jeziah), and if they do not, fight them. . . . Now you, the king, pay the tributes and submit, otherwise the sword would decide between us.[3]

When the Arab armies fanned out across the ancient world in the seventh century, they overcame most of the resistance offered by opposing armies. But the speed of advance in different directions was uneven. The geography and terrain hindered the pace of progress and conditioned the direction and scope of the conquests. The Muslim armies overran North Africa but were discouraged from expanding southward by the inhospitable Sahara Desert. In the north, the absence of maritime capacity limited Arab expansion to land expeditions. The primary directions of northern expansion were northwestward into Syria and northeastward into Iraq. From Syria, the armies could go south into Egypt and then either continue south up the Nile or west toward Morocco, or else they could go north into Asia Minor. While the eastward march into Iraq and Syria and the westward march into Maghreb were swift, the Arab armies failed to make major headway northward to Constantinople. Geographic conditions and the technical superiority of the Byzantines—including their use of flame-throwing devices known as "Greek fire"—checked the advances of the Arab columns.[4]

In the east, the Arab armies conquered Persia as far as the great rivers of Central Asia, but the craggy massif of the Hindu Kush stopped them. Although many invading hordes had used the Hindu Kush defiles to invade India, the only serious Arab invasion was in Sind, through the desert of Makran, where they faced no mountainous barriers. Arabs also sailed from Siraf and Hormuz in the Persian Gulf along the coast to the mouth of the Indus River.

Initially, most of these military thrusts into distant lands were raids for plunder, not occupation. The invading hordes were too few to occupy the invaded lands and mostly limited their presence to collecting tributes from subdued rulers. The unsteady power of the center was more adapted for conquest than assimilation, as the area—overrun by the hard-to-control invading hordes—was too vast to be held in permanent subjugation. Conscious of their weakness, the Arabs spared no effort to proselytize the tenets of Islam, which alone were capable of welding together communities differing widely in race, language, and customs. Still, it took more than two centuries to assimilate the conquests.

The Arab armies of conquest arose from small and fragmented tribal fighters and developed into a formidable military machine by the beginning of the eighth century. With the growth of Islamic civilization, the military cultures of the conquered lands, including Byzantine, Persian, Khorasan, and Central Asian Turks, were integrated into the most advanced military system of the time. The evolving military establishment not only became the basis of a universal model adapted across the Muslim world of the middle ages but also strategically outwitted the Western knight-based military culture during the Crusades (1095–1290), which came on the heels of the Arab-Byzantine and the Seljuq-Byzantine wars. The most distinctive features of the Arab Muslim's military doctrine were the rapid concentration of forces in the war zone and fast advance by mobile forces to the battlefield. Time was the major factor in achieving strategic military advantages.

Except for a few small kingdoms such as the Hira (or Heera) in the northeast and that of Ghassan in the northwest of the Arabian Peninsula, which were in contact with the Persian and Byzantine Empires, there were no regular and standing armies in the nomadic society of Arab tribes. Tribal wars were fought by the members of the community with available personal weapons. During the life of the Prophet Mohammad, the Muslims' army included available members of the community, which amounted to 313 infantrymen at the Battle of Badr in 624 AD. By the end of Mohammad's life, this army increased to several thousand. The Muslims fielded an army of 30,000–40,000 cavalry and infantry at the Battle of Yarmouk (southeast of the Sea of Galilee) against the Byzantines in 634 AD.[5] Arab sources speak of a force of 150,000 during the rule of Mohammad's immediate successors.[6] The army of the Umayyad Caliphate (661–750) was known as perhaps the world's foremost military power.

The Muslim Arab Armies

The Muslim army was organized into a regular force and put under a separate department for the first time under the Caliph Omar (634–644), a process that was completed by Abd-al-Malik ibn Marwan (646–705) of the Umayyad dynasty.[7] At that time, the army was classified into a regular paid force and a volunteer corps that was employed at the frontiers of the Islamic Empire. Known as *motawi'a*, these forces were sustained and rewarded by the spoils of war.[8] Later converts from the conquered lands swelled the ranks of the Arab Muslim armies. During the conquest of Persia, some 12,000 elite Persian troops converted to Islam and served within the Arab ranks during the invasion of the Persian Empire. Earlier, about 4,000 Greek Byzantine soldiers converted during the conquest of Roman Syria and served as regular troops in the conquest of both Anatolia and Egypt. Coptic converts were employed in Egypt, and Barbers were recruited into the regular army in Africa. During the Umayyad period, slave soldiers made up an important part of the royal guards of the caliphs who in later years played a major role in the court politics of the Abbasid Caliphate.

As the Arab Muslim armies launched their conquest of the powerful empires of the time, they were technically inferior to the opposing militaries. Qualitatively and strength-wise, they were no match for the Sassanid and Roman armies. But over time they learned and adapted advanced weapons and combat methods and introduced certain innovations.

Initially, the bulk of the Muslim army was composed of infantry, and Arab leaders relied heavily on their foot soldiers. In the Prophet Mohammad's first battle, his army was exclusively an infantry force with only two horses and 70 camels. As the empire extended, the cavalry became a dominant component of the army. Arabs quickly adopted the use of stirrups by the cavalry. The stirrup was long ignored by Greeks and Romans, although it provided horsemen the ability to use heavier lances with a greater shock impact and increased the effectiveness of mounted bowmen.

Arab light cavalry armed with an 18-foot lance was very mobile and responsive, with the ability to engage and disengage the enemy and turn back and attack again from the flank or rear. This tactic later inspired the development of the Arabic knightly discipline and ethical code known as *Furusiyya* in the middle ages. This combination of martial arts and equestrianism was practiced particularly during the Crusades and the Mamluk period (eleventh—thirteenth centuries). *Furusiyya* implied races of mounted archery practiced from Afghanistan to Muslim Spain. The light cavalry, with its high mobility, also proved amazingly effective as advance guards, patrolling detachments, and flank security. Such sprightly "hussars," mostly used as *tali'ah* (advance guard), outmaneuvered the Byzantine army in the conquest of Syria. The method was emulated by later dynasties in the Muslim world, including the armies of Saffarids, Ghaznavids, and Ghorids in Afghanistan in the ninth to thirteenth centuries.

Initially, Arab armies were organized on a tribal basis. Each tribal contingent was led as a unit by the tribal chief or his deputy. In later times, the organization developed into a more sophisticated system. Like other earlier eastern armies, the Arab army was organized on a decimal structure. The troops were grouped in tens commanded by a *'areef*, hundreds led by a *naqib*, thousands commanded by a *qayed*, and ten thousands by an *amir*.[9] The combat and combat support component of the expeditionary forces included the foot soldiers (*rijal*), horsemen (*fursan*), archers (*rumat*), patrol (*tali'ah*), camel corps (*rukban*), and foraging parties (*nuhhab al-mu'an*).

The principal weapons were swords, infantry long spears (*rumh*), and shorter cavalry spears (*harba*). The use of bows and arrows was a distinguishing feature of Arabs' tribal culture. Archery was highly esteemed and commended in the Prophet's sayings and other religious traditions.[10] Bows, made locally in different parts of Arabia, were about six feet long, like the English longbow. The use of composite bows was not uncommon. The maximum effective range of the traditional Arabian bow was about 500 feet. During the conquest of the Sassanid Empire, Arab archers using very heavy arrows with armor-piercing capability at a short distance outperformed the Persians' light arrows. Later, other types of bows, including Central Asian recurve short bows, became available as the Islamic empire expanded. Early Muslim bowmen were foot archers who proved to be highly effective against cavalry. In Khorasan and Central Asia, lightly armored but highly mobile archers were integrated into the armies of local Muslim dynasties.

Arab military tactics evolved from those of the typical small tribal host seeking local dominance into massive operations by large forces of combined arms. The early Muslim armies fought in rank formations. Later, in the Umayyad period, they adapted Roman combat tactics by dividing the army into small squadrons known as *kata'ib* (battalion in today's Arab armies), each of which could support other similar units. Although horses and camels facilitated mobility, the emphasis was fighting on foot. When the troops were attacked by cavalry, they would form a spear wall, kneeling with the ends of their spears in the ground beside them with the points sticking up toward the enemy. As the enemy horses moved upon them, they would rise and jab at the horses' faces.[11]

The combat formation in battle was structured into right (*maimana*) and left (*maisara*) wings, the center (*qalb*), and the stem (*saaqa*). In marches, the advance guard (*muqademah*) and rear guard (*mut'kherah*) were added to the formation. The usual combat tactic of the infantry, known as *al-karr-wa-farr*, was to make repeated charges and withdrawals using arrow barrages from a distance while advancing into close combat using spears and swords. The aim of infantry action was to weaken and wear down the enemy, creating the conditions for a final blow by a flanking charge by the cavalry to encircle the enemy forces. Initially, the cavalry was deployed in reserve waiting for the infantry to soften the enemy ranks. Once the enemy ranks were disrupted, the cavalry would be unleashed to deliver a crushing thrust. But later, with the expansion of the empire and deployment of armies over long distances, the cavalry dominated the battlefield, with infantry playing the supporting role.

Reducing fortified cities was attempted by scaling walls, undermining defenses, and using siege engines. The siege engines were introduced into Arab armies in the early years of their conquests. They included large catapults (*manjaniq*) and smaller ones (*arrada*), as well as the siege towers (*dababah*) and battering rams.[12] The catapults were used to discharge stone and fire balls into the enemy fortifications while the 70 to 150-foot-high wheeled wooden towers were driven up to the foot of the besieged fortification and then pierced the walls with a battering ram. Once the gap was bridged, the infantry attacked. The rams were used to shatter gates and to destroy spear holes in the walls. In the siege of the Persian capital of Ctesiphon, the Arabs constructed twenty siege engines on the spot and used them in the attack.[13] In the 712 siege of Daibal in Sind, the Arab army's large catapult named *'arous* (the "bride") was operated by 500 men. The engine destroyed the enemy's 240-foot-high temple with only two shots.[14]

The Arab armies maintained a high level of discipline, strategic prowess, and devotion during the reign of the *Rashidun* caliphs, when major conquests were made. Early Muslim armies stayed in encampments away from cities because Caliph Omar feared that they might get attracted to wealth and luxury and start accumulating wealth and establishing dynasties. During his life, Mohammad gave various injunctions to his forces and adopted practices for the conduct of war. The most important of these were summarized by Mohammad's companion and successor, Abu Bakr, in the form of ten rules for the *Rashidun* army:[15]

> Stop, O people, that I may give you ten rules for your guidance in the battlefield. Do not commit treachery or misuse spoils of war. Do not deviate from the right path or seize public property. You must not mutilate dead bodies. Neither kill a child, nor a woman, nor an aged man. Bring no harm to the trees, nor burn them with fire, especially those which are fruitful. Slay not any of the enemy's flock, save for your food. You are likely to pass by people who have devoted their lives to monastic services; leave them alone.

When the spoils of Persia were laid at the feet of the second Caliph Omar, he wept and said: "I fear all this wealth and luxury will in the end ruin my people."[16] And when Ziyad, who had escorted the treasure to the capital, asked the caliph's permission to march against Khorasan, he answered: "I would prefer to see insurmountable mountains between Iraq and those other lands, so that they could neither attack us, nor could we attack them."[17] But as the march of the Arab armies gained momentum, they swept across vast areas beyond the "mountains." Meanwhile, as the empire expanded and an unrelenting struggle for power and competing claims of legitimacy dominated the politics of the Muslim world, the original unity of the Arab army failed to survive. A series of civil wars known as *fitna* in the second half of the seventh century and during the eighth century, in addition to the rise of slave armies, undermined the discipline and morale of the army, which eventually led to the fragmentation of the Islamic Empire two centuries later. Arab conquests in later times saw major excesses and massacres of people in conquered lands. In 705, after capturing the Central Asian commercial city Paykand, the renowned Arab commander Qutayba ibn Muslim sacked the city, massacred the men of fighting age, sold off women and children into slavery, and amassed an enormous amount of spoils.[18] Later, in 712, Qutayba's brutality in Samarkand and Khwarazm exceeded even the terror of Paykand. The eleventh-century Kwarazmian scholar al-Biruni compares the events with a barbarian sack, as the Arabs proceeded to massacre most of the upper classes that had fomented the revolt and destroyed a great many objects of Kwarazmian culture.[19]

The Arab Conquest of Afghanistan

In the middle of the seventh century, Muslim Arab armies, pursuing the defeated Persian king Yazdegerd III, encountered the people of the lands occupied by modern Afghanistan. Although it took another decade before the last Sassanid monarch was killed in Merv, the arrival of Arab armies in 642 opened the way to the conquest of Afghanistan.

The political conditions in and around Afghanistan at the period of the Arab conquests were very complex. As the sixth century wore on, the weakening of the Sassanid influence in the south and the drooping grip of the Western Turks in the north gave rise to local semi-independent dynasties that ruled in separate provinces on both sides of the Hindu Kush. In the north, the native Kushano-Ephthalite principalities were reconstructed in Tokharistan (northeastern Afghanistan), Badghis, and Herat under the intermittent suzerainty of the Turks and the Sassanids. In Transoxiana and Tokharistan, the Turks' influence was often limited to the appointment of military governors and collection of tributes while the native princes and local *dehqan* (local ruling nobles) remained in power. The ninth-century Persian geographer Ibn-i Khordadbeh (870– 912 AD) lists about two dozen local rulers who governed different cities and regions in Khorasan, Transoxiana, and eastern provinces.[20]

In the south, two local dynasties ruled the area from Sistan in the southwest to the Indus basin in the east. The Kabul and Gandhara region was under the rule of the Buddhist and then Hindu dynasty, called the "Kabul Shahis" since the fifth century. The Chinese traveler Hsuen Tsang, who passed through the area around 632 AD, described the ruler of Kapisa-Kabul, whom he had personally met, as a devout Buddhist and a Kshatriya (Hindu ruling and military elite) and not a Turk, as suggested by al-Biruni some four hundred years later.[21]

The area between Sistan and Zabulistan up to the limits of Kabul was ruled by a dynasty identified as Zunbils and Rutbils by early Muslim authors. Zunbils were the descendants of the southern Hephthalites

(Ephthalites). Their territory included an area between what is now the city of Zaranj in southwestern Afghanistan to Kabul, with Zamindawar and Ghazni serving as the capitals. The Zunbils dynasty is believed to have been related to the Kabul Shahis. The rulers of this dynasty were sun-worshipers. Their shrine of Zoon (sun god)—from which their name is derived—was located about three miles south of Musa Qala in Helmand.[22] Furthermore, the title Zunbil can be traced back to the Middle Persian original Zunn-datbar, or "Zun the Justice-giver." The geographical name "Zamindawar" would also reflect this, from the Middle Persian Zamin-i datbar (Land of the Justice-giver).[23] Many other inhabitants south of the Hindu Kush practiced Buddhism and other religions including Zoroastrianism and Nestorian Christianity.

The eastward advance of the Arab armies, after the defeat of the Sassanid army at the Battle of Nahavand in 642, followed two divergent strategic axes running through the wide plains to the north and south skirting the Great Salt Desert in the center, virtually impassable by large forces. The most important road was the northern Khorasan route, which stretches from Hamadan to Tehran and on to the greater Khorasan plains reaching northern Afghanistan and Central Asia. The other route lay far to the south, linking the western Iranian plains to the Fars and Kerman Provinces extending to Sistan and southern Afghanistan. The two conquest routes again swerve north and south on the two sides of the Hindu Kush Mountains. The geography determined the directions of the Arab invasion beginning in 642. In the north, the invasion was directed from the strategic base of Merv, which was occupied by the Muslims in 650–651, toward northeastern Afghanistan (Tokharistan) and Transoxiana (*mawara un-nahr*). The southern axis was used to conquer southern Afghanistan and its southeastern extension into Sind. The operation along this route was launched from strategic bases at Kerman and Sistan. The two axes converged in western Afghanistan at the Sistan-Herat plain but remained divergent on the east side due to the mountain barriers of the Hindu Kush.

Military operations on both axes were directed by the Arab governor of Khorasan centered in Merv, who reported to the governor of Iraq in Basra. But there were times that the governors and military commanders were appointed by the caliph and reported directly to the center of the caliphate. The main effort in the conquest focused on the northern axis due to its political, strategic, and economic importance. There, the Amu Darya (*Jayhoun* in medieval Arabic) and Syr Darya (*Sayhoun* in Arabic) basins encompassed major political centers of Iranian and Turkic power north of the Hindu Kush. It was also the strategic frontier of nomadic hordes that constantly threatened the settled areas to the south. The economic importance of this area was due to the trade routes that crisscrossed the region connecting China to the west through Khorasan and to India across the Hindu Kush and the Kabul Valley. The area's major cities, including Herat, Balkh, Bukhara, and Samarkand, were the political and economic hubs of the region. The southern axis led to areas with natural obstacles, including craggy massifs in the northeast and barren deserts in the southeast. Early Arab authors considered Sistan greater than Khorasan, which had "more expanded borders, many warlike tribes, difficult terrain and larger populations."[24] However, the strategic and economic significance of the area did not match those in the north. For this reason, the conquest along the southern axis was slow and hardly reached Kabul until the late ninth century.

The Arab conquest and the spread of Islam in Afghanistan featured three distinct phases:

1. Military conquest and colonization.
2. Increasing political authority of the Islamized native powers and their influence in shaping the politics of the Islamic Caliphate.
3. The rise of independent Muslim dynasties in Afghanistan.

The first phase opened with the Arab armies' pursuit of Yazdegerd III into Sistan and Khorasan in 642 AD and lasted until the end of Umayyad rule in 750 AD. This period was the expansion of the Arabian Empire through military conquests, during which Arab governors and generals led sporadic raids along the two conquest routes (northern and southern) into modern Afghanistan to reduce local powers and force them to pay tribute. In the later years of this phase, as Arab influence increased, the conquerors began to colonize major cities through settlement of Arab tribes and military occupation. The process expedited proselytization and the emergence of local Muslim communities linked to metropolitan power centers.

Military Campaigns on the Southern Axis

The Arab invasion on the southern axis through Sistan was the continuation of the Arab governor of Basra Abdullah ibn Aamir's eastward drive in pursuit of Yazdegerd III as he fled to Khorasan through Sistan in the false hope of raising a new army to fight the invaders. Sistan in the sev-

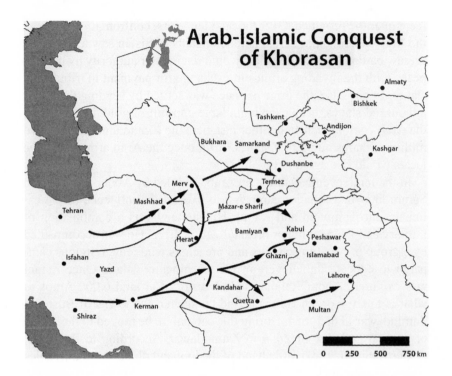

Arab-Islamic Conquest of Khorasan

enth century covered a large area extending from the modern Iranian province of Sistan to the provinces of Farah, Nimruz, and Helmand in Afghanistan and the Baluchistan Province of Pakistan, with its center at Zaranj, now a southwestern Afghan city near the border with Iran.

In 644–645, the Arab army led by Asem bin Amr advanced on Sistan. Several towns along the difficult road across the edge of the Great Salt Desert submitted and made terms with the victors. But Zaranj, the capital of Sistan, stood up against the intruders. Zaranj was a well-fortified city with an impregnable citadel. Both the city and its outer settlements were walled, and the city had five gates. It was ringed by a deep ditch of water for further protection.[25] The Muslims blockaded the city and eventually forced the natives to make peace and pay tribute to the Arab government in the province.[26] Accordingly, the invading force pulled out while taking full security measures to protect their columns from attacks by fortresses that were not part of the peace deal.

But less than five years later, after the death of Caliph Omar (644), Sistan broke into revolt. Caliph Uthman directed Abdullah ibn Aamir to reconquer the province. Over the next ten years, confrontation between the Arab Muslim conquerors and defendants of Sistan saw a pattern of seesaw battles. The local leaders would retain their authority by making peace with the invading armies in exchange for payment in tribute and slaves. In one case, the price of peace was settled by sending the victor a thousand slaves, each carrying a large cup full of gold demanded by the Arab commander. In another instance, the tribute amounted to two million dirhams and 2,000 slaves.[27] But once the Arab armies left, the locals would rise again in revolt.

In the mid-seventh century, an Arab army led by Abdur Rahman ibn Sumra launched a major campaign to expand the influence of the caliphate into Helmand and Kabul. His strategy was a combination of military action and a major proselytization drive. He was accompanied by a group of Muslim scholars and preachers who led a religious campaign to educate unbelievers in the teachings of Islam. Once Zaranj was captured, Abdur Rahman led an army of around 6,000 Arabs to what is today modern Helmand and conquered the towns of Bust and Zamindawar in 653–654. During this campaign, he moved to the shrine of the sun god *Zun* or *Zoon* in Zamindawar. According to Ibn Athir, Abdur Rahman "broke off a hand of the idol and plucked out the rubies which were its eyes in order to persuade the *Marzban* of Sistan of the god's worthlessness." The Arab general explained to the *Marzban* that "my intention was to show you that this idol can do neither any harm nor good."[28] Now the people of southern Afghanistan began to embrace Islam for the first time.

Failed Advance to Kabul

Abdur Rahman continued his advance to Ghazni and Kabul. This was the first time the Arab armies entered the limits of the Kabul Shahis' territory. As the Muslim columns reached the suburbs of Kabul, the Kabul Shah strengthened the protective walls built on the hills around the city[29] and confronted them with nearly 30,000 horses and seven elephants.[30] The Arabs pushed the Kabulis into the city and surrounded the fortified town while their siege engines came into action to reduce the defenses. The catapults made a breach in the city's western defenses at the present-day De-Mazang Gorge, which was widened during the night. On the next day, after getting reinforcements, the invaders poured into the city. Kabul fell to the Muslims. However, unable to retain control of the city, the Arab army left, only to return the next year to deal with the defiant Kabul ruler. During this episode, when Abdur Rahman captured Kabul, he left a body of Muslim preachers under Tamim ibn Qays Ansar to proselytize the faith and spread Islamic teachings. But soon after the departure of the Muslim army, a crowd, including the followers of Hinduism, Shaivism, and Buddhism as well as those who were forcefully converted to Islam, made a night assault on the Muslim preachers and slaughtered them all. From that time on, the site of the massacre at the eastern corner of old Kabul was turned into a shrine highly revered by the Muslim people of Afghanistan.

The future Arab penetration into Zabulistan and Kabul proved inconclusive. For years, the governors of Sistan were engaged in clashes and seesaw battles with *Zunbil*, the ruler of Zabulistan, including Helmand and Kandahar, which blocked the advance of Arab armies to Kabul. More than once, the raiding Arab columns, which sought to tax local rulers, ended up buying their way out of encirclement by the fierce native fighters.

The Death Valleys of Zabulistan

In 695 AD, Caliph Abdul Malik appointed Hajjaj ibn Yusuf governor of Iraq with authority over Khorasan and Sistan. Known for his draconian administration, Hajjaj decided to get tougher in dealing with the defiant rulers of Sistan and Kabul. He sent Obaidullah ibn Abi Bakra with the Kufa and Basra armies to Sistan and ordered him to advance on Zabulistan and Kabul and subdue their defiant rulers. According to Tabari, Hajjaj instructed Obaidullah to fight Zunbil (Ratbil) with all the troops he had under his command and not return from the area until he had laid waste the land, destroyed Zunbil's strongholds, killed his fighters, and enslaved his children.[31] As the Arab columns set out on their advance, they soon met a perilous situation similar to what their predecessors experienced. Zunbil withdrew before them, luring them further and further into the rugged terrain while removing all the food supplies. When the Arab army was about 70 miles from Kabul, around Ghazni, the die was cast. Zunbil blocked all roads and passages and entrapped the invaders in a rugged mountainous stockade. Realizing his precarious situation, Obaidullah opted for peace, which cost him a high price: paying Zunbil a sum of 700,000 dirhams, giving hostages (including three of his sons), and taking a solemn oath not to invade Zunbil's land again. However, some of the Arab forces decided to fight the enemy despite the unfavorable conditions. This suicidal decision cost them very heavy losses. Out of 20,000 soldiers with armor-clad horses, only 5,000 returned, and the army won the dubious title *Jaish al-Fana* (Army of Destruction).

The battle in Ghazni was the most disastrous setback for Arab forces since the beginning of their conquest. Alarmed by the defeat of his army, Hajjaj reported the near-destruction of his Muslim army to the caliph and strongly recommended that a large and well-equipped army from Kufa and Basra be sent to punish the infidels immediately. Otherwise, he warned, the enemy would become bolder and attack all areas under Muslim control. He also cautioned that, if Zunbil mobilized the local population, all Arab gains might be lost.[32] After the approval of the caliph, Hajjaj formed an army of 20,000 men each from Kufa and Basra. The 40,000-strong expeditionary force was so thoroughly armed and elegantly equipped that it was called *Jaish Tawawis* (Peacock Army). In 699–700 AD, Hajjaj appointed Abdur Rahman ibn Ash'ath, a distinguished Arab nobleman and general, commander of the Peacock Army.

Taking note of the experience of his ill-fated predecessors, Abdur Rahman moved forward prudently, securing his flanks and back as he advanced toward Zabulistan and Kabul. Zunbil enacted his usual strategy of luring the intruders into rugged mountains, but the Arab leader was taking measures to avoid entrapment. This slowed progress, making it difficult for him to reach Kabul before the onset of winter, when snow blocks the mountain defiles. So Abdur Rahman decided to stop at a middle stage short of Kabul and resume the advance after the winter. Meanwhile, he sent an advance detachment to Kabul to test its defenses. The detachment succeeded in penetrating into the city but faced resistance from overwhelming forces within Kabul. Fighting between the Muslims and Kabul soldiers continued along the Kabul River. Local tradition has it that during the fighting a Muslim holy man named Lays ibn Qays ibn Abbas was fighting with two scimitars and leading his men to victory until he fell in battle. He is remembered by the title *Shah-i Doh Shamshira* (King of Two Swords). A mosque built later near the tomb of the Muslim martyr in downtown Kabul is named after him—the Shah-i Doh Shamshira Mosque. The Arab incursion was repelled by the Kabul defenders.

Abdur Rahman reported his advance and setback at Kabul to Hajjaj and recommended that he resume his campaign against Kabul in the spring after the snow melted. Hajjaj responded angrily, accusing Abdur Rahman of cowardice and incompetence. He ordered him to continue the operation immediately and then to garrison the army in the Kabul area to complete the occupation. Abdur Rahman felt that Hajjaj's reaction was a gross insult and, after winning the support of his troops, renounced Hajjaj and mutinied against him. He ended hostilities with Zunbil and made an alliance with him.[33] Zunbil offered him protection if he failed in his war with Hajjaj. The Peacock Army under Ibn al-Ash'ath's leadership returned to Iraq, where it fought Hajjaj. Although the mutiny was eventually defeated by the Syrian Umayyad army, it marked the end of major military campaigns in southern Afghanistan until the fall of the Umayyad rule in 750 AD. Islamization of major centers in eastern Afghanistan was achieved by the local Muslim dynasties of Saffarids and Ghaznavids in the ninth and tenth centuries.

Campaigns on the Northern Axis

In 641 AD, the Arabs on the northern axis headed toward northern Afghanistan and Central Asia. The initial purpose was to capture or kill the fugitive Sassanid king Yazdegerd III, who was on the run toward the eastern confines of Khorasan to raise a new army. It took the invading army nearly a decade to clear its passage through the resisting strongholds in the Nishapur–Herat–Sistan Triangle and establish forward military bases in the region. The Arab penetration of the area during this phase amounted to raiding expeditions in which the cities overrun by the invading hordes were forced to pay tribute to their new masters. However, after the death of Caliph Omar, the conquerors faced a general insurrection throughout the area that continued until 652. The Arab governor at the time, Abdullah ibn Aamir, launched a major campaign to reconquer Sistan and Khorasan and force the region to acknowledge the caliph's suzerainty. The war in Khorasan and Transoxiana proved to be the toughest and the longest of all the early Arab campaigns. From the capture of Merv in 650–651, which became the base of future campaigns and the capital of the Arab Governorate of Khorasan, to the final battle at Talas in 751 that solidified the Arab military gains, the region constantly resisted Arab domination for a full century. Major cities in the area repeatedly changed hands as the conquered challenged the authority of the conquerors whenever they saw an opportunity.

The Geopolitics of the Military Campaigns

The Arab campaign in Khorasan and Soghdiana was shaped by four geographic and political realities of the time. First was the geographic proximity of Tokharistan and Soghdiana and the strategic importance of

The Extent of Islamic Khorasan

Cisoxiana (*ma dun al-nahr*)—the territory south and west of the Amu Darya River. Control of this region is indispensable to the conquest of Central Asia. Second was the absence of a dominant power in the region. Third was the political disunion of local principalities. And fourth was the long distance between the region and the imperial center with the resulting complexity of control.

Although the Arabs called the lands north of the Amu Darya (Oxus) *mawara un-nahr* (What Is Beyond the River), the river has never been a barrier to the movement of imperial armies from either side. The tenth-century Arab geographer Muqaddasi surveyed the crossing points on the Amu Darya and counted twenty-five such sites excluding the northernmost point in Khwarazm.[34] The Amu Darya flows within the bounds of ancient Iranian-Zoroastrian civilization extending from the Syr Darya (Jaxartes) in the north and the Hindu Kush Mountains in the south. As H. A. R. Gibb writes, "The Oxus is a boundary of tradition rather than of history."[35] In the past, from the Achaemenid emperor Cyrus to Alexander the Great, the northern border of Iran rested on the Syr Darya (Jaxartes), not on the Amu Darya (Oxus). It was on the banks of the former where Cyrus and Alexander built their border outposts to protect the settled areas in the south against raids by nomadic hordes from the steppes. Even when the Jaxartes border was crossed by invaders, the blocking positions to contain them were not on the Amu Darya but rather on the Murghab River. True, the legends of ancient Iran depicted in the epic of Firdausi's *Shah-Nama* identify the Amu Darya as the boundary between Iran and Turan. But the legends—mainly based on *Khwday-Namag* (Book of Kings), which was a late Sassanid period compilation—were influenced by the presence of the Western Turks in the area at that time, which probably influenced the acceptance of the Oxus as the boundary between Iran and Turan.

Geographically, the middle Central Asian settled tract between the Jaxartes River in the northeast and the Hindu Kush Massif in the south is divided by the Hissar Mountains into two distinct areas. The northern section covers the fertile valley of Zarafshan and other smaller streams that flow down the northern slope of the watershed; the southern sections include the Oxus basin between the Pamir and the western plains stretching to Jawzjan and Faryab. The former is known as Soghdiana and the latter as Tokharistan. Tokharistan straddles the Amu Darya from its eastern confines to the plains west of Balkh. Named after the Tokharis, who are mentioned among the races who overthrew the Greco-Bactrian Empire in the second century BC, Tokharistan during the period of Arab conquest embraced all the provinces on both banks of the Amu Darya that were economically dependent on Balkh.[36] The territory of northern Tokharistan included the independent principalities of Chaghanian, Termez, Qubadian, Khutalan, and others; southern Tokharistan consisted of the greater Balkh and Badakhshan principalities. In the 630s AD, the Chinese traveler Yuan Chwang (Hieun Tsiang) found the country divided into twenty-seven petty states under separate rulers.[37]

The Arabs' conquest of Soghdiana and the Jaxartes region was hinged on control of Tokharistan. It became possible only after Arabs completely subdued lower Tokharistan. Thus, the center of gravity of the Arab invasion was focused on lower Tokharistan along with the western principalities of Jawzjan, Faryab, Merv-ar-Rud, Gharjistan, and Herat. The early Arab expeditions met strong resistance in these cities, which were repeatedly attacked by Arab raiding columns. For this reason, the Arabs always regarded Balkh—the old religious capital of the Kushan Empire and site of the famous Buddhist shrine of Nawbahar—as the capital of the "Turks" or the assumed dominant power in the region. According to Gibb, Balkh was in fact "the center of what we might almost term as the 'amphictyony' of lower Tokharistan, combining strategic and commercial importance with religious veneration. Long after the

Nawbahar had been destroyed by ibn Aamir, the sentiment continued to exist in the country."[38]

At the time of the Arab conquest of Khorasan and Central Asia, there was no single dominant power in full control of the region. The Western Turks' empire, centered in the Ili and Chu Valleys (today's Kyrgyzstan and Kazakhstan), maintained nominal sway over semi-independent principalities ruled by native princes in both Soghdiana and Tokharistan. All the principalities acknowledged the Khan of the Western Turks as overlord and paid tribute to him, but until the rise of Turgesh power in 716 AD, no major Turkish army ever came to help the local princes in their war against the Arabs. The area was divided into several small states formed together in a loose confederacy like that of the ancient Greek city-states. Their common interest in the Chinese silk trade, with its major hubs in Samarkand, Paykand, near Bukhara, and Kesh, bound the principalities into a union. Common outside threats impelled these otherwise competing territories to join in a unified front. The house of Samarkand, with closer ties to the Turkic overlords, often played a linking role among the regional power centers. Similarly, in Tokharistan the chief military authority over the separate principalities was vested in the Turkish Shad (Turkish Viceroy), the eldest son of Jabghu or Yabghu (king) of the Western Turks, who had his seat in what is modern Kunduz in northern Afghanistan. In later years, when the power of the Western Turks declined, the whole territory was integrated into an independent kingdom under a son of the former Shad who founded the dynasty of Jabghus of Tokharistan, whose suzerainty was acknowledged from the Iron Gate (Temir Darvoza, in modern Uzbekistan) to Zabulistan.

The political disunion of the region favored the Arab conquerors, who often succeeded in concentrating their forces progressively against separate power centers for their piecemeal reduction. The domestic situation prevented effective public backing of competing local dynasties, which taxed the population to support their courts, armies, and efforts to maintain or expand their realms in a highly competitive environment. The people were also assessed extra taxes to support the tribute paid to Arab overlords. Popular discontent would move the population to welcome a strong and unified Arab government, especially in later years when they saw that large segments of the Arab armies were their own kinsmen.

The long distance between the center of the caliphate and Khorasan made exercising central control over military campaigns difficult. The governors of Khorasan were allowed much leeway in waging military campaigns and governing the conquered lands. The personal leadership and military skills of the Arab governors figured prominently in the progress of the conquest of Khorasan and Soghdiana. This was not always positive due to Arab commanders' internal rivalries that sometimes led to civil war among the tribal contingents of the Arab army in Khorasan. For example, after the death of Caliph Yazid in 683, three main tribal groups in Khorasan represented by Mudar, Rabi'a, and Bakr ibn Wa'il engaged in a fierce struggle for control of the province. Abdullah ibn Khazim, the head of the Mudar, took power in Merv and made war on his rival tribes, who had fled to Herat and established themselves there. After a year, Abdullah overcame his enemy's defenses and massacred 8,000 of the Rabi'a and Bakr members. The tribal war in Khorasan spread to Basra, home to many of the same tribal peoples. It took the Umayyad Caliphate center about eight years to restore its power in Khorasan. The center did this by arranging for the killing of Abdullah ibn Khazim, who had declared himself the ruler of Khorasan in defiance of the caliph.[39] Later, his son Musa led a rebellion from his base in Termez (Tirmidh) that lasted another eight years. The geographic isolation of the region tempted certain governors of Khorasan to defy the center and rise in rebellion. Even the illustrious career of the renowned Arab conqueror of Central Asia, Qutayba ibn Muslim, ended with his assassination by fellow Arabs after he revolted against the caliph and insulted fellow Arabs for not joining him in the rebellion.

The century-long war in Khorasan and Central Asia comprised a series of campaigns that began with the Arabs' plundering raids followed by their military conquest, which was temporarily reversed by a counteroffensive and concluded with the reconquest of the regions by Arab armies in the middle of the eighth century. Modern authors describe the war as a four-phase campaign.[40] The first phase is characterized by a period of fragmented raiding expeditions with little occupation. The second phase was a decade-long (705–715) campaign under the renowned Arab commander Qutayba ibn Muslim Bahili to conquer and garrison the conquered lands in the region. The third phase (716–737) was marked by the counteroffensive of resurgent Turks and the local princes to reverse the Arab gains. The fourth phase was Arab reconquest in which Arab armies established the caliphate suzerainty by accommodating local princes and recognizing their internal self-rule and status. This phase was completed by the Arab victory in a battle at the Talas River in 751 over the Chinese Tang dynasty army that sought to control the strategic area of Central Asia. The Battle of Talas marked the end of the Tang dynasty's western expansion and was the farthest point of western territorial expansion by the Tang or any prior or subsequent Chinese dynasty.

The Initial Raids

The progress of conquest in Khorasan was influenced by the domestic situation at the heart of the Umayyad Empire. The civil wars (*fitna*) of 656–661 following the assassination of Caliph Uthman and the subsequent struggles over his successor, and the conflict of 683–685 among the Umayyads for the control of the caliphate, all but halted the military campaign in Khorasan. This led to a general insurrection and then rejection of Arab rule.

In the initial wave of expansion under the caliphs Umar and Othman, the Arab armies reached Herat and the banks of the Oxus River but did not firmly control the area. With the murder of the last Sassanid monarch, Yazdegerd III, in 651 near Merv,[41] the Arab conquest of the Sassanid Empire was complete. The semi-independent ruler of Merv, Mahuya, surrendered to the approaching Arab army, which occupied Merv and turned it into the capital of the Arab province of Khorasan. The Arab governor of Basra, Abdullah ibn Aamir, launched a major campaign in Khorasan in 654. An expeditionary force of 4,000 Arabs and 1,000 Persians led by Ahnaf ibn Qays met stout resistance from a 30,000-strong allied army from lower Tokharistan—including contingents from Faryab, Jawzjan, and Taleqan—forcing the Arab columns to retreat to Merv ar-Rud on the Murghab River (the modern Bala Murghab District in Afghanistan's Badghis Province). Tabari relates how the Arab commander managed to win the battle against superior enemy numbers by using terrain to his advantage. According to the story, on the eve of combat, as Ahnaf was contemplating how to deal with an enemy force six times larger than his own, he received an unsolicited and unexpected suggestion from one of his soldiers. Ahnaf was strolling though the camp when he overheard a conversation in a tent where a group of soldiers were cooking dinner. During a discussion of the situation, one of them suggested that the "Amir should avoid facing the enemy in the open since our small force will be easily overwhelmed and surrounded. Instead he should take a position in a narrow passage between the Murghab River on the left and the mountain on the right where the enemy will not be able to deploy a force larger than our own. We can beat a force equal to us in numbers."[42] Ahnaf took the advice and deployed his forces on the banks of Murghab at a point near modern-day Maruchaq where the Murghab Valley widens about two or three miles across.[43] The road from Merv to Bala Murghab crosses the river at Maruchaq and follows the right bank to Qaraol Khana and Bala Murghab. It was there that Qasr-i Ahnaf Castle was later built.[44] In the Murghab battle, which took place at night, the Arab army routed the Tokharistan legions and pursued them down to Faryab.

Meanwhile, another Arab expeditionary force under al-Aqra' ibn Habis overran Jawzjan, Faryab, and Taleqan. Ahnaf advanced to Balkh and failed to break its strong defenses. A peace deal was concluded whereby Balkh agreed to pay a tribute of 400,000 dirhams. Smaller columns raided other cities, including Samangan and Khwarazm, with little success. With the departure of the raiding columns, general insurrection broke out, headed by a Herati leader named Qaren who, according to Tabari, mobilized a 40,000-strong army (which seems highly exaggerated unless he counted the local population who rose in defiance of the enemy) and fought Arab forces sent from Nishapur. The revolt, coupled with the first Muslim civil war, caused the Arabs to evacuate Khorasan.

In 671, Ziyad ibn Abu Sufyan (Mu'awiya's adopted brother) sent a large host of troops and Arab settlers numbering 50,000 to Merv to establish a colony. Using this city as their base, the Arabs launched military campaigns into Tokharistan and across the Amu Darya into Central Asia. However, the invading columns did not occupy the conquered cities and returned to their base in Merv that winter. Far from being part of an integrated strategic plan, the military campaigns were often fragmented and aimed at targets of opportunity. In 673, Caliph Mu'awiya I appointed his 25-year-old nephew, Obaidullah ibn Ziyad, the governor of Khorasan and, two years later, also put him in charge of the governments in Kufa and Basra.[45]

Obaidullah pursued a two-pronged campaign strategy that included consolidating Arab control in Tokharistan and then using it as the base for military expeditions across the Amu Darya into Soghdiana. In 674, he launched the first known invasion of Bukhara by Muslim Arabs. In Bukhara at that time, the mother of an infant heir to the throne, known as the Khatun (Lady), acted as the regent and had become the central figure in the principality.[46] In spite of the assistance the Khatun received from the Turks, the Arab army defeated the natives, and Obaidullah ordered the trees uprooted and the villages destroyed. To save her city from destruction, the Khatun asked for peace. The price for such peace was one million dirhams. The Arab governor departed with the money and took 4,000 captives with him.[47] Obaidullah's successors followed his example, and in 676 Sa'id ibn Othman pushed the Arab conquest more deeply into Transoxiana, reduced the Soghdians, and took fifty young nobles as hostages.[48] Although the Arabs made inroads into Samarkand, Khuttal, and Tirmidh (Termez) and made them tributaries, there were no advances for five years. But a tribal feud among Arabs in Khorasan provided the opportunity to the princes of Transoxiana to regain their independence.[49] The second civil war (during the height of the empire, 680–692) impeded the caliphate's intervention to restore control in Khorasan until 705, when the governor of Iraq, al-Hajjaj ibn Yusuf, appointed Qutayba ibn Muslim Bahili as the governor of Khorasan. The appointment opened a new phase of the Arab conquest in Khorasan and Central Asia.

The Decade of Qutayba's Conquest and Pacification

Although the Arabs had projected power for many years into Khorasan from their regional capital at Merv, their hold on the country north of the Amu Darya was very fragile. Their incursion into Bukhara and other parts of Transoxiana (*mawara un-nahr*) were mostly raids and their authority in the area petered out with the departure of the main body of the army back to Merv. The military campaigns of Qutayba from 705 to 714 not only brought most of the Khorasan and Central Asia under firm Arab control but also achieved major gains in spreading Islam across the conquered lands. The military campaigns were phased into operations to consolidate the Arab sway in Cisoxiana (*ma dun al-nahr*), particularly Tokharistan, and occupation of major centers of power in Transoxiana including Bukhara, Samarkand, Shash (Tashkent), and Khujand. In the last phase of the campaign, Qutayba established frontier outposts on the Syr Darya (Jaxartes) and in the Ferghana Valley to check the movement of the Turks and Chinese.

After reducing resistance in Tokharistan, Qutayba returned to Merv and launched a major campaign to conquer the main center of power in *mawara un-nahr*. Between 705 and 714, the Arab armies were engaged in fighting for control over the major cities in the Zarafshan Valley, including Bukhara, Samarkand, and Kesh. In a series of well-planned campaigns lasting from 706 he 709, the Arab commander subdued Bukhara, and then from 710 to 712 he reduced Samarkand. According to Narshakhi, Qutayba conquered Bukhara four times; each time after the Muslims withdrew, the population rose in rebellion.[50] After the fourth seizure, Qutayba decided to colonize the city and settled Arab tribes there. Accordingly, he made the people give half of their houses and fields to the Muslims, and he divided the city among the Arab tribes; a part was given to the Rabi'a and Mudar tribes and the remainder to the Yemenites.[51]

Qutayba massacred all the fighting men, carried off the rest of the population and sold them into slavery, and destroyed the city. According to Tabari, Qutayba returned to Merv with such enormous spoils that they exceeded in value all the booty that had been taken by the Arabs in Khorasan. The riches enabled the Arab leader to rearm his troops for new military operations.[52]

In 713, Qutayba moved farther east and made inroads in the Ferghana Valley. Over the next two years, Qutayba directed his military efforts farther north and moved to the Jaxartes Valley, apparently to control the Silk Road extending from China to Central Asia through the Ferghana Valley. In 713, as the fighting season arrived, a 20,000-strong Arab army supported by the native contingents moved in two columns to the banks of the Jaxartes. One column, composed of native levies, marched on Shash (modern Tashkent) while the second column, led by Qutayba, took the Arab sword to Khujand and on to the Ferghana Valley. Tabari writes that Qutayba penetrated into Chinese-held territory up to Kashghar, although this is questionable.[53] As the Arabs renewed their raids in the Jaxartes provinces the following year (714) from a new base in Shash, their initial efforts were not conclusive. Furthermore, the operations were disrupted by the death of Governor Hajjaj, a strong supporter of Qutayba. Seeing his patron gone and unsure about his position under a new administration, Qutayba disbanded his army and returned to Merv.

Qutayba—the man who conquered Transoxiana for the empire—met his end in dramatic fashion. The death of his patron Hajjaj and the ascendance of his archenemy Suleiman bin Abd al-Malik to the throne frightened Qutayba about his future. In a state of utter panic, he halted the conquest of Ferghana and mutinied against the new caliph. Despite Qutayba's favored standing among the native levies, the Khorasani Arabs refused to support him. The opposition, led by the Tamim tribe and their leader Waki' ibn Abi Sud al-Tamimi, killed Qutayba along with his family and supporters in 715.[54] Waki' succeeded as governor and ordered the army back to Merv, where it was disbanded. The death of Qutayba was a turning point in the Arab conquest of Transoxiana during which an increasing number of natives joined the Arabs' cause.

The decade-long military campaign of Qutayba in Central Asia was marked by systematic atrocities against the populations of the conquered lands.

The Turkish Counteroffensive

During the next twenty years, there was a reversal of the Arabs' gains in Central Asia partly due to the counteroffensive undertaken by the revived Turkish power, the Turgesh, a Turkish tribal confederation that rose to power after the decline of the Western Turkic Khaganate and managed to build a short-lived polity from 699 to 766. In 719, the native Iranian and Turkish leaders of the region appealed to China for help in their war against the Arabs. Although the Chinese were not yet prepared to intervene directly in remote areas west of their borders, they encouraged the Turgesh confederacy to get involved in the region. Consequently, the Turgesh attacks, assisted by the native forces of Transoxiana, began in 720 and continued for more than a decade. The attacks were launched by mobile bodies of cavalry with apparent Chinese support against Arab garrisons. Meanwhile, the local populations and their princes turned against the Arabs due to their harsh and cruel treatment and their breaching of existing agreements. Further Arab tribal feuds in the region reduced their military power and weakened their grip on the area.

Efforts by the Arab rulers to suppress the rebellion with great brutality failed, and the Arabs suffered a major disaster in 724 in an attempt to capture Ferghana. The Arab forces were defeated and chased in hot pursuit across the Jaxartes. This disaster, known as the Day of Thirst (*yaum al-'attash*), came as a serious blow to Arab prestige in Central Asia and marked the last aggressive expedition by Arabs in Transoxiana until 739.[55] Meanwhile, other Arab efforts to punish rebellions in different locations on both sides of the Amu Darya did not succeed. Neither did the Arabs' conciliatory policies, including the abolition of taxation of native converts, bring any relief. As the carrot-and-stick policy failed, the Arab armies' military operations stopped and even reversed over the next several years. Finally, in 728, the Turgesh invasion and local uprisings forced the Arabs out of most of Transoxiana except for the areas around Samarkand.

One of the major battles during this period was fought in July 731 at Tashtakaracha Pass in modern-day Uzbekistan. There the Arab army and the Turgesh forces fought the Battle of the Defile, a three-day bloody encounter that ended with a decisive defeat of the Arab forces.

The Arab *Reconquista*

The situation changed in the Arabs' favor following the assassination of the Turgesh king, which led to the disintegration of the Turgesh polity. At the same time, a shift in the policies of Arab governors—showing increased respect for local populations and building friendly relations with local leaders and princes—paved the way for the Arabs to regain control and further expand their rule from 739 until the end of the Umayyad Caliphate.[56] By then, Umayyad power had reached its uppermost limits, beyond which it could not be governed from Syria and Iraq. Consequently, the Ferghana Valley and the provinces of Shash (modern Tashkent) and Ushrusana (the area between Samarkand and Khujand) remained as the border outposts of the Islamic world for centuries.[57] Meanwhile, Bukhara and Samarkand became important bases of Islamic culture and centers of learning. During the Arab conquest, Samarkand and Bukhara were inhabited mostly by Iranian people, whereas the steppes across the Syr Darya and the mountainous lands to the east were occupied mostly by the more warlike Turkish tribes, which discouraged further Arab expansion.

However, by the middle of the eighth century, the westward expansion of the Chinese Tang Empire threatened Arab control over Central Asia. In 750, as the Umayyads had just been overthrown and their successor caliphate, the Abbasids, were consolidating their power, the Chinese army, supported by local forces, marched westward, overrunning several cities and states in eastern Turkistan. The invading forces not only eyed control over the Jaxartes River but also had the ambition to dominate the whole of Central Asia. The nascent Abbasid Caliphate, with its power base in Khorasan, within striking distance of the enemy, had to deal with the Chinese threat. The Abbasids' victory over their rivals, the Umayyads, in 750 freed up the army to concentrate against the advancing Chinese army. The opposing forces met in a major showdown in July 751 in the valley of the Talas River near today's Taraz in Kazakhstan. The strength of the Arab army, led by Ziyad ibn Salih, is inflated to 200,000 by Chinese sources, while Arab records put the Chinese forces at an inflated number of 100,000. Considering the logistics, the real sizes of the opposing forces might have been half the recorded numbers. The Chinese army under its Korean general, Ko Sonji, was supported by 20,000 Qarluqs mercenaries who had defected to the Muslim side during the battle and attacked the Tang army from close quarters. Consequently, the Chinese army met a devastating defeat, and only 2,000 of the Tang troops managed to return to their territory.

The outcome of the Battle of Talas resulted in major political changes in the region. It marked the end of Chinese power in the west and frustrated the last attempt at restoring an independent Soghdiana with Chinese support. As W. [V. V.] Barthold writes, the Battle of Talas is "undoubtedly of great importance in the history of Turkistan as it determined the question which of the two civilizations, the Chinese or the Muslims, should predominate in the land."[58] The situation opened the way for further assimilation of Khorasan and Soghdiana into the Muslim *umma*. There is also a tradition that Chinese prisoners captured in the battle helped in the transfer of papermaking technology to the Middle East and eventually Europe.

Khorasani Influence in Shaping the Politics of the Islamic Caliphate

The Arab conquest of Khorasan and Sistan in the seventh and early eighth centuries, along with consistent proselytizing, made steady progress in replacing local practices of Zoroastrianism and Buddhism with the Islamic faith. The pious Caliph Omar II (r. 717–720) invited the princes of the conquered lands in Khorasan and Soghdiana to embrace Islam on the condition that they should have the same rights as other Muslims. Two decades later, in 737, Barmak, the hereditary administrator of the renowned Buddhist monastery of Nawbahar (Nava Vihara) in Balkh, followed by many leading landowners (*dehqans*), converted to Islam. The Islamization of the region provided opportunities for the local population to penetrate the civil and military administration of the conquered lands. Furthermore, the Arab rulers increasingly recruited non-Arab converts into the military and raised native levies and auxiliary military forces to augment the Arab armies. The more the native forces integrated into the new order, the stronger became their influence in local politics. Among the Khorasani converts, Hayyan an-Nabati rose in status to become the foremost military leader of Khorasani conscripts and the chief negotiator with Soghdian principalities. Throughout Qutayba's governorship of Khorasan (705–715), Hayyan held a prominent position in his campaigns and acted as his chief negotiator.[59]

Khorasan, Soghdiana, and Sistan were remote and hard to control from the center and gradually drifted away from close central control. As the eighth century proceeded, the growing native Muslim communities, as well as the Arab settlers in the area, became detached from the center and moved closer to one another culturally—the Iranians became Islamized but not Arabized, while the Arabs adopted certain strains of Iranian culture.

Moreover, the tribal divisions within the Arab armies in Khorasan fostered rivalries and competition among tribes for local resources and political standing. The people of the conquered lands, who had unsuccessfully struggled to preserve their independence in the face of the Arab invasion, refocused their efforts to become autonomous within the dominant system. They saw hardly any prospect of achieving their goals under the Umayyads, who treated them as second-class citizens. The Arab campaign was originally waged to spread the faith but turned into raids to gain loot and to impose heavy taxation to satisfy the extravagance of the ruling class. In some cases, the Umayyad rulers imposed the poll tax (*Jizya*) even on those who had embraced Islam.[60] According to Tabari, Abdur Rahman ibn Ziyad, who served two years as governor of Khorasan, amassed 20 million dirhams. Caliph Yazid (r. 680–683) offered him the choice of being held to account and losing the wealth he apparently acquired illegally or being removed from his post.[61] Abdur Rahman chose the latter option. In an earlier case, Yazid's father, Mu'awiya, dealt in the same way with Ibn Aamir, who had returned from ruling the region with enormous wealth.[62]

As the Khorasanis saw little prospect of winning influence under the Umayyads, they opted to tap into other sources of power within the empire and support the cause of the rival Abbasids dynasty (the descendants of "Abbas," an uncle of the Prophet). They also made common cause with the Shi'ites by pretending devotion to the family of the Prophet (*ahl-i bait*). The social and political intricacies in the Muslim world provided legitimate causes to underpin their struggle for political influence. The Umayyad dynasty was gradually degenerating because, in the words of the fourteenth-century Muslim historiographer Ibn Khaldun, the improved revenues led to the abundance of "bounties and salaries," life became more relaxed and the character of tribal warriors softened, giving way to laziness and corruption. The situation, he wrote, reached a point where the elites were competing for material gains while government expenditures were exceeding revenues. These two factors paved the way for disintegration of the polity, opening opportunities for certain groups to mobilize new forces to challenge the power of the declining dynasty.[63]

In Khorasan Province, there was a deep bitterness toward the Umayyads for murdering so many of Ali's descendants. A native Khorasani saddler named Abdur-Rahman, who assumed the name of Abu-Muslim, became the main advocate of the house of Abbas and mobilized large masses—both Khorasanis and Arabs—in support of the Abbasids' cause. On June 17, 747, he raised the black flag of rebellion in Merv, and within a few months, in the words of Robert Payne, "the whole patiently acquired empire which had endured for ninety years toppled over and went to its death."[64]

Events moved rapidly. The last Umayyad caliph, Marwan II, was defeated on the Zab River, between Mosul and Arbela. It was in January 750 when the 120,000-strong army of Abu-Muslim and Abul Abbas crushed his force. Flying the banners known as the "Cloud" and the "Shadow," the revolutionaries moved like cloud and shadow, pouring out of Khorasan and Persia onto the plains of Iraq and to the coasts of Syria. Soon, Arab garrisons in Khorasan were disaffected, and the provincial governor, Nasr ibn Saiyar, made a desperate appeal to Marwan for assistance. When no relief force arrived, Merv fell—and the road was open to Iraq. Abul Abbas Abdullah headed the Abbasid house, and when the army under Abu-Muslim reached Kufa, he emerged from hiding and was elected caliph.

The Abbasid Revolution, as a landmark event in the annals of Islam, has been the subject of extensive studies since its occurrence in the middle of the eighth century. Far from being merely a dynastic change and a shift of power from the Umayyads to the Abbasids, the momentous uprising marked a new era in the history of Islamic civilization. It was the first Islamic revolution heralding cataclysmic changes and serving as a prototype for later insurrectionary movements in the Muslim world. The nature of transition from Umayyad to Abbasid rule can be characterized by the hallmark features defining the political identity of the two dynasties. Whereas the former was considered a predominantly Arab empire, the latter attempted to build a unified dominion through a universal Islamic community.

It is important to draw on the fundamental changes that took place in political, social, and economic life across the Islamic world during the Umayyad period. Rapid expansion of the empire during this period gave way to competing demands by different forces, which were involved, at different levels, in the Arabs' political, religious, and military domination of foreign lands. Lack of Umayyad capacity to respond to sometimes conflicting demands deepened the rifts and intensified disputes among rival factions. On the one hand, the victorious Arab tribes were embroiled in fierce competition for power and material gains; on the other, the religious movement began to factionalize, backing rival contenders for political power. Meanwhile, the non-Arab converts in conquered nations sought to fight for equal political rights and economic opportunities under the tenets of Islam. The leadership of the Abbasid Revolution mobilized various dissident forces, each of which had a stake in overthrowing Umayyad rule. Therefore, it will be a mistake to look for "dominants" in listing the causes of the Abbasid Revolution. In fact, the revolt was fueled by a synergetic combination of several factors, which led to the victory mainly through joint and coordinated action. In the words of Montgomery Watt, the victory of these forces is considered as the driving force behind fundamental changes in the social and political structure of the empire.[65]

With a large influx of Iranian ideas into the Arab system, the influence of Khorasanis and Persians in the Abbasid administration increased. As the caliphs of the house of Abbas emerged from Khorasan, they adopted many customs and rituals of the Iranian royalties. The situation lifted the political standing of the Khorasanis, while the Arabs began to lose their influence not only in the army and at court but also in society. Armies from Khorasan dominated caliphate military forces and played key roles in caliphate military campaigns across the empire.[66] Abu-Muslim, the first non-Arab governor of Khorasan under Islamic rule, consolidated his power in Khorasan and Transoxiana. His rising popularity began to alarm the Abbasid court, which owed its elevation to the throne to him and his Khorasani followers. Right after the caliph's brother, Abu Ja'far Mansur, visited Merv, the court became alarmed at the influence and independence of Abu-Muslim. Upon accession to the caliphate, Mansur planned the assassination of the Khorasani leader. According to Tabari, Mansur also held personal jealousy and animosity toward Abu-Muslim.[67]

The eventual murder of Abu-Muslim caused widespread resentment, particularly in Khorasan. The fallen hero became a legendary figure for many in Khorasan and Persia, and his soul on earth inspired several rebellions led by his followers (some of whom claimed that he had not died and would return). Abu-Muslim's followers did not consider him to be simply a military and political leader; to them he was a religious figure equivalent to an imam in Shi'ite terminology. One of them was

Sunpadh (Sinbad), a close associate and a general of Abu-Muslim in Nishapur who rose in rebellion in 755. Another insurgent, al-Muqanna', in Khorasan launched an uprising in 777 against Caliph al-Mahdi. Known as the Veiled Prophet, who inspired Thomas Moore's *Veiled Prophet of Khorasan*, al-Muqanna' (real name Hashim ibn Hakim) was a cloth-pleater-turned-commander in Abu-Muslim's army. He claimed to be an incarnation of Abu-Muslim after he was murdered. For this he was taken to Baghdad and imprisoned, but upon release he returned to Merv and commanded a great following that at one point numbered 50,000 men including Khorasanis, Transoxianans, Turks, and others.[68] Muqanna' was wearing a veil in order to cover the glaring "light" of his face, but his enemies claimed that he wore it to hide his ugliness (being one-eyed and bald). Known locally as *sapid jamagan* (wearers of white raiment), his Mazdakite followers wore white clothes in opposition to the Abbasids' black. Al-Muqanna' was instrumental in forming the Khurramiyya sect, which claimed Abu-Muslim to be the Mahdi and denied his death. The rebellion was finally crushed in 786.

While these rebellions were based on extremist religiopolitical tenets, resentment over how the Abbasids dealt with a Khorasani hero survived for a long time. More than a century later, when Amir Yaqub Laith Safar launched his campaign against the Abbasid Caliphate, he used the Abbasids' murder of Abu-Muslim as one reason to defy the legitimacy of Abbasid rule over Khorasan.[69]

For the next several generations, the story of Khorasani leaders' influence in the Abbasid administration saw many ups and downs. Several prominent figures from Khorasan rose to the highest levels of power, only to fall suddenly as the caliphs saw their increasing influence as a threat to their own authority. One such influential Khorasani clan actively involved in caliphate affairs was the Barmakid dynasty. The Barmakids, a prominent family from Balkh, wielded great political power under the Abbasid caliphs of Baghdad. The progenitor of the family, Barmak (an Arabized form of Sanskrit Pramukha), was the hereditary administrator of the Buddhist monastery of Nava Vihara in Balkh. A son of Barmak, Khalid, embraced Islam, supported the Abbasid Revolution, and became vizier under the first Abbasid caliph, Abul Abbas, and a general under the second, Caliph al-Mansur. Khalid's son Yahya, who helped Harun al-Rashid secure his throne, rose in rank to become the most powerful man in the empire. The Barmakids were highly educated and respected for their administrative skills, splendor, and generosity throughout Arabia, Persia, Transoxiana, and the Levant. Yahya served as vizier under Caliph Harun al-Rashid, and Yahya's sons Fazl and Ja'far were the actual rulers of the caliphate for seventeen years and Harun's intimate friends. Different members of the great family are featured in the *Arabian Nights* fables. In his anecdotes from the early caliphs' time, Mas'udi wrote that the Barmakids

> were the crown and ornament of their age. Their generosity passed into a proverb; adherents thronged to their court from every side, and multitudes centered their hopes on them. Fortune showered upon them a prodigality of favors. Yahya and his sons were like brilliant stars, vast oceans, impetuous torrents, beneficent showers. Every kind of talent and learning was represented in their court and men of worth received a hearty welcome there. The world was revived under their administration, and the empire reached its culminating point of splendor. They were a refuge for the afflicted and a haven for the distressed.[70]

But the Barmakids' ascendancy to the highest level of power suddenly reversed in 803 as their patron, Caliph Harun al-Rashid, unceremoniously sacked and destroyed their all-powerful dynasty. Arab sources claim that the reason for Harun's action was linked to a personal family matter between him and Ja'far Barmakid. They maintain that the caliph, who was fond of his sister Abbassa and his close friend Ja'far, wanted both to be with him in private meetings at the same time. To permit this, Harun had married Abbassa to Ja'far on the condition that the marriage remained purely nominal without consummation. But Abbassa, being in love with Ja'far, secretly bore him a child. When the news reached Harun, he became so angry that in a fit of rage he put Ja'far to death, imprisoned the whole Barmakid family, and confiscated their enormous wealth of property. But other authors, including Tabari and Ibn Khaldun, link the fall of the Barmakids to an increasing fear by the caliph of the growing power, influence, wealth, and extravagant spending of the Barmakids, which drew more and more people to their political constituency and fostered the army's allegiance to them. Meanwhile, the jealousies within the court contributed to Harun's suspicions about the potential threats of the Barmakids' power to his own authority.[71]

Less than a decade after the tragic downfall of the Barmakids, another Khorasani leader, Tahir ibn Hussein, played a key role in securing the throne for Harun's son Ma'mun during his war of succession with his brother Amin. But despite his services to Ma'mun, Tahir fell out of favor with the caliph and wished to return to Khorasan and gain independence from the caliphate. Tahir sought help from the vizier Abi Khalid to obtain for him the post of governor of Khorasan. The vizier, citing impending security problems in Khorasan and the weakness of its governor, Ghassan, suggested to the caliph that he take new measures and recommended that Tahir be appointed to the important post. Ma'mun agreed and appointed Tahir as governor of Khorasan in 821. Ma'mun sent a confidential eunuch with Tahir to serve as the postmaster. The eunuch was also given the mission to poison his new master if "he remarked anything suspicious in his conduct."[72] About two years later, after Tahir established himself in the government of Khorasan, he failed to read the Friday prayer *khutba* in the caliph's name, thereby signifying an act of independence. The next morning he was found dead, poisoned by Ma'mun's agent.[73] Ma'mun, however, thought it wise to confirm Tahir's two sons Talha and Ibrahim in the governorship, and together they ruled Khorasan as a semi-independent kingdom—a prelude to the rise of independent Muslim dynasties in Afghanistan.

6 Decline of the Abbasid Caliphate and the Rise of Local Muslim Dynasties, 921–1215 AD

The rise of the Tahirid dynasty in Khorasan coincided with the decline of the Abbasid Caliphate's control over the empire's peripheries as the thrust of Arab projection of power declined in the middle of the eighth century. The decline gave way to the rise of autonomous local dynasties that, over the course of time, regarded the "Commander of the Faithful" more as a spiritual leader than as a temporal overlord. The waning of the political power of the caliphate notwithstanding, the religious influence of the office became more prominent. The caliph was regarded as the heir of the Prophet, whereupon the authority of the most powerful monarchs cowered before his hallowed grandeur. He was able to legitimize the authority of local monarchs and expansion of their power in the Muslim world or to delegitimize them. Thus, local independent rulers used the caliphs' blessing as an instrument of legitimacy in their competing schemes for expansion.

The process of political fragmentation was furthered by the simultaneous weakening of the center and the strengthening of the peripheries. On the one hand, local governors appointed by the caliph grew too powerful to be dictated to by the center. On the other hand, the vacuum created by the waning control of Baghdad was filled by local leaders who led successful uprisings or asserted independence. In Afghanistan, the former case was exemplified by the rise of Tahirids (821–873) and Samanids (819–999), the latter case by the Saffarids (861–1003).

The emerging local dynasties that based their rights only on the sword often saw building and maintaining large armies as their path to survival within a volatile political environment. Maintaining large armies required finances that were often unavailable locally and had to be acquired from other areas, usually through military invasion and conquest of resource-rich countries. Thus, the race for power through expansion became the hallmark of interaction among the competing regional powers in and around Afghanistan. Eventually, control of conquered lands required more military forces and the need for more funds. Therefore, the local Muslim dynasties that rose to power in Afghanistan between the ninth and thirteenth centuries—including the Tahirids, Saffarids, Samanids, Ghaznavids, and Ghorids—were based mostly on military power manifested in maintaining large armies.

The Rise and Fall of Local Muslim Dynasties

Meanwhile, competing demands for survival and growth led to clashes among these powers. These demands shaped the history of the rise and fall of successive dynasties in Afghanistan. The Tahirid dynasty, established by the Herati general of Ma'mun in 822, ruled over Khorasan from Nishapur and was overthrown by the rising power of the Saffarids of Sistan in 872. The latter dynasty, which rapidly exploded into power, bringing vast areas in Khorasan, Afghanistan, Fars, and Tabaristan under its rule, met its swift decline at the turn of the tenth century at the hands of the Samanids. The emerging empire of the Samanids projected power from their base in Transoxiana across the Amu Darya to Khorasan, Sistan, and Fars. About a century later, the rise of the mighty Ghaznavid Empire, centered in Ghazna (Ghazni), eventually ended Samanid control of Khorasan and its peripheries. The waning power of the Ghaznavids in the middle of the twelfth century gave rise to the power of the Ghorid dynasty. It chipped away at the power of the Ghaznavids until their fall later in the century.

Beside the internal struggle for power among local dynasties in Afghanistan during this period, the omnipresent push of nomadic Turkic hordes from the north continued to pose a constant challenge to the power of states in the south. The Samanids were overthrown by the Qarakhanids and the Uighur Turkic dynasty that belonged to the Qarluq tribal confederation. The confederation ruled in Transoxiana and Central Asia (999–1211). The Ghaznavids were challenged by the Seljuqs and the Ghorids by the Khwarazmids. Among these, the dynasties in the east, with room to expand toward India, were in a favorable position to compensate their losses in the north and west with gains to the east. The early Ghaznavids and the Ghorids had an advantage over their rivals, with their ability to tap into the wealth of India and Khorasan to fund military operations. In any case, the situation kept Afghanistan in a state of militarization that often hindered the development of nonmilitary institutions.

Military Institutions

The nature of military institutions and their conduct was intricately linked to the sociopolitical nature of the society. The constant rise and fall of ruling dynasties and the prevalence of an unstable security environment reinforced a state of localism in political, social, and military life. While state armies focused on dynastic interests, nonstate local groups and factions emerged that took on paramilitary tasks and local interests and sometimes acted as outlaw bands or sources of local resistance. As in other Muslim cities in the Middle East, the neighborhoods in towns in Afghanistan were the building blocks of social life. These *mahallas* (neighborhoods) were more a sociopolitical entity than a physical or geographical unit. The population of a given district often shared the same ethnic and religious background, while patronage relations often bound individuals and families inside the neighborhood or city quarter to one another. Since such groups and factions often shared certain strongly held political or religious views or were pursuing some common social purpose, they found innate solidarity and cohesiveness, which is termed by Ibn Khaldun as *'assabiyya*. According to Muqaddasi (or Maqdisi), in Nishapur the factions based in the city's west and east were in "frightful bigotry against any other sect." He wrote that there the Shi'as are pitted against the Karramiyya. He highlighted the presence of fanaticism in Sijistan (Sistan), where the followers of Abu Hanifa confronted the followers of al-Shafi'i. In other major cities of Khorasan, including Herat, Sarakhs, Nesa, Merv, Abiward, Balkh, and Samarkand, similar factional discords prevailed.[1]

One of the most crucial and distinctive features of these neighborhoods was that they ensured the protection and physical security of their populations. They often did so through informal associations of young men from the quarters. These groups were found throughout the Muslim cities between the ninth and the fifteenth centuries, and they frequently took on a paramilitary nature. These groups were named differently in different regions, such as *ahdath*, *'ayyaran*, *zu'ar*, *'usab*, or *shutar*.[2] While they were meant to serve local communities, such groups could easily descend into extortion and other abuses as the social order deteriorated. Nevertheless, they also frequently policed their respective quarters against thieves and protected them against outside threats and abusive state functionaries. At times, the authorities even used gangs as a kind of local militia. In addition, *ahdath*, *'ayyaran*, and their like sometimes engaged in welfare and charitable activities and generally endeavored to improve the condition of the poor and less privileged elements of urban society.[3]

In Afghanistan, such *assabiyya*-based factionalism was connected to the emergence of paramilitary bands and military-style sporting organizations, such as *zorkhaneh*, or "the house of strength." *Zorkhanehs* were, and are, gyms that feature strength training, group exercise, and martial arts such as wrestling. The *zorkhanehs* also have a spiritual and moral code, featuring prayer, respect, self-discipline, and love of country. The existence of such groups was not limited to urban areas, but the bands were also active in rural areas and on the borderlands of the Muslim territories where they waged *ghaza* to expand the frontiers of the faith. As Clifford Bosworth writes, Khorasan and Transoxiana in the tenth and eleventh centuries provided large numbers of *ghazis* for such activities as manning the *ribats* (border strongpoints) on the fringes of the Central Asian steppes and the Ghaznavid campaigns in India.[4]

One of the legendary local paramilitary groups in Afghanistan was the *'ayyaran*. The *'ayyaran* were people associated with a class of warriors in Iraq, Persia, Khorasan, and Sistan during the ninth–twelfth centuries. The word literally means "vagabond," and in Persian sources the *'ayyaran* are variably described as irregular fighters, rogues, highwaymen, and robbers[5] to noble-minded highwaymen, or generous, clever, brave, modest, pious, chaste, hospitable, and generally upright persons. Sometimes the *'ayyaran* were associated with *futuwwa* (medieval Islamic organizations) located in cities. There are numerous fables of Samak-i-'Ayyar in Persian folklore representing a positive and chivalrous character of the *'ayyaran*.[6] The traditions of the *Kakahs* (chivalrous) of Kabul, as well as of the *dzwan* (magnanimous) and *dzwani* (magnanimity) in Pashtun societies, are other characterizations of this class of vigilantes. The *'ayyaran*'s activities were prominent during times of weak government and civil war, when their role as a military force most likely made them fight on opposing sides. The Saffarids (861–1003) of Sistan, the first independent non-Arab Muslim state in Afghanistan, were in fact an *'ayyaran* dynasty, as the founder of the kingdom, Yaqub ibn Laith, was a leader of the *'ayyaran* of Sistan.

The Saffarids

In his valuable study of the Ghaznavids, Bosworth characterizes the Ghaznavid Empire in Mahmud's reign "as something like 18th Century

Prussia—an army with a state."[7] But the achievements made by the kings of Ghazna in developing nonmilitary state institutions, as well as their efforts to revive and nurture the Persian cultural heritage, including the Persian language, show that the empire was far from being a purely militarized state. In fact, the Saffarid dynasty, at least under Yaqub, is more qualified for such characterization and even more as "a leader with a state." The rise of the Saffarids to imperial power was as rapid as their downfall within half a century. Their explosion to power was greatly linked to the strong leadership of Yaqub ibn Laith, who was known for his iron discipline, his prompt actions to serve justice, fearlessness in battle, affection for his followers, chivalrous treatment of his prisoners, and unparalleled toughness in the field. One of his opponents, Hasan ibn Zayd, the ruler of Tabaristan, called him the "anvil" on account of his iron character.[8] Yaqub and his three brothers, 'Amr, Tahir, and Ali, hailed from the village of Qarnin located at a distance of one day's march from Zaranj, the capital of Sistan.[9] Yaqub is known as "Saffar" (coppersmith) due to his father's trade and his earlier occupation before he became an *'ayyar* and then a local warlord. He was the leader (*sarhang*) of an *'ayarran* band that at times acted as highwaymen. But he was also known for his Robin Hood–type generosity to the poor and kindness in the treatment of his prisoners.[10] Yaqub became one of the most popular heroes of Khorasan and Iranian history for overthrowing the rule of the Arab overlords and challenging the authority of the Abbasid Caliph by leading his army against Baghdad.

Freelancing in the internal conflict in Sistan, Yaqub ibn Laith ibn Mu'addal wielded power in the province and was given charge of the provincial army. This opened the way for Yaqub to ascend to the position of the Amir of Sistan. After consolidating his power in Sistan, Yaqub conquered Herat, Kerman, and Fars between 867 and 879, and the caliph invested in him the viceroyalty of Balkh and Tokharistan and all the country as far as the Indian frontier. Then Yaqub moved east to establish his rule over an area that had never been fully conquered by the Muslim Arab armies. The early Arab governors of Sistan had at times penetrated as far as Ghazna and Kabul, but these had been little more than plundering raids. There was a fierce resistance from the local rulers of these regions, above all from the line of Zunbils who ruled in Zamindawar and Zabulistan and who were probably linked to the southern Ephthalite or Chionite kingdom of Zabul. In the seventh and early eighth centuries, these Zunbil kings inflicted sharp defeats on the Muslims. The Zunbils were linked with the Kabul shahs of the Shahi dynasty; the whole Kabul River valley was at this time culturally and religiously an outpost of the Indian world, as it had been in the earlier centuries during the heyday of the Buddhist Gandhara civilization.[11]

Raising the cause of spreading the faith of Islam, Yaqub marched against the Zunbil dynasty of Zamindawar and Zabulistan (Helmand and greater Kandahar). He killed Zunbil in battle, captured Ghazna (which he rebuilt), and in 870 captured the city of Kabul, where he took an idol from the city's great temple and sent it along with other trophies from Bamian as a present to the caliph. This was the first systematic effort to spread Islam into Afghanistan and to the borders of India long after the expansion of Arab Muslims into eastern Afghanistan had stopped. In 872, the Saffarid king moved north across the Hindu Kush passes and seized Balkh—another first in linking up the northern and southern axes of Muslim advance into Afghanistan. Furthermore, for the first time Ghazna and Kabul were fully reduced by a Muslim army. This forced the Shahiya kings to move their capital east to the Indus basin. The expedition also extended the authority of the Saffarid Empire to Sind and Makran in the south.

A year later, in 873, Yaqub overthrew the Tahirid dynasty, which was favored by the caliphate court. After defeating Muhammad ibn Tahir and taking him prisoner, Yaqub entered Nishapur in August of the same year. According to Gardizi, when Yaqub marched on the capital of the Tahirids, the Tahirid ruler, Muhammad ibn Tahir, stated to him that, if he had come by the order of the caliph, he should present his credentials so that he could deliver the government to him—otherwise he should return. Yaqub responded by showing his sword, saying "this is my order and my standard."[12] However, the influence of the Tahirids in Baghdad circles was too strong to allow the caliph to condone the rapid rise to military power of the Saffarid king. Thus, the caliphate's policy, regarding Yaqub's military conquests, vacillated between approval and disapproval. On the one hand, the caliph could hardly afford to ignore the power of the Sistani monarch and antagonize him; on the other, he was fearful of Yaqub's assertive and independent manners and wanted to keep him at a distance. With the passage of time, suspicion and animosity crept into relations between Yaqub and the court in Baghdad. The caliph hoped that the orthodox and obedient Samanid could be used against the Saffarids. But as the menacing activities of Yaqub had alarmed the caliph, Baghdad awarded Yaqub the viceroyalty of Khorasan, Tabaristan, and Jurjan, Ray, and Fars and military command of Baghdad. But even this failed to induce Yaqub to cancel his march on

Baghdad. According to Tarikh-i Sistan, Yaqub held a deep distrust of the Abbasid Caliphate, which he considered a polity whose rule was based on "wrong-doing and deceit, seen in what they did to Abu-Salama, Abu-Muslim, the Barmakid family and Fadl ibn Sahl, despite everything which these men had done on the dynasty's behalf. Let no one ever trust them."[13]

Yaqub's dramatic military expedition against Baghdad was a unique event in the annals of the Abbasid Caliphate. Caliph Mu'tamid tried to discredit Yaqub in the eyes of Muslims and mobilized them against him. He even displayed the garment of the Prophet to bless his cause and evoke spiritual support. Meanwhile, he fielded a 150,000-strong army under his brother Muwaffak to stop Yaqub, who had led his 100,000-man army in two columns from Khuzestan north to the plain of Hormuz. The two armies finally faced each other at Dayr al- 'Aqul on April 8, 876. The battle began with a race to seize control of a series of hills that separated the two armies. The Abbasid advance troops gained control of the high ground from where they engaged the Saffarids with a withering shower of arrows. Although Yaqub's forces eventually dislodged the Iraqis from the hills, they suffered heavily. By late afternoon, Yaqub was wounded three times in his arms and neck, and the fate of the battle was sealed in favor of the caliph's army. Yaqub had to leave his baggage on the battlefield, which was looted by the *mawali*. Yaqub pulled out his wrecked army to Khuzestan in the hope of raising a new force to renew his march on Baghdad. The caliph sent proclamations accusing Yaqub of being an outlaw who had moved away from the faith. He even claimed that some of Yaqub's banners on the battlefield had displayed the Christian symbol of the cross.[14] But Yaqub showed his steadfastness in his faith even in such a difficult time.

Three years later, the caliph dispatched an embassy mission of goodwill to Yaqub, who lay dying with his sword by his side and a crust of bread and onions ready to be served for his meal. His answer to the caliph was sharp and assertive: "If I live, the sword shall decide between us. If I conquer, I shall do as I please. If I die, I would be freed from you and you from me. If thou art victorious, bread and onions are my fare, and neither thou nor fortune can triumph over a man accustomed to such a diet."[15] Yaqub did not live long and died on June 5, 879, in Gundishapur (Jundishapur), a village 14 kilometers southeast of Dezful in Khuzestan. He suffered from colic disease and had refused treatment when advised to undergo it.

Yaqub was succeeded by his brother 'Amr, a former "muleteer" who like his brother was a tested military leader. He made peace with Caliph Mu'tamid, who legitimized him as the viceroy of Khorasan, Fars, Isfahan, Sistan, Kerman, and Sind. As a convenient diplomacy, 'Amr also tried, unsuccessfully, to make peace with the Tahirids, who were favored by the caliphs. Meanwhile, the Saffarids' relationship with Baghdad was based on mistrust and suspicions. In 885, the caliph again declared Mohammad ibn Tahir the viceroy of Khorasan. Tahir had already conquered Nishapur in 882, forcing 'Amr to retire to Sistan. The caliph even cursed 'Amr publicly and ordered the imprecation to be repeated in the mosques.[16] But the Saffarids' power base proved to be too strong to be discounted; four years later, in 889, Baghdad restored the authority and legitimacy of 'Amr,[17] only to annul it again a year later. Undaunted by these setbacks, 'Amr continued to fight, and after overrunning Fars and capturing Shiraz, he dropped the name of the Muwaffak, the heir apparent, in *khutba* and added his name. Soon after this, in 892, with the accession of Caliph Mu'tadid, 'Amr was finally recognized the lawful ruler of Khorasan and the standards of viceroyalty was sent to him from Baghdad.

But 'Amr was not content to rule only over Khorasan and wanted Transoxiana to be added to his realm. This was the case for the past governors of Khorasan, including the Tahirids. In 898, he asked the caliph to grant him the right of viceroyalty over the Samanid rulers of Mawara un-Nahr. Although the caliph favored the Samanid rulers of Transoxiana, he publicly approved 'Amr's request and in the presence of Khorasani pilgrims read the decree appointing 'Amr the viceroy of Transoxiana (while hoping that 'Amr would be defeated in trying to claim his right to rule over the Samanids).

As expected, Ismail defied 'Amr Laith's demand to submit to his authority, and in the spring of 900 the two armies faced each other in Balkh. Ismail was reportedly significantly outnumbered, with 20,000 horsemen against 'Amr's 70,000-man cavalry. Narshakhi reports that Ismail had 12,000 cavalry and 30,000 volunteers from Turkistan and Ferghana.[18] But his horsemen were ill-equipped, with most having wooden stirrups, while some had no shields or lances. 'Amr-i Laith's cavalry, by contrast, were fully equipped with weapons and armor. Despite fierce fighting, 'Amr was captured; some of his troops switched sides and joined Ismail; and his horse got stuck in mud as he was fleeing the battlefield.[19] Ismail wished to keep 'Amr captive, but the caliph demanded that he should be delivered to him for punishment. 'Amr was sent to Baghdad, where he was executed in 903. The caliph granted

Ismail power over Khorasan, Tabaristan, Ray, and Isfahan. Thus ended the empire built by the two Saffar brothers. Although their dynasty ruled Sistan at times, Sistan was mostly under the suzerainty of the Samanids and then the Ghaznavids in the tenth and eleventh centuries.

Both Yaqub and 'Amr founded their power on the sword and focused on the army as the most important element of the state. And, in fact, the rapid rise to power of their dynasty was facilitated by the effectiveness of its military machine. Yaqub and 'Amr were skilled military commanders and charismatic leaders. They were seasoned soldiers toughened by operating under harsh and contentious conditions. Meanwhile, they pursued a simple way of life, thereby setting an example to their troops and avoided encumbering their armies with unnecessary baggage. Yaqub slept on an old saddlecloth with his head on his shield and ate coarse food, the staples of the Sagzi diet: barley bread, rice, leeks, onions, asafetida, and fish.[20]

The Saffarid Army

The nucleus of the Saffarid army consisted of local Sagzi (Sistani) troops and of 'ayyaran bands, while Yaqub incorporated former Kharijites from northern Sistan and Badghis into his army as a special unit known as the jaysh al-shurat. As mentioned in chapter 4, the infantry of Sistan was renowned since Sassanid times, and more than a century later the Ghaznavids employed Sagzi infantry in their army of conquest. With the expansion of the Saffarid state, the army attracted mercenary troops from far and wide eager to plunder and to serve a rising power. In this way, the Saffarid army speedily became multiethnic, similar to those of contemporary powers such as the Samanid state and the Abbasid Caliphate. A group of Arabs, as well as an Indian contingent, served under Yaqub and 'Amr.

Following contemporary military organization in the eastern Muslim world, the Saffarids increasingly used slave troops (ghulams, mamalik) drawn from different nationalities. Yaqub and 'Amr similarly welcomed capable soldiers of any race into the ranks of their troops. In addition to the Sagzis and Khorasanis, there were not only the ubiquitous Turks but also Arabs, Indians, and people from the Indo-Afghan borderlands. The Saffarids were probably the first to recruit Afghans (Pashtuns) from eastern Afghanistan into the army. They also raised peasant levies (hasharha-yi rusta'i), which were pressed into service in times of need but were often of dubious fighting quality. Yaqub's increasing reputation attracted large bodies of the Kharijites of Sistan and Badghis and several of the former commanders of the Tahirids and the *'ayyaran* leaders of Khorasan who rallied to his side.

Like other contemporary rulers, the Saffarid amirs had a body of palace *ghulams*, probably in large part Turkish, who were used as an elite force and for ceremonial occasions. Yaqub bin Laith had a bodyguard of 2,000 slaves armed with weapons captured from the Tahirids' treasury in Nishapur.[21] (They were a counterbalance to the tribal-based contingents whose loyalty was not always trusted. This system of slave armies was institutionalized throughout the Islamic world from North Africa to India.[22] According to Nizam al-Mulk, the Abbasid Caliph al-Mu'tasim (833–851) had 70,000 Turkic slaves in his army, many of whom reached the high command rank of Amir.[23]) Both Yaqub and 'Amr were keenly interested in the acquisition and training of these *ghulams*. According to Mas'udi, watching the progress of these young slaves' education was Yaqub's sole diversion as he had no interest outside his military career. 'Amr reportedly trained young slaves and then attached them to his chief commanders as spies, preceding the Ghaznavid use of such spies (*mushrifs*). 'Amr is reported to have owned 10,000 palace *ghulams* at his death, but this figure seems exaggerated.[24]

To maintain morale and discipline in the army, the Saffarid kings ensured that the troops were paid promptly and in full. These payments were made after a general inspection (*'ard*) of the troops, their equipment, and their horses. Gardizi offers an account of the inspection ceremony, when the *'Arid* (or head of the department of the army) inspected everyone, from the amir himself downward, before payment. On hearing the two large drums, the whole army assembled in front of the *'Arid*. Sacks of money lay in front of the *'Arid*, and the *'Arid*'s assistant had a list of the soldiers and called out their names. The first person called was 'Amr Laith, the amir himself, who reported to the bench. The *'Arid* made a close inspection of his horse and equipment, then expressed his approval and gave him 300 dirhams. 'Amr placed the money in the leg of his boots and said "*alhamdu lelah* (God be praised) that he had permitted me to serve faithfully the Commander of the Faithful and hath made me worthy of his favors." After this, 'Amr took his seat on an elevated site and watched the rest of the inspection process.[25] The review ceremony is reputedly a Sassanid institution[26] continued by the Muslim Iranian dynasties that became a standard procedure in later centuries.[27]

The tactics of the Saffarid armies were significantly influenced by the unconventional warfare techniques mastered by the plebian components of the army, including the *'ayarran*, the Kharijites, and other irregular bands. Yaqub and 'Amr both had started their military career as insurgent fighters and shared their experience with their comrades-in-arms when they rose to command large, regular forces fighting conventional wars. The army often tried to move lightly to facilitate fast marches over long distances and practiced the indirect approach in the field when fighting enemy forces.

In a battle to control Fars in 869, Yaqub swiftly marched on Shiraz to overthrow the government of Fars. The ruler of Fars, Ali ibn Hussein, had deployed his 15,000 troops in a defile, which was flanked by a mountain on one side and by a river and marshlands on the other. Reportedly, the Shirazis were confident about the impregnability of their defenses against attackers no matter how numerous they were. Yaqub knew the strength of the enemy's defensive position and avoided a frontal attack. He camped a mile away from the enemy position and, after a thorough reconnaissance of the terrain, decided to go around the enemy position and attack it from the rear. Under the astonished eyes of the defenders, Yaqub swerved toward the marshland, ordered his troopers to take the saddles off the horses and swim across the stream following a dog he had unleashed to test the way through. Before the Fars army could react, Yaqub led his army onto the far bank in a flanking movement to the rear of the enemy's dispositions. The battle was swift and decisive; the enemy forces had to abandon their positions, which were threatened by the enemy from behind. Part of the enemy troops retreated to Shiraz; their leader, Ali ibn Hussein, was taken prisoner. Yaqub marched on and captured Shiraz and an enormous amount of booty.[28]

The Samanids

The fall of the Saffarids from power opened the way for the expansion of the Samanids' authority far beyond their home turf in Transoxiana, which they had held since 819. The progenitor of the dynasty, Saman Khuda, a Zoroastrian noble who was founder and ruler of the village of Saman in Balkh, had to leave his hometown and take refuge in Merv under the protection of the Arab governor of Khorasan, Assad ibn Abdullah (735–738). In return for the governor's support, Saman converted to Islam and named his son Assad after his Arab protector in gratitude. In 819, Assad ibn Saman's four sons were rewarded with provinces in Mawara un-Nahr for their service to the Abbasid caliph Ma'mun. They helped crush the rebellion led by Rafi' ibn Laith, the governor of Samarkand, who was the grandson of the last Umayyad governor of Khorasan, Nasr ibn Saiyar. His son Nuh was appointed governor of Samarkand; Ahmad ruled Ferghana; Yahya governed Shash (Modern Tashkent); and Elyas governed Herat.[29] The Saman brothers were confirmed in their posts by the Tahirid dynasty of Khorasan (821–873). After the overthrow of the Tahirids' rule by Yaqub Laith, the Abbasid caliph Mu'tamid granted the administration of the whole of Transoxiana to Ahmad's son Nasr in 875—a year that marks the foundation of the Samanid dynasty. More than two decades later, Nasr ibn Ahmad's brother and successor, Ismail (r. 892–907), overthrew the Saffarids in Khorasan in the year 900 and established the Samanid Empire in Transoxiana and Khorasan with Bukhara as its capital.

At the peak of their power, under three great amirs—Ismail (892–907), Ahmad (907–913), and Nasr (913–943)—the Samanids controlled a vast territory extending from the Jaxartes Valley in central Asia to the Persian Gulf and from the borders of India to the vicinity of Baghdad. It included Transoxiana, Khorasan, as well as Ray, Isfahan Tabaristan, Kerman, Sistan, Kabulistan, Ghazna, Kandahar, and all the way to the Suleiman Mountains in southeast Afghanistan.

The contemporary Muslim sources are very sympathetic and favorable to the Samanids. The bias is visible in Muqaddasi's words: "They (Samanids) are among the best of kings in conduct and knowledge," he wrote, "among the sayings of the people: If a tree were to revolt against the house of Saman, it would wither."[30] Similarly, Ibn Hauqal, a tenth-century Muslim geographer, praised the dynasty for its excellent administration. "In all the eastern lands," he wrote, "there is no kingdom whose borders are better defended, whose population is more numerous, whose material possessions are more extensive, whose internal affairs are better regulated."[31] The bias is said to have been prompted by the Samanids' promotion of law and order, religious orthodoxy, and the continuation of traditional, hierarchical society. Their traditionalist approach to political and social issues made them more appealing to the influential social groups than to the plebian Saffarids, who they regarded as base militants. In the words of Barthold: "The complex state of organization introduced or restored by Ismail was in any case better adapted to the interests of the aristocracy than general equality under the power of a military despot, as under the Saffarids."[32]

Under the loosely centralized feudal government of the Samanids, Transoxiana and Khorasan prospered with a notable expansion of industry and commerce. Persian literature flourished, historiography was encouraged, and the foundations of Iranian Islamic culture were laid. The Samanids promoted the arts and supported the advancement of science and literature, thus attracting scholars and men of letters. They revived the Persian language and made it the language of bureaucracy. Samanid rulers were patrons of the orthodox Sunni sect of Islam and enjoyed the caliphate's moral support. During their rule, Bukhara was a rival of Baghdad in its glory.

The Samanid government structure was modeled on the Abbasid Caliphate. As Narshakhi[33] relates, the government bureaucracy included nine central departments that were replicated in the provincial governments. These departments included the office of the vizier, which headed the whole bureaucratic system like a prime minister. Other departments were in charge of the revenue and treasury (*Mustawfi*), correspondence (*'amid ul-Mulk*), the police (*Sahib u-shurat*), the postmaster (*Saheb-i Barid*), internal intelligence (*Ishraf*), the amir's personal affairs (*mamlaka-i-khas*), the religious police (*Muhtaseb*), and the judicial system (*Qadi*).

The Samanids ruled directly over Transoxiana, which covered the valleys of the middle Amu Darya (Oxus), Zarafshan, and middle Syr Darya (Jaxartes) Rivers. While Khorasan was linked to Transoxiana, practically it fell under the control of powerful military leaders (*Sepah-Salar-i-Khorasan*), some of whom were of Turkish slave origin such as Tash, Begtuzun, Fa'q, and Alptigin. Other provinces were ruled semi-independently by hereditary local amirs who were under loose control of the Samanid kings. According to Muqaddasi, the amirs of Sistan, Khwarazm, and Gharj al-Shar, Juzjan (Jawzjan), Bust, Ghazna, and Khuttal did not pay land taxes to Bukhara but sent gifts only while their rulers availed themselves of the land taxes.[34]

As in other contemporary dynasties, the core of the Samanids army consisted of Turkish slave soldiers (*ghulams*). The Samanids and the caliphs themselves used their Turkic slave soldiers as the praetorian guard at the center of the empire and, increasingly, as governors in the provinces. The employment of slave soldiers in the royal guards and other military organizations was a common trend in other parts of the Muslim world at that time and long after. Such military classes often became so influential that they shaped imperial politics and at times even seized government power and formed their own ruling dynasties. During this period, Turks and Slavs were the two main sources of military slaves. The Samanids, with their proximity to the trans-Jaxartes steppes, had better access to Turkish slaves for their armies. The rulers preferred

Turkic *ghulams* not only for their military ability and skills but also for loyalty untainted by other allegiances. The slaves were taken either during wars or as part of the tribute from the vassal states. They were also acquired through the slave trade that flourished along the frontiers of the Muslim territories. Samarkand reportedly maintained important slave markets in the ninth and tenth centuries. Some prominent slaves rose to high levels of power such as Alptigin, the founder of the Ghaznavid kingdom, who was sold to Ahmad ibn Ismail Samani. One of Alptigin's successors was the Ghaznavid monarch Sebuktigin, who was originally a slave brought from the Issyk Kul, in today's Kyrgyzstan, to Nakhshab, where he was bought by Alptigin.

The restructuring of the court organization under the Samanids included the establishment of a personal guard for the sovereign consisting mainly of Turkish slaves purchased to man the unit. The process of development and promotion of the guardsmen is described by Nizam ul-Mulk in his illustrious *Siyasat-nama* (Book of Government). He wrote that, during the first year of service, the slave served on foot as a groom. The second year he was promoted to a horse-rider. He received better weapons, equipment, and clothing in succeeding years until he was promoted to the rank of *Withaq-bashi* (commander of the tent), which he shared with three other men. Afterward, the slave was gradually elevated to the rank of *Khayl-bashi* (section commander) and *Hajib* (commander). The whole court establishment was headed by the chief *Hajib* (*Hajib-i-buzurg*), who was one of the first dignitaries in the kingdom.[35] Slave soldiers also reached the highest positions in the army. Narshakhi tell us that one, Sima 'l Kabir, who was a slave of Nasr and Ismail's father, was promoted by Ismail as commander in chief of his army.[36]

Throughout the Samanid Empire's century-long rule, security challenges facing it came from three directions. In the north, the rising power of the Qarluq Turks posed a continuous threat to the Samanids' northern border in Ferghana and the upper Syr Darya Valley. In the south, communication and control difficulties contributed to rebellions by disaffected nobles and military commanders—particularly when the grip of the center weakened over the peripheries. And in the west, the Samanids and the Buyids struggled over control of the lucrative regions of Central Iran.

The security challenge in the north was a persistent one. It was the border of Dar al-Islam, reached by Arabs in the eighth century and then handed over to the Samanids' control. It was a volatile frontier that was intermittently penetrated by the nomadic hordes of the steppes. The expansion of the Muslims' control over Central Asia and their successful containment of the Turko-Chinese advance into the region were facilitated by the motivating force of *jihad* and the drive to spread the Islamic faith in the region. Meanwhile, the campaign brought the conquerors material reward in the form of plunder and tributes collected from the conquered areas. When the power of the Arabs' thrust toward Central Asia abated in the early ninth century, the vigor of *jihad* was transmitted to the Samanids, who took over the control of the region from their caliphate overlords. The pious Samanids continued to acknowledge the caliphs as their suzerains and send regular tribute to Baghdad. Islam's penetration of these eastern borderlands was then consummated by the wholesale conversion of the Turks. This culminated in the Islamization of the Turkic dynasty of the Qarakhanids, who eventually supplanted the decaying Samanid dynasty in the late tenth century.

The earlier Samanid amirs pursued a forward policy aimed at securing a well-protected frontier against the Turks of the trans-Jaxartes steppes. The security of the borderland was vital for ensuring trade interests and the safe passage of caravans. In 893, Ismail ibn Ahmad extended his control to the frontier region of Ushrusana and brought it under the direct control of Bukhara. He then moved farther north and captured and sacked the capital city of Qarluq Turks in Talas (modern Taraz in Kazakhstan) and converted a Nestorian church into a mosque. Later, Ismail and his successors spread Islam among the inhabitants of the area, which led to the conversion to Islam of some 30,000 tents of Turks. In the middle of the ninth century, Ferghana was conquered and Islamized, as was Isfijab (today's city of Sayram near Shymkent in southern Kazakhstan).

With the expansion of the empire in Khorasan and Persia, the Samanids' security policy on the northern borders of Transoxiana shifted to a defensive posture aimed at containment of incursions and maintaining the dynasty's authority and prestige among the inhabitants of the steppes. The Samanids had little incentive to raid farther north because the main reward of such raids was the acquisition of slaves, but there was no motivation to risk mounting raids in an area where the nomads had no towns and valuables to pillage and the raider could be drawn into the deep steppes without gaining enough to make the effort worthwhile.

However, the borders remained hot and vibrant. *Ghazis* conducted small-scale informal military campaigns to spread the faith. The *ghazis* were volunteer fighters for the faith who deployed along a chain of border strongpoints known as *ribats*. After the governor of Samarkand, Nuh ibn Assad, wrested control of Isfijab from the Turks in 840, the city became a linchpin in the broad zone of defensive forts built to protect the Samanid Empire from nomadic raiders. Muqaddasi numbered these *ribat*s at 1,700, manned by volunteers from Bukhara and Samarkand. They built outer walls to protect the crops of the inhabitants from raiders. But the towns were not only military outposts. Traders from Bukhara and Samarkand constructed large caravanserais for themselves in Isfijab (Sayram).[37] Ushrusana had many *ribats*; and those in Dizak were manned by *ghazis* from Samarkand. The defense of Baykand, a vital point on the Bukhara–Amul road, guarding communication with Khorasan against the Oghuz of the Qara Qum, was a communal obligation of the villages of the Bukhara oasis, who manned the *ribats* of Baykand in winter when the attacks of the hungry infidels intensified.[38]

While the northern military frontier gave dominance to the military class in the social hierarchy, the south was influenced mostly by politics so that the local rulers and the *dehqan* class of small landowners exerted significant political influence. Khorasan was a sphere of politico-military dynamism, and a major source of state revenue, that played a decisive role in the rise and fall of the Samanid Empire. The governor of Khorasan, based in Nishapur, also held the post of the commander in chief of the army, which was the most influential position in the state. He had a major say in appointing the vizier and other high officials of the government and even was instrumental in winning allegiance to a new amir in Bukhara. As noted earlier, most of the commanders of the Khorasan army were Turks who wielded enormous power as the authority of the center declined in the middle of the tenth century. Controlling Khorasan from the seat of the empire in Transoxiana was a challenge. Although there were twenty-five suitable crossing points on the Amu Darya,[39] and the choice of Bukhara as the seat of the Samanid state facilitated easy and direct access to Khorasan through the Amul crossing point leading to Merv, most of the remote areas in the south were hard to control from Bukhara. With the fall of the Saffarids, the districts south of Hindu Kush, including Kabul, Ghazna, Zabulistan, Rokhaj (Kandahar), and Bust, reverted to their local leaders.

During the rule of Amir Abdul Malik (954–961), the kingdom was plagued by rebellions from the Turkish military leaders who firmly cemented their dominance in Khorasan. Upon Abdul Malik's death in 961, the Turkish chief Alptigin, who held the command of the army of Khorasan, tried to put Abdul Malik's son on the throne but was thwarted by the rival court eunuch Fa'iq, who made Abdul Malik's brother, Abu Salih Mansur, the king of the Samanids. The situation caused Alptigin to feel threatened. He tried to enforce his will by the sword, but the new amir won over some of his officers and forced Alptigin to give up his planned advance on Bukhara. But the new amir did not let him go freely and dispatched a 12,000-strong cavalry force against him. Alptigin met the royal army near Kholm Pass (the Tashqurghan gorge in the Afghan province of Samangan) in April 862 and emerged victorious. He not only defeated the Bukhara army but also captured a maternal uncle of the amir and several other important officers. However, the defiant Turkish warlord could no longer see a future for himself in Bukhara and decided to establish himself somewhere out of reach of his offended overlord and carve up a territory to rule. He seized control of Bamian and marched on Ghazna. There, he founded the Ghaznavid kingdom in the heart of the Afghan mountains after defeating its local ruler, Abu Bakr Lawik—possibly of Kushano-Ephthalite lineage.

In the west, the Samanids had to deal with the rival Persian Ziyarid dynasty of Tabaristan that came to power in 927 as well as the expanding Buyids of Iraq and western Persia, who moved eastward, establishing their rule over Ray, Kerman, Tabaristan, and Gorgan between 943 and 981. Amir Mansur ibn Nuh, who succeeded Abdul Malik as the new Samani monarch, was a feeble ruler who presided over the rapid decline of the kingdom during his lifetime. The Buyids and Ziyarids defied the authority of the Samanids and captured their dominions in the west. The Samanids influence in Sistan disappeared completely as well.

Thus, the power of the Samanids gradually declined—economically by the interruption of the northern trade, and politically by a struggle with disaffected nobles in Khorasan. Meanwhile, the weakened Samanids became vulnerable to pressure from the rising Turkish powers in Central Asia, where a clan of Uighur tribes founded a formidable state that stretched from East Turkistan to the Aral Sea. The state was known as Qarakhanids, and their rulers were called Ilak Khan. Toward the end of the tenth century, the Qarakhanids, under their king, Satok Bughra Khan, embraced Islam and pushed westward from their capital in Kashghar. They occupied the greater part of Transoxiana and deposed the Samanid amir Mansur II. Bukhara fell to them in 999, and the last Samanid ruler, Ismail II, after a five-year struggle against the Ghaznavids in the south and the Qarakhanids in the north, was assassinated in 1005.

The Ghaznavid Empire

The kingdom that Alptigin founded in Ghazna rapidly expanded under his successors. Alptigin died in 963; after an interval of thirteen years, during which his son and two of his slaves succeeded to the throne, Sebuktigin, the son-in-law of Alptigin and one of his trusted slaves, assumed power. He reigned over an expanding territory that, in the eleventh century, developed into the largest Muslim empire after the disintegration of the Abbasid Empire. Sebuktigin mobilized the neighboring Afghan (Pashtun) tribes under his banner and added large districts to his dominions, extending from Peshawar in the east and Bust in the west. The rise of the Ghaznavids coincided with the decline of the Samanids, whom the rulers of Ghazna still acknowledged as their suzerain. In 994, responding to an appeal from the Samanid prince of Bukhara for help against the encroaching Turks, Sebuktigin saw a new opportunity for expanding his influence in Khorasan. His reward for quelling the revolt in Herat was the transfer of Balkh to his control and the appointment of his son Mahmud as commander of the troops of Khorasan. Thus, the Ghaznavids' territories practically spread to the Amu Darya in the north and Khorasan in the west.

Sebuktigin was the first Muslim ruler who launched the invasion of India over the traditional northwest route. Earlier, in 712, the Arab incursion into India went through the southern advance route. The Umayyad general Mohammad ibn Qasim led the invasion, which extended barely beyond Sind and Multan. As Stanley Lane-Poole writes, it was "only an episode in the history of India and of Islam, a triumph without results."[40] But the invasion of the tenth century was the first in some five hundred years when foreign armies once again marched the hilly roads of the Khyber Pass and the valleys of Tochi and Gomal into the Indus Valley and beyond. Sebuktigin's military victory over Jaipal, the Brahman raja of the Gandhara Valley and Punjab, opened the gate for further penetration into the subcontinent, which was completed under his "idol breaker" son Mahmud.

Sebuktigin died in 997, but he did not leave his throne to his oldest son, Mahmud. After a yearlong war of succession, Mahmud defeated his younger brother Ismail, to whom his father had bequeathed the kingdom. Mahmud, a seasoned 27-year-old soldier and an experienced commander of the army of Khorasan, was a staunch Sunni Muslim. His campaign against the "idolaters" of India brought him rich stores of treasure and captives that furthered his power and polished his religious credentials in the eyes of fellow Muslims. It also earned him the blessing of the caliph in Baghdad who bestowed on him the title of *yamin-ad-dawlah*, "the right arm of the state." His dynasty is known to historians as the Yamini dynasty. His contemporary author Abdul Jabar

'Utbi (d. 1023) states that, on the occasion of receiving the title from the caliph, Mahmud made it a duty to himself to undertake every year an expedition into India to spread the faith of Islam.[41] He earnestly fulfilled this pledge by leading seventeen military expeditions into India during his reign. Consequently, the army was considered the main pillar of the state power, which continued to expand as new territories were added to the empire and additional riches from conquered lands loaded the state coffers. The military invasion of India spread Mahmud's authority from the Indus River to the plains of Jumna.

Meanwhile, the Samanids' power had ended in Central Asia, and the Qarakhanid Turks who replaced them were successfully contained by the army of Ghazna. In the west, the decaying power of the Buyids crumbled before the marching Ghaznavid armies, which seized Ray, Isfahan, and some provinces in Iraq. Thus, the Ghaznavid kingdom grew into the largest empire established after the dissolution of the Abbasid Caliphate. During more than three decades of Sultan Mahmud's rule, his state of Ghazna, Bust, and Balkh under the suzerainty of the Samanids expanded into an empire that stretched from Iraq and the Caspian Sea to the Ganges River and from the Aral Sea to the Indian Ocean, covering an area of nearly three million square miles.

The State and the Army

The Ghaznavid state was founded and expanded mostly by the sword. Because of its strong martial orientation, the army was considered the main pillar of state power. The state military machine continued to develop as it conquered new lands and enormous stores of plundered treasures to fill the state coffers. A dynasty of Turkish slave origin, the Ghaznavids became highly Persianized and adopted an Islamo-Iranian identity. In the meantime, their military culture preserved some of the nomadic ethos of the Central Asian steppes.

The Ghaznavid army was characterized by three main features: the dominance of the slave soldiers; the ethnic diversity of the military forces; and the focus on high mobility for rapid concentration and movement of forces over long distances.

The Ghaznavids, like neighboring Muslim dynasties, made wide use of soldiers of slave origin in the armed forces. They served both as soldiers and as officers, who often rose to higher positions in the civil and military administration of the state. The founder of the dynasty, Alptigin, himself of a slave background, was helped by a 3,000-strong army of slave soldiers to establish his kingdom in Ghazna in 961. The *ghulams* were favored for their military ability and personal bond to their chief, which ensured loyalty. The hardy Turks from the steppes, who were endowed with high qualities of toughness and bravery, mostly filled the ranks of the slave contingents. With the expansion of the empire in India, thousands of Hindu slaves were added to the corps. The slave soldiers came from remote places in Central Asia and India and had few local connections and interests. Furthermore, the *ghulams* created a counterbalance to the influence of native nobles, whose loyalty was tempered by their traditional local interests.

However, the system entailed potential dangers. Commanders of large slave contingents could be tempted to defy authority and serve personal ambitions. The Samanid Empire was seriously undermined by the power struggle among powerful slave leaders in Khorasan, including the Simjuris, Tash, Fa'iq, and Alptigin. The Samani amir Ahmad ibn Ismail (907–914) was murdered by his *ghulams*. Having learned from the experience of their Samanid predecessors, the Ghaznavid rulers closely watched their military leaders and censored the commanders who were suspected of purchasing large numbers of slaves. When Sultan Mas'ud was informed that Ahmad Inaltigin, the commander in chief of the army of India, was acquiring Turkish slaves for a possible rebellion, he immediately replaced him with a Hindu officer named Tilak.[42]

The slave contingents of the Ghaznavid army were under command of an officer known as the *Salar-i Ghulaman*, or "the head of the slaves," a rank next in grade to the commander in chief of the army—the *Hajib-i Buzurg*. Within the slave corps, the personal bodyguards of the sultan constituted a special contingent known as *ghulaman-i saray, ghulman-i khas*, and *ghulaman-i Sultani*. Their number grew. Jawzjani reports that the *ghulaman-i saray* under Sultan Mahmud numbered 4,000, which lined up with 2,000 on each side during ceremonial occasions at the court.[43] Sultan Mas'ud deployed 6,000 of them in his battle against the Turkmens near Balkh.[44] The slave soldiers were either acquired during battles or purchased from Transoxianan markets.

There were also other slave units, including Tajiks, Khorasani, and Indian *ghulams*. The number of Hindu *ghulams* significantly increased after Sultan Mahmud's Indian conquests, and they were constantly replenished after each campaign. The sultan brought many Hindu *ghulams*, which numbered 55,000 after his conquest of Kanauj in 1018. The slave contingents usually fought as a unit and were used in key positions in the center of the battle line. Often, the slave units were tasked with more difficult combat missions that the regular forces could hardly accomplish.

Another distinct feature of the Ghaznavids' military organization was its ethnic diversity. The army consisted of contingents of Turks, Arabs, Dailamis, Khorasanis, Khalaj, Afghans (Pashtuns), Indians, and Kurds. The diversity in the military structure was praised by some leading contemporary chroniclers for its synergic military effectiveness and expediency of control. "Sultan Mahmud had established a military organization," wrote Nizam ul-Mulk "that consisted of different nationalities such as Turks, Khorasani, Arab, Indian, Dailamis and Ghorids. In the field, these hordes encamped separately at night under their own guards so no group would make a move due to the presence of other groups. During the battle, each ethnic military horde would fight bravely to preserve its good name in competition with the other national contingents."[45] Therefore, Nizam ul-Mulk advised that a mono-national army should be avoided, for it only leads to plots and mutinies.

Among the diverse elements of the army, the Turks dominated the leadership, while the Iranians dominated the bureaucracy. The Turkish combatants were recruited from different Turkic tribes of Central Asia and those who settled in Khorasan. Indian foot and cavalry troops were increasingly deployed as the Ghaznavids extended their reign into India. The tough Dailami mountaineers made excellent foot soldiers similar to the Sagzis of Sistan. The Arabs were some of the best horsemen and played key roles in advance detachments and advance guards. Kurds and Arabs were often grouped under a single commander and assigned to important military missions.[46]

One of the major developments of this period was the increasing recruitment of Afghans (Pashtun) into the army and their deployment in the military campaigns in India. Although Yaqub Laith Saffar was the first Muslim ruler who enlisted Afghan tribesmen on a large scale in the army, the Ghaznavid state and army established a much wider relationship with the Afghan tribes, who at that time lived between the Hindu Kush and the Indus Valley, with their geographic center around the Suleiman Mountains. Sebuktigin recruited thousands of Afghans into his army; they assisted him in defeating the Hindu Shahi king Jaipal in Laghman and Nangrahar, driving him out of the Kabul Valley and capturing an amount of immense booty, including 200 elephants.[47] The role of the Afghan tribes widened significantly under his son Mahmud as the Afghan highlanders embraced Islam and rallied around the sultan's banner in spreading the faith in India. Furthermore, 'Utbi states that Afghans formed part of Mahmud's army during his expedition to Balkh.

Operational mobility and the capability to deploy armed forces rapidly in the right place at the right time ensured the dominance of the cavalry forces in the army, predeployment of large forces in strategic areas, and the establishment of a reliable logistics system. The cavalry constituted the bulk of the Ghaznavid army. Its effectiveness in quick deployment, its usefulness in deep reconnaissance missions, its battlefield mobility, and its effectiveness when charging enemy ranks were all of high military value. The troopers were armed with bows, battle axes, maces, lances, and long curved swords known as *qalachurs*, the weapon of choice of the Turks.[48] The lasso (*kamand*), which was a typical weapon of the pastoral herdsmen and was used in ancient Iranian armies (see chapter 2), continued to be used by Ghaznavid horsemen against the Indians and the Turkmens.

Bayhaqi relates that a considerable part of the cavalry was composed of double-mounted troopers, with the second horse carrying equipment, food, and water and providing a spare mount.[49] Obviously, such a system required a large number of horses that were mostly acquired from northern Afghanistan, Central Asia, and the Pashtun areas around the Suleiman Mountains. Many horses were sent as gifts by the tributary princes. The *mir-akhor*, the officer in charge of the royal stable, also maintained a large pool of remounts. Upon the death of Mahmud, when his son Mohammad took temporary charge in Ghazna, his brother Mas'ud asked him to send him 20,000 horses from the reserve stores.

Besides the cavalry, the Ghaznavid army had permanent infantry forces that fought on foot but could be mounted on camels for long-distance campaigns. They were praised for their fighting ability in difficult terrain, for reducing and breaking fortresses, and for fighting in pitched battles. The elite infantry soldiers mostly included Dailamis of the Caspian area, Sagzis of Sistan, and Afghans (Pashtuns) of the eastern highlands who were often recruited locally. The foot soldiers were armed with bows, spikes, spears, and wide shields. Their effectiveness in close combat was highly praised. They were granted similar respect similar to that earned by the Swiss foot soldiers in medieval Europe who outmatched the mounted chevaliers in combat.

The Ghaznavids were the first Muslim dynasty to use elephants in large numbers for battle and to integrate their use in combat. The Ghaznavids acquired elephants during their Indian conquests and learned how to use them more effectively on the battlefield. Elephants provided a suitable observation post to watch the battlefield during a melee or confused combat conditions. The elephant-borne bowmen and spearmen targeted enemy soldiers as the beast closed with the enemy. The use of elephants at the front of the battle line and when leading the charge had a demoralizing effect on enemy cavalry. 'Utbi describes the action of Sultan Mahmud's elephant in his battle with Ilak Khan in Balkh with these pompous words: "His elephant seized the standard bearer of Ilak Khan and tossed him into the air, and, with weighty fury and extreme might humbled the men under his feet, and with his trunk hurled them from the back of horses and tore them to pieces with his teeth."[50] However, the Indians' overreliance on elephants in battle limited their flexibility and undermined their maneuverability. The Ghaznavids and later the Ghorids integrated the use of elephants into their mobile tactical theory and used them in combination with their versatile cavalry and infantry units on the battlefield.

Although the military service was highly organized, there is no definitive information about the ranks of the military officers in the Ghaznavid military hierarchy. The sultan was the commander in chief, and immediately under him was the commander of the army of Khorasan. Every province had a commander of the local troops. In a survey of the Ghaznavid military activities recorded in the primary sources, Nazim suggests that the lowest military rank was the *khail-tash*, who commanded ten horsemen. Above him were the *qa'id*, who commanded a *khail*, probably of one hundred horses, the *sarhang*, who was the commander of five hundred horses, and the *Hajib*, who was the officer commanding an army.[51] But *khail-tash* was apparently a functional designation; in the last battle of Sultan Mas'ud with the Seljuqs, the advance guard of the Ghaznavid army consisted of 500 *khail-tash*, who fought as a single unit at Dandanqan. Bayhaqi lists the *khail-tash, Naqib, Sarhang*, and *Hajib* as military ranks but does not define their exact level of command.[52] We know that the military ranks in some armies before the Ghaznavids (Achaemenids) and after them (Ghorids and the Delhi Sultanate, Mongols, and the Timurids) were organized on a decimal basis (ten, hundred, thousand, and ten thousand). It is highly probable that the Ghaznavid army also adopted the system.

The size of the Ghaznavid army gradually increased with the expansion of the empire. Nazim estimated that the peacetime army under Mahmud was probably 100,000, which would be augmented with thousands of wartime volunteers and military contingents contributed by the provinces.[53] Gardizi indicates that in 1023 the army inspected in Ghazna numbered 64,000 cavalry and 1,300 elephants, excluding the armies of the provinces and those on garrison duties.

Siege warfare and the reduction of walled cities and fortresses figured prominently in the Ghaznavids' military campaigns in India. The common tactics in such battles was to surround the besieged cities and forts and eventually scale the walls or gain access to the city through the gaps created by mining or siege engines such as ballistae (*'arada*) and rams (*kharak*). To support such operations, special units of miners, engineers, and foot soldiers were trained and organized.

The military tactics of the Ghaznavid armies were based on the general military culture of the time in the Muslim world as transmitted to the rulers of Ghazna by the Samanid sovereign of early Ghaznavids. We know from 'Utbi that, when Sebuktigin fought against the Hindu Shahis in Gandhara Valley, he divided his slave soldiers into groups of 500 who attacked successively. About two hundred years later, Sultan Mohammad Ghori applied similar tactics in fighting the Rajput army in India by using three groups of light cavalry and a reserve contingent of heavy cavalry to attack successively, with the reserve launching the final strike.[54] Nearly six hundred years later, this combat tactic was used by Ahmad Shah Durrani while fighting the Maratha army in the historic Battle of Panipat in 1761. This application was apparently inspired by the tactics of *karr-wa-farr* of the early Islamic armies, which was a series of repeated cavalry charges and withdrawals using arrow barrages from a distance, culminating in close combat using spears and swords.

The Ghaznavids continued the Samanid system of paying the salaries of their civil and military officials quarterly in cash and avoided paying them in land grants (*iqta'*), which could lead to the emergence of hereditary feudal franchises with a potential threat to the power of the center—a system that became a prominent governance feature of the Seljuqid dynasties in the eleventh and twelfth centuries. When proceeding on an expedition, every soldier was required to make his own arrangements for food and supplies and was paid his salary in advance for such arrangements. Otherwise, the soldier's salary (*bistgani*) was paid quarterly, often during the review (*'ard*) ceremonies.

The enormous size of the Ghaznavids' territory and the need to deploy troops rapidly in the right place at the right time necessitated advanced basing of military forces in strategic locations. Major concentrations of forces were placed in Khorasan, India, Balkh, Bust (*Lashkari Bazar*), and Ghazna. Local governors and tributary princes were required to contribute military contingents during campaigns conducted close to their territories. Furthermore, a reliable logistics system was essential to the needs of the army. Sultan Mahmud is credited with being a skillful planner and logistician. These skills contributed to his success in waging war in distant areas using his strategic bases.

Ghaznavid Military Conquests

Mahmud's most celebrated campaign among the Muslims was his next-to-last expedition in 1025–1026 to conquer the legendary temple of Somnath and to destroy its widely venerated idol. For this, he would win the title of *but-shekan* (idol breaker). For many years, Mahmud had heard of the religious significance and the wealth of the temple of Shiva, the Moon-Lord, at Somnath on the coast of Kathiawar. Reports said that the wealth of the temple far exceeded the treasures of any shrine he had hitherto conquered. But the religious importance of the temple of Somnath also inspired Mahmud to elevate his religious credentials in the Muslim world by destroying the most celebrated symbol of idolatry. The temple of Somnath was situated on the promontory of Gujarat, in the vicinity of Diu (one of the possessions of the Portuguese during the colonial period that was reclaimed by India in 1961). The Somnath was endowed with the revenue of 10,000 villages; 2,000 Brahmans were consecrated to the service of the idol, which they washed each morning and evening in water from the distant Ganges. The temple was also served by 300 musicians, 300 barbers, and 500 dancing girls. Three sides of the temple were protected by the ocean; the narrow isthmus was fortified by a natural or artificial precipice; and the city and adjacent country were inhabited by a most devoted and fanatic population.

The march to Somnath from Ghazna through Multan across the desolate Rajputana Desert proved to be extremely tough, although the actual battle and the capture of Somnath were quick and easy. Mahmud led an army of 30,000 cavalry and a large number of volunteers to conquer the legendary temple of Somnath on the Gujarat seacoast in India; his logistics preparation (particularly the provision of water to supply his men and horses across the waterless Thar Desert in Rajasthan) remains an ingenious but questionable undertaking in the annals of military history. He is said to have provided each trooper with two camels to carry water for him. Additionally, the sultan supplemented these arrangements by establishing a major reserve of water carried by 20,000 camels—this made for quite an inflated number of beasts, about 80,000, that could stretch along tens of kilometers on the road. Then he undertook a monthlong advance across the burning and parched desert.[55]

Despite the huge pack-animal trains, the numbers do not add up.

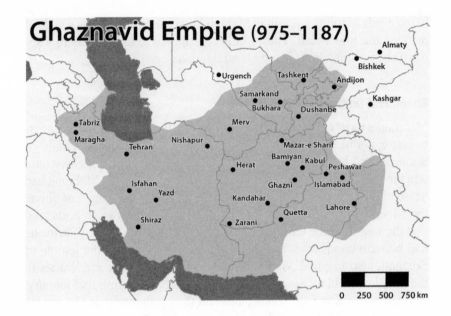

Ghaznavid Empire (975–1187)

Estimated daily water requirement for one soldier is a half-gallon, or five pounds. The number for a horse is 8 gallons, or 80 pounds. The maximum load carried by a camel is 350 pounds. This means the total water available at the beginning of the desert was 28 million pounds. Assuming that there were 30,000 cavalrymen and at least 15,000 followers, the total daily water requirement for such an army would be about nine million pounds; that would consume all the water supply in three days unless the water was resupplied during the march or the army lived on one-tenth of the standard ration, which would be hard for animals, particularly for horses, to survive. So, either the real number of the troops was far lower than claimed, or the baggage train was larger than reported. In 1880, during the second Anglo-Afghan war, the loss of the British army's 90,000 camels devastated the transport herd in Northwest India. In later years, the burden of heavy trains hindered the tactical action of the Ghaznavid troops in fighting the Turkmens in Khorasan.

The sultan arrived at Somnath on January 9, 1026. The king of Somnath fled with his entourage, leaving the temple under the protection of 50,000 poorly armed faithful with little military training. With a zealous confidence in Shiva, the Hindus greeted the Muslims with contemptuous laughter, but the following day, as 50,000 Brahmans defended the Somnath fortress, Mahmud surrounded the fort with his troops and, using a heavy barrage of arrows, drove the defenders away from the walls while his infantry scaled them. The Ghaznavid ladder-bearing infantry mounted the temple ramparts and poured into the fortress. Fifty thousand Hindus suffered for their faith as the soldiers sacked and devastated the sacred shrine. The temple was constructed of wood and enshrined a huge stone *lingam* (an erect phallus representing Shiva), which the conqueror broke apart; he plundered the enormous wealth and treasures endowed to the shrine. Two large fragments of the idol were dispatched to Ghazna to be used in building steps at the entrance of the great mosque.[56]

The destruction of Somnath was a psychological setback to Hindus and India and encouraged future invaders from the west to lead their armies across the plains of Hindustan. Mahmud won the battle with surprise, a cavalry charge, better logistics, and the motivation of *jihad*. The fall of the Hindu temple made Mahmud a champion of Islam for centuries afterward.

The main factors contributing to Mahmud's military gains were the lack of unified power in India, the use of obsolete tactics by the Hindu armies, and the *jihad* fervor of the Muslim fighters that brought thousands of volunteers from Central Asia and Khorasan to the ranks of the sultan's army of conquest. India, at that time, was divided into numerous kingdoms, many of which were feuding with one another. They included the Brahman kings of Gandhara and Punjab, the Tamara dynasty in Delhi and Kanauj, the Buddhist Palas of Magadha on the lower Ganges, the survivors of the Guptas in Malwa, and other principalities in the midlands and in the south.

Modern Indian and Western authors also point out the failure of the Indian armies to adopt new warfare techniques and to develop proper military forces to implement them.[57] In his book *Problems of Indian Defense*, K. M. Panikar writes that "so long as the preeminence of the elephant remained and the horse was used in war mainly for drawing chariots, Indian military methods were adequate for India's own defense." But, he adds, "the Hindu armies[,] based mainly on ponderous elephants and numerous but untrained infantry, broke before the cavalry charge of the Turk and later Mughal invaders. The heroism of individual warriors and the training of elephants were of no avail."[58] The superiority of the Ghaznavid and the Ghorid strategies and tactics was due primarily to their well-organized cavalry and their skills in archery. The combination of the two provided mobility and firepower, enhancing tactical effectiveness and flexibility to the extent that even in retreat the horsemen were able to turn in the saddle and shoot at the pursuing enemy. As mentioned earlier, the invention of the stirrup in Central Asia led to a revolution in military capability in ancient times. Before the introduction of the stirrup, many armies used horses for drawing chariots and transporting warriors. At that time in India, horses were not as effective as elephants, since a rider on an elephant could shoot arrows from his seat atop the beast or use javelins and other weapons. With the appearance of the stirrup, the situation changed drastically in favor of cavalry. With his feet firmly secured in the stirrup, the horse-rider could stand up while riding and shoot arrows or swing a sword without falling off the horse.

Furthermore, Vincent Smith suggests that the strategic and tactical stagnation in the Indian art of war caused the country to suffer repeated defeats in the face of invasions from the west. He wrote that

> no Hindu general in any age was willing to profit by experience and learn the lesson taught by Alexander's operations long ago. Time after time enormous hosts, formed of the contingents supplied by innumerable Rajas, and supported by the delusive strength of elephants, were easily routed by quite small bodies of vigorous western soldiers, fighting under one undivided command, and trusting chiefly to well-armed mobile cavalry. Alexander, Muhammad of Ghor, Babur, Ahmad Shah Durrani, and other capable commanders, all used essentially the same tactics by which they secured decisive victories against Hindu armies of almost incredible numbers. The ancient Hindu military system, based on the formal rules of old-world scriptures (*shastras*), was good enough for use as between one Indian nation and another, but almost invariably broke down when pitted against the onslaughts of hardy casteless horsemen from the west, who cared nothing for the *shastras*. The Hindu defenders of their country, although fully equal to their assailants in courage and contempt of death, were distinctly inferior in the art of war, and for that reason lost their independence. The Indian caste system is unfavorable to military efficiency as against foreign foes.[59]

Sultan Mahmud's continual engagement in India did not distract him from the northern and western expanses of his empire. In the north, the fall of the Samanids to the Qarakhanids left the northern borders exposed and threatened. However, after the Qarakhanid ruler Ilak Khan invaded Balkh in 1007, Mahmud led an army of Turks, Afghans, Indians, and Khalajs to the Oxus (Amu Darya) River and defeated the Qarakhanid army in an intensely contested battle and drove it across the Oxus. Henceforth, the Qarakhanids made no further incursions and the river remained the border between the two states. Ten years later, internal troubles in Khwarazm prompted Mahmud to conquer the province on the delta of the Amu Darya and to bestow it to a Turkish chief, Altuntash. The province remained in his family for a generation. The Ghaznavids continued to pursue a strategy of containment in the north.

To the west, the decaying Buyid dynasty of Fars and Iraq provided the opportunity for Mahmud to annex its Persian territories. The Ghaznavid army overran the area in 1029 and captured Ray, Isfahan, Hamadan, and several provinces in Iraq. These areas remained under the Ghaznavids until they were lost to the rising Seljuq power.

The Ghaznavids combined early Arab Islam with their nomadic culture from the Central Asian steppes. As Bosworth notes, the Ghaznavids present the phenomenon of a dynasty of Turkish slave origin that became culturally Persianized to a perceptibly higher degree than other contemporary dynasties of Turkish origin such as the Saljuqs and Qarakhanids.[60] Sultan Mahmud is remembered in history not only as a military leader of genius, compared by Nazim with Alexander the Great,[61] but also as a great patron of the arts, science, and literature. He presided in Ghazna over a stately and cultivated court. The sultan founded and endowed a university at his capital, where mosques, palaces, and public buildings surpassed those of any city of the time. His court encouraged men of science and art including leading poets and writers, who descended on Ghazna from different corners of the Muslim world. In the words of Stanley Lane-Poole: "Napoleon imported the choicest works of art from the countries he subdued to adorn his Paris; Mahmud did better, he brought the artists and the poets themselves to illuminate his court."[62]

Sultan Mahmud died in 1030 and left the empire to his son Mohammed. Mohammed was challenged by his much stronger brother Mas'ud, who finally prevailed and blinded and imprisoned his mild and affectionate brother. Despite his personal bravery, Mas'ud was unable to preserve the empire. While overengaged in the Punjab, he disastrously ignored the real threat building in the northwest in Khorasan. The Seljuq Turkmens, who migrated from across the Syr Darya in the tenth century to the borders of Khorasan, were allowed by Sultan Mahmud to settle in areas around Merv. Throughout the reign of Mas'ud, the Seljuqs strengthened their standing and turned into a security threat.

In 1040, Mas'ud finally moved against the Seljuqs. There was a decisive battle between the two sides near Merv. The Seljuqs, under their leaders Tughrul and Chaghri Beg, harassed the army of Ghazna in Sarakhs with hit-and-run attacks and cut its supply lines and water sources. The exhausted 50,000-man army of the Ghaznavids met the enemy's 20,000 troops at Dandanqan between Sarakhs and Merv in May 1040.[63] The Turkmen surrounded Mas'ud's army and blocked the passes behind it. Then they began cavalry charges on all sides, causing panic in the enemy ranks. Mas'ud desperately tried to keep his forces together; despite his personal heroic action on the battlefield, his legions fled. He returned to Ghazna broken and disappointed, only to rush off to India to raise a new army and face the enemy again. He left Ghazna with his family and treasures, but as he reached Hasan Abdal in the Indus Valley, his guards mutinied, plundered his treasure, and imprisoned their ruler. They later murdered him.

The Battle of Dandanqan opened the way for the Seljuqs to occupy Khorasan without much resistance. About ten years later, they captured Isfahan, which led to the establishment of what was later known as the Great Seljuq Empire. The rise and rapid expansion of the Seljuqs' power replicated the Arabs' empire-building conquest streaming out from the opposite direction. The Seljuq Turks advancing from the eastern borders of Khorasan rapidly penetrated as far as Asia Minor, which became their permanent home. The Seljuqs overran the scattered and decaying dynasties in Persia and Iraq and planted the seeds of a much larger Ottoman Empire that lasted more than six centuries. However, the Seljuqs' rule in Khorasan was transient and was overthrown by the passing waves of the Turkmen Ghuzz nomadic invasion and then by the rise of the Ghorids and Khwarazm Shahids later in the twelfth century.

In the year 1058, one of Mas'ud's sons, Ibrahim, ascended the throne in Ghazna, and during his forty-year rule (1058–1098) he reestablished a truncated empire on a firmer basis by making peace with the Seljuqs based on restoration of cultural and security relations and political marriages. The reigns of Sultan Ibrahim and his successors saw a period of sustained tranquility for the empire. Although it lost its western lands, it was increasingly sustained by riches accrued from raids across northern India. In 1116, the Seljuq sultan Sanjar temporarily took possession of Ghazna as protector of Bahram-Shah against his brother Arslan-Shah, who were locked in a war of succession to the Ghaznavid throne. There was no danger of occupation by the Seljuqs, as they saw more attractive lands to the west and the extension of a dynasty that was branching out toward the Syrian and Mediterranean vastness. The real threat to the survival of the Ghaznavids came neither from the west nor from the east. It came from the heart of their realm—the hilly country of Ghor.

The Rise of the Ghorids

Ghor encompasses the mountainous country of the upper Harirud and Murghab Rivers and the hilly confines of Farah, Helmand, and Uroz-gan Provinces in the central mountainous tract of modern Afghanistan. The cul-de-sac geography of Ghor, with its craggy peaks and deep valleys, made the mountainous tract a natural fortress with limited access from the surrounding lowlands. For most of its history, Ghor lay outside the path of invading armies and was spared by the Arab Muslim conquerors in medieval times as they marched along the main routes on the two sides of the Hindu Kush, bypassing the Ghorids and their pagan practices. There is little information about the province before the Ghaznavids conquered the area in the early eleventh century and Islamized the population.[64] The Ghaznavids left the province to its local chieftains, as a vassal of Ghazna, out of whom the Shansabanis (Middle Persian: *wishnasp*)[65] rose to prominence in the later eleventh century. They made Ghor, with the capital at Firozkoh (most likely located around the magnificent Minaret of Jam, in the Sharak District of the Ghor Province) becoming the center of the Ghorids' powerful empire in the twelfth century. The origin of the Ghorids is wrapped in myths and legends. The ethnic roots of the people have been the subject of contradicting views. Some link them to Afghans (Pashtuns),[66] while others believe them to be an eastern Iranian people of Tajik stock.[67]

A disputed Pashto-language manuscript, *Patta Khazana* (Hidden Treasure), said to have been discovered by the late professor Abdul Hai Habibi in 1944, contains an anthology of Pashto poetry that dates the earliest Pashto literature to the eighth century in Ghor and claims that Ghorids were Pashto-speakers.[68] It is claimed that *Patta Khazana* was authored in 1729 on the basis of older scripts. Many of the literary figures featured in the book are also mentioned in other credible sources. However, given the records of the chroniclers of the Ghorid dynasty and other medieval Muslim sources, it is hard to prove the genuineness of certain passages in the book and its content related to some Pashto poetry allegedly presented in the court of the Ghorids. The manuscript has not been authenticated by most scholars of Oriental studies.[69] Meanwhile, it is agreed that the Ghorids spoke a different language, since the

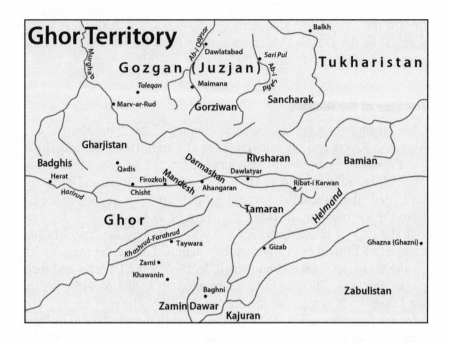

Ghaznavid prince Mas'ud, during his 1020 campaign in Ghor, had to employ local interpreters to communicate with the Ghorids.[70]

After Sultan Mahmud conquered Ghor in 1010, the Suri horsemen of Ghor joined his army and fought for the empire in many battles, particularly in India. But as the empire weakened and Mahmud's successors lost much political and military ground while facing the Seljuq hordes, the Ghorid princes became more assertive and independent. Signs of weakness in the state became apparent when Mas'ud III died in 1115 and an internal struggle between his sons ensued. Bahram-Shah defeated his brother, Arslan, for the throne at the Battle of Ghazni in 1117 thanks to the help of the Seljuq sultan Sanjar. But Bahram-Shah was the last Ghaznavid king to rule from Ghazna. During his thirty-five years of rule, the deterioration of relations between Ghazna and Firozkoh led to open hostility that resulted in the downfall of Ghaznavid power in Afghanistan. The troubles started when Qutbuddin Mohammad, one of the Ghorid princes, took refuge in Ghazna after having a dispute with his princely brother. He was well received in Ghazna and was married to the sister of Sultan Bahram-Shah. The sultan, however, suspected him of planning a plot against his power and had him poisoned. Hearing the news of the tragedy, Saifuddin Suri, the ruling prince of Ghor, decided to avenge the death of his brother. In 1048, he attacked and defeated Bahram-Shah, who fled to Kurram. Saifuddin thereupon established himself as ruler in Ghazna and appointed his brother Bahauddin Sam the governor of Ghor.

Not long after, Bahram-Shah returned with a new army and surprised and defeated Saifuddin Suri, who surrendered on the condition that his life be spared. Bahram-Shah, however, broke his pledge and beheaded the ill-fated captive after having him paraded around town in a humiliating display. In response to Bahram's treacherous act, 'Alauddin Hussein, the younger brother of Suri and the chief of the Ghorids, launched a campaign against Ghazna and, after three fiercely fought battles at Zamindawar and near Ghazna in 1151, routed the army of Bahram-Shah and captured Ghazna. In a wild fury of vengeance, 'Alauddin burned the beautiful capital of the Ghaznavids to ashes. The city, known as *'rous al-bilad* (the bride of cities) was subject to seven days of pillaging and raping during which 60,000 inhabitants were killed. All the tombs of the Ghaznavid sultans, with the exception of those of Mahmud, Mas'ud, and Ibrahim, were broken open and their remains burned as the victor celebrated his triumph and his dark vengeance. He held drunken parties featuring wine and music, where the musicians sang poems written for the occasion by the Ghori prince himself. One of the lyrics read that "the world knows that I am the king on the earth. . . . I wanted to flood the land with the blood of the Ghaznin thugs like a Nile River. . . . But they are also the elderly and the children for whom my youthful fortune feel mercy!"[71] For this merciless conquest, 'Alauddin received the dubious title of *Jahan-suz* (World Burner).

'Alauddin ruled at Firozkoh until his death in 1161. His son succeeded him, and after his death two years later 'Alauddin's nephew, Ghiasuddin ibn Sam, took over the throne in 1163; under his leadership, the Ghorid Empire reached its territorial extent and peak of power. Ghiasuddin recovered Ghazna from the mob of Turkmen Ghuzz in 1173–1174 and seated his brother Mu'izuddin Mohammad (also known as Shahabuddin and Mohammad Ghori) in Ghazna on the ruined throne of Mahmud. From his military base at Ghazna, Mohammad Ghori expanded his territory through military conquests in India.

In the west, Sultan Ghiasuddin, assisted by his brother, extended his rule over Sistan and the Kerman branch of the Seljuqs. Furthermore, he established control over Herat. The Ghori sultan's main thrust, however, was in western Khorasan, where he clashed with the Khwarazm Shahs, who had carved out a principality in the region and were backed by their

Qara-Khitai suzerains. In 1192, he defeated the Khwarazm monarch near Merv and took over his territories. In later years, the Ghori sultan established his rule over most of the towns of Khorasan down to Bestam in Qumes. Meanwhile, the Bamian branch of the Ghorid dynasty secured Balkh and Tokharistan from the Turkish vassals of the Central Asian Qara-Khitai khanate (1124–1218).

The Ghorids' Military Establishment

As with preceding dynasties in Afghanistan, the Ghorid Empire was based on its military power and expanded mostly by exploiting the decaying authority of the Ghaznavids in eastern Afghanistan and the decline of the Seljuqs in western Khorasan. The empire was built on the ruins of the Ghaznavids and adopted the main elements of the Ghaznavids' military establishment. The Turkish *ghulams* (slave soldiers) component of the Ghorids army not only played a key role in the expansion of the empire but also became an instrument of perpetuation of the empire in northern India after the Ghorid state disintegrated in the west. Shahabuddin Ghori was keen on purchasing the best Turkish slaves. Once, when a deal to buy one named Shamsuddin Iltutmish did not go through, the sultan made sure that no one else purchased the slave. He finally got the slave, who rose to power in the early thirteenth century and founded the Shamsia dynasty of the Delhi Sultanate. The Ghori sultan used to train his slaves personally, and when they proved themselves he freed them and appointed them to military command and government posts. One of them was Shamsuddin Iltutmish, who was freed after his heroic action in a battle in India.[72]

One of the key elements of the army was the guards division, known as the *jandar*, which was considered the most trusted and loyal corps of the army. *Jandar* literally means "bodyguard," a designation still in use in some Persian-speaking places. According to Mohammad Qasim Hindu Shah, *jandars* were mostly Turkic slave soldiers but were often commanded by a high-ranking noble known as *sar-jandar*.[73] The dynasty was more eager than its predecessors to hire Turkic *ghulams*, some of whom they elevated to positions of power. Some former slaves succeeded their masters as the sultans in their Indian dominions.

The core of the Ghorid army was the cavalry, which was distinguished by its high mobility and shock action. The troopers were skilled in shooting arrows while riding. The light cavalry was used to charge the enemy lines in running battles, whereas the heavy cavalry, clad in steel armor, was employed to deliver a penetrating blow on the enemy as he was weakened after the hit-and-run attacks of the light forces. This method of warfare earned the army a decisive victory over the Rajputs in the Battle of Tarain in 1192. Other segments of the army included the infantry, siege engines, and elephants acquired during military campaigns in India.

The Indian Conquest

The Ghorids laid the foundation of Muslim occupation in India. Mu'izuddin Mohammad Ghori, who began ruling from Ghazna in 1174, used that city as a launching pad for the invasion of India. His campaigns through the Gomal Pass in 1175 extended his rule into Multan and Uch, and by 1182 he subdued the whole of Sind down to Daibal and the seacoast. After his unsuccessful advance in Gujarat, however, he shifted his attention to the northern approaches to India, making Punjab his objective. His armies made progress on the northern route by capturing Peshawar in 1179. Seven years later, Mohammad Ghori defeated and captured Khusrau Malik, the last of the Ghaznavids in Lahore, and sent his prisoner to Firozkoh. By 1186, Mohammad Ghori had overpowered his Muslim rivals in Sind and Punjab and was ready to turn to the Hindu principalities in northern India. This marked the end of the era where the Turkish conquerors of the previous centuries pursued a policy of assimilation between the Turks and their Hindu subjects. The Ghorids abandoned this policy, since the Afghan Muslims, supported by numerous Turks, were full of religious zeal and eager to destroy the "Hindu infidels."[74] This was the beginning of a new phase in Indian history, one that led to the establishment of Muslim governments in India that had varying degrees of expansion and lasted for more than six centuries.

The opening stage of the campaign pitted the Ghorid Muslim army against the legendary Rajput Hindus. As Mohammad Ghori seized and garrisoned Sirhind on the main road from Lahore to Delhi, he came face to face with the entire force of the Rajputs led by Prithviraj (1149–1192). Prithviraj was the chief of the Chauhan dynasty, which had succeeded the Tomaras in Delhi and Ajmer. *Rajput* means "son of a king," and the Rajputs were born fighters who fought to the death; many of their principalities in northern, central, and western India rarely submitted more than nominally to the Muslim rulers. The Rajputs formed the military caste of the ancient Hindu social order and preserved their old feudal system. With their deep-rooted military traditions, the Rajput military structure was clan-based. Each clan "division" had its hereditary leader who served the raja as their men served them. The hierarchy was cemented by bonds of kinship and military devotion that facilitated control in both peace and war. However, as noted by Jaywant Joglekar, the Hindu rulers had an unbounded faith in their elephants as an instrument of war. It was beyond their comprehension that a battle could be fought without war elephants. As a result, they did not think that it was necessary to study the organization of cavalry and battle techniques based on it.[75] Therefore, the Hindu rulers often depended on the weight of numbers and sticking to the stereotypical combat technique of applying pressure with massive numbers in a headlong charge.

However, true to their traditions and experience with the cavalry tactics of Central Asia, the Ghorids' army had an unlimited faith in their well-organized cavalry and the firepower of their bowmen. The Rajputs had neglected this combination of fire and maneuver to their disadvantage. Sultan Ghiasuddin Balban (r. 1266–1287), the ninth sultan of the Mamluk dynasty of Delhi stated: "I know that no [Indian] ruler can raise his hand against the army of Delhi [Sultanate] because the armies of the Rais and Ranas though consisted of a lakh [hundred thousand] *paikas* [footmen] and *dhanuks* [bowmen] cannot face my army. Barely six or seven thousand horsemen of Delhi are enough to ravage and destroy them."[76]

The most decisive battle between the Ghoris and the Rajputs was the Battle of Tarain, also known as the Battle of Taroari, fought in 1192 in Tarain near Thanesar in present-day Haryana (about 150 kilometers north of Delhi).

A Battle that Changed India

The most decisive battle of Mohammad Ghori in India was his fateful encounter with the Rajputs led by Prithviraj (1149–1192), chief of the Chauhan dynasty that had succeeded the Tomaras in Delhi and Ajmer, the Battle of Tarain (or Taroari). The outcome of the battle had far-reaching consequences that shaped the future of India. Following an initial military setback against the Rajput coalition led by Prithviraj in 1191, Ghori mobilized a force of 120,000 Afghan (Pashtun), Tajik, and Turk troopers[77] into India to face about 150 Rajput chiefs who had assembled with their levies on the battlefield. "They swore by the water of Ganges that they would conquer their enemies or die martyrs to their faith."[78] The contemporary sources exaggerated the number of the Rajput army at 300,000 horses, 3,000 elephants, and innumerable foot soldiers.[79] Neither side may have fielded more than 60,000–70,000 combat troops on the battlefield, excluding the camp followers and service details. The two sides came face to face at Tarain (Taroari) in 1192.

When the Ghori's army reached the vicinity of the intended battlefield, the Rajput chief advised him to return and spare the lives of his men from a "definite annihilation." As a measure of deception, Ghori sent the Rajput leaders a request from his brother Sultan Ghiasuddin, whom he served merely as a general, for truce pending his permission to retreat. Overconfident about their strength and believing that Ghori was intimidated, the Rajput leaders relaxed the security around their camp. Taking advantage of the unwary enemy, Ghori launched a surprise attack before the ranks of the Rajputs swelled with the arrival of additional forces. The Ghorids' logistical constraints inside enemy territory precluded a drawn-out campaign, and it was in the interest of the Ghorid army to fight a decisive battle as soon as the next day. The Ghorid leader left the infantry, heavy detachments, banners, royal canopy, and trains nine miles behind in the main camp and led his picked cavalry in an attack on the enemy camp. Early in the morning, as the inhabitants of the sprawling Rajput camp on the plain of Tarain were looking forward to another peaceful day, the leading detachment of the Ghorid cavalry descended on the unprepared Rajputs, who were busy in morning ablutions and were taken by surprise. The Hindu troops in the depth of the extensive camp were alerted in time to mount and form a battle line.

As the Rajput forces were recovering from the shock of the surprise attack, Mohammad Ghori regrouped his forces into five divisions. The first four were made up of 10,000 light cavalry troops wearing light armor, skilled in shooting arrows while riding. The fifth division consisted of 12,000 heavy cavalrymen clad in steel armor, kept in reserve for the final blow.[80] The light cavalry divisions were to advance to within bowshot range of the enemy and discharge their arrows against the center of the enemy line; as the enemy advanced with their elephants in front for close combat, the attacking horsemen were to fall back swiftly. The cavalry columns were also instructed to attack the enemy flanks jointly if one of the divisions was pursued by the enemy line and exposed its open flanks. The idea was to engage the enemy by different columns in hit-and-run attacks, wearing down the momentum of its advance. It was a typical running cavalry battle mastered by the Central Asian horsemen and aptly used against the confused Rajputs, who were captive to their stagnant combat traditions. The Ghorid cavalry's Arab, Khorasani, and

Turkmen horses outdid the enemy horses in stamina and endurance. The combat action was a match between a Ghorid army that combined maneuver and firepower in hitting the enemy versus a Rajput force that was ponderous, moved slowly under the elephants' protection, and lacked the skill of shooting arrows while riding. So while the Rajputs were intent on forcing the enemy into close combat and trampling them under the feet of their elephants, the Ghorid cavalry avoided close combat; when the enemy cavalry did charge, they gave ground. When the Rajputs halted, the Ghorids resumed the charge and kept attacking the Rajputs' ranks on their exposed flanks.

By the evening, the running battle had exhausted the Rajputs to the point that they could hardly withstand a heavy cavalry charge. Mohammad Ghori launched his final blow with his 12,000 heavy cavalry reserve. The final strike was decisive. The cavalry charge created great confusion in the enemy ranks and destroyed their morale. Once the Rajput army was boxed in, it was massacred. Many Rajput leaders fell, and Prithviraj fled the battlefield but was chased and captured near Sirsuti and executed. The Rajputs were totally routed and suffered heavy losses as the Ghorid cavalry plowed into the enemy ranks, cutting down the numerous foot soldiers who merely swelled the ranks but added little in combat skills.

The outcome of the battle sealed the fate of northern India for many centuries to come. It paved the way for the establishment of the Muslims' Delhi Sultanate; except for the hills and deserts of Rajputana, no Hindu chief ruled in the north until the rise of the Sikh maharaja Ranjit Singh in the early nineteenth century. As Vincent Smith puts it: "All the numerous subsequent victories were merely consequences of the overwhelming defeat of the Hindu league on the historic plain [Taraori] to the north of Delhi."[81]

The victory led to the annexation of Ajmer, Hansi, and Sirsuti. Temples and idols were destroyed and mosques were built. Qutbuddin Aibak, a *ghulam* of Mohammad Ghori, was appointed viceroy of India, where he and the sultan expanded their territory in the greater part of northern India. Furthermore, Gwalior, Badaun, Kalpi, Kalinjar, and Anhalwara in the south came under Ghori control.

The deaths of Sultan Ghiasuddin in 1203 and of his successor, Sultan Mohammad Ghori, in 1206 marked the decline of the Ghorid Empire, which lost much ground in Khorasan and suffered a decisive defeat against Khwarazm ruler Sultan Mohammad (r. 1200–1220). Meanwhile, different sections of the multiethnic army rose in support of different

The Battle of Tarain, 1192

Phase I - The disposition of opposing forces

Phase 2 - The rout of the Rajput Army

Ghori Army	Rajput Army	
△ Armored Cavalry	◇ Cavalry	⬡ Elephants
◇ Light Cavalry	▢ Infantry	ⅼⅼ Guns

contenders to the throne. The last Ghori rulers were under suzerainty of the Khwarazm monarch Sultan Mohammad, who finally drove them out. All the Ghorid lands, except their possessions in India, fell under the Khwarazm-Shahids' control in 1215—a few years before the Mongol invasion, which finally overthrew the Khwarazm-Shahid Empire.

The rise of the Ghorids from a highland chiefdom to a vast empire stretching from Gorgan in Persia to Bengal in India was a remarkable achievement. The short-lived empire played a significant role in Islamic history. Despite their relatively short period of imperial rule, the Ghorids made an unparalleled penetration into India. Their expansion to the west and north, however, was challenged by the Khwarazmids, who had greater access to the fighting men on the inner Asian steppes. The Ghorids finally lost in the west and gained in the east. Their legacy proved to be the most lasting in India. Compared to Sultan Mahmud's penetration into India, the Indian conquests of Mohammad Ghori were much wider and far more permanent. Of the two invasions, Mahmud's had left little trace and was, in fact, a series of victorious raids; when its thrust was spent, it had little force remaining to hold even a single province. Mohammad Ghori benefited from building a solid base in Punjab, which served as an anchor for his steady advance inside the subcontinent. After the demise of the Ghorid Empire, the territories it had conquered were consolidated under other Muslim rulers. Until the Indian mutiny in 1857, there was always a Muslim king seated on the throne in Delhi.

7 The Mongol Cataclysm, 1220–1370

"They came and they destroyed, they burned, and they slew, they trussed up the loot and they left." With these harrowing words, Juwayni, a contemporary chronicler, quoted a survivor describing the Mongol cataclysm that befell the prosperous cities of Transoxiana, Khorasan, and Afghanistan in the early thirteenth century.[1]

The tsunami of the Mongol invasion came to the region in early 1220, the Chinese Year of the Dragon, unheralded and unforeseen, taking the Muslim states and the rest of the world completely by surprise. Soon it spread in leaps and bounds across the lands, engulfing the whole area in devastating waves of fire and bloodshed. The invasion marked the beginning of the conquest of the Muslim states in Central and West Asia that eventually consumed virtually all of Eurasia. Although a conflict between the Mongol Khan—Chinggis—and the sultan of the Khwarazm Empire—'Alauddin Mohammad—initiated the invasion, the conquest extended far beyond the limits of the Khwarazmid state. Over four years (1219–1223), the Mongols massacred millions of local inhabitants, enslaved hundreds of thousands of others, turned vast farming lands into killing fields, and destroyed the irrigation systems. The impact of the destruction continues even today in Afghanistan.

At the turn of the thirteenth century, two major empires were forming on the two sides of the Asian Continent. In the east, Chinggis Khan, a leader among numerous obscure Mongol chiefs, rose to prominence in the remote vastness of the Central Asian deserts after gaining control of his own tribe and then establishing its absolute supremacy over the wild mounted herdsmen of the desolate plains of Mongolia. In the first decade of the thirteenth century, he built a massive nomadic empire that extended from the Sea of Japan to Balkhash Lake in the west. Born as Temujin on the banks of the Onon River in Mongolia (not far from Mongolia's modern capital, Ulaanbaatar), Chinggis Khan unified many of the nomadic tribes on the Central Asian plateau, north of China, who were divided into several tribes and confederations, including the Naimans in the west, the Merkits in the north, the Tanguts in the south, the Tatars in the east, the Khamag Mongols (whole Mongols) in the Mongolian plateau, and the Keraits in the south. These tribes were all prominent in their own right and often hostile toward each other, preoccupied with raids, revenge attacks, and plunder.

During less than two decades, Temujin overwhelmed the other tribes, either by defeating them in war or winning them over through deal-making and by delegating authority based on merit and loyalty rather than family ties. Furthermore, he incorporated members of the defeated tribes into his extended tribal confederacy and its military machine. By doing so, he won a major following that acclaimed him as the Supreme Khan of all the Turko-Mongol tribes in the great *quriltai* (tribal council) of 1206—the Chinese Year of the Tiger.[2] There, Temujin assumed the new title "Chinggis Khan," or "very mighty chief." During the next ten years, Chinggis Khan led successful campaigns against the Chinese dynasties and in 1215 marched triumphantly into the streets of Yanjing (today's Beijing).

In the west, the Khwarazm-Shahid dynasty of Transoxiana, Khorasan, and Persia rapidly expanded into a vast empire after throwing off allegiance to the Qara-Khitai Empire in Central Asia. Within fifteen years, the Khwarazmian sultan, 'Alauddin Mohammad Khwarazm-Shah, seized control of most of Persia down to the Zagros Mountains, took Transoxiana from the weakened Qara-Khitais in 1210, and shifted his capital to Samarkand. Five years later, he conquered much of the Ghorids' territories in Afghanistan, pushing the successors of Mohammad Ghori to the east, where they established their northern Indian kingdom—a state known as the Delhi Sultanate (1206–1526).

Following his initial conquest of China, Chinggis Khan turned his attention westward to deal with the rebellious tribes of Merkits and Naimans, which were driven out of Mongolia, fled west, and established themselves in Irtysh-Qipchaq and East Turkistan, respectively. In 1215–1216, the Mongol Khan dispatched an army of several thousand men (10,000 or more) under his experienced generals Subedai and Toquchar against the Merkits in the Qipchaq steppes. Chinggis Khan's oldest son, Juji, led the expedition. This expedition coincided with a military campaign led by Khwarazm-Shah against the Merkits, whom he considered intruders into the borders of the Khwarazmian dominions. A chance clash between the two powers erupted in the Qipchaq steppes while a detachment of Mongols was in hot pursuit of the Merkits. Being under strict order to avoid confrontation with the Khwarazmians, the Mongol commander assured 'Alauddin that he was only pursuing their enemy and had no intention of fighting him. But 'Alauddin considered the Mongol move as an encroachment on his territory and attacked the Mongol force. The fight ended inconclusively. The following day, the Mongol detachment left the area. Chinggis Khan did not wish to take military action against Khwarazm-Shah while he was engaged in the Chinese campaign. Both sides considered the clash to be an accident, and it did not lead to war. Nevertheless, the brief encounter struck fear in the heart of Khwarazm-Shah, who, after seeing the ferocity of the Mongol fighters, noted that a much stronger power was lurking on his borders and capable of attack. Although his fears subsided over time, 'Alauddin embarked on a major espionage effort to size up his mighty neighbor. Thus, the Mongols' westward drive brought them in contact with the Muslim Khwarazmian Empire, and by the year 1215 Chinggis Khan's frontiers met those of 'Alauddin Mohammad in Central Asia.

The power base of the two empires was drastically different. The Mongols had coalesced into a cohesive, confederated nation governed by reformed nomadic rules and a strictly enforced civil and military discipline. The nation was backed by a well-organized army that had adapted new military skills from their steppe wars and its encounters with the armies of the settled areas. The Mongols not only refined the traditional battlefield tactics of the steppes, which was based on mobility and encirclement conducted by mounted archers, but also acquired siege engines, explosives, and technical expertise, which added significantly to the effectiveness of their military.

However, even though the Khwarazm-Shahid Empire looked vast on the map, it was weak and disjointed inside. The expansion of the empire was rapid, but its consolidation into a cohesive state had yet to occur. According to several Islamic sources, the empire possessed a 400,000-strong army; the number represented regular military forces but may also have included paramilitary and provincial forces. A modern author estimates that the actual number of the Khwarazm-Shah army could hardly exceed 40,000.[3] The real number may be between 100,000 and 150,000 deployed across a population of about five million. In any case, it was an odd assortment of different national contingents dominated by the nomadic Qanquli and Qipchaq Turks from the area between the Aral and Caspian Seas whose horse-archery skills made them the best soldiers in the army. These mercenaries, evolved into the state military aristocracy, were loyal more to the sultan's powerful mother, Turkan Khatun, a princess of the Qipchaq Turks, than to the sultan or the state. The ethnic mix of the military included Central

Asian Turks, Khalaj and Afghan (Pashtun) tribesmen, Khorasanis, and Persians, a fact that made the coherence of the military extremely shaky. The mercenary army constituted the sole support of the throne and was favored by the sultan over the civil elements of the state. The predatory nature of the Qipchaq and Qanquli mercenaries undermined the morale of other native contingents. Further, the sultan was in open conflict with the Abbasid caliph al-Nasir in Baghdad, whose lack of spiritual support and hostility undermined the legitimacy of the sultan in the eyes of his Muslim subjects. Neither was he on good terms with the clergy, particularly after he murdered the noted Sufi mystic Sheikh Majduddin Baghdadi (Baghdadaki), a disciple of Sheikh Najmuddin Kobra (the founder of the Kobrawiya order of Sufis), in 1216.[4]

Having overwhelmed his rival powers in Asia, Chinggis Khan saw no immediate threat to his dominions. He was aging and could have lived in peace within his vast and unified empire. However, a powerful empire with an enormous military machine could hardly resist the temptation to grow greater. Neither could such a great power maintain peace among the militarized nomad tribes without keeping them engaged in more wars and plunder. Tribes that had been unified in war were liable to disintegrate into infighting in the absence of incentives provided by the conquest of new lands. In fact, the unification of the Mongols under one supreme leader had set the stage for the nation to overflow its pastoral borders and to flood out over its sedentary neighbors, as had the previous empire-building nomads in Asia. Before Chinggis Khan unified most of the nomad tribes into a Mongol confederacy, the people of Mongolia were organized into tribes with no identified boundaries separating tribal territories. They were incessantly on the move in search of grazing lands and water for their sheep and horses.

Between 1180 and 1220, Mongolia experienced a drop in the mean annual temperature that shortened the growing seasons for grass.[5] The situation may have forced the Mongol hordes to move westward, away from their traditional pastures, clashing with the Muslim lands across the Syr Darya. Furthermore, Chinggis Khan's wars with China had disrupted the trade on which the nomads depended for the supply of goods. And finally, Chinggis Khan's own ambitions and his beliefs in fulfilling a Shaman-based messianic mission to rule the known world could have been the motive behind his conquest. But it is not known whether Chinggis Khan deliberately planned expansion to the west, or if Khwarazm-Shah's brutal massacre of Mongol-sponsored traders in

1218 provoked the Mongols' deadly machine to destroy their Muslim neighbors.

Khwarazm-Shah had his own ambitions for expanding his empire to the east. After annexing parts of the Qara-Khitai territories in Transoxiana, he was vying for influence in East Turkistan and dreamed of conquering China. When the rumors of Chinggis Khan's conquest in China reached him, the sultan dispatched an embassy mission to the Mongol court to get information about the extent of his power in the east. According to Jawzjani (1193–1260), who had spoken with the leader of the Khwarazmian mission, Bahauddin Razi, it was basically a fact-finding mission. The envoy reached Chinggis Khan after Beijing had already fallen to him (1215) and he was still present in China. Jawzjani quoted the envoy as saying that signs of terrible devastation were seen everywhere in the area. He noted that the bones of massacred people formed "whole mountains; the soil was greasy with human fat and the rotting of the bodies caused an illness from which some of Bahauddin's companions died. At the gate of Peking, lay a vast heap of bones. The envoys were told that on the capture of the town 60,000 girls threw themselves from the walls to avoid falling into the hands of the Mongols."[6] The report brought back to Samarkand seemingly contained a significant dose of exaggeration, yet the harrowing description of Mongol brutality sent a message of fear through the Khwarazmian lands.

Chinggis Khan received the Khwarazmian envoys graciously and asked them to inform Khwarazm-Shah that he considered him the ruler of the west as he himself was the ruler of the east. He also desired that there should be peace and friendship between them and that merchants should be free to travel from one country to another.

Khwarazm-Shah responded favorably to the friendly messages of Chinggis Khan and expressed his willingness to expand trade relations between the two lands. Soon after this, a large group of some 450 Mongol-sponsored merchants arrived in the border town of Otrar on the Syr Darya River. According to Jawzjani, the caravan included 500 camels laden with goods consisting of gold, silver, Chinese silk garments, beaver skins, sables, and other articles. The governor of Otrar, Inalchuq, titled Ghayir Khan, a powerful Qanquli Turk and a close relative of Turkan Khatun, was tempted to seize the enormous wealth of the caravan. He detained the merchants and reported them as spies to the sultan. They may well have been spies, as the Mongols used merchants for spying. (Khwarazm-Shah himself did the same.) The sultan, without any hesitation, ordered the execution of the presumed spies. When a lone survivor took the news of the massacre to Chinggis Khan, he sent a three-member embassy mission to Khwarazm-Shah and demanded that, if the offense against the Mongol-sponsored merchants was not ordered by the sultan, then he should hand over the governor of Otrar to face punishment. The sultan's ruthless answer was to murder one of the three envoys and to burn the beards of the remaining two. War was now inevitable, and a *quriltai* (council) called by Chinggis Khan determined to go to war against Khwarazm-Shah. Possibly Chinggis Khan was also encouraged to proceed by the invitation of the Abbasid caliph al-Nasir, who was a deadly enemy of Muhammad Khwarazm-Shah—the latter having attempted to displace him and to put a follower of his own on the throne of Baghdad.[7] In the spring of 1219, Chinggis Khan set out from Karakorum for the west. He summered in Irtysh and gathered an army of some 150,000 horsemen and made final preparations to launch his invasion in the autumn—the Chinese Year of the Rabbit.

The Mongol Military Structure

The source of Chinggis Khan's extraordinary power was an army that had emerged strengthened after many long years fighting the steppe wars. Most of its soldiers and officers had fought for him over three decades, and he had established close bonds with them. It evolved into a formidable military machine that not only brought competing tribal warriors together but also served as a nation-building mechanism giving new identity to the isolated tribal herdsmen and providing them with a universal sense of belonging to a world-conquering people. As David Morgan suggests: "To speak of the Mongol army is really no more than to speak of the Mongol people in one of its natural aspects."[8] The army-state relationship was cross-functional and complementary. The structural reforms that Chinggis Khan introduced into the organization of the Mongol army helped hold together disparate groups of nomadic tribes and mold them into a militarized nation. Chinggis Khan divided the tribal soldiers into units under different leaders to break up their social and tribal connections so that there was no division based on heritage or tribal alliances. Promotion was based on merit. In this new social structure, the new military units of a thousand men replaced traditional tribal identities and, in the process, transformed a steppe confederation into an army that conquered an empire.[9]

As in many medieval armies in the region, the Mongol army was organized on the decimal system. Even though the Mongols inherited many of the military traditions of previous nomadic empires, they also developed a more refined system of raising their army and developing it. The smallest unit was a section of ten troops (*arban*; Persian: *daha*). Ten of these sections constituted a squadron of 100 men (*jaghut*; Persian: *sadah*), and ten squadrons were grouped into a regiment of 1,000 horsemen (*mingan*; Persian: *hazara*). However, as the *mingan* represented both a social-tribal and a military unit, the actual size of the force it fielded varied.[10] The largest unit was the *tumen*, which, according to *The Secret History of the Mongols*[11] and Juwayni, was a division of 10,000 troops that could operate as an independent force.[12] But, as Larry Moses suggests, most of the numbers used in *The Secret History of the Mongols* are of a legendary nature. He notes that *tumen* refers to 10,000 soldiers, peoples, and tribes, but the unit is also used to express immensity, not a literal number.[13] *The Secret History* contains examples of *tumen* commanders with two, three, or four *mingans*.[14] Two to five *tumens* would form an *ordu* (army), from which the word "horde" is derived. *Ordus* were commanded by khans or their generals (*noyons*). This command structure proved to be highly flexible and allowed the Mongol army to attack en masse or divide into several smaller groups to engage separate enemy targets simultaneously or outflank and encircle major enemy concentrations. The hierarchical organization of the army facilitated close control and coordination.

An elite force, called *kishik* or *kishig* (guards), was senior to all units. They functioned as the imperial guard as well as a training cadre for officer cadets. Some prominent Mongol commanders, such as Subedai, started their careers there. The *kishik tumen* was kept in reserve under direct command of the commander in chief. Under Chinggis Khan, the *kishik* evolved into one of the Mongol Empire's most important institutions. It grew from a unit of a few hundred men into a formation 10,000 strong.

The army was supplemented by auxiliary forces that provided combat support and logistics services to the army. During their military campaigns in Central Asia and Khorasan in the thirteenth century, the Mongols used prisoners as a protective screen in front of their ranks. During siege operations, prisoners (*hasher*) were also forced to fill the moats, assemble the siege engines, and service catapults and ballistae. The tactic is borrowed from the Khitans, a local tribe with a long history that established the Liao dynasty in Liaodong in the early tenth century. The Khitans compelled civilian laborers to lead the way in attacking fortified cities.[15]

The Mongol military consisted entirely of cavalry, which was suitable for fast-paced combat on the steppes. Most of it was a lightly mounted force with six of every ten troopers being light cavalry horse-archers. The remaining four were heavier cavalry with lances for close combat after the archers had disrupted the enemy ranks. Each Mongol trooper usually maintained three or four horses, which they changed often to travel at a fast pace for days without stopping or wearing out the animals. This arrangement made the Mongol army the fastest force of its time. Outfitting the horsemen with multiple mounts, however, made the Mongol army vulnerable to shortages of fodder, particularly in arid or forested regions. Thus, the nature of the terrain and the horse itself dictated their way of war. It was on the steppes and open prairies that the mounted warriors felt at home, and they had to keep moving to ensure sufficient grazing for their massive horse herd.

The Muslim chroniclers of Chinggis Khan's military campaigns often exaggerated the number of Mongol armies. Judging from the number of military units (*mingans*) and the Mongols' population patterns, the number of armies Chinggis Khan and his commanders fielded comprised tens of thousands, not hundreds of thousands. According to one estimate, the total Mongolian population in the thirteenth century was around one million, of which males of military age represented no more than one-fourth.[16] Such a population can hardly field armies numbering hundreds of thousands. It is more reasonable that the armies that fought battles were often of several thousand or tens of thousands of fighters.

The number of *mingans* listed in *The Secret History of the Mongols* is about one hundred in 1206. Rashiduddin records 129 *mingans*, or 129,000 men, in Mongolia at the death of Chinggis Khan, excluding forces deployed abroad. Therefore, it is estimated that the total number of the military manpower was no more than 250,000. The number increased later as the empire extended further.

The Mongols' way of war, as a nomadic activity, was shaped by the horse, and their campaigns were influenced by their way of war. This was what the Huns practiced centuries before them; this was what the Phrygians honed in ancient times and what the Khitans used in the tenth and eleventh centuries in China.[17] The Mongols perfected these combat tactics under Chinggis Khan. It was the horse that gave the Mongol hordes the power and the organization to conquer China and the Muslim states and to reach the gates of Central Europe. Their way of war emerged from their way of life. The same techniques that were necessary for survival in a herding and hunting environment were applied with little deviation in warfare. Juwayni (1226–1283) wrote that the hunt is analogous to the Mongol way of war in every detail.[18]

As the empire expanded, people from the conquered lands swelled the ranks of the Mongol army, although the nomadic Mongol-Turkic cavalry remained the core component of the force. The use of infantry, raised among sedentary populations for garrison duties, gave the Mongol army wider variety and greater flexibility and allowed it to greatly expand the empire. Artillery consisted of missile-throwing machines and mechanically operated siege engines, including catapults and ballistae. The engines could be disassembled for easy transportation as pack artillery and then reassembled on the battleground. But in later years in Europe, they recruited engineers to build the machines on the spot. Their corps of engineers was vital to their conquests. Initially, siege engineers were Chinese, but as the Mongols advanced into Muslim Central Asia and the Middle East, they incorporated Arab, Persian, and Armenian engineers. Adoption of technology was one of the important facets of Mongolian warfare. Siege engines helped attack fortified cities in Transoxiana and Khorasan.

Another unique characteristic of the Mongol army was its reduced dependence on cumbersome supply trains despite the constant requirement for forage for the large reserve of horses that always accompanied the soldiers. Mongols' ability to live off the land and, in extreme situations, off their animals (mare's milk especially) made their soldiers logistically self-reliant. As they moved, they milked the animals, slaughtered them for food, and fed themselves by hunting and looting. According to Jawzjani, Chinggis Khan, before embarking on war with Khwarazm-Shah, decided that each section of ten troopers would carry their own food rations to sustain them during a three-month march. This included the dried meat of three sheep, a supply of water, and *qumiz* (kumiss) made of fermented mare's milk.[19] Marco Polo (1254–1324) wrote that the Mongol warriors could travel ten days without stopping to make a fire or heat food, that they drank horse's blood, and that each man carried with him ten pounds of dried milk. Each soldier would put a pound of dried milk in a leather flask of water each day to make his meal. The motion of riding shook the contents violently and produced a thin porridge for dinner.[20]

Mongol soldiers were subject to strictly enforced discipline standards applied equally to all with no exceptions. They were perfectly obedient to their chiefs and were maintained at small expense. In the words of Juwayni: "So patient in hardship and grateful for comfort, so obedient to its commanders both in prosperity and adversity; and this not in hope of wages and fiefs nor in expectation of income or promotion. . . . In war all fight bravely, from the lowest to the highest warrior."[21]

And finally, the Mongol soldier was extremely tough and resilient—seasoned under the most difficult conditions. Marco Polo states that no people on earth could surpass them in fortitude under difficulties or show greater patience under wants of every kind. They could support every kind of privation, and, when needed, they could live for a month on the milk of their mares and upon such wild animals as they may chance to catch. Their horses were fed upon grass alone and did not require barley or other grain. The men could remain on horseback for two days and two nights, without dismounting, sleeping in the saddle while their horses grazed. The Mongol soldiers left a mythical impression in the minds of their contemporaries in the Muslim world. Enumerating the qualities of the Mongols, a contemporary author, Vassaf, wrote that "they had the courage of lions, the endurance of dogs, the prudence of cranes, the cunning of foxes, the far sightedness of ravens, the rapacity of wolves, the keenness for fighting of cocks, the tenderness for their offspring of hens, the wiliness of cats in approaching, and the impetuosity of boars in overthrowing their prey."[22] This is similar to the suggested traits of the nomadic warrior depicted more than two centuries earlier in the *Qutadghu Bilig*.[23]

The primary weapon of the Mongol forces was their native bow, which was a recurved bow made from composite materials (wood, horn, and sinew) and was, at that time, unmatched for accuracy, force, and reach. It could shoot an arrow more than 500 meters, while targeted shots were possible at a range of 200–230 meters, which marked the optimal tactical approach distance for light cavalry units. Mongol archers used a variety of arrows depending on target and distance. Special heavy arrows were used for penetrating chainmail and some metal armor at close range. The bow and arrow was a weapon with which Mongols were the most expert, being accustomed, from childhood, to employ it in their sports and to use it from horseback. They also carried a second bow with greater precision for use on foot. The troopers carried three quivers of arrows of different diameters and with different arrowheads for shooting at different ranges and engaging various targets, ranging from armor-protected troops to unprotected people.

The Mongols' battle tactics were a combination of maneuver by light horsemen, bow-shooting from a distance, and cavalry charges by heavily armed mounted soldiers. Such tactics worked well in the steppes but were inadequate against trained and resolute armies in settled areas. Mongol success against the Khwarazmians was due in part to the strategic and tactical mistakes of their enemies, who often withdrew into the defenses of their walled cities instead of facing the Mongols in pitched battle. From the outset, therefore, they traded maneuver for protection behind the walls. But fortifications could be breached, and walls could be scaled. The Khwarazmian army was piecemealed into several garrisons defending major cities and towns, whereas the Mongol forces had the freedom to sequence their operations, concentrating superior forces against individual enemy targets. This left the population outside the cities unprotected, and it was massacred by the Mongols as they laid siege to the walled towns. Civilians who fled from the suburbs to the cities for protection added to the population inside, overstraining supplies and reducing the capacity to withstand long sieges.

The Mongol army's operational techniques were flexible and agile. Psychological warfare and deception were distinct features of their operational methods. They often spread terror and fear to enemy towns and cities to break resistance and made deceptive moves to create confusion in the minds of enemy commanders and thereby achieve surprise. The use of feint retreats to lure the enemy into unfavorable situations was widely practiced by Mongol commanders.

Swarming Westward

In 1219, Chinggis Khan gathered an army in northern China and, after leaving his generals to continue the war with the Chinese and appointing his youngest brother, Temuge Otchigin, to take charge in Mongolia, he moved west with his generals Subedai, Chepe, and Toquchar leading the vanguard in the long march to the Khwarazmian lands. The speed of Chinggis Khan's march across the Altai Mountains impressed contemporary observers. The Mongol army arrived on the border in just three months rather than the expected four. In the summer of 1219, Chinggis Khan concentrated his forces at Balkhash east of Lake Baikal and mobilized an engineer corps, composed mostly of Chinese experts, to operate siege engines in anticipation of siege warfare. The size of his army was exaggerated at 600,000–700,000 by contemporary Muslim chroniclers.[24] As noted earlier, given the size of the Mongolian population, and the possible number of men of military age in the thirteenth century, the invading army may have numbered between 150,000 and 200,000, of which at least 15,000 were part of the army's engineer parks.[25]

Some modern authors suggest that Chinggis Khan's military operation against the Khwarazmian Empire was launched along two converging strategic axes on the two sides of the Tianshan Mountains, with the

main effort centered in the north under the khan himself and a supporting action in the south led by Subedai and Chepe Noyon.[26] While such
an offensive operation was launched in the south, a separate move a year
earlier (2118) by Chepe Noyan aimed at clearing eastern Turkistan from
the forces of the fugitive Naiman chief Kuchlug, who was chased and
finally killed in Badakhshan.[27] This way, the Mongol column came to a
position to threaten the Khwarazmian Empire at its southeastern flank
while Chinggis was moving with the main body from the north.[28]

Chinggis Khan spent the summer of 1219 on the plains in the north
between the Qara Irtysh and Kobok Rivers, where the horses grazed, fat-
tened, and rested. In autumn, when the weather cooled off and the usual
fighting season (autumn-winter) began, the khan with all of his sons
moved along the main route through the Dzungarian Gate, separating
the Barlik Range from the Ala-tau (Colorful) Mountains. The Dzungarian Gate is a geographically and historically significant, 50-mile-long
mountain pass between China and Central Asia and has been described
as the one and the only gateway in the mountain-walls that stretch from
Manchuria to Afghanistan over a distance of 3,000 miles. Throughout history, torrential waves of nomadic invaders, including the Huns,
passed through this natural gate. It was the only defile wide enough (7–
10 miles) to accommodate the passage of hundreds of thousands of herd
animals and large armies packing their tented city. From there the main
army took the caravan route westward, where allied contingents from
eastern Turkistan, including troops from Almaliq, Uyghur, and Qarluq
lands, joined the Mongol army. The first objective was Otrar, the site of
the massacre of the Mongol trade caravan that became the casus belli.

Facing the massive enemy forces, Khwarazm-Shah failed to draw
up a comprehensive defense plan. While the Mongol Khan was trying
to draw the Khwarazm-Shah out of his multiple urban strongholds into
the open for a pitched battle, the latter did not trust his ethnically mixed
forces to face the enemy in a major battle. Furthermore, Khwarazm-
Shah's plan was based on the flawed assumption that the Mongols
would be interested only in plundering the country and would withdraw
after looting the districts surrounding the major cities without risking a
drawn-out siege of walled towns. He assumed that the Mongols lacked
the capability to reduce fortified cities. This illusion gave him a false
hope that he would get an opportunity to launch a counterattack from his
defensive enclaves. He was proved wrong on both counts. The Mongols
were there to pillage and destroy every major city and massacre their
entire populations to eliminate all potential sources of resistance. They

came with hundreds of siege engines and thousands of warriors with the expertise to reduce fortified towns they had acquired in their wars in China.

In any case, Sultan Mohammad Khwarazm-Shah did not have any easy options and failed to adopt a well-conceived strategy in time to face the enemy. Defense on the banks of the Syr Darya River would provide a natural barrier, but many big cities on the far bank of the river would be lost to the enemy. A defensive line across the river to save the northern cities would have put the forces in a position with a broad river to their back with the risk of annihilation if defeated. And finally, a position on the steppes astride the Qara-Tau Mountains was too risky because the area was suitable for the enemy cavalry while the army would be limited to one supply line there and a single retreat route through Arys Pass. Defense on the Amu Darya River meant giving up the major cities of the empire in Transoxiana, including the capital (Samarkand). Seeing few suitable strategic options, Khwarazm-Shah violated every known and tested principle of war and spread out his army in several detachments locked up in major cities along the Syr Darya River and in Transoxiana, leaving the freedom of action to the Mongols, who concentrated against separate targets and destroyed them sequentially.

At a war council called by the sultan, an alternative option discussed was defending on the Amu Darya River or pulling back across the Hindu Kush Mountains to Ghazni to entrap the enemy in mountainous country. Khwarazm-Shah did not see any of the suggested options working under the circumstances. He was not sure of the loyalty of all the segments of his army, particularly after Chinggis Khan duped him by forging a letter from the generals loyal to the sultan's powerful mother offering collaboration with the Mongol Khan. The deception worked, and the sultan became so alarmed that he lost the will to face the enemy in the open.

Khwarazm-Shah garrisoned major cities north of the Syr Darya with strong contingents and strengthened major urban centers in Transoxiana. Otrar (also called Farab) was garrisoned with 20,000 troops. In Samarkand, 40,000 local infantry and thousands of Qanquli cavalry guarded the walls. Bukhara was defended by some 30,000 troops. The real number of these garrisons is hard to verify but may have been less than the suggested numbers. The sultan also ordered recruitment of militias and collected the entire annual taxes three times in one year to fund additional forces. He ordered a wall to be built around the city of Samarkand that, according to contemporary author Ahmad Nesawi, was to extend more than 30 miles to protect not only the town but also its suburbs.[29] But the intended militias were not fully raised in time. And the protective wall was not completed before Khwarazm-Shah left the scene and fled west in the hope of building a new army to face the enemy.

Phasing the Military Campaign

Chinggis Khan's invasion unfolded in four phases. In the first phase, he reduced the border cities along the Syr Darya, hoping to draw Khwarazm-Shah out of his defenses into a major battle. In the second phase, the bulk of the Mongol army crossed the Syr Darya River and conquered and destroyed the main centers of enemy power, including the capital, Samarkand. In the third phase, the Mongol army crossed the Amu Darya into Khorasan and destroyed the main cities in that area, including Balkh, Merv, Nishapur, and Herat. The fourth phase involved mopping up and defeating the final resistance in Khorasan and Afghanistan. These phases were completed in four years from 1219 to 1223.

In the first phase, the main objective of the Mongols' military operation was to secure the Syr Darya frontier from its upper confines to the Aral Sea. When the Mongol army reached the *Qara-Tau* (black mountain) Mountains east of the Syr Darya, it divided into four corps. The first corps of several *tumens* (10,000–15,000 troops) and the Uyghur division under Chinggis Khan's sons Chaghatay and Ogdai rode through and laid siege to Otrar, the border-security fortress at the mouth of the Arys River. The second corps of three *tumens* (8,000–12,000 men) under the command of Khan's eldest son, Juji, wheeled down the Arys Valley, passed Otrar, and turned northwest down the right bank of the Syr Darya with Jend (now a decayed village near Qizil Orda in south-central Kazakhstan) as his main objective. The third corps (5,000 troops) followed the main body to Otrar and then turned southward down the river and laid siege to Benaket, the crossing point to Samarkand. The fourth corps, about 50,000 strong, under Chinggis Khan himself with his youngest son, Tolui (Tulai), acting as chief of staff, encamped north of the hills. The concept of the operation was to seize control of the riverine towns on the two flanks of the Otrar-Bukhara axis and then punch through across the river to the heart of Khwarazm-Shah's power base in Transoxiana.

While the siege of Otrar was in progress, Chinggis Khan led his army to Bukhara, skirting the Qizil Qum (Red Sands) Desert (in today's Uz-

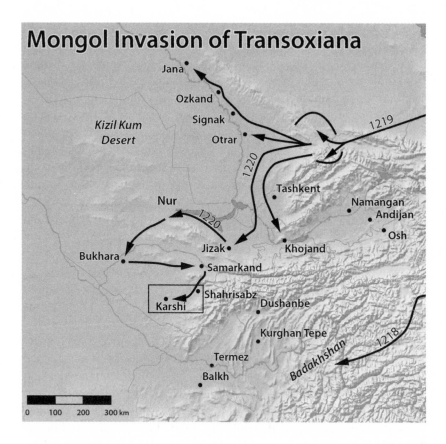

bekistan southwest of the Aral Sea) and bypassing Samarkand to split the Khwarazmian army. Some modern authors suggest that Chinggis Khan cut across the desert and descended on Bukhara.[30] But the contemporary sources at the time indicate that he crossed the Syr Darya at Benaket and followed the route along the margins of the desert and reduced Zernuq and Nur before appearing before the walls of Bukhara, driving thousands of captives (*hashar*) as protective screens in front of his mounted hordes.[31]

Bukhara, a longtime center of trade, scholarship, culture, and religion, was a major pillar of Khwarazmian political power. The "City of Good Fortune," as it was known in ancient times, won the epithet of *Bukhara-i-Sharif*,—"Noble Bukhara"—during the Islamic period. We know from Ibn Hauqal that in the tenth century Bukhara was surrounded by two walls, including a four-mile inner ring and a nearly 50-mile outer enclosure with several palaces, parks, gardens, and suburban villages located between the two walls. At the time of the Mongol invasion, Bukhara had a fortified citadel and was well garrisoned with more than 30,000 troops, including 12,000 horsemen. Many people from outlying districts had fled the Mongols and poured into Bukhara, swelling the population and increasing the strain on the city resources, particularly stores of food and water. This restricted the ability to sustain a long siege. After capturing cities along the way, Chinggis Khan laid siege to Bukhara in February 1220. The city commander (Gur-Khan) led an attack on the Mongols at sunrise to prevent them from erecting the siege engines. But the attackers who broke through the Mongol lines were pursued, and a small part of it was forced back into the city after suffering heavy losses. The following day, a group of city elders and religious figures—excluding the commander, who continued to hold out in the citadel—was sent out to make terms with the Mongol Khan. After the submission of the population, the city doors were opened.

The next day, Chinggis Khan rode to the city and headed straight to the great mosque and entered it on horseback. There, he asked if this was the sultan's palace; on being told it was the house of God, he dismounted, climbed the steps, and announced in a loud voice to his followers, "The hay is ready to cut, give your horses fodder." It was a cynical invitation to plunder. The boxes in which copies of the Quran were kept were converted into mangers, and the sacred books were trampled under the horses' hoofs. Meanwhile, the imams, religious scholars, sheikhs, and sayyids were compelled to hold the horses' bridles.[32] Then Chinggis Khan harangued the population from the pulpit of the mosque, announcing that he was the scourge of God sent to punish them for their sins. "You have committed great faults," he said, "and the great ones among you have committed sins for which I am the punishment of God. If you had not committed great sins God would not have sent me upon you."

Then he asked the people to disclose all their hidden treasures. This was the prelude to the sacking of the city. The inhabitants were ordered to leave the town with only their clothes so that it might be more easily pillaged, after which the spoils were divided among the victors. They herded the people into groups and massacred all except those who the Mongols needed. These were forced to march with the conquerors. "It was a fearful day," recorded Ibn Athir. "One only heard the sobs and weeping of men, women, and children, who were separated for ever; women were ravished, while many men died rather than survive the dishonor of their wives and daughters." The Mongols ended by setting fire to all the wooden buildings in the town.[33]

But the citadel did not surrender and continued to fight the invaders. Chinggis Khan ordered the Khwarazmian army out of town and instructed his troops to reduce the citadel. The Mongol soldiers, who fought superbly in open plains, were no match for the city's defenders. There, they became engaged in heavy street fighting and night attacks from the citadel assisted by the citizens. Frustrated with the lack of progress, Chinggis Khan ordered his army to set the city on fire and raze it to the ground. As Juwayni reports, a man who had escaped the carnage of Bukhara and reached Khorasan summarized the ordeal of the ill-fated city by saying "they came and they destroyed, they burnt and they slew, they plundered and they departed."[34]

Chinggis Khan kept the able-bodied people of Bukhara to serve as a protective shield during his advance to Samarkand, the capital of the Khwarazm Empire. The khan left a commander named Taush as *darugha* (governor) of the ruins of Bukhara and marched on Samarkand. The fall of Bukhara in such a short time shocked Khwarazm-Shah. As the Mongol detachments went out rampaging villages and towns across Transoxiana, the sultan, in utter panic, decided to leave Samarkand and Transoxiana and move west, hoping to muster a new force for a comeback. His son Jalaluddin, the only resolute and brave leader in the family, unsuccessfully tried to dissuade him from going west. Failing in that attempt, he demanded that the army stay with him to face the enemy on the Amu Darya. But the sultan had made his decision.

Hearing the news of the sultan's flight, Chinggis Khan dispatched three *tumens* (10,000 troops) under his three generals, Subedai, Chepe, and Toquchar, to pursue him as long and as far as necessary. Long before the arrival of the Mongol columns, Khwarazm-Shah left the banks of the Amu Darya and made a westward dash to Nishapur, which he reached in mid-April 1220, and began making preparations to raise an army, assuming that the Mongols would not cross into Khorasan. The pursuing Mongol force crossed the Amu Darya at Kilif and followed the sultan's trail to the west and was getting closer to the fleeing monarch. So, after staying less than a month in Nishapur, the sultan was on the move again and, under the guise of going hunting, rushed to western Persia. The Mongols' close pursuit continued as Khwarazm-Shah withdrew to the difficult terrain of Mazenderan and finally ended up on a Caspian Sea island, totally stripped of property and almost unattended except by some members of his family, including his gallant son Jalaluddin. The shah confirmed Jalaluddin as his successor before dying on January 10, 1221. Jalaluddin immediately left with his three brothers for Mangishlaq on the Caspian Sea and then traveled to Urgenj. There, his claim to the throne was challenged by the Qanquli-dominated army, which backed his brother. Jalaluddin decided to leave with 300 troops commanded by Timur Malik, the stout Khujand commander who had escaped through the Mongol lines. Jalaluddin fled to Nessa, near today's Ashgabat in Turkmenistan, and evaded the Mongol security screen and finally reached Ghazni through forced marches; he began preparations to face the Mongol threat in a new showdown.

Causing Khwarazm-Shah's wild flight, and the Mongol generals' relentless chase, became a major accomplishment for the Mongols. Although the Mongol generals Subedai and Chepe never caught up with the fugitive king, they extended the Mongols' reach to vast areas in the west, thereby paving the way for later incursions into Europe. They triumphantly marched through unfamiliar territories with a relatively small army without maps and still won the submission of major towns in Persia and Iraq, crushed the kingdom of Georgia, and pressed on into southern Russia. In their wake, they appointed military and civil administrators under Chinggis Khan's suzerainty before he recalled them in 1223, whereupon they returned via the northern coasts of the Caspian Sea.

After the destruction of Bukhara in February 1220, Chinggis Khan rode to the capital of the Khwarazm Empire. Marching along the fertile valley of Zarafshan, the Mongol army pillaged its way to Samarkand—the jewel of *Mawara un-Nahr*. Samarkand was not only the traditional and political capital of Transoxiana; it was also one of the greatest centers of Islamic culture and a major commercial hub in Asia. As one of the oldest inhabited cities in the world, Samarkand prospered throughout its history due to its location on the trade route between China and the Mediterranean known as the Silk Road. The walled city was three miles in circumference with eight iron gates and was garrisoned by some 30,000 Qanquli Turkmen and 50,000 local Tajiks, Turkmen, Ghori, Khalaj, and Qarluq troops under command of the governor, Taghday Khan, brother of Turkan Khatun. There were also 20 war elephants attached to the army. Soon after his arrival in the vicinity of Samarkand, Chinggis Khan was joined by the two other corps that had returned from reducing Otrar and ravaging the Khwarazmian towns along the Syr Darya and in northern Transoxiana. The joint forces converged on the capital and invested it with an overwhelming force.

As part of a deception plan, the Mongols lined up the prisoners (*hashar*) that they had been driving to serve as laborers and as a protective screen in front of their ranks. The Mongols issued flags to each ten prisoners so that they appeared to be Mongol soldiers in an immense army. When Ogdai and Chaghatay joined the khan's army, they brought with them more crowds of captured inhabitants from Otrar who were also used as dummies in the deception plan. Although the Mongols put on an impressive deception, on the third day of the siege tens of thousands of the Samarkand garrison sallied out to attack the enemy, only to fall into the Mongols' ambush. The Mongols killed them to the last man.[35] Then the Turkish mercenaries, who thought they would be treated as compatriots by the Mongols, deserted with their families and property. After this betrayal, the local inhabitants decided to surrender and sent a deputation headed by a religious elder, Shaykh al-Islam, to the Mongol camp to announce their submission. The Mongols entered the city. Chinggis Khan rode to the main mosques and gave immunity to 50,000 under the protection of Shaykh al-Islam. The citadel, however, held out and was taken by assault after the Mongols undermined part of the wall. But before the fall of the fortress, garrison commander Alp Khan made a sortie with 1,000 troops and managed to break through the Mongol forces and eventually joined the sultan's armies. The rest of the defenders were massacred within the fort. Then the 30,000 Qanquli Turkish troops who had surrendered earlier and were taken into service by the Mongols were herded onto an open space and massacred along with their officers. Samarkand was captured on the day of Ashura.[36]

Then, as was their usual practice, the Mongols ordered the inhabitants to leave the city while they plundered it. About 30,000 artisans captured in the city were assigned to the khan's sons as slaves. An equal number were herded as *hashars* for military works and transport service. Some 50,000 citizens were freed after they ransomed themselves for 200,000 dinars (gold coins), while the districts in the provinces were nearly depopulated.

The Conquest of Khorasan and Afghanistan

The Mongol conquest of Khorasan—the area south and west of the Amu Darya (Oxus) down to the eastern coasts of the Caspian Sea—was a difficult and lengthy campaign. This was not only because of its geographic location between Persia and India and its topographic nature from the highlands of Hindu Kush to the lowlands of the central Iranian desert and the plains of the Helmand basin but also due to the independent localism that required the Mongol armies to fight for every city and

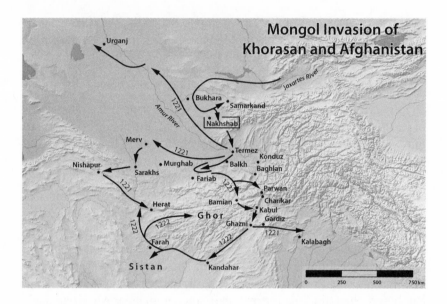

every fortress using drawn-out siege operations. Mongol armies that felt at home on the plains of Central Asia found themselves faced with the highlanders of Ghor, Ghazni, and Parwan at the foot of the Hindu Kush. There, they were forced to fight the first pitched battle since they invaded the Khwarazmian territories. Khorasan was a vast area, and its political and economic power was based in four major cities: Balkh, Merv, Nishapur, and Herat. The Mongols pursued a predictable way of war in Khorasan. They usually called on the inhabitants of the targeted cities to surrender, which did not always guarantee that the lives of the people would be spared. Failing surrender, the Mongols would besiege and blockade the towns until they reduced them, in which case the inhabitants—except those who were deemed of some use for the invaders—would be massacred and their city destroyed. To pressure the besieged towns, the Mongol hordes would usually ravage the districts to isolate the cities politically and economically. But still, some of the besieged towns and fortresses in Khorasan and Afghanistan held out for many months and even years.

After sending a plundering detachment to smaller cities in Transoxiana in late spring of 1220, Chinggis Khan rested for the summer in the oasis of Nakhshab (modern Qarshi in southern Uzbekistan).[37] At the end of the hot season, Chinggis Khan dispatched Toquchar, his son-in-law, with two *tumens* (5,000–6,000 troops) to follow up on the conquest of the territories overrun by Subedai and Chepe in the spring during their pursuit of Khwarazm-Shah. Chinggis Khan himself left his camp and descended into the Amu Darya (Oxus) basin across the Qara Tagh Mountains. He had to travel through the narrow Darband Defile, known as the Iron Gate (Temir Darvoza). The passage through the pass, which is about 20 yards wide with cliffs rising to 150 yards on both sides, has been a major challenge faced by the armies moving across the hills between Qarshi and Termez. Because of this, some armies avoided the defile and opted to cross the Amu Darya at Kilif, located on today's Afghanistan-Turkmenistan border. But the Mongol armies were determined to remove all obstacles in their path and could not afford to bypass the strong city of Termez, on the other side of the pass, which controlled the passage to Balkh.

After eleven days, the Mongols breached the strong defenses of Termez, massacred the inhabitants, and looted the city. The brutality of the carnage is epitomized by a story recorded by Juwayni stating that a certain old woman promised the killers a rare pearl if they spared her. When they asked for the treasure, she answered that she had swallowed it. Then the Mongols ripped her body open and retrieved the precious pearl from her stomach. Thinking that others might have swallowed jewels in the same way, Chinggis commanded that dead bodies be eviscerated thenceforth.[38]

From the ruins of Termez, Chinggis Khan led his army to Balkh, "the Mother of Cities," as its ancient epithet described it. Balkh was the roundabout of lower Tokharistan and the traditional political center of eastern Khorasan. As Ferdousi, the tenth-century author of the epic *Shah-Nama*, noted, in ancient times Iran regarded Balkh as the Arabs revered Mecca. Balkh's political reputation and its strategic location might have been the reasons for Chinggis Khan's reluctance to spare the city despite its submission to the Mongols. Contemporary sources also refer to the fact that the Mongol Khan did not want to leave a potential threat on his flank, since tidings of the efforts of Jalaluddin Khwarazm-Shah, the son of Sultan Mohammad, was reaching his camp. Under the pretext of conducting a census, the Mongol Khan directed the people of Balkh to assemble outside the town, but as they were herded outside the city, all were brutally slaughtered by the Mongol troops. The city was then pillaged and burned and all its defenses demolished.[39]

Chinggis Khan passed the winter between Balkh and Badakhshan, plundering and destroying all the key towns and places of potential defiance. Now, three major tasks lay ahead before he could ensure the destruction of all resistance in Khorasan. First, he had to neutralize Urgenj (Urgench), which was left intact at the Syr Darya Delta near the Aral Sea. That city was considered to be the power base of the Khwarazmian polity. Second, the submission of the other major cities in Khorasan—most of which had recovered from the Mongols' initial blows and rose in resistance—had to be completed. And third, renewed efforts by the new shah of the Khwarazmian Empire, Jalaluddin Mungaberti (or Mungaberdi—"God Given" in Turkish), the son of the deceased Sultan 'Alauddin Mohammad Khwarazm-Shah, had to be addressed. The threatening situation in Khorasan at the beginning of 1221 forced Chinggis Khan to take immediate actions.

In Urgenj, signs of anti-Mongol activities became more visible. The arrival of Khwarazmian princes after the death of their father alerted the Mongol Khan to possible trouble on his flank. In January 1221, he ordered an army under his three sons Juji, Chaghatay, and Ogdai to Urgenj. Arriving with the army's main body, the Mongol princes called on the defenders to surrender. The defenders rejected the demand. Several attempts by the besiegers to reduce the defenses of the city failed, resulting in heavy losses for the Mongol army. The siege lasted six months, extending into the summer, before the Mongols succeeded in mounting the walls and defeating the garrison. The garrison, along with the inhabitants, was put to the sword, and the city was flooded by diverting the course of the Amu Darya River. The army of the princes then returned in response to urgent calls from their father.

In Khorasan, the situation was not going well for the Mongols. The army under Toquchar, sent to Khorasan earlier in the autumn of 1220, failed to achieve its goal of reducing the defiant cities there. The Mongol commander himself was killed in his attempt to besiege and reduce Nishapur, the capital of Khorasan. In January 1221, Chinggis Khan ordered his youngest son, Tolui (Tulai), to take four *tumens* (10,000–15,000 troops) and finish the job in Khorasan. The campaign in Khorasan proved to be one of the bloodiest invasions of the time. It targeted the most populous cities, which, in addition to their urban populations, had accommodated large numbers of refugees from outlying districts who had crowded into the towns seeking protection from the Mongol onslaught. In just three months the Mongol army devastated the three main cities of Nishapur, Merv, and Herat.

Merv fell in February following sporadic skirmishes between the Mongol detachment and local Turkmen contingents. Although the city made peace with the victors, Tolui broke the deal as his army entered the city. The population was massacred; the city was looted and razed to the ground. Some 5,000 inhabitants who had escaped by hiding in cellars and underground watercourses were later smoked out by a Mongol detachment and put to the sword. The renowned Muslim geographer Yaqut, al-Hamawi (1179–1229), who left Merv just before the invasion and revisited the city after the disaster, wrote that the city's splendid palaces and other buildings "were effaced from the earth as lines of writing are effaced from paper, and these abodes became a dwelling for the owl and the raven; in these places the screech owls answer each other and in the halls the winds now moan responsive to the simoom [a strong and dry dust-laden wind]."[40] About a century later another geographer, Hamdullah Mustawfi, described Merv by saying that "the people here are much given to fighting, and the city now is mostly in ruins."[41]

The destruction was repeated in Nishapur, which fell in April. The home of many scientists, philosophers, and poets, Nishapur was identified as one of the greatest centers of knowledge and culture during the early Islamic period. The fame of some of its celebrated natives, including Omar Khayyam (1048–1131) and Fariduddin 'Attar (1145–1221), extended far beyond its borders. The Mongols' decision to destroy the celebrated town was made in advance. A year before, Chinggis Khan's son-in-law Toquchar met his death at Nishapur as he unsuccessfully tried to reduce the defiant city. His widow was now accompanying the army to make sure her husband's death was avenged. Unnerved by the brutality of the enemy, which had forced the peasantry to erect the siege engines under fire and drove them in front of its ranks to serve as arrow fodder, the commander of the city sent a deputation led by the chief judge of Khorasan to Tolui to offer submission. But having already made the decision to wipe out Nishapur and its inhabitants, Tolui rejected the peace offer and continued the fierce assault. Continuing their determined attack, the Mongols poured into the city at several points, and the street battles turned into a massacre and genocide. Tolui had heard that during the destruction of Merv many people had saved their lives by lying down among the corpses, so he ordered all bodies beheaded and constructed three pyramids (*kala-munar*), one of men's heads, a second of women's heads, and a third of children's heads. Then the walls and buildings were pulled down. The killing and destruction continued for fifteen days, during which no one's life was spared. Even the dogs and cats in the city were killed. Of the inhabitants, only a few hundred men who were skilled artisans were left alive. The place disappeared altogether, and the Mongols sowed barley on the site. Lest some should find refuge in underground places, troops were left near the ruins to slay anyone who might creep out later into the daylight. Nishapur never returned to its glorious days.

Leaving Nishapur in utter ruin, Tolui sent a detachment to Tus, the home of Ferdousi, the highly revered Persian poet and author of the *Shah-Nama*, the national epic of greater Iran. Tus shared the fate of Merv and Nishapur and was turned into ruins after being looted by the Mongol hordes. The Mongol army then turned east and marched against Herat—the last city standing among the quartet of Khorasani cultural titans. Herat takes its name from *Hariva*, the Avestan name for the Hari Rud River, translating as the "Golden River." Herat's prosperity was linked to the fertile valley of the Golden River that gently meanders through the verdant havens of the province. Herodotus (484–425 BC) described it as the breadbasket of Central Asia. It was the site where Alexander built the Alexandria Aria, denoting its ancient name. Herat, as a political and commercial roundabout, connected West Asia with Central and South Asia. It is not unusual that Rumi (1207–1273) called Herat "the pearl of Khorasan."[42] According to Mustawfi (1281–1349), prior to the Mongol invasion, during the time of the Ghorids' rule in Herat (1148–1215), there were 12,000 shops, all of them fully occupied, 6,000 public bathhouses, 359 colleges, and 444,000 houses inhabited by a settled population.[43] But the Mongols' double destruction of the celebrated town (1221 and again in 1222) eventually turned it into ruins—the signs of which are visible even today.

On his way to Herat, Tolui ravaged the area with raiding parties that he sent around the countryside. He sent a messenger named Zanbour in advance to call for the submission of the city. The governor, Malik Shamsuddin Mohammad Jawzjani, rejected the call and put Tolui's messenger to the sword. Predictably, that event presaged the brutal retribution to come. After its destructive march, the Mongol army camped before the ramparts of Herat and laid siege to the town. Saif Herawi wrote that there were 190,000 fighters in Herat ready to defend their town, surely an inflated number.[44] Governor Shamsuddin had determined to fight the enemy to the last. For eight days after the siege started, the Heratis put up a desperate resistance to the Mongols' assault, which was launched simultaneously from all sides. The defenders fought from the walls and repeatedly sallied out until the gallant governor fell while repulsing one of the enemy's storming parties. Then the city sent a deputation to Tolui offering peace. Tolui consented and, surprisingly, spared the inhabitants and slaughtered only the 12,000-man garrison. It is likely that the reason for his leniency was his hasty recall by Chinggis Khan to deal with an emerging threat posed by Jalaluddin Mungaberti, the son of Sultan Mohammad Khwarazm-Shah, whom he succeeded and who had raised a new army in Ghazni to face the Mongol conqueror.

The fall of these great cities resulted in a massive loss of civilian life, as the Mongols had no intention of taking prisoners. Contemporary sources put the number of people killed in Nishapur and Herat alone at more than four million.[45] Given the population of the area and the size of Khorasan's major cities, such numbers are grossly inflated. The major cities in the thirteenth century were hardly populated by more than 30,000–70,000 at the most. For example, the population of Nishapur in the early eleventh century was estimated at 30,000–40,000.[46] The population of Herat is exaggerated even in greater proportions by the fourteenth-century chronicler Hamdullah Mustawfi, who claims that prior to the Mongol invasion there were 444,000 houses occupied by a settled population.[47] But during the Mongol invasion, tens of thousands of refugees from the suburbs and outlying areas swelled the population of the major cities and protected towns.

The historical demographers Tertius Chandler and Gerald Fox estimate the populations of some major cities in Central Asia and Khorasan at the beginning of the thirteenth century. These include Samarkand at 80,000–100,000; Nishapur, 70,000; Merv, 70,000; Balkh, 30,000; Herat, 40,000; and Otrar, Urgenj, and Bukhara unknown but less than 70,000.[48] Juwayni reports that about 1.2 million of the population were massacred in Urgenj. The number of Merv's citizens killed after the city surrendered to Tolui's army is claimed to be 1.3 million. Given the estimated populations of the cities and the limited time the Mongols spent to execute their killing spree, these numbers sound incredible.[49]

John Mann's calculations suggest that in the thirteenth century the population settled in the total territory of Khwarazm and Khorasan—with about twenty major cities and a thousand small and big villages—is estimated at five million. He assumes that, if 25 percent of the people were killed in the invasion, then perhaps 1.25 million were massacred in that area over two years. He concludes that the number of deaths was still "one of the biggest mass killings in absolute terms in history; and in proportional terms, perhaps the biggest, an equivalent of the 25–30 per cent population cut meted out by Europe's greatest catastrophe, the black death."[50]

The fall of the major cities in Khorasan failed to end the anti-Mongol resistance. Taking advantage of rugged terrain and strong fortresses, many towns in Ghor, Gharjistan, Bamian, Ghazni, Parwan, and some other remote areas continued to resist repeated attacks by Mongol detachments. One such fortified town, located at a key strategic position, was Taleqan and its hard-to-reach fortress, the Nusrat Koh. Some modern authors have mistaken the location of this city with the Taleqan of Tokharistan situated east of Balkh. It stood at a seven-day journey west of Balkh on the lofty hill Koh-i-Nuqrah, meaning the "Silver Mount," after the presence of a silver mine on its top. Hudud Al-'Alam (982 AD) makes distinctions between the Taloqan of Marv Rud and the one in Tokharistan. He wrote that the western Taloqan was located in the frontier of Guzganan (Jawzjan).[51] Ibn Hauqal reports that Taleqan was located at a three-day journey from Merv ar-Rud (modern Murghab) in the west and at the same distance from Sheberghan in the east.[52] Medieval Muslim geographer Estakhri described the distance from Balkh to Taleqan in the west as six stages. He put Merv ar-Rud at the same distance from Taleqan and wrote that the Taleqan lies among mountains and has running water and gardens.[53] These descriptions place the Taleqan of Khorasan at a point not far from today's Maimana at the foot of the Turkistan Range, which stands on the main east–west highway of ancient Khorasan.[54]

In the spring of 1221, Chinggis ordered several detachments to reduce the resisting cities and fortresses around Ghor, Gharjistan, and Tokharistan. The route of most of these expeditions ran past Nusrat Koh. The defenders often sallied out to attack the passing Mongol columns while local 'Ayarran (public commandos) raided and ambushed enemy forces for plunder. After months of failed ventures, Chinggis Khan decided to move personally against the stronghold. From his camp at the Nu'man hills and Ka'ab plains between Balkh and Taleqan, the khan led his forces to Nusrat Koh. The defenders had vowed to fight to the last for "attainment of the glory of martyrdom."[55] The Mongols finally overcame the besieged and burst into the town, massacred the rest of the inhabitants, and destroyed the fortress. The siege lasted between seven and ten months, according to contemporary authorities.[56] While Chinggis Khan was destroying Nusrat Koh, his son Tolui joined his father after ravaging the major cities of Khorasan.

Ghazna Emerges as a New Center of Resistance

In the winter of 1221, Ghazna (Ghazni), the renowned center of power in medieval Afghanistan, became a thriving anti-Mongol bastion, drawing several Khorasani military leaders who had lost their battles against the Mongols. Military activities in the city surged after the new Khwarazmian king, Sultan Jalaluddin Mungaberti, headed to the town to mobilize native forces and the remnants of the old regime's army and retake the field against the Mongol invaders. During the rule of his father, Sultan Mohammad II, Prince Jalaluddin oversaw the eastern provinces of Ghor, including Ghazna, following their annexation from the last Ghorid ruler in 1215. Therefore, Jalaluddin maintained a strong connection to the city and commanded wide support among various tribes and ethnic forces in the area. But the political and military upheavals that rapidly consumed the area, along with the Mongol blitzkrieg through Transoxiana and Khorasan, created an unstable political environment. A power struggle between Ghorid, Khwarazmian, and Turkic warlords led to a volatile military situation.

Malik Ikhtiaruddin Khar-post, an experienced and valiant Ghori leader, was in command of Ghazna. The malik raised about 130,000 horsemen, "all brave soldiers and completely armed, with the intention of undertaking" offensive operations against Chinggis Khan's forces, which at that time were encamped at the Pushtaht-i-Nu'man between Balkh and Taleqan.[57] However, he was overthrown and assassinated by his main rival in power, Amin Malik, the former governor of Herat and a leader of a Qanquli Turkish division fighting Mongols in Sistan. The tragedy undermined the military preparations and caused major political confusion. Most of the troops raised by Malik Ikhtiaruddin were disbanded and dispersed, and the government in the city changed hands several times.

Meanwhile, Sultan Jalaluddin Mungaberti was on the road again, heading south from Urgenj to Nishapur. He reached Nishapur in February 1221 and stayed briefly before the Mongol army under Tolui arrived. The shocking influence of the Mongol invasion and massacres made it difficult for Jalaluddin to raise an army in Khorasan, so he headed southeast to Sistan on the way to Ghazna, his potential power base. After leaving Nishapur, he felt that his small party was being trailed by Mongol scouts, who he managed to evade by forced marches covering 120 miles in one day from Nishapur to Zuzan northwest of Herat. Then, eluding the enemy intelligence, Jalaluddin proceeded to Sistan, where Amin Malik joined him with his 10,000 Qanquli troops and continued on to Ghazna, where they arrived in the early spring of 1221.

The sultan was received warmly in Ghazna and was able to settle the internal disputes that haunted the politics in the city. Many tribal contingents consisting of Turks, Ghori, Tajiks, and Khalaj as well as the highlanders from the surrounding hills, including Ghilzai Pashtuns, joined his cause. This soon coalesced into a major army of 60,000–70,000 troops.[58] Jalaluddin's chronicler Mohammad ibn Ahmad Nesawi notes that with 30,000 troops Jalaluddin entered Ghazna, where another army of the same size joined him. This new army consisted of Turkmen under Saifuddin Aghraq, Afghans under Muzaffar Malik, Balkhi troops under A'zam Malik, and Qarluqs under Hasan. The combined forces were now a significantly large army under a capable leader, which worried Chinggis Khan. To deal with this emerging threat, the Mongol Khan recalled his sons from the military expeditions in Khwarazm and Khorasan. His sons Chaghatay and Ogdai returned from Urgenj and other places on the Amu Darya while Tolui came from Herat. But his eldest son, Juji, defied the order due to being superseded by Ogdai during the Urgenj campaign and moved deeper into the steppes north of the Aral Sea and began to establish the khanate of Qipchaq, known later as the "Golden Horde." He never again saw his father. The combined Mongol army went into the neighboring mountains for its summer encampment and in the autumn of 1221 began the campaign against Sultan Jalaluddin Mungaberti.

From the Plains of Parwan to the Banks of the Sind River

The Hindu Kush massif was the major barrier separating the Mongol forces from Jalaluddin's area of influence south of the mountains. Control of the Hindu Kush passes was critical to both sides. Both occupied advantageous geographic positions there. Jalaluddin moved his camp to Parwan south of the Hindu Kush to control all major routes that extended from there to Kabul and Ghazna in the south, to Baghlan and Bamian in the north, and to Nangrahar and Peshawar in the east. Chinggis Khan ordered a strong advance detachment of possibly 8,000–10,000[59] troops commanded by his adopted brother Shiki-Qutuqu to observe the activities of Jalaluddin and to secure the passes across the Hindu Kush. The detachment took a direct route to the northern foot of the Hindu Kush, where one of its reconnaissance parties moved forward as far as the village of Wallian in the Andarab area. Jalaluddin's forces destroyed the detachment almost to the man. Shiki-Qutuqu pushed forward and crossed the Hindu Kush through the Wallian Pass and descended onto the Parwan plains near the confluence of the Ghorband and Panjsher Rivers. At that point, the Mongol advance forces came face to face with Jalaluddin's army.

The military action in Parwan was greatly influenced by the nature of the terrain. It was not suitable for cavalry charges, the Mongols' tried-and-true tactic. The first day of the encounter ended inconclusively as both sides attempted to get into a suitable position on the Parwan plains (between today's Charikar and Jabul-Seraj) and across the farmlands and orchards between the mouth of the Ghorband Valley and the Panj-sher River. The Mongols, with their backs to the mountain walls, had limited lines of retreat through the Panjsher and Ghorband Valleys, whereas Jalaluddin's army enjoyed a vast area of maneuver to the south as well as access to support bases in the rear.

Preparing for the next day, the Mongol commander ordered dummy figures mounted on spare horses so that it would appear at first glance that the Mongols had been significantly reinforced. However, Jalaluddin's army depended more on tactical superiority than numerical dominance. Accordingly, Jalaluddin ordered his first ranks to dismount, for archers on foot were superior to mounted bowmen on terrain that was unsuitable for cavalry. Dismounted archers and infantry bowmen could effectively launch showers of arrows against mounted troops. The Mongols opened the battle with an attack on the left wing of the army of Ghazna, only to receive a withering rain of arrows from the dismounted cavalry, and were forced to retire in confusion. Next, the Mongol army advanced along the entire battle line, and a fierce fight between the foot archers of the army of Ghazna and the mounted Mongol warriors ensued. As soon as the Mongol attack was repulsed, Jalaluddin ordered his line to remount and charge. The result was a rapid breakdown of the Mongol ranks and a desperate struggle to withdraw through a few narrow defiles. Jalaluddin won a complete victory; less than half of the Mongol troops escaped. The rest fell in the battle or were taken prisoner and killed after being tortured.

Even though Jalaluddin won the military battle, he lost the political game. The victory was thwarted by his own failure to keep the heterogeneous force together after the battle. Had he maintained his united army, he would have gained the opportunity to block the advance of Chinggis Khan with a fair chance of success. The Battle of Parwan was the first major test of the Mongol forces' ability to face an enemy in a pitched battle on difficult terrain in Afghanistan. They lost miserably. A dispute over the division of the spoils of war between Amin Malik of the Qanquli Turks and Saifuddin Aghraq of the Turkmen led to a personal argument during which the former struck the latter across the face with his riding whip. The dispute turned into ethnic tensions, which Jalaluddin

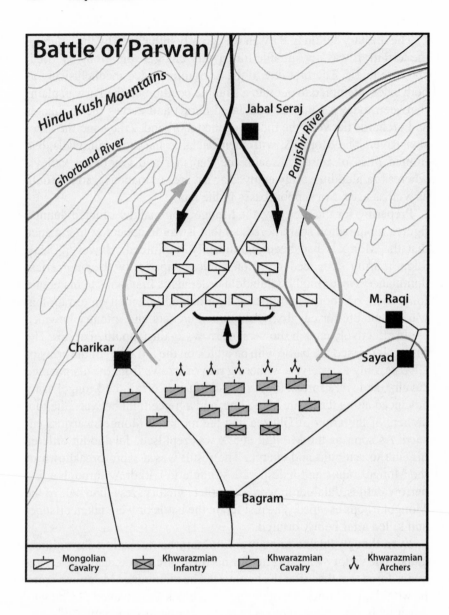

Battle of Parwan

Hindu Kush Mountains

Ghorband River

Jabal Seraj

Panjshir River

M. Raqi

Charikar

Sayad

Bagram

Symbol		Symbol		Symbol		Symbol	
	Mongolian Cavalry		Khwarazmian Infantry		Khwarazmian Cavalry		Khwarazmian Archers

failed to resolve. Consequently, a large portion of the army, including the Turkmen contingents of Saifuddin Aghraq and those of A'zam Malik and the Afghan highlanders under Muzaffar Malik, abandoned Jalaluddin's camp. He was left with only 20,000 Qanquli Turks under Amin Malik and some other troops to face roughly 70,000 Mongol troops under Chinggis Khan. Jalaluddin decided to retreat to the east in the hope of getting another chance to deal with the enemy.

Meanwhile, the combined Mongol army under Chinggis Khan and his three sons left its summer camp around Taleqan in early autumn and moved south behind the advance detachment that had deployed earlier to the Hindu Kush. Contemporary sources offer conflicting accounts of the khan's passage and the route he took to reach Ghazna, Jalaluddin's stronghold. Given the sequence of Chinggis Khan's military operations and the geography of the area, it is likely that he moved from the vicinity of today's Maimana south to the fortress of Gurziwan in Faryab Province, where he faced stiff resistance. It took him a full month to destroy and massacre its inhabitants. From there, the Mongol army took a southeasterly route through the Haftad-Gardesh Pass to the Balkhab District in modern Sar-i Pul Province down to the Yakawlang District and finally to Bamian. In recent years, this network of backroads was often used by drug traffickers in Afghanistan to transport their loads across the Hindu Kush.

Chinggis Khan's advance was hindered by the city of Bamian, the ancient center of Buddhism and a place widely renowned for its massive statues of Buddha carved in the cliffs that flanked the Bamian Valley. During the Islamic period, Bamian became one of the bastions of power in central Afghanistan and was one of the capitals of the Ghorid Empire in the twelfth century. Bamian could hardly resist the overwhelming Mongol forces that had laid siege to it. Much worse, a single incident sealed the town's fate. During a survey of the defenses of Bamian, an arrow from the walls struck and killed Chinggis Khan's favorite grandson, Moatugin, the 12-year-old son of Chaghatay. Chinggis vowed to spare no one in the city. Over seven days, the walls were battered down, scaled, and assaulted. Chaghatay's wife is said to have led the assault. When the city fell, the town was totally destroyed, no prisoners were taken, no booty was collected, and even the dogs and cats in the city were killed.[60] The signs of the Mongol holocaust are visible even today in the ruins near the modern city of Bamian. The ruins are known among the people as *shahr-i gholgola* (the city of screams), supposedly because screams can still be heard in the deafening silence of the rubble. Bamian was thus destroyed, although the statues of Buddha survived, only to be demolished nearly eight centuries later in 2001 at the hands of the Taliban, linked to the global terrorist network al-Qaeda.

Leaving the lifeless city of Bamian behind, Chinggis Khan led his army through the Ghorband Valley to Parwan, where he inspected the site of his advance army's disastrous defeat at the hands of Jalaluddin. Moving at breakneck speed, the Mongols headed for Ghazna with few stops along the way. But when they reached the town, they learned that Jalaluddin had left fifteen days before, traveling eastward and intending to move across the Indus River.

On his way to the Indus, Jalaluddin called on his supporters in Afghanistan to join him for a final showdown with the enemy. But Chinggis Khan was fast on his trail, blocking reinforcements from reaching Jalaluddin and trying to stop him from crossing the river. It was a race against time. To slow down the Mongol advance, Jalaluddin, according to Mohammad Nesawi, made a night attack on the enemy's vanguard at Gardez and cut it down almost to a man. Nevertheless, he failed to delay the Mongols long enough to gain the time and space needed for an unimpeded crossing of the Indus. Citing the contemporary chroniclers of the historic fourteenth-century figure Tamerlane, some modern authors suggest that the Battle of the Indus took place at the point where Tamerlane later crossed the Indus to invade India (1398)—a place below the Nilab crossing north of Kalabagh.[61] Another nineteenth-century survey of the Indus identifies Nilab as the point where Tamerlane crossed the river.[62] The sequence of events and the geography, however, suggest that Chinggis Khan may have followed the main route from Ghazna to Gardez in the east and from there moved along the well-trodden Touchi Valley to Bannu and reached the Indus River at Kalabagh in today's Mianwali District of the Punjab Province of Pakistan. When the Khwarazmian forces reached the riverbank, the boats intended for crossing had not yet arrived, and the Mongol hordes caught up with them. Jalaluddin's 30,000 troops were pitted against a Mongol army that was more than twice as large. There was no time to cross, so Jalaluddin deployed his army for battle in a suitable location, with its left wing anchored on a mountain that extended to the river and was hard to cross or turn, while its right wing was protected by a bend in the river against flank attacks. Being superior in numbers, the Mongol army formed an arc around Jalaluddin's battle line.

The battle began at dawn on November 24, 1221, with a Mongol attack across the entire front.[63] Jalaluddin's right wing, under Amin Malik, repulsed the attack by the Mongols' left wing, while Jalaluddin himself broke Chinggis Khan's center. For a time, the Mongol conqueror was in personal peril, since a horse was killed under him during the struggle. Although Jalaluddin was able to hold his own and even win a victory,

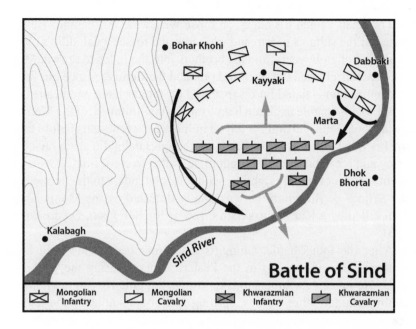

Battle of Sind

| Mongolian Infantry | Mongolian Cavalry | Khwarazmian Infantry | Khwarazmian Cavalry |

his lines were being threatened from two sides. Chinggis Khan ordered 10,000 chosen men under Bela Noyon to cross the mountain on Jalaluddin's left at all costs. The Mongols crept over the cliffs and pushed forward until they were in the rear of the weakened left wing and center of Jalaluddin's position. Then, Chinggis Khan led his reserve cavalry force against Jalaluddin's victorious right and contained it while launching simultaneously a flank attack against Jalaluddin's left wing to link up with Bela Noyon's force. The Mongols closed in from both sides. At this point, the Khwarazmian force was nearly surrounded with the river at its back. Jalaluddin rallied 7,000 men and made a desperate charge that pushed back the Mongol attack for some distance. Jalaluddin then turned, quickly jumped on a fresh horse, threw off his armor, and raced to the Indus. His horse leaped from a high bank (given variously as from 20 to 60 feet above the water).[64] With his shield on his shoulder and his standard in his hand, he plunged into the Indus and safely reached the far bank. Impressed by the gallant move of his enemy, Chinggis Khan spurred to the riverbank, gazing at the fleeing prince. He could not resist admiring his defeated foe and even forbade his soldiers from shooting arrows at him. He exclaimed: "How could Shah Mohammad [Khwarazm-Shah] be the father of this man!"[65]

The khan vented his anger on those who were left behind. He disposed of the sultan's harem and treasures and tossed Jalaluddin's eldest son, a lad of eight years, and his brothers into the Indus to drown. Mongol generals crossed the river and pursued the fugitive prince but failed to capture him. Jalaluddin disappeared on the far bank and headed for Delhi. Being unable to obtain help from Sultan Iltutmish, of the Mamluk dynasty of Delhi, Jalaluddin stayed in India for a few years before making his way back to western Persia. Although Jalaluddin again raised an army and reestablished his kingdom, he failed to consolidate power. He spent the rest of his life fighting Mongols, pretenders to the throne, and the Seljuqs of Rum until he was finally defeated by the Mongols and then killed by a Kurdish assassin hired by the Seljuqs in Diyarbakir in 1231.

After the Indus battle, Chinggis Khan marched up the right bank of the Indus and camped in the Peshawar plain during the winter of 1222. He sent a detachment to take Multan but failed to capture it. More columns raided other valleys, chasing Jalaluddin's allies in the region. Amin Malik was finally caught and executed. Jawzjani reported that Chinggis Khan wished to take a shortcut to China and reconquer the Tangut Empire in that northwestern Chinese province. But Sultan Iltutmish of Delhi refused to cooperate, and the terrain and severe climate frustrated the plan.[66] Renewed resistance in Afghanistan forced the Mongol Khan to return west, and in the early spring of 1222 he set up camp in Kabul, from where he launched a new campaign to subdue resurgent native forces in Afghanistan.

"Coming Back to Life"—Renewed Anti-Mongol Uprisings

Jalaluddin's victory against the Mongol forces in Parwan resonated across Afghanistan, inspiring many cities and towns to revolt against the brutal enemy. In Khorasan, Ghor, and Sistan, local rulers, who mostly acted independently after the fall of the Kwarazmian kingdom, put the Mongol-appointed governors (*darugha -shahnas*) to the sword and rose in rebellion. The resistance was particularly widespread in the mountainous tracts of Ghor and Gharjistan and the western city of Herat. When the news reached Chinggis Khan, he expressed his anger by asking "from whence have these people whom I have killed come to life again?" He then ordered that henceforth "the heads of people shall be separated from their bodies, in order that they may not come to life again."[67]

Chinggis Khan ordered his son Ogdai to destroy Ghazna, which he himself was unable to deal with earlier while pursuing Jalaluddin. Ogdai moved at the head of several *tumens* and dispatched raiding hordes to rebellious cities and fortresses. He personally invested Ghazna and, after capturing the town, drove the inhabitants out under the pretext of taking a census and then slaughtered them brutally, except for the artisans, who were spared to serve the victor. The population of Ghazna at the time can be estimated from the reported presence of 12,000 madrasas in the city.[68]

A strong army commanded by Ilchi Kadai moved to take and destroy Herat. The force is said to have numbered 70,000,[69] though that number is questionable. Given Chinggis Khan's military campaign in the autumn of 1221 into the winter of 1222 in eastern Afghanistan, and the size of his available army, it seems it would have been impossible to spare such a large army for operations in Herat, even if some contingents were contributed to the force from other Mongol camps. Furthermore, the distance from Ghazni to Herat by the shortest road through the troubled Ghor territory is about 600 miles, which might have taken a large army with enormous logistics requirements more than a month to reach despite the Mongols' rapid movements. It is likely that the force was not more than 20,000.

Herat was spared a year earlier when it submitted to Tolui; he had killed 12,000 of Jalaluddin's adherents instead. Since then, the Heratis had repaired the defenses and stored away arms and supplies under the pretext that they were for Mongol use should the need arise. In early spring 1222, the Mongols laid siege to Herat after ravaging the districts around the city. The defenders were led by Malik Mubariz-u-Din, who had moved to Herat after his city, Firozkoh, was captured and destroyed by the Mongols. The Heratis fought desperately, knowing what their fate was if they failed. The murderous siege lasted six months and seventeen days. The inhabitants suffered enormously. Faced by the hardship of a tight blockade and relentless attacks, influential citizens who wanted to surrender won increasing support, and dissension within the ranks of the garrison hampered the defense. Finally, the city opened its gates to the Mongols, who entered Herat on June 14, 1222. They began a weeklong orgy of executions, pillaging, burning, and destruction during which, according to Jawzjani, 1.6 million people perished.[70] Chinggis Khan received the choicest plunder, plus several thousand young slaves. A few days after the Mongol army departed the devastated city, it sent back a detachment of 2,000 troopers to the ruins of Herat to wipe out any remaining signs of life. The detachment found 2,000 miserable wretches who had survived the cataclysm. They soon met their deaths under the Mongols' swords. Sixteen persons who had taken refuge in a steep mountain returned after the Mongols were gone and joined a few others who also came back. Forty survivors took refuge in the ruins of the main mosque of the city.

During these renewed military operations in Afghanistan, Chinggis Khan was encamped in Parwan south of the Hindu Kush, where he was visited by a Chinese Taoist monk, who reported that the khan stayed there until October 3, 1222.[71] As Sultan Jalaluddin was still active in Lahore, the khan ordered Bela Noyon with two *tumens* (5,000–6,000 men) to sweep through Punjab; at the same time, he sent Chaghatay with another force of equal size south to push through Baluchistan and Makran to the Indian Ocean. Neither force caught up with Jalaluddin, who had left for western Persia. Bela Noyon marched to Multan and then wheeled north through Firozpur and Lahore, but the oppressive summer heat forced the Mongols to return to the hills. Similarly, Chaghatay rode through Baluchistan to Tez on the coast but had to move north, where he lost many men from starvation and thirst in the Makran Desert. After reaching Sistan he divided his force, one half heading to the Hindu Kush, where it joined the main Mongol camp, while he himself led the remainder to Farah and thence to Bukhara.

The War of the Fortresses

The year 1222 was one of the most terrible periods ever experienced by the mountain fortresses of central Afghanistan as the Mongols penetrated through the most rugged districts of Ghor and Gharjistan to reduce the impregnable mountain fortresses between Ghazna and Herat. Although the Mongol detachments failed to capture any of these remote strongholds by frontal assault, they starved to death thousands of inhabitants by siege. For centuries, these fortresses were the bastions of resistance to outsiders and the key to controlling the adjacent valleys. Invading armies might control the foothills of the Hindu Kush, but they usually left the central alpine vastness free. When the Mongol armies penetrated the area, they had to keep the major citadels besieged for months and years. Why did the invading Mongols tie up their contingents for such a long time when they had other strategic priorities? One assumption is that the Mongols had no keen interest in capturing and garrisoning the remote fortresses, but because such strongholds were the key to controlling the more attractive and fertile plains and pastures below, they could hardly leave them in hostile hands. Furthermore, some fortresses in Gharjistan dominated the main routes in the north between Balkh and Merv ar-Rud and had crucial security significance.

In the summer of 1222, after the destruction of Herat, the Mongol army divided into two divisions. One division marched into Sistan, and the other advanced east into the territory of Ghor and appeared at the foot of the fortress of Kaliun, which stood about 80 miles northeast of Herat[72] near the border with Badghis.[73] The place was known later on as Nerretu[74] (Nerre-tau)—a possible Mongolian name.[75] Kaliun's fortifications were extremely strong. The only access to the stronghold was through a high narrow ridge where men had to climb single file to reach the fort. The place was beyond the reach of arrows and of stones shot by catapults. Following three failed attacks to reduce the fortress, the Mongols set up a blockade, which according to Jawzjani lasted more than a year. The inhabitants depended on a diet of dried meat, clarified butter, and pistachio nuts until they were starved to death inside the fortress before it fell to the attackers.

Soon, the fortress of Fiwar faced a similar fate. This fort was located about 40 miles from the Kaliun in the Qadis (Kadis) District, which is still known by the same name in the Badghis Province bordering Herat and Ghor Provinces. Unable to take the stronghold by assault, the Mongols blockaded the fortress until virtually all the inhabitants were starved to death. Jawzjani writes that when the Mongols entered the fortress there were not more than seven men alive, and out of them four or five were sick.[76] Thus the two strongest fortresses in Ghor fell.

Firozkoh, the seat of government of Ghor, resisted the initial attacks by the Mongol detachments and forced them to retire from the city in 1221. But when Chinggis Khan ordered his son Ogdai to crush the renewed resistance in Ghor and Khorasan in 1222, a body of Mongol troops made a surprise assault on Firozkoh and massacred the population after capturing the city. Firozkoh, the capital of the Ghorid kings, which had made a great name in Khorasan as the historical powerbase of the Ghorid Empire, was completely destroyed by the Mongol hordes and never recovered. The magnificent Minaret of Jam, still standing in the Sharak District of Ghor Province, is suggested to be the location of the lost city of Firozkoh.

The defenders at the fortress of Tulak, southwest of Firozkoh, defeated the Mongols. According to Jawzjani, the inhabitants of Tulak waged a four-year war against the Mongols, during which Jawzjani himself participated on several occasions, and reported that Tulak never fell into the hands of the Mongols. With the departure of Chinggis Khan for Mongolia in 1223, military activities in remote areas slowed down, and for a while there was calm across the mountain valleys. In later years, the Tulakis obtained the mandate of self-rule from the Mongol Khan, Guyuk Khan (r. 1246–1248), under Mongol suzerainty.

Marching Homeward

Far from experiencing a peaceful homeward journey, the Mongols left a bloody trail of devastation as they passed through ruins on their return eastward. Chinggis Khan destroyed more human life than any other known conqueror. In Transoxiana, Khorasan, and Afghanistan, he massacred hundreds of thousands or millions of people over four years. There is no strong evidence that the mass killings were inspired by religious or racial animosity; they represented a thirst for power, instincts for pillage, and sheer revenge. Still, according to Muslim chroniclers of the time, Chinggis's armies massacred 5–6 million people during four years—an average of more than 4,000 souls each day. Although such figures are much exaggerated, the carnage was clearly enormous, and the disaster did not end there. For decades and centuries, the devastating aftermath of the invasion continued to take heavy tolls on the population in the affected lands. Many of those who survived in the ruined cities or took refuge in remote mountain havens must have perished from the inability to obtain shelter or food, since the area could not support life and was depopulated. Quick recovery was hampered by the destruction of the irrigation systems and the lack of a sufficient labor force to keep the canals free from silt and restore the farmlands in Khorasan to agriculture. The situation led to a gradual process of desertification of once fertile and verdant suburbs and adjoining valleys around major urban centers. Merv, Nishapur, Herat, Balkh, Bamian, Ghazna, Bukhara, and Samarkand barely recovered after centuries, while some places never regained their resourcefulness. When Ibn Battuta visited the area in 1333, he described Kabul as a village and Ghazna—once the capital of a vast empire—as ruins.

The Mongols' massacre matches other mass killings in history. In the words of John Mann, "What happened in Merv, in Urgench [Urgenj], and across the region suggests a comparison with the Nazi Holocaust itself, for there are some terrible similarities in the attitude of Teloi's Mongols and that of those who perpetrated the Final Solution."[77]

Chinggis Khan died in August 1227 after defeating the Tangut kingdom. According to his wishes, his body was returned to his birthplace
in Mongolia and buried there without a trace. The bulk of his approximately 130,000-strong central army passed to his son Tolui, while the
rest was divided among his other sons, his brothers, and his mother.
The impact of the destruction caused by Chinggis Khan's invasion
of Transoxiana and Khorasan lasted for centuries. His bitterness over
Khwarazm-Shah's massacre of his merchants had snowballed into an
extreme viciousness vented against its subjects. He lived and died amid
bloodshed, fire, and destruction. In his review of Chinggis Khan, Harold
Lamb noted that "to visualize this man we must actually approach him,
among his people and on the surface of the earth as it existed seven
hundred years [sic] ago."[78] So to Lamb, Chinggis Khan remains "a good
deal of mystery. . . . Did Genghis Khan have a profound plan for the
conquest of the world, or was he an inspired barbarian? We only know
that he was wise, with a wisdom that proved terrible to the world we
live in."[79] Rashiduddin Fazlullah, a contemporary chronicler at the time,
recorded an account of Chinggis Khan's debate with two of his top commanders on "what makes a man the most happy and satisfied person?"
When he was unconvinced by the views of his colleagues, he defined a
man's gratification in these words: "The greatest joy is to conquer one's
enemies, to destroy them, to seize their property, to see their families in
tears, to ride their horses and to possess their daughters and wives."[80]

Upon the death of Chinggis Khan, the Mongol armies were spread
across a vast area stretching from the Caucasus to China. Some divisions were engaged in the Caucasus and southern Russia while others
were roaming the devastated expanses of Central Asia, Khorasan, and
Afghanistan. There were yet more divisions locked in wars to expand or
consolidate the Mongols' control in the Chinese provinces. The absence
of an overall strong leader such as Chinggis Khan threatened the unity
of command that had existed under the late khan. Although Chinggis
Khan appointed his son Ogdai as his successor and advised his brothers against infighting, his descendants failed to resist the temptation of
competing for dominance at the expense of their kinsmen a few years
after his death. Chinggis Khan divided the conquered lands among his
sons at the end of his life, but there were no well-defined borders, and
this made infighting in later years inevitable. The division was more
of a clan-based allocation than territorial distribution. The khan appointed tribes and clans deployed in certain loosely defined *urdus* to
each son where the borders met one another. The Mongol khanate, ruled

by the descendants of Chinggis Khan's eldest son, Juji (d. 1226–1227), in the steppes north of the Black Sea and the Caspian and known as the Golden Horde, bordered the territory of the descendant of Tolui, a younger son of the khan, known as the Ilkhanids. Meanwhile, the territory of Chaghatay, the second son of Chinggis Khan, which covered Kashghar (now the Xinjiang-Uyghur autonomous region of China), the Transoxiana, Badakhshan, Balkh, and Ghazna, known as the Chaghatay khanate, touched on the lands claimed by the Il-Khans and the Golden Horde, causing occasional collisions among them.

The immediate successors of Chinggis Khan—his sons—who shared the empire did not survive long after their father's death. His eldest son, Juji, died shortly before his father's death. True to his father's decision, Tolui made every effort and arrangement to help Ogdai mount the seat of overall Mongol rulers, the Khaqan, in 1229. He died three years later in 1232. Ogdai and Chaghatay both died in 1241. An interregnum of four years followed Ogdai's death as a rivalry among the cousins led to stagnation during the regency period preceding the election of Ogdai's son Guyuk Khan as a new Khaqan in the *quriltai* of 1246. Two years later, following Guyuk Khan's death, the Mongols' imperial power shifted to the sons of Tolui. Tolui fathered four sons; the eldest of them, Mungke (Mangu), was elected the great Mongol Khan (Khaqan), and the succession thus passed over the sons of Guyuk. Mungke appointed his brother Qubilai (Kublai) to rule the conquered provinces of China, where he founded the Yuen dynasty, while another brother Hulagu (Hulaku) was appointed the ruler in Persia, and he, too, founded a dynasty known as the Ilkhans.

During the thirteenth century and the first half of the fourteenth century, the territory of today's Afghanistan was divided between the dominions of the Chaghatay khanate of Central Asia and the Ilkhanids of Persia. The western and southern provinces of Afghanistan, including Herat, Farah, Kandahar down to Baluchistan, and Sind, were ruled by the Ilkhanids, while the northern, northeastern, and eastern parts of Afghanistan, including Balkh, Badakhshan, Kabul, and Ghazna and other eastern districts, were considered part of the Chaghatay khanate. The military history of Afghanistan during this period features three major trends.

1. Clashes of rival Mongol khanates along their loosely defined borders.
2. The struggle of native principalities to survive amid competing Mongol colonists.

3. The massive displacement of the population and the changing social and political landscape.

The Clashes of the Khanates

In Afghanistan, the clashes among the Mongol khanates mostly involved the Chaghatay khanate and the Ilkhanids. However, while the former was often engaged in a power struggle in the east with the houses of Ogdai and Tolui, the latter was pulled into drawn-out conflicts in the west against the Mamluks of Egypt and the Seljuqs in Asia Minor. The Ilkhanids also had to deal with occasional incursions by the Golden Horde's armies into the north, mostly around the Caspian Sea. The intensity of inter-khanate power struggles in two divergent directions somehow spared Transoxiana, Khorasan, and Afghanistan from becoming the battlefield in major confrontations.

In the early fourteenth century, internal disturbances in both khanates and the rise of native principalities limited the capability of the Chaghtayids and the Ilkhanids to project power outside their territories. The Chaghtayids were split into eastern and western khanates, which were engaged in a constant power struggle. The Ilkhanids, as noted above, were engaged in a series of factional disputes and internal disturbances during the reign of Abu Sa'id (1316–1335) that undermined the integrity of his state and fragmented its central power.

The Native Kurt Dynasty

By the turn of the fourteenth century, the Mongol khanates exercised waning control over their peripheries. The local Kurt dynasty that had ruled over Herat, Ghor, and surrounding territories in Khorasan as a vassal to the Mongol overlords began in 1345 to stand up against the Ilkhanid kings. The Kurts were of native Ghori origin, and their lineage traced back to Tajuddin Uthman Marghini, the brother of 'Izzuddin Umar Marghini, the vizier of Sultan Ghiasuddin Mohammad ibn Sam (d. 1202) of the Ghorid Empire.

In 1263–1264, the Kurtid king established compliant relations with Hulagu, the Ilkhan leader, after some initial troubled encounters. Three years later, he accompanied Hulagu's successor, Abaqa Khan, in his war against Berke of the Golden Horde in 1266 in Baku and Darband and his expedition against Buraq Khan of the Chaghatayid khanate in 1270, where he fought gallantly and was reconfirmed as the ruler of greater Herat.

One of the major features of the reign of the founder of the dynasty, Malik Shamsuddin, was his long campaign to spread his authority into the lands his contemporaries called "Afghanistan," which covered the territories of the Pashtun tribes who were settled in the mountainous valleys and plains extending from the Indus River to Hindu Kush in the north and part of Baluchistan in the south. In his nine-year campaign (1249–1257), the Kurtid malik led expeditionary forces against several strongholds of "Afghanistan" to force the tribes to acknowledge his authority and pay him tribute. The Afghan tribes, who considered the Kurt ruler merely a vassal of the Mongol commanders, resisted his demand, claiming that "they had refused to pay taxes and tribute to Chinggis Khan how could they submit to his surrogates in the region."[81] Malik Shamsuddin led a long series of military campaigns into the territories of "Afghanistan" for temporary gains but no major strategic shifts.

Shamsuddin's dynamic son Fakhruddin was a patron of literature but also extremely religious. He is remembered for his brave stand against the Mongol overlords and his revolt against the Ilkhan Uljaytu at the turn of the fourteenth century. Shortly after his ascension, the ilkhan sent a force of 10,000 in 1307 to take Herat. The impregnable citadel of Herat (*Qala-i-Ikhtiaruddin*), which has been restored in recent years, was gallantly defended by Fakhruddin's commander Mohammad Sam. Fakhruddin, however, tricked the invaders by letting them occupy the city and then destroying them in close street-to-street combat. The Mongol commander Danish Bahadur was killed in the process. The account of this event, detailed by contemporary chroniclers, is a fascinating story of bravery, deception, treachery, and psychological warfare used by both sides. Although Uljaytu eventually brought Herat under his rule following the death of Malik Fakhruddin, the battle marked the beginning of the end of the Ilkhans' suzerainty over the Kurtid dynasty.

Fakhruddin's brother Ghiasuddin succeeded him. The most notable event of his reign (1307–1329) occurred during the invasion of Khorasan by Prince Yassaur Nikudari, who crossed the Amu Darya and overwhelmed the Ilkhanid army, which was defending the narrow defiles of Murghab. Yassaur plundered Khorasan as far as Mazenderan. However, after a protracted struggle in which Malik Ghiasuddin played a major part as an ally of the Ilkhans, Yassaur was compelled to withdraw to his appanage. His relative, Kepek Khan, of the Chaghatay khanate, who had an old grudge against him, killed the renegade prince.[82]

The decline of the Ilkhanids beginning under Abu-Sa'id (1316–1335) opened an opportunity for the Kurtids to act assertively and expand their influence in Khorasan. Mu'izzuddin Kurt (1331–1370) led two successful campaigns to Kirman and forced it to capitulate. The independence of the dynasty, however, was short-lived, as the successor of Mu'izzuddin, Ghiasuddin Pir Ali (1370–1389), faced the rising power of Amir Timur (Tamerlane), who at first treated him as a friend in 1376 then moved against him five years later. Timur occupied Herat and imprisoned Malik Ghiasuddin in Samarkand and finally killed him in 1389, ending the dynasty that had ruled from Herat for about a century and a half.

Massive Social Displacements

During the century after the Mongol flood subsided, major portions of the population in Khorasan and Afghanistan migrated to more secure areas in Punjab and northern India or drifted southwest to Persia, which had escaped the Mongol devastation. Meanwhile, large hordes of Turko-Mongol nomads found a home in the depopulated valleys and plains of the area and took control of the limitless lands that turned into steppes. The ruined cities of Khorasan attracted settlers from areas in the west that were not affected by the invasion. Meanwhile, the Mongol princes and aristocracy roamed Khorasan and Afghanistan, camping in places as they pleased and treating local leaders as their vassals.

The Kurt maliks conducted major rebuilding efforts in Ghor and Herat. Some of the descendants of Chinggis Khan also contributed to the effort. Ogdai, the Khan's immediate successor, was interested in rebuilding Herat, and in 1237 he sent some cloth weavers, who were exiled by his father from Herat to the eastern Turkistan town of Besh-Baligh, back to Herat to begin the repopulation of the city. The exiles returned home, restored agriculture, and repaired the irrigation systems in the province. They grew cotton and sent some of the cloth to "Afghanistan" (the land of Pashtun tribes) to raise funds for purchasing agriculture tools.[83]

One of the most debated issues related to this period of Afghanistan history is the origin of the Hazaras. They are commonly believed to have been the remnants of the Mongol military that settled in the areas devastated and depopulated by Chinggis Khan's army and his successors. The Hazaras' physical profile, facial bone structures, and parts of their culture and some words in their language resemble those of Mongolians and Central Asian Turks. The Mongolian ancestry of Hazara tribes is partially supported by genetic tests. "Hazara" most

likely derives from the Persian word for "thousand," which contemporary sources such as Rashiduddin used as the translation of the Mongol
word *ming* (or *Mingan*), a military unit of 1,000 soldiers at the time of
Chinggis Khan and afterward.[84] About 160 years after Chinggis's invasion, Tamerlane encountered elements of Hazara and Sadha military-
tribal units in upper Helmand and Urozgan who had settled in the area
during the invasion and later during the Chaghatayid period.[85] Modern
western authors, including Elphinstone, Burnes, Bellew, and Barthold,
believe that the Mongols settled their *Mingan* (Hazara) units to conquer
and colonize mountainous areas of Afghanistan. They later adopted the
local language and religion and were joined by other units which took
the Hazara designation to identify themselves along with the military
integration of tribes named after their commanders such as the *Hazara-
i Nikudari, Hazara-i Jermani, Hazara-i Aughani, Hazara-i Toumani,
Hazara-i Nawroozi, Hazara-i Khulm* and so on. This view is shared
by some modern Hazara authors in Afghanistan.[86] Faiz Mohammad
Kateb, the prominent Hazara writer of the twentieth century, considers
the Hazaras of Mongol and Tatar descent, which are divided into twelve
main tribes, or *Dai*. The first five of them are grouped into the Saada-
Soyka tribal confederacy including Dai-Zangi, Dai-Kundi, Di-Mirdad,
Dai-Miraksha, and Dai-Mirak. Five others are united in the Saada-Qabr
tribal confederation, which includes the Dai-Chopan, Dai-Khatay, Dai-
Nuri, Dai-Miri, and Dai-Folad. The Jaghori and Behssud are the two
other tribes divided into several subtribes.[87]

    The Hazara population of Afghanistan commonly believes that they
are of Mongolian stock and take pride in their "Mongolness."[88] They
definitely consider themselves Mongols,[89] and approximately 10 percent of their dialect contains Mongolian roots or usage.[90] Babur, the
founder of the Mughal Empire in the early sixteenth century, recorded
the name "Hazara" in the *Babur-Nama*. He referred to the populace of
Hazarajat, which he located west of Kabul as far as Ghor. He further
notes that the Hazara and Nikudari are settled in the Ghazni Mountains,
and some of the Hazaras there speak the Mongolian language.

    A field anthropological study of the Hazaras of Afghanistan by an
American scholar in 1938–1939 attests to the Mongol roots of the Hazaras. The author, Elizabeth Bacon, wrote: "That they were Mongoloid
was attested by their sparse beards and high cheekbones. That they were
Mongols seemed probable enough in view of the general history of the
area. That they were descended from military garrisons left in Afghani-

stan by Chinggis Khan in the early part of the thirteenth century AD, as is frequently stated by European writers, seemed open to question."[91]

What is commonly accepted by most scholars, however, is that the Hazaras are a mixed group. This is not entirely inconsistent with their descent from the Mongol military forces. For example, Nikudar Mongols settled in Afghanistan and mixed with native populations who spoke Persian. A second wave of mostly Chaghatayid Mongols came from Central Asia. They were followed by other Mongol groups, associated with the ilkhanate, who were driven out of Persia. The Timurids joined all of these in Hazarajat, where they mixed with the local, mostly Persian-speaking, population, forming a distinct group.

8   Timur and the Timurids, 1335–1526

The decline of the Ilkhanid dynasty in Persia in the middle of the fourteenth century coincided with the fragmentation of the Chaghtayids' power in Central Asia. Thus, the vast empire built by Chinggis Khan and his descendants disintegrated into competing regional states until another nomadic conqueror rose from the ruins of the Mongol Empire. He reconfigured the broken pieces of the Mongol dominions into a new empire that rivaled that of Chinggis Khan in territorial scope and its lasting impact on societies throughout Asia. Amir Timur, known to the West today as "Tamerlane," rose to imperial power at the end of the fourteenth century, bringing under his rule a massive area that extended from Turkey in the west to India in the east.

The rise of Timur to power amid the turmoil of Transoxiana and Persia in the second half of the fourteenth century has long fascinated students of medieval Islamic history. Timur's ascent from a petty tribal standing to a world-class conqueror in a relatively short time makes the story of his life intriguing for scholars and the public alike. The very name "Tamerlane" has invoked legendary imaginations. He is the protagonist of Christopher Marlowe's dramatic epic *Tamburlaine the Great* (1590) and Edgar Alan Poe's poem "Tamerlane" (1827).

What makes Timur's life and his military exploits remarkable is the way he roller-coastered to the heights of authority against all odds utilizing the constant power struggles in his homeland. His ability to build an enormous military machine almost from scratch facilitated his sweeping military conquests and made him the master of vast territories extending from Central Asia to Anatolia and from Russia to India. Deciphering the secrets of the Turkic conqueror's rapid ascendance to power, as Beatrice Manz noted, requires a review of Timur's political and military status in the Ulus Chaghatay and the sources of his power that brought him first to the top of his tribe, then gave him control of the Ulus and finally enabled him to conquer most of the known world.[1]

Timur was a blend of contradictory personal behavioral traits. Although he had little formal education, he was keenly interested in scholarship and enjoyed such refined activities as the game of chess. He supported and generously rewarded learned men, artists, and scholars. He was a formidable destroyer and an avid builder at the same time. He enhanced his capital, Samarkand, with splendid palaces and buildings and adorned the metropolis with every splendor of the age. He constructed important public works elsewhere. Though a devoted Muslim with a distinctive respect for the mystics, he acted with extreme brutality against Muslims of the vanquished cities, erecting bloody pyramids using the heads of the massacred population as a grisly sign of his victory. He won the trust and respect of his army by setting the example of physical and moral strength, valor, perseverance, and heroism.

Timur was the last of the great nomad conquerors, and yet much about his military feats stems from his association with settled areas. This makes him different from other nomad conquerors who originated in the steppes and conquered settled lands. Timur's Turkic tribes conquered the region, yet Timur formed his empire by manipulating both steppe and sedentary traditions and institutions. Timur kept close ties with his tribe, the Barlas, and other Turko-Mongolian groups of Transoxiana throughout his life. Militarily, he was more related to the nomadic elements than settled areas, whose resources he used to further his empire-building effort. As Beatrice Manz suggests, the Ulus Chaghatay khanate was of central importance to Timur's life, as its nomads made up the core of his army and its traditions determined his goals.[2]

As a conqueror and empire builder, Timur ranks among the few great warriors who have global impact throughout history. Sir Percy Sykes evaluates Timur's achievement as "unsurpassed by any Asiatic conqueror."[3] To Harold Lamb, Chinggis, Timur, and Alexander the Great are "the masters of war upon the stage of the world. Their feats of arms may have been duplicated by others in miniature but never upon the earth as a whole."[4] However, the legacies of these three great military leaders—Alexander, Chinggis, and Timur—differ enormously, as do the ways each ascended to imperial power. Alexander mounted the throne before he embarked on his empire-building venture. Chinggis Khan was the master of a strong polity at home prior to launching his imperial conquests. Timur's rise to power was incremental, with many ups and downs. Had it not been for his exceptional perseverance, he would have been forced out by the power struggles on several occasions. His fortunes shifted from having a commanding position in the

Transoxiana to being exiled from the region and wandering in Sistan as a soldier of fortune. He wrote in his alleged autobiography that "from the twelve year of my age I suffered distresses, combat difficulties, took fixing measures and vanquished armies; experienced mutinies amongst my officers and soldiers; was familiarized to the language of disobedience which I opposed with policy and with fortitude and hazard my person in the hour of danger; until in the end I vanquished kingdoms and empires and established the glory of my name."[5]

Timur was a resolute and ambitious leader whose ability to survive in a turbulent political environment and whose carefully calculated opportunism contributed to his ascent. The power structure inside the Ulus Chaghatay, where Timur emerged as a tribal figure, and in neighboring lands, which Timur eventually conquered, was extremely fragmented. While his contemporaries were trying to wield power by using traditional and conventional methods, Timur changed the rules of the game by transforming the very foundation of the prevailing political landscape and mobilizing much wider resources of power in support of his ambitious plans.

The Rise to Power

Ulus Chaghatay, where Timur began his career, was a loose confederation of Turko-Mongolian tribes that came into being with the breakup of the Chaghatayid khanate after 1334. The Chaghatayid khanate included the territory of Chinggis Khan's second son, Chaghatay, which extended from Issyk Kul Lake and the Ili River in the east to the Muslim lands of Central Asia and Transoxiana in the west. Cultural rifts and internal disputes among the Turko-Mongolian tribes that inhabited the eastern and western areas of the khanate led to its split into two parts. The western segment consisted of the Transoxiana and the territories south of it (including Balkh, Qunduz [Kunduz], Baghlan, and Qandahar [Kandahar]) and became known as Ulus Chaghatay. The eastern part became known as Jatah, or Mughulistan. The Ulus Chaghatay was initially ruled by the khans of the Chaghatayid house and then by a succession of tribal leaders (amirs) who usually ruled in the name of puppet khans.

In political terms, the Ulus Chaghatay was divided into two north–south tribal camps based on the opposite sides of the Amu Darya. The northern camp included the Yasa'uri and the influential Barlas and Jalayir tribes. The more cohesive south, dominated by Qara'unas amirs, grouped the Qara'unas, Arlat, Apardi, and Khuttalani tribes. The Selduz tribe wavered between the two camps. The region was dominated by the south from the time the Qara'unas leader, Amir Qazghan, took over Ulus leadership (1346). In 1370, with the assumption of power by Timur, the leadership shifted to the north. The political life of the Ulus Chaghatay was controlled by tribal chiefs who exerted influence using the military power and economic resources that they controlled. Therefore, the personality of leaders and their abilities to seize opportunities were the keys to power.

Timur, the son of Amir Turghai, belonged to the Barlas, one of the four tribes known from the time of Chinggis Khan.[6] The Barlas tribe traced its origin to Qarachar Barlas, head of the Chaghatay regiments.[7] Timur was the member of an important clan but did not have a leading position in the tribe,[8] which was led by Haji Beg. His ascendancy to tribal leadership at the age of twenty-five did not come from within but from without. In 1360, when the Chaghatayid khan of Mughulistan, Tughluq Timur, invaded Transoxiana, the tribal leaders within the Ulus either fled the area or swore allegiance to the invading khan. The occasion presented an opportunity for Timur to gain the leadership of his tribe. While Haji Beg fled to Khorasan, Timur attended the khan's court, which installed him as the leader of his Barlas tribe.[9] The event underscored the importance of outside support in winning a power struggle in an unstable political environment—one of the tenets that Timur never hesitated to use when achieving his goals.

Using his tribal position, Timur forged an alliance with several tribal leaders in Transoxiana and joined with the leader of the Qara'unas, Amir Hussein, the grandson of Amir Qazghan who ruled the Ulus Chaghatay in 1346–1347. However, when Haji Beg returned from exile, Timur lost his leadership position despite the help he had received from his local allies.[10] Seeing the tribal support shifting toward Haji Beg, Timur decided not to defy his opponent but to acknowledge his authority in order not to lose his position in the tribe. Survival through patience and perseverance was another component of Timur's rise to power.

The Chaghatayid khan of Mughulistan, Tughluq Timur, invaded Transoxiana a second time. This invasion improved Timur's position. He not only regained his leadership of the tribe and command of the Barlas *tumen* at Kish but also became an aide to the Moghul khan's son, Ilyas Khwaja, who represented him in the Ulus.[11] As the rule of the khan became increasingly unpopular in Transoxiana, Timur decided to join the forces opposing the Mughulistan khan. He cooperated with Amir Hussein against the Moghuls. Parting ways with prospective losers was another element of Timur's long-term rise to power.

The failure of Timur and Amir Hussein's opposition to the Moghuls forced them to leave Transoxiana with a few followers. During this first of many periods of exile, Timur developed political and strategic partnerships with several power centers in Khorasan, including the Kurt dynasty of Herat. In Sistan, he served as a soldier of fortune supporting the local ruler against his opponents. He was wounded in the leg, thereby winning the dubious nickname "lame" (*lang*) as an attachment to his name, Tamerlane (*Timur-i lang*, or "Timur the Lame"). Later, Timur was able to regroup several Ulus Chaghatay tribes who were eager to cooperate with Timur and Amir Hussein against the tyrannical rule of the Moghuls, who had deprived them of their local independence. Choosing the best times to disengage and then to return and strike back constituted another tenet of Timur's scheme of political maneuvering.

As strategic conditions in Transoxiana became favorable for a political comeback, Timur and Amir Hussein embarked on another campaign to control the Ulus. Mustering their army in Qunduz, they launched their attack across the Oxus and defeated the army of Ilyas Khwaja at Pul-i Sangi. The momentum gained there enabled the forces of Hussein and Timur to chase the Moghuls out of Transoxiana. In 1364, Amir Hussein assumed the leadership of the Ulus Chaghatay and, as usual, appointed a Chaghatayid prince, Kabil-Shah, as a puppet khan to legitimize his rule. Timur and Amir Hussein were now the supreme power among the Turko-Mongolian tribal confederation in Ulus Chaghatay. But the duumvirate soon faced complications. As the leader of Qara'unas, Amir Hussein's power base was in the south. Timur had his power base at Qashqa-darya and had significant influence in the north. Sharing power with Hussein was simply not appealing to Timur. The dissatisfaction soon came out into the open and led to a series of military clashes.

Timur unified the tribes in Transoxiana. His successful attack on Hussein in Balkh marked the end of a long power struggle between the two leaders representing the north and south in the political alignment of the Ulus Chaghatay tribes. Hussein's death marked the rise of Timur as the head of the Ulus Chaghatay in 1370. Timur then became an in-law of a direct descendant of Chinggis Khan when he took Hussein's widow, Saray Mulk-Khanum, daughter of Amir Qazan (d. 1346), the last Chaghatay khan of Transoxiana, as his fourth wife. For the rest of his life he called himself Timur *Gurgan*, or "son-in-law of the Great Khan." It was also at this time that Timur assumed the title *Sahib Qiran* or "Lord of the Auspicious Conjunction."

Timur derived legitimacy by supporting the Chinggisid line and stressing his links to the Great Khan's house. He installed a puppet Chinggisid khan, in whose name he ruled. Furthermore, in his conquests of the Islamic world, he never hesitated to play the religious card to justify his conquests by honoring spiritual leaders, building shrines, and even claiming divine blessing and approval. He claimed to have been chosen by God to rule over the known world.[12] Timur sought spiritual blessings from the Islamic holy figure Baba Shukrullah of Andkhoy prior to his campaign against the Kurt dynasty in 1381. Earlier, his claim to power was bolstered by support from another religious leader, Sayyid Baraka.[13]

Initially, Timur seemed to be just another leader who had established his rule over the tribal confederation of the Ulus Chaghatay. But what marked Timur as a different type of leader was his ability not only to maintain his grip on power but also to expand it into a great empire. The Ulus tribal leaders were traditionally opposed to a powerful centralized leadership. They cooperated with contenders for Ulus leadership who used it for personal gains and wielding influence within their own tribes. Timur transformed the system into a centralized power. By incorporating the tribal forces—including the powerful Qara'unas troops of his fallen rival Amir Hussein—into his own army, Timur changed the Ulus Chaghatay from a turbulent tribal confederation into a loyal army subordinate to himself. Furthermore, by launching military campaigns beyond Ulus Chaghatay lands, Timur directed the might of the tribes toward areas outside the region, a move that contributed to stability at home. So Timur kept the loyalty of the Turko-Mongolian tribes, which constituted the core of his military might, through constant military conquests and furthered his military gains by efficient use of available resources.

Timur's Military Machine

The core of Amir Timur's army was from the main Tatar tribes, including the mighty Barlas kin of the amir. They were born as skilled riders, rich in horses but poor in amenities out in the harsh environment of the steppes. About a century before the rise of Timur, they led a nomadic life and were constantly on the move. The drive to raid and plunder their settled neighbors was engrained in their nomadic lifestyle. Their pride emanated from skill with the sword, making them a formidable force for destruction. "By experience it is known to me," wrote Timur, "that only those warriors are worthy of having command and leadership positions who are skilled in fighting and defeating the enemy, never waver in facing the foe, direct their men under the most difficult moments and lead them to victory in the most trying conditions."[14] From the numerous Tatar tribes and clans, 12 tribes constituted the base of the standing army, while 28 other tribes contributed military hordes during the war.[15] The confederation of these 40 tribes was augmented by contingents from other peoples from the conquered lands.

Timur's military structure was organized on a decimal basis. The lowest unit (*daha*) was composed of ten troopers commanded by a section leader (*oun-bashi*). A unit of 100 troopers (*sadha*) was led by a squadron commander (*yuz-bashi*). A larger unit of 1,000 mounted soldiers (*ming-hazarah*) was commanded by a regimental commander (*ming-bashi*). The *tumen* was the largest field formation and grouped together ten regiments. Various-sized armies and expeditionary forces were composed of *mings* and *tumens*. In his military and political institutes (*Tuzukat-i-Timuri*), Timur notes that he awarded the commanding ranks to 330 officers, of whom one had the top rank of *Amir-ul-Umara*, four were ranked *Beglar-Begi*, and the rest were appointed the leaders of ten, a hundred, and a thousand troopers.[16] Twelve other military commanders (amirs) were each in charge of a unit ranging from 1,000 troopers up to 12,000. The number of troops in units was increasing by 1,000 as it moved from the first unit to the twelfth. This way, the amir of the first unit commanded 1,000 troops, while the amir of the twelfth unit had 12,000 soldiers under him.[17]

Timur's army was mostly a mounted force; each trooper was supplied with two horses for uninterrupted mobility. Higher ranks required more horses, while the *Amir-ul-Umara* required no less than 300 horses. The troops wore armor consisting of a fine steel mesh of Persian manufacture and pointed steel helmets with steel nose guards and straps that fastened under the chin to protect the neck. Their shoulders were covered by double-mail plates, and some of the horses had leather or mail body curtains and light steel headpieces. The bow was the most important weapon. The troopers carried long bows for use on foot and short bows for mobile use from the saddle. The five-foot-long dismounted bow was used against heavy targets. They used arrows of different lengths, weights, and tips. The arrows were also used for projecting fire and naphtha. Heavier and triple-tipped arrows were used against armored targets, as they could penetrate armor. Besides the universal bow (or bows) strengthened with horn or spliced with steel, the soldiers carried curved swords or straight, double-edged Persian blades. Contemporary chroniclers report the use of incendiary firepots. These may have used gunpowder or a naphtha compound. The spears used by the Tatar soldiers were sometimes the light 10-foot lance with a small tip. Other shorter and heavier spears had an iron knob on the butt, intended for smashing through armor. Most of the riders carried iron maces.[18] Timur's siege engines were portable and carried by pack animals. The engines could reduce the strongest fortresses such as those the Tatars faced in Kalat and Tikrit.[19]

Timur was almost constantly on the march and usually brought part of his court with him on campaigns. His army moved as a mobile camp. There were 18 soldiers to a tent. Each soldier was supplied with his weapons, a saw, an axe, an awl, thread with ten needles, and one leather knapsack. Each five *bahadurs* (guards) shared a tent. The higher ranks each had their own tent.

The salaries (known as "subsistence") of the soldiers and officers were measured by the value of horses. A trooper would draw his pay equivalent to the value of his horse, while the soldiers of Timur's special guards (*bahduran*) were each provided an amount equal to the value of two to four horses. The *oun-bashis* received ten times the allotment of a trooper. The *yuz-bashis* received twice the rate of *oun-bashis*. The *ming-bashis* received three times as much as the *yuz-bashis*. The *Amir-ul-Umara* received ten times the subsistence of the highest officer under him. The wages of infantry and cavalry soldiers were paid annually or biannually in cash; the *oun-bashis* and *yuz-bashis* received their pay through written orders, which were redeemed from the cash revenue of the cities and states. The subsistence of the *ming-bashis* was provided through land grants in provinces, and that of the *Amir-ul-Umara* was granted through revenue from the frontier provinces.[20]

Having a passion for chess, Timur preferred to face his enemy in a pitched battle. His combat formation on the battlefield was also inspired by his interpretation of chess. He invariably divided his battle formation into the right wing (*branghar*), the center (*qol*), and the left wing (*jranghar*). Each wing was composed of several columns moving in a box surrounded by advance, flank, and rear security elements. He devised a range of different battle formations used for facing enemy forces of various sizes.[21]

There is no evidence that Timur ever assembled more than 200,000 men at one location. The Tatar records mention numbers only occasionally: 70,000 men in the later campaign in Persia, 90,000 who went into India, and 200,000 mustered for the last campaign into China. The list of the various amirs and commanders at the Battle of Angora (Ankara) would indicate a strength of from 80,000 to 160,000.[22]

The Conquest of Afghanistan

The regions surrounding Timur's power base were politically and militarily fragmented and easy to conquer. In Afghanistan, the northern and eastern provinces were ruled by several Turko-Mongol warlords who eventually submitted to Timur. In the west, the government of the Kurt dynasty (centered in Herat) had freed itself from the sway of the waning Ilkhanid rule but was locked in a power struggle with another local dynasty. That dynasty was the Sarbadaran of western Khorasan, which had also emerged after the decline of the Ilkhanid rule. The last Kurt ruler, Malik Ghiasuddin Pir Ali (1370–1389), maintained friendly ties with the Tatar lord while he was consolidating his power in Transoxiana. Taking advantage of internal strife in the Sarbadaran state, centered in Sabzevar, Ghiasuddin seized the city of Nishapur in 1375. During his expansion of territory to the west, Ghiasuddin's relations with Timur remained friendly, and Timur even proposed a marriage between his niece and the Kurt ruler's son Pir Mohammad. The marriage took place in Samarkand in 1376. But Timur wanted the malik to be his vassal rather than merely a friend. Soon after, when Timur invited Ghiasuddin to one of his annual councils, the latter refused to attend, claiming preoccupation with the Shia population of Nishapur. But the malik's refusal meant noncompliance with a vassal's status to his superior. The situation pressed Timur to move against Herat, especially as he received emissaries from several of Ghiasuddin's rivals in Khorasan, including Sarbadaran, encouraging him to intervene there.

The lord of Samarkand embarked on his Herat campaign in 1380. In the autumn, he dispatched an advance army of 50,000 strong under his son Jalaluddin Miran-Shah to secure the routes to Herat and establish advance posts for the campaign that was planned for the spring of 1381. The prince crossed the Amu Darya and secured the districts across the river, including Balkh and Sheberghan, from where he raided the Badghis country and seized many horses, cattle, and sheep to supply the upcoming military operation. Meanwhile, the ruler of Herat ordered the city defenses strengthened and the outer city enclosed within an eight-mile defensive wall.

When Timur launched his campaign in April 1381, the entire area across western Khorasan was in a defiant mood. The Tatar army was not short on enemies and had to fight for every town. The battle for the region turned into a series of bloody encounters in fortified towns that lasted for several years. Timur decided to break the centers of resistance around Herat before moving against the malik's capital. He wheeled west from Murghab to Kosuya to cut off Herat from Nishapur, which the Kurt ruler had garrisoned after seizing it from the failing Sarbadaran dynasty. After taking Kosuya, Timur turned east but was halted by the well-defended city of Foshanj west of Herat. The Lord of the Tatars laid siege to the city, filled the moat, and positioned his siege engines to batter the ramparts. The defenders fought back until Timur's siege engines made several gaps in the walls and his rams broke the city gates.[23] Then the besiegers scaled the walls and poured inside. Timur was wounded twice in the ensuing battle. Finally, the intruders overwhelmed the garrison, massacred the population, and leveled the town during a weeklong orgy of carnage.

Herat was much stronger and ready to fight the invaders. Malik Ghiasuddin had mobilized the entire citizenry to take part in defending their town. The Tatar army reached Herat after plundering the surrounding villages and towns. Expecting a drawn-out siege, Timur deployed his army inside a fortified encampment facing the city walls.[24] The Herati defenders did not sit idle, and while Timur was sizing up the defenses of the city, a host of Ghorid daredevils, led by their chief, Talik, sallied out and attacked the enemy camp. The fighting was vicious and lasted until dusk, when the Ghorids returned to the city. The night was far from quiet, however, as another band of Herati fighters streamed out of the Khwaja Abdullah Ansari Gate under the cover of darkness and launched a surprise attack on the Tatars' camp.

Skirmishes continued for four days until Timur assembled his full might before the city walls. While the Tatar hordes attempted to mount the walls, a detachment of Tatars moved to the Marghin District and discovered an access to the city where the Enjil stream access flowed into the town. This was close to the Enjil Gate, where Malik Ghiasuddin was leading his men in combat. The Tatars' pressure at the walls and their push through the Enjil access forced the defenders off the ramparts. The malik moved his forces into the inner city. Timur's forces took some

2,000 prisoners, whom the *Sahib Qiran* (Lord of the Fortuitous Conjunction—as Timur was titled) treated very well and even rewarded so
that they could take his message of peace to the rest of the citizens with
the promise of safe conduct for those who surrendered. Timur's clever
move divided the population. Inspired by the instinct of survival and
reluctant to die for the sake of Ghiasuddin's rule, most of the population submitted to the victor. Timur seized the opportunity to call on the
Kurtid ruler to make peace, citing the friendly relationship that existed
between them in the past. Ghiasuddin saw few choices and agreed to
submit to the authority of the Tatar chief in March 1381.[25] Timur ordered the destruction of the inner and outer walls of Herat. Then he
seized the treasures and fortunes accumulated over the centuries by the
Ghorid and Kurtid dynasties. He ordered that the historic Iron Gates
of Herat, which displayed the titles and honorifics of its past rulers, be
transported to his hometown of Shahr-i Sabz. Taking Herat was a major
step in the conquest of Khorasan, but it was just the initial step. After
consolidating his grip over Nishapur, Sabzevar, and Asfrain, Timur returned home, only to reappear the following winter (1382) to deal with
uprisings in the western Khorasan towns of Sabzevar and Kalat. After
suppressing the rebellious cities, Timur sent Malik Ghiasuddin Kurt and
his family into exile in Samarkand.

The peace proved fragile and fleeting. Soon the area around Herat
and Sistan rebelled again. Timur had appointed Mohammad Ghori,
son of Malik Fakhruddin Kurt, the governor of Ghor. A year later,
Mohammad attacked Herat to end the Tatar occupation. Timur's appointed administrator (*darugha*) had to take refuge in the citadel—the
Ikhtiaruddin fortress. The rebels set fire to the fortress gate and forced
out the garrison, which they then put to the sword. Timur's son, Prince
Miran-Shah, was encamped at Panjdeh on the Murghab River. He dispatched his best generals, Amir Haji Saifuddin and Amir Aq'bouq'a,
with their troops to bring the Heratis back into the fold. The prince
followed his generals immediately, bringing more troops to Herat. The
defenders fought the Tatars in a street-to-street battle before they were
overwhelmed. Miran-Shah went on a killing rampage and, following
his father's custom, erected pyramids of the heads of the slain defenders
(*kala-munar*). Meanwhile, Timur crossed the Amu Darya at Termez and
led a large army southwest, where most of Khorasan was in revolt. In
Sabzevar, Sheikh Dawood Sabzevari had killed Timur's *darugha* Taban
Bahadur; in Kalat, Amir Wali had rebelled and the Sistanis were defying

the Tatars. To contain the uprising, Timur attacked several cities simultaneously. From his assembly area on the Murghab River, he dispatched one column under Amir Sheikh Ali and Uch-Qara Bahadur to reduce Kalat and ordered Prince Miran-Shah, assisted by Amir Haji Saifuddin and Amir Aq'bouq'a, to move against Sabzevar. Timur himself headed for Herat, from where he intended to move south and bring the Sistanis into submission.

In Herat, Timur ordered the massacre of its citizens. But after negotiations, he allowed the city to ransom itself. Many Heratis died under the torture of Timur's tax collectors, who enforced the fulfillment of the agreement.[26] Before moving south, Timur went to Sabzevar, which had recently surrendered to Prince Miran-Shah. There, Timur had 2,000 captives buried alive and built more gruesome pyramids with the heads of the butchered citizenry. This was a warning to any other towns in revolt. Still, the brutality failed to cow the population. Timur faced increasing popular resistance as he moved south into Sistan. The natives were not blind to the military supremacy of their enemy and the odds they faced. Still, they believed that resisting the intruders was the right thing to do. Shami, a chronicler of the Timur court, collected tales of desperate resistance by the inhabitants of towns faced with the Tatars' onslaught.[27] In Farah, the city governor surrendered to Timur, but the population did not. They boldly attacked the invaders, only to be overwhelmed and massacred by the Tatars.

The Tatars plundered the area and moved to Zaranj, the capital of Sistan. The city surrendered to Timur, but this failed to break the peoples' resistance. As the Tatars were celebrating their victory, 5,000 Sistanis sallied out and fought the enemy in the open before they were repulsed. Qutbuddin, the local ruler of Sistan, opened talks with Timur to negotiate peace terms. The parleys, however, were interrupted by another attack by the citizens on the Tatar camp. Timur's army lured the attackers into ambush sites, inflicting heavy losses and forcing them back into Zaranj. The next day, Timur's army lined up in full force before the walls and surrounded the city. At nightfall, many Zaranj citizens (perhaps thousands) opened the gates and launched a surprise attack on the Tatar camp. The Tatars feigned retreat, opened their ranks, and drew the attackers into a planned kill zone. During the ensuing battle in the darkness, both sides sustained losses before the local forces made it back into the city. The following day, the defenders, imitating their enemy's ambush tactics, lured an advancing column of the Tatars, which was led by a Tatar prince, inside the city gates, where it was encircled. The column was rescued by a 1,000-strong force under Aq-Timur Bahadur.

Following several clashes, the Sistan Qutbuddin came out of the city and went into Timur's camp to come to terms with him. Peace with the enemy, however, was not what the city population wanted. While Qutbuddin was still in the Tatars' camp, some 30,000 (a number that might be inflated by a factor of ten) Sistani nationalists poured out of the gates and wreaked havoc within the Tatar ranks. Taken by surprise, Timur arrested Qutbuddin and rushed to take command of his army, which was scrambling to regroup and face the attackers. During the clashes that followed, Timur lost his mount in the melee when it was struck by an arrow from the Sistani foot bowmen. When the Tatars finally forced the assailants back into the gates, Timur began a deliberate reduction of the city. His siege artillery went into action, punching openings in the defenses. Ladder-bearing attackers seized the gaps and scaled the walls. Soon the streets were filled with Tatars, who massacred the population. Timur ordered the religious community and some others to be spared. They were sent to Farah. Qutbuddin and other dignitaries of Sistan went into exile in Samarkand. Timur leveled Zaranj, the historical capital of Sistan, and destroyed the Rustam water dam, thereby turning the fertile land into desolate and lifeless ruins. This was the second devastation of Sistan (it was ravaged by Chinggis Khan about 160 years earlier). The area has never returned to its verdant and populous past.

From Sistan, Timur led his army east across the Helmand River to Bust and Garmsir. Contemporary accounts suggest that Timur reduced certain towns and fortresses in upper Helmand and Urozgan, where he encountered elements of *hazara* and *sadha* military-tribal units that had settled in the area during Chinggis Khan's invasion and later during the Chaghatayid period.[28] Farther east, the Afghan (Pashtun) tribes of the Suleiman Mountains defied Timur's rule, stirring the Tatar leader to launch a punishing expedition against their mountain abode. Contemporary accounts indicate that Timur attacked one of their main fortresses, most likely in today's Zabul or Paktika Provinces. In the fierce fighting, some of Timur's prominent amirs were killed or wounded; Timur massacred the inhabitants after he captured the fortress. Timur then captured Kandahar, hanged its governor, and ordered the destruction of the fortress of Qalat. These expeditions completed Timur's conquest of Afghanistan, which opened the road to his invasion of Persia in the west and India in the east during the following years. Timur spent the winter in Kandahar and returned to Samarkand in the spring of 1384.

Conquest of Persia and West Asia

During the next twenty years, Timur's armies triumphantly marched through the plains of Persia, the mountains of the Caucasus, and the vastness of Mesopotamia, the Levant, and Anatolia. Timur invaded northern and southern Persia during two separate campaigns. In his first campaign (1384–1387), he swept across northern Iran, and after spending the summer of 1386 in Tabriz, he crossed the Aras River and occupied Armenia and Georgia, capturing Nakhchivan, Aras, and Tiflis (Tbilisi). Then he sacked Van, the capital of the rising Qara Qoyunlu (Black Sheep) Turkmen dynasty, and advanced on Isfahan. Timur's capture of the city of Isfahan from the Muzaffarid dynasty is noted as his utmost brutality. When Isfahan surrendered to Timur in 1387, he treated it with relative mercy, as he normally did with cities that surrendered. However, when the city rioted against Timur's punitive taxes by killing the tax collectors and some of Timur's soldiers, Timur ordered the massacre of the citizens. This resulted in a death toll of at least 70,000 people whose severed heads were built into pyramids reinforced with mud and brick.[29] According to Shami, an eyewitness counted more than 28 towers constructed of about 1,500 heads each. The towers were lined up along the outer wall of Isfahan.[30]

In his second campaign in 1393, Timur conquered southern Persia. At Shiraz, a Muzaffarid prince, Shah Mansur, charged Timur's army with a few thousand armor-clad horsemen and even struck the Tatar emperor twice on his helmet. But the prince was finally killed by Timur's son Shah-Rukh. Timur had all Muzaffarid princes put to death except for a few, who were blinded by their relatives instead. This marked the end of the Muzaffarids, a native Iranian dynasty that came to power following the breakup of the Ilkhanids in 1314. This was followed by the downfall of yet another local dynasty that rose to power after the demise of the Ilkhanids. The Jalayir Turko-Mongol dynasty ruled over Iraq, Kurdistan, and Azerbaijan. The last ruler of the dynasty, Sultan Ahmad, fled his capital of Baghdad to Egypt as Timur approached the city. The Tatar chief occupied Baghdad, and although he spared the city for a price, eight years later the *Sahib Qiran* sacked the legendary city of the *Arabian Nights* and massacred the population.

Timur's Ventures Far Afield

Besides conquering the territories of the defunct Ilkhanid and Chaghatayid khanates, Timur led two major campaigns in the west and two in the east. To the west he fought the Golden Horde and crushed the rising power of the Osmanli Turks (Ottomen) in Turkey. In the east, he conquered northern India and sacked Delhi and attempted to conquer China. The military and political consequences of his victory over the Golden Horde were decisive, as it finally fragmented the Mongol khanate. But his crushing defeat of the Ottoman sultan Bayezid Yildirim in Angora (modern Ankara) failed to end the Ottoman Empire, which soon recovered from the shock of Timur's onslaught. Neither did Timur's conquest of India lead to the dissolution of the Delhi Sultanate, which continued under a new dynasty. And finally, Timur did not survive to pursue his goal of overrunning China, although he had dispatched a 200,000-strong army across the Syr Darya to lead the campaign.

Timur's military face-off with the Golden Horde was the most decisive war he fought in the west. He led two campaigns against Toqtamish Khan (d. 1406), the last overall khan of the Golden Horde.[31] Although Timur had extended support to Toqtamish (Tokhtamysh) against his warring rivals and helped him gain the leadership of the Horde, the alliance did not last long. On his accession to power, Toqtamish fell out with Timur over the possession of Khwarazm and Azerbaijan where his borders met those of Timur.

In his two campaigns between 1393 and 1398, Timur fought the Golden Horde army under Toqtamish once near Moscow and then again in the Caucasus, which resulted in the defeat of the rival power and destruction of Sarai—the capital of the Golden Horde—and Astrakhan, thereby fragmenting the power of the unified Juji khanate.

Five years later, Timur launched his invasion of India, a land rich in wealth but often poorly protected. Apparently what lured Timur to India was the appeal of plundering a rich country and surpassing Chinggis Khan's conquest to the east. In a battle near Delhi in December 1398, Timur defeated the young Sultan Nasiruddin Mahmud, the last ruler of the Turkic Tughluq dynasty (1320–1414), and entered Delhi, where his soldiers plundered the city. The citizens rioted in protest of the amount of treasure demanded by the Tatars to ransom their city. The Tatars sacked the city, massacred thousands of the inhabitants, and left the place in ruins. According to Zafarnama of Yazdi, some individual Tatar soldiers took 150 slaves, including men, women, and children. The victors also took an immense amount of spoils, including precious stones, pearls, gold, silver, money, and other valuables. Timur's campaign extended to the Ganges River and other surrounding areas, where the Tatars massacred thousands of Hindus.

The Indian conquest and the defeat of the Delhi Sultanate was one of Timur's greatest victories, surpassing the Indian adventures of Alexander the Great and Chinggis Khan. Timur's invasion and destruction of Delhi prolonged the chaos, famine, and anarchy that already consumed India, and the city would not recover from the great loss it suffered for almost a century. One historian noted that Timur inflicted more misery on India than had ever before been inflicted by any conqueror in a single invasion.[32] On the eve of his departure from India on March 6, 1399, Timur appointed a local ally, Khizr Khan Sayyid, as his viceroy in India. In a few years, Khizr Khan restored the Delhi Sultanate as the Sayyid dynasty, which lasted for thirty-seven years. Timur's invasion of India was more a plundering campaign than a conquest.

Soon after the Indian conquest, Timur embarked on another major campaign in the west that culminated in the fateful Battle of Angora (Ankara) with the mighty Ottoman sultan Bayezid Yildirim (the "Thunderbolt"). Before meeting the sultan on the battlefield, Timur consolidated his authority in West Asia by invading Syria, where he sacked Aleppo and captured Damascus after defeating a Mamluk army in 1400. The Tatars massacred the city's inhabitants, except for the artisans, who were deported to Samarkand. Then Timur ravaged Christian Armenia and Georgia again, enslaving more than 60,000 locals and depopulating many districts. Timur next crossed into Asia Minor to face a stubborn resistance at Sivas. The defenders were forced to capitulate. Timur ordered 4,000 Armenian soldiers buried alive and ran over women and children with his horsemen. Then he turned his attention to Baghdad, the capital of the headstrong Sultan Ahmad Jalayir. When the city fell on June 20, 1401, he ordered a great massacre in revenge for the death of many notable officers of his army who had perished during the siege. The contemporary chronicler Ibn 'Arabshah noted that Timur ordered that each soldier bring the heads of two inhabitants of Baghdad to build his usual skull towers. He noted that the number of Timur's soldiers on this occasion was 20,000 and estimates the number of victims at 90,000.

In February 1402, Timur marched to meet Bayezid and succeeded in outmaneuvering him before the battle. Faced with a Tatar enemy greatly superior in numbers, the Ottoman generals advised the sultan to follow their traditional military tactic—withdraw for several days into the mountains and assume an advantageous defensive position, thereby forcing the enemy to fight the Ottomans at a place of their choosing.[33] But Bayezid was impetuous and incautious and preferred to meet the enemy head-on. The Ottomans moved east to Sivas and took up an advance position to await the enemy. Timur, however, outfoxed him by evading and encircling the Ottoman forces and marched against them from their rear. This way, Timur forced the enemy to turn around and meet him near Angora at a place of the Tatars' choosing. As the exhausted and thirsty Ottoman army came out of the waterless country and reached the walls of Angora, they faced an enemy that was now well entrenched toward the east. The outcome of the battle was already sealed. When the battle was joined, the Anatolian Tatar cavalry, which was deployed in the frontline of the Bayezid army, deserted and joined their kinsmen. This depleted the Ottoman army by a quarter of its total force. The battle was a desperate attempt by the Ottomans, and even the daring personal action of Bayezid could not save the day. The Ottoman army was defeated and fled. Bayezid was Timur's captive. Timur spared no effort in humiliating the ailing sultan who died in captivity after a few months (1403).

Timur's decisive victory gave the beleaguered Byzantines a reprieve and saved Constantinople, which had been under a fifty-year Ottoman siege until 1402. Timur dispatched a column to capture Bursa, the capital of the Ottomans, and he himself marched on Smyrna, which was held by the Knights of Saint John. Obsessed by the desire to emulate the *ghazi* traditions of the Islamic Ottomans, Timur stormed the city, put the garrison to the sword, and catapulted the heads of the knights onto the decks of two European ships in the harbor.[34]

Before leaving Anatolia for Samarkand, Timur prepared to fulfill his last eastward expansion: the invasion of China. On returning home, he mobilized a 200,000-strong army and ordered it to march eastward. But as the army crossed the Syr Darya at Otrar, Timur fell ill and died on February 18, 1405, without conquering China. He was seventy years old.

Timur had to overcome enormous obstacles, outmaneuver a host of powerful contenders, and break the military might of numerous dynasties to build his empire. He spent almost all his life on the battlefield and personally commanded his armies in major campaigns. But the empire he founded with so much effort soon disintegrated after his death. Timur's success stemmed from his personal leadership and his ability to maximize the impact of available resources.

Timur has been judged in different ways. His court chroniclers portray him as a ruthless but just ruler. His critics, including his biographer Ibn 'Arabshah, ferociously vilify him as a wanton destroyer. Among modern historians, Berthold Spuler believes that Timur's career was devoid of any higher purpose than war and predatory raids.[35] V. Barthold agrees that Timur did not have a Turkish national goal and that his objective was to conquer as much land as possible. Nevertheless, Barthold credits Timur as a builder and as a man of arts.[36] To Beatrice Manz, Timur's career is a constant effort to create a "state dependent on his person, made up not of allies giving provisional loyalty, but subjects owing it."[37] Rene Grousset asserts that the story of Timur is an expression of a "farsighted Machiavellianism, a consistent hypocrisy based on and identified with reasons of state. He is a Napoleon with the soul of a Fouche, a Phillip II descended from Attila. A devout yet a dashing soldier and an experienced and prudent leader, the friend of artists and men of letters, savoring Persian poetry like a Shirazi."[38]

Timur's lifelong pursuit of military conquests left him little time to build viable state institutions that ensured the continuity and integrity of the empire that he painstakingly built over thirty-five eventful years. He was the sole character behind his major decisions, with little contribution from ministers and advisers. Maintaining an empire intact is often harder than building it. This can hardly be achieved by a single strongman. Harold Lamb noted that while Chinggis Khan "shared his responsibility among ministers and generals . . . the Tatar leader accepted all responsibility himself. After his death Chinggis' commanders Subedai, Chepe Noyon, Mukhuhli and Bayan enlarged the empire, [whereas] Jaku Barlas, Saifuddin, Shaikh Ali Bahatur and others never accomplished such results for Timur." Timur's disregard for the fundamentals of statecraft haunted his descendants with unrelenting rivalries and blood-spattered power struggles.

Timur's Descendants

Timur outlived two of his four sons. Jahangir and Umar Shaykh predeceased him, while his third son, Miran-Shah, died soon after his father, leaving only the youngest son, Shah-Rukh, who ruled Khorasan from Herat, as his immediate descendant. Although Timur had designated his grandson, Pir Mohammad, son of Jahangir, his successor, Shah-Rukh ultimately succeeded to power following an interregnum of four years. Making Herat his imperial capital, Shah-Rukh appointed his son, Ulugh Beg, the governor of Transoxiana (with its capital in Samarkand) and set about undertaking major projects to restore the damage caused by years of war and bloodshed. The rehabilitation amounted to a comprehensive physical, social, and cultural revival of the conquered lands, healing the wounds inflicted by Timur's destructive sword. Politically,

Shah-Rukh was able to rule over the greater part of the empire built by his father and successfully brought rebelling princes back into line and submission. Timurid rulers continued to dominate Persia, Afghanistan, India, and much of Central Asia, though the Anatolian and Caucasian territories were lost by the 1430s.

The thirty-seven-year reign of Shah Rukh (1409–1447) and that of his astronomer son Ulugh Beg in Samarkand (1409–1449) were the "renaissance of art" under the cultured Timurid princes. Because Persian cities were desolated by wars, the seats of Persian culture were now in Samarkand and Herat, cities that became centers of Timurid reconstruction. Shah-Rukh undertook rebuilding efforts throughout the empire, restored the walls of Herat, and adorned his capital with magnificent buildings. His cultured wife, Gauhar Shad, was his main partner in his renewal efforts. Soon, Herat became a cultural magnet drawing men of arts, poets, and scholars from all over the empire, turning Herat into the cultural hub of Khorasan and Central Asia. In Samarkand, Ulugh Beg was also a great patron of the arts and learning and made Samarkand a Mecca for scholars, men of letters, and artists who flocked to his court from all corners of Persia. Samarkand was one of the gems of Asia. Today, the remains of the observatory built by the astronomer-king in Samarkand continues as a major tourist attraction in Uzbekistan.

Shah-Rukh was succeeded by his son Ulugh Beg, who could not hold power long. His nephew 'Alla u-Daulah seized Herat and took Ulugh Beg's son, Abdul Latif, hostage. Although Ulugh Beg eventually drove out the pretender and freed his son, the Uzbeks sacked Samarkand. Ulugh Beg's son rebelled in Balkh, imprisoned his father, and murdered him in 1449 using a Persian slave. One year later, a servant of Ulugh Beg's killed the patricidal prince. This ended a relatively peaceful period following the death of Timur during which a greater part of the empire stayed together. The second half of the Timurid dynasty saw a gradual disintegration of the empire. Internally, the Timurid princes quickly fell into disputes and civil wars, and many of the governorships became effectively independent. Externally, the vassal states broke away and new powerful dynasties emerged in Persia and Central Asia. In the west, the Turkmen dynasties of Qara Qoyunlu (Black Sheep) and Aq Qoyunlu (White Sheep) alternately dominated eastern Anatolia and northwestern Persia. The Caucasus broke away.

Amid the ongoing turmoil, Abu Sa'id, a grandson of Timur's third son, Miran-Shah, seized power and mounted the throne of Samarkand in 1452. During the next fifteen years, he defeated every rival and emerged as the unquestioned master of Transoxiana. But this did not last long. Two years later, he failed in his venture to intervene in Azerbaijan and was captured by the local pretender and handed over to his family enemy, Prince Yadgar Mirza (Shah-Rukh's son), who had him put to death. Abu Sa'id's son, Sultan Ahmad, would ascend the throne, while his brother Omar Shaykh settled in Andijan in the Ferghana Valley. Sultan Ahmad ruled by making compromises with the nobles until his death in 1494. Shortly before his death, he marched on Andijan to seize the holdings of Omar Shaykh, who had died in an accident in 1494. There, he was to face his young nephew Babur Mirza, who had succeeded his father at the age of twelve. The sultan died before reaching Andijan, and Babur took prompt action to defend his territory. From that time on, Babur emerged as a major actor on the political scene in Transoxiana and Afghanistan. In Samarkand, Sultan Ahmad's brother Mahmud, who had slaughtered his five nephews to win the throne, died after a reign of six months, and the country once again plunged into civil war. Mahmud's son Baisunghur succeeded him as Babur Mirza expanded his territories and captured Samarkand.

Meanwhile, in Herat, the last of the Timurid princes and the greatest patron of arts, Sultan Hussein Bayqara (r. 1469–1506), presided over a prospering center of Khorasan. Supported by his illustrious vizier, Amir Ali Sher Nawai, he turned his capital of Herat into a major center of the arts and literature and sponsored many great names, including the world-class miniature painter Behzad, the poet Jami, and the historian Mirkhwand.

By 1500, the divided Timurid Empire had lost control of most of its territory and in the following years was effectively pushed back on all fronts. Persia fell quickly to the Shi'ite Safavid dynasty of Shah Ismail I, who ruled during the following decade. Much of the Central Asian lands were overrun by the Uzbeks under Mohammad Khan Shaybani, who conquered the key cities of Samarkand and Herat in 1505 and 1507 and founded the Shaybani dynasty.

Meanwhile, in the course of ongoing family rivalries, Babur was dislodged from his home in Ferghana as well as from his other territories in Transoxiana. After years of wandering (*qazaqilar*), he reappeared on the scene and temporarily seized control of Samarkand—only to be defeated in 1501 by his most formidable rival, Shaybani. Three years later, at the head of a new army made up mostly of Badakhshani troops, he crossed the Hindu Kush and captured Kabul from its local Turko-Mongol ruler. It was from his base in Kabul that he eventually invaded

India and defeated Sultan Ibrahim Lodi of the Afghan Lodi dynasty. His victory at Panipat in 1526 founded the Mughal Empire of India or, more precisely, the Second Timurid Empire.

Babur never gave up the fight for his Transoxiana homeland against the usurper Shaybanids, who drove him out of his native country. While sitting on the throne in Kabul, Babur united with Sultan Hussein Bayqara of Herat to confront the Shaybanids. The death of Sultan Hussein in 1506, however, delayed that venture. Furthermore, a rebellion forced him to return to Kabul from Herat. Meanwhile, Mohammad Shaybani was defeated and killed by Shah Ismail in 1510, and Babur used this opportunity to make another attempt to reconquer his ancestral Timurid territories. Over the next few years, Babur and Shah Ismail would form a partnership to take over parts of Central Asia.

Failed Attempts by the Shaybanids to Form a Nomadic Empire

Before closing this chapter, we look at the last attempt by the Shaybani Uzbeks to form a nomadic empire in Central Asia with the goal of projecting power to the south. Mohammad Khan Shaybani (1451–1510) is known to history as the founder of the Uzbek dynasties of Central Asia that ruled Transoxiana until the Russian conquest in the nineteenth century. Paradoxically, his historical distinction stems more from his failures rather than his political achievements. A descendant of Chinggis Khan through the Juji lineage, Mohammad Shaybani was the last Chinggis-Khanite leader to attempt unification of Central Asia and Persia under a Turko-Mongol empire. In spite of his sudden burst into power—which made him master of western Turkistan, Transoxiana, Ferghana, and Khorasan—Shaybani's efforts to build the last nomadic empire in the region were thwarted by the emergence of the Safavid dynasty in the south and the rise of the Kazak nomadic state in the north. Meanwhile, the rise of Shi'ism in Iran and its politicization under the Safavid dynasty clashed with a strong messianic Sunnism emanating from Central Asia. This added depth to the existing geographic and ethnic divide between Central Asia and Persia.

There are several primary sources focusing on Mohammad Khan Shaybani and the Shaybanids. They provide accounts of the Uzbek khan's campaigns as well as insight into the political and military affairs of the Shaybani dynasty.[39] Among them, the *Mehman-Nama-ye Bokhara* was written for Mohammad Khan Shaybani by Fazlullah Ibn

Ruzbehan Khonji in 1509.[40] The author began writing the book in 1508 in Bokhara and finished it in Herat in 1509.[41] The book details Shaybani's campaigns against the Kazaks, his roaming the steppes across the Syr Darya, his return to Samarkand, and his further military ventures to Mashhad and Tous in Khorasan. The author accompanied the Uzbek khan in most of his campaigns and offers an elaborate description of Shaybani's court and his administration. The book is a particularly good source on two important trends of the time: the continuing power struggle between the Uzbeks and Kazaks in Central Asia, and the politicization of religion to advance political ambitions by both Mohammad Shaybani and Ismail Safavi.

Fazlullah traces the source of constant Uzbek-Kazak animosity to the desertion of two vassal chiefs, Qarai (Girai) and Janibeg, from the camp of Abul-Khayr Khan Shaybani (1411–1468), who had established Uzbek rule over a vast area extended from Tobolsk to the Syr Darya. Qarai and Janibeg led many nomads out of the Uzbek khanate to the east, acquiring wide swaths of grazing land from the Chaghatay Mongol khans. They were called "Kazaks" (Qazaqs), meaning "adventurers" and "renegades." It was the son of Janibeg, Baranduk (Baranduq) Khan, who founded the Kazak state and waged a drawn-out war with Abul-Khayr's grandson Mohammad Shaybani. Fazlullah's account is one of the few original sources that provide much detail about the Uzbek-Kazak conflicts at the beginning of the sixteenth century.

Another important issue is the religious basis of Shaybani's war on the Safavids and the Kazaks. Fazlullah laces his tome with numerous juristic vignettes justifying Shaybani's military conquests based on Sunni jurisprudence (*Fiqeh* and *Kalam*).[42] The author's selection of *Fiqehi* and *Kalami* issues for discussion is linked closely to his Sunni bias and anti-Shi'ite prejudice. His hidden agenda in writing the book seems to be an emphasis on the religious obligation of Mohammad Shaybani to uphold the cause of "real" Islam against the "apostates." He considers the Safavi Shi'ites worse than Christian heretics (*afranj*)[43] and worthy of annihilation. His self-made fatwas encouraged Mohammad Shaybani to fight a holy war against the Safavids.[44] These fatwas readily suited Shaybani's political agenda, as they provided religious legitimacy for his ambitions.

Fazlullah depicts his benefactor as the divine agent charged with the holy mission of protecting and promoting Sunni Islam facing the "Shi'ite heresy" in the south (the Safavids) and the "Kazak apostasy" in the north.[45] He calls Mohammad Shaybani the Almighty's viceregent (*Khalifat-u-Rahman*) and the Living Imam (*Imam-e Zaman*).[46] The latter is apparently aimed at overriding Ismail Safavi's self-proclaimed religious credentials.[47] The basis of the Safavid monarch's militant theology was the supremacy of Shi'ism through force of arms. He claimed to be enjoying divine blessing and being appointed as the representative of the Hidden Imam (*Imam-e Ghayeb*), thus combining in his person both temporal and spiritual authority.

The ardent religiosity encompassing the Shaybani-Safavi confrontation led to unprecedented violence. It was clearly reflected in Ismail Safavi's mutilation of the dead body of his opponent after he was killed in the Battle of Merv (1510).[48] The effects of religious hostility left a lasting impact on social and political developments in the region. Babur's failure to restore Timurid rule in Transoxiana following the death of Mohammed Shaybani is attributed to his dealing with the Safavids, whom the Sunnis of Central Asia bitterly despised.[49]

Despite the lifelong animosity between Babur and the Uzbeks, his *Babur-Nama* gave a relatively balanced version of the battles against Shaybani rulers. His book also offers a wider perspective on a turbulent political scene in Central Asia dominated by a relentless power struggle involving the Uzbeks, local Chaghatay Mongol rulers, and Timurid princes. Babur's clashes with Shaybani in Samarkand and Ferghana are discussed in detail.[50]

To conclude, we can state that Mohammad Shaybani represented a turning point in the history of Central Asia. In fact, it was the historical ramifications of Shaybani's failure that made him a distinct figure in the region's history. The period between the sixteenth and nineteenth centuries brought major changes to the political landscape of Central Asia. The region that fostered the emergence of several empires in the past gradually declined into one of history's backwaters. The rise and growth of three major empires in the region we discuss in chapter 9— the Safavid, Ottoman, and Indian Mughal Empires, known collectively as the "Gunpowder Empires"—greatly influenced the future of Central Asia. The situation changed the historical trend in which Central Asia–based empires projected power to the south while expanding their rule to larger areas in the Middle East and India.

The impact of the fall of Mohammad Shaybani at the hands of Ismail Safavi is summarized by Rene Grousset (1885–1952). He writes that the event "made a considerable impact in the East. That the restorer of Iranian independence should have killed the restorer of Turko-Mongol power—that the heir of the great Sassanid kings should have defeated and slain Chinggis Khan's grandson—was a sign that the time had changed and that, after many centuries of invasions patiently endured, the sedentary was beginning to get even with the nomad and cultivation was winning against the steppe."[51]

9   Afghan Tribes and the Gunpowder Empires, 1500–1709

The military history of Afghanistan in the sixteenth and seventeenth centuries is marked by a three-way persistent struggle for dominance among the three regional powers that carved up the territory of today's Afghanistan into separate spheres of control. "Gunpowder Empires" refers to three major Islamic powers—the Ottomans, Safavids, and Mughals—which were dominant from the fourteenth through the seventeenth centuries, undertaking important military exploits using newly developed firearms, especially cannons and small arms, to build imperial power. As the Safavids of Persia (1501–1722), the Mughal Empire of India (1526–1857), and the Uzbek khanate of Central Asia (1500–1876) fought on their peripheries for dominion over Afghanistan, the native populations inside fought a desperate struggle for survival. They did survive, but the empires did not. Beginning at the turn of the eighteenth century, the Afghan tribal confederations not only forced the occupying empires out of the country but also marched triumphantly into the imperial capitals and made them capitulate to their authority. First, the Ghilzai Pashtuns of Kandahar cast off the yoke of the Safavids and took the war to the heart of the Persian state. They toppled the Safavid dynasty and captured its capital, Isfahan, in 1722 and ruled its territory until 1730. Twenty-six years later, Ahmad Shah Durrani (r. 1747–1772), the founder of the rising Afghan Empire, marched on Delhi in 1756 and turned the weakened Mughal Empire into a vassal holding of the Durrani state centered in Kandahar. Meanwhile, Afghans forced the Uzbek khanate out of northern Afghanistan and contained its power north of the Amu Darya River.

During the first part of this period of Afghanistan's history, the political situation was dominated by the military actions among competing empires aimed at securing their landholdings against the incursions of rival powers. Most of the military operations were inspired by security imperatives because Afghanistan was situated on the region's geopolitical fault line. The tripartite power struggle centered on three subregional domains:

1. The Uzbek-Safavids battleground in Khorasan in the northwest.
2. The Safavid-Mughal arena in Kandahar in the southwest.
3. The Uzbek-Mughal frontline in Badakhshan and Balkh in the northeast.

In the first subregion, the Safavids fought the expansion of the Uzbeks to the key cities of Khorasan, including Herat, Mashhad, and Nishapur. The second domain was the battleground of the Safavids and the Mughal Empire for control of Kandahar, which stood on the southern route to the Mughals' dominions in India. In the north and northeast, the Mughal Empire of India engaged in fierce competition with the Uzbeks for control over Balkh and Badakhshan. Certain areas were under the firm control of one or another competing state. Kandahar changed hands several times between the Safavids and the Mughals, yet the former never challenged the authority of the latter in Kabul. Furthermore, the Mughals never intended to expand as far west as Herat, which was often under the Safavids' domination. In the north, the Uzbeks and the Mughals fought persistently for control over Badakhshan and Balkh, yet the Uzbeks rarely crossed the Hindu Kush Mountains into the Mughals' dominions in the south, whereas the Mughal rulers practically gave up any ambition to make inroads into their ancestral home north of the Amu Darya River. Thus, during the sixteenth and seventeenth centuries, the subregional power struggles pitted different contending states in the region one against another.

The military actions by the troika in and around Afghanistan, however, were not the main thrust of their strategies; mostly they were of supporting actions. The Safavids' main effort was concentrated in the west and northwest, where they faced the expanding authority of the Ottoman Empire and Tsarist Russia. The Mughal Empire was involved heavily in expanding and consolidating its power across the vastness of the Indian subcontinent and was interested in keeping its links to Central Asia through Afghan territory that was secured and unchallenged by neighboring states. The Uzbek khanate's main strategic vulnerability was to the north and northeast, where it faced the growing Kazak khanate (1456–1847) beyond the Syr Darya River and the rising power of the Oirat Empire (1619–1858) of western Mongols based in northwest China and eastern Turkistan. All these competing powers were trying to keep their adjoining peripheries stable and safe inside Afghanistan. The trends of sixteenth- and seventeenth-century military history in Afghanistan should be studied within this context of imperial struggle.

Among the major players of this period, the Mughal Empire was most

238 Chapter Nine

engaged in Afghanistan, and with the Afghan tribes, for several reasons. First, the Mughals, initially, built their state in northern India on the ruins of the Afghan dynasty. That dynasty was defeated by Babur in 1526 at the Battle of Panipat. The Afghan tribes never gave up their efforts to regain power. Second, the vital territorial link between the Mughals' Indian dominions and their natural power base in Kabul and northern Afghanistan was controlled by Afghan tribes who constantly attempted to block the passage of the Mongol armies. Third, when confronting the Safavids in the south and the Uzbeks in the north, the Mughals needed to enlist the support of the Afghan tribes. And finally, the Mughal Empire eventually weakened and became a vassal of the Afghan state under the Afghan emperor Ahmad Shah Durrani.

The Turko-Afghan Legacy in India

The Mughals' interaction with the Afghans played against a backdrop of more than three centuries of Afghan involvement in the affairs of India. Afghans had become a major actor on the political scene of the subcontinent. The fall of the Ghorid dynasty, after the disintegration of their empire in Afghanistan and Khorasan in 1215, moved the Turko-Afghan power base of the Ghorids into northern India. Sultan Shahabuddin Mohammad Ghori (1150–1206) conquered northern India at the end of the twelfth century, and his lieutenants expanded this realm during the early thirteenth century. During more than three centuries of rule by the Turko-Afghan dynasties in India (1206–1526), thirty-four Muslim kings ruled from Delhi. For one-third of this period, Afghan (Pashtun) sultans sat on the Delhi throne. During those centuries when Afghanistan was dominated by the successors of Chinggis Khan (1227–1370) and then by Amir Timur and his descendants (1370–1510), the principal Afghan rulers did not rule in their homeland but instead reigned in India. Along with the Afghan sultans in Delhi, there were Afghan military leaders commanding large Afghan contingents, mostly made up of Ghilzai (Khalji) and their Bittani kinsmen. These constituted the influential nobility within the Turko-Afghan ruling class in India. This situation inspired many Afghans (Pashtuns) and other ethnicities in Afghanistan to move eastward into India to seek employment or to serve as soldiers of fortune. The Muslim rulers, who were constantly engaged in expanding their territories, were never short of fighting men.

During this period of India's medieval history, five Turko-Afghan dynasties ruled in India. The slave kings (Mamluks), led by Qutbuddin Aibak (1206–1210), consolidated the Ghorids' conquered lands between Ghazni and Bengal. Afghans under Bakhtiar Mohammad Khalji founded a subdynasty in Bengal. Aibak was succeeded by his able slave and son-in-law Sultan Shamsuddin Iltutmish (r. 1211–1236), whose rule coincided with Chinggis Khan's invasion of Afghanistan. Iltutmish is credited with containing the Mongols at Punjab and maintaining the integrity of the Sultanate between the Sind River and Bengal. Another great name of the dynasty was Ghiasuddin Balban (r. 1266–1286), who is known for his strict enforcement of law and bringing order and normality to the sultanate territories. The dynasty is also known for putting the first Muslim woman sultan on the throne of Delhi. Sultana Razia (r. 1236–1240), the daughter of Iltutmish, succeeded him and proved herself to be no less a sovereign than the other good administrators before she met her tragic death at the hands of jealous nobles.

The Mamluk dynasty was succeeded by the Afghan Khalji dynasty (1290–1320); its second sultan, Alauddin Khalji (r. 1296–1311), expanded the Delhi Sultanate to central India for the first time. His military commanders made several raids into southern India, spreading Muslim rule farther into the Hindu provinces in the south—a trend that continued for centuries.[1] Under the Khaljis, imperial policy allowed the Hindu kingdoms to survive as vassals, a policy that was changed under the succeeding Tughluq dynasty. Alauddin is also remembered for defeating the Mongol incursions into India, which on one occasion, in 1297, reached the gates of Delhi. The Khalji sultan met the 200,000-strong Mongol army near Delhi and forced it to retire after a fiercely contested battle.

The ultimate expansion of Muslim rule in India came under the third dynasty of Tughluq Turks (1320–1414). During the nearly century-long rule of the house of Tughluq, the authority of the Delhi Sultanate extended to all corners of the subcontinent. The second sultan of the dynasty, Mohammad Tughluq (r. 1325–1351), extended the borders of his kingdom to the southern extremities of India.[2] As the power of Delhi was overextended in all directions, it became increasingly difficult to rule the territories from the center. Over the succeeding decades, several provinces revolted and asserted their independence. However, the fragmentation that weakened central control did not enfeeble Muslim rule in India, since nearly all breakaway provinces were in fact controlled by Muslim rulers. There was no significant opportunity for Hindu kingdoms to cast away the yoke of Muslim authority. Consequently, the Tughluq sultans who unified most of India under Muslim rule also saw central authority truncated into a small principality around Delhi by the end of the fourteenth century, when Amir Timur invaded India and plundered Delhi (see chapter 8). Under Mohammad Tughluq, the rule of the sultanate had extended to all India except for small territories in Orissa, Kathiawar, and Kashmir. About half a century later, it was so constricted that a contemporary of one of the last Tughluq rulers, Sultan Nasiruddin Mahmud (r. 1390–1398), defined it thus: "The rule of the world-lord extends from Delhi to Palam." Palam is 16 kilometers (about 10 miles) southwest of Delhi, where Delhi's international airport is located today.[3]

As discussed in chapter 8, Amir Timur appointed a local ally, Khizr Khan Sayyid, as his viceroy in India; he founded the Sayyid dynasty (1414–1451) in Delhi. The devastation of the country by the Timur invasion was too destructive and far-reaching to be repaired by his vassals in a short time. During the relatively brief history of this dynasty, which witnessed rule by four separate members of the house, the sultanate was fatally weakened and the Sayyids, of Arabian descent, were mostly engaged in quelling rebellions and defending the shrinking territories of the sultanate. Meanwhile, Bahlol Lodi, the mighty leader of the Lodi Afghans, wielded significant strength with the help of his Afghan-dominated army and rose to power in Punjab and Multan. As the area under the control of the last Sayyid ruler extended hardly 40 miles from Delhi, Bahlol marched on Delhi in April 1451 and proclaimed himself sultan when the last Sayyid ruler, Alauddin Alam-Shah (r. 1445–1451), voluntarily abdicated his throne.

Bahlol Lodi founded the fifth and the last dynasty of the Delhi Sultanate, which lasted three-quarters of a century (1451–1526). The Afghan leader came to power during a very difficult time. He was faced with the challenge of bringing the breakaway provinces back into line. As Ishwari Prasad writes, Bahlol restored the political prestige of the Delhi Sultanate.[4] But most of his achievements were of a military nature and were accomplished through the services of some forty Afghan tribal chiefs, who were treated as equals. Bahlol was able to restore Delhi's authority in neighboring principalities, including the northeastern Sharqi Sultanate (the Eastern Kingdom) based at Jaunpur in Uttar Pradesh, which was not only the home of the strongest army in India at the time but was also known as a major center of Urdu and Sufi knowledge and culture fostering excellent communal relations between Muslims and Hindus.

Faced with many challenges by multiple centers of power around the Delhi Sultanate, Bahlol made attempts to organize an Afghan-dominated army. In a *firman* (edict) recorded by Abbas Sarwani (ca.

1579) in his *Tarikh-i Sher Shahi* (The History of Sher Shah), Bahlol stated that "Hindustan can be held by somebody who rules over a nation with tribes. Let every Afghan tribesman bring his relatives leading a life of indigence, let them come and take up estates in Hind [India], relieving themselves from straitened circumstances and supporting the state against powerful enemies."[5] In response to Bahlol's *firman*, large numbers of Afghan tribes—mostly the Lodi's fellow Ghilzais such as Lodi, Lohani, Niazi, Marwat, and Bittani plus some tribes from the other major branches of Afghans (Pashtuns) including the Sarabanis and the Karlanis—flocked down onto the plains of India. The tribal colonization scheme, however, was of temporary value. The policy facilitated Bahlol's tribal-based administration but empowered tribal leaders to the extent that they became hard to control by Bahlol's son Sikandar Lodi (r. 1489–1517), who succeeded him. The son's efforts to reinforce central authority caused resentment among the tribes, who carved up spheres of influence for themselves in the provinces. The situation led to internal confusion and disarray under the last Lodi king, Ibrahim Lodi (r. 1517–1526). Ibrahim's policy of reducing the power of Afghan nobility through arbitrary and strict decisions alienated powerful Afghan leaders. The discontent finally inspired Daulat Khan Lodi, the powerful governor of Punjab, to invite Babur to invade India and to extend his support to him.[6]

The Muslims' rule in India was basically a colonization enterprise powered by better use of military forces and the religious inspiration of the *ghazis* (volunteers fighting for their faith). The sultanate ushered in a period of Indian cultural renaissance by facilitating the fusion of Indo-Muslim cultures with lasting syncretic monuments in religion, architecture, literature, music, and fine arts. The Urdu language, in which "urdu" literally means "horde" and "camp" in various Turkic tongues, was born during this period as a result of the intermixing and interacting of speakers of local Prakrit vernaculars with Muslim immigrants speaking Persian, Turkic, Arabic, and Pashto. But religiously and culturally, the Hindus suffered heavily during the centuries of Muslim domination. Thousands of Hindu temples and deities were destroyed, and in some cases Hindus were forced or coerced to convert to the victors' faith. As Joglekar, an Indian author and journalist, argues, the Hindu rulers never understood the true nature of the Muslims' domination, which was basically a military invasion by the Central Asian tribes whose military triumph made Islam a dominant faith. "To save Hindu religion and culture from the Islamic onslaught," he states, "the military defeat of the Turks was necessary. Therefore, as long as such military defeat was not inflicted, till then Hindu society could not remain immune from the Islamic aggression."[7]

Despite their enormous resources and the advantage of being the natives of the land, the Hindu kingdoms successfully challenged the Muslim rulers very rarely. Even when the grip of the central government of the Delhi Sultanate weakened, the Muslim governors of far-flung provinces, who were mostly Turks and Afghans, not only maintained sway over Hindu principalities but also expanded their territories. In the fourteenth century, provincial India split up into numerous independent Hindu and Muslim states. Six great Muslim dynasties remained supreme in Jaunpur (the Sharqi Sultanate), Bengal, Oudh, Malwa, Gujarat, and the Deccan Plateau. These dynasties covered almost all major parts of the subcontinent down to its southern extremities. After Mohammad Tughluq (r. 1325–1351) expanded the authority of Delhi beyond the Vindhyas Range into the Deccan Plateau, southern India came under Muslim rule, and a few years later, with the weakening of central control by the powerful Muslim state (the Bahmani Sultanate or Bahmani Empire, 1347–1527), emerged as one of the great medieval Indian kingdoms. It was the first independent Islamic kingdom in southern India established under an Afghan ruler, Hasan Gangu. It dominated the south from coast to coast.

The rise of the Bahmani Sultanate coincided with the formation of the Vijayanagara Hindu kingdom (1336–1646) in the south as the culmination of attempts by the southern powers to ward off the Islamic invasion of the south. In the words of one modern Indian author, Vijayanagara was established for the purpose of saving southern India from being completely conquered by the Muslims. Another reason was to save the Hindu religion, allow for its natural development—at least in this corner of India—without molestation from outside agencies, and finally to save as much of India's culture and learning as possible.[8] And yet the kingdom never succeeded in winning a victory over the overwhelming power of the Bahmani Empire, which repeatedly forced the Hindu Empire to pay tribute to the Bahmani sultans. Even after the Bahmani Sultanate split into five states in 1518,[9] the Hindu rajas in the south failed to hold their own against the united front of these separate states and suffered a decisive defeat in the historic Battle of Rakshas-Tagadi (January 5, 1565) on the Krishna River.

These repeated Hindu setbacks have a military explanation. The Turks and Afghans possessed powerful cavalries and used cavalry-based battle tactics. Furthermore, as in the Battle of Rakshas-Tagadi, the

Muslim armies had superior artillery, and their cavalry was better armed and better mounted and excelled in horsemanship. According to Hindu sources, in 1442, a council called by the Vijayanagara king identified the superiority of the Muslims in the strength of their horses, which were of Arabian and Khorasani stock, and the Bahmani sultan's great hordes of excellent archers. There were only a few well-trained archers in the Hindu army. Vijayanagara's population, revenue, and the numerical strength of its army exceeded those of the Bahmani kingdom.[10] The emperors of Vijayanagara had the largest infantry force in India, which could also be used effectively as foot archers against enemy cavalry charges, but the rajas did not pay much attention to train it into a more powerful instrument of war. In fact, all the divisions of the Hindu army would make a simultaneous attack upon the enemy, and the battle was either won or lost in that single charge. The Muslims protected themselves with a furious discharge of their artillery, which decimated the Hindu ranks. They followed this with a vigorous charge by the cavalry and elephants, which decided the outcome of the battle.[11] It is likely that an often-quoted Hindu prayer is a reflection of this period. The prayer beseeches divine deliverance from "the venom of the cobra, the teeth of the tiger and the vengeance of the Afghan."

The Mughal Empire and the Afghan Tribes

The military history of the Mughal Empire in India, and its dealings with the defiant Afghan tribes within India and on the communication routes to Kabul and Kandahar, reflect some of the same difficulties experienced by the rulers of the Delhi Sultanate and their partners in India. But there was one major difference: the sultanate was involved mostly in the Indian hinterland. The Jhelum River was its western border, and the Turko-Mongol princes prevailed beyond that. The Mughals, who ruled India after the Turko-Mongol princes, were faced with outside rivals from beyond the Indus River, from inside Afghanistan, and later on from the Europeans in the east advancing from the southern and eastern Indian seaports.

The Mughal conquest of India arrived in the wake of many previous invasions launched from Afghanistan. Historically, the powers that held control over Afghanistan were in a strategically advantageous position to project power eastward into India through the Hindu Kush passes and then overrun the northern Indian plains. Conquest was often easily achieved but hardly sustained. A rich but poorly protected India made

the invasion an attractive and rewarding venture for conquerors coming from the west. An ongoing power struggle among Indian princes
and local rulers—particularly in the absence of a sovereign authority—tempted some regional princes to invite outside powers to intervene. This usually led to foreign invasions. From Alexander the Great
(356–323 BC), who was encouraged and supported by the king of Taxila
to invade India, to Sultan Mohammad Ghori (1150–1206), who was inspired by a call from Raja Chakra Deva of Jammu[12] to conquer northern
India, most invaders were assisted by competing princes on the subcontinent. Similar collaborations were recorded between Babur and Indian
rulers, including Daulat Khan Lodi, the powerful Afghan governor of
Punjab, and Maha-Rana Sanga (1484–1527), the mighty Rajput prince
of Mewar.[13] Following the initial waves of the invasion, however, the
invaders either returned home laden with plunder or stayed in the conquered lands to rule. Alexander the Great, Chinggis Khan, Tamerlane
(Amir Timur), and Nader Afshar (1688–1747) belong to the first class,
while Sultan Mahmud of Ghazni, Sultan Mohammad Ghori, and Babur
represent the second.

The first class of conquerors became powerful plunderers that disrupted and pillaged the land with no long-term occupation. The second
group of invaders would increasingly get locked into a drawn-out political and military struggle to unify separate principalities into a central
colonial state. Within a sociopolitical geographic environment, an alien,
military-based colonial power could hardly settle internal conflicts
through peaceful means and often resorted to military force, at least
at the outset. This made civil strife and intermittent revolts inevitable
in spite of the efforts of Emperor Jalaluddin Akbar (1542–1605), who
brought some religious and cultural harmony through the introduction
of *Din-i-Ilahi* (the Divine Religion).[14] While this reconciled the Hindus—including the Rajputs and Marathas—with the Muslims, less than
a century later, during Aurangzeb's rule (1658–1707), the crackdown on
Hindus and the persecution of non-Muslims undermined the integrity of
the state and paved the way for its eventual decline. Finally, the powerful Rajput prince Maha-Rana Sanga invited Babur to invade India and
collaborated with him in his conquest. But once the Rajput raja saw that
the Timuri prince intended to establish permanent Muslim rule in India,
he became one of the first native leaders to challenge the conqueror and
fought him in March 1527 at the historic Battle of Kanwa near Agra.
The Indian nationalists lost the battle, but Kanwa was just the begin-

ning. Similarly, Babur failed to sway the Afghan nobles, who considered him and his dynasty as usurpers after the fall of the Lodi dynasty following the Battle of Panipat in 1526. The Afghans held prominent positions in India for more than three centuries and had put two dynasties on the Delhi throne that lasted about a century.

The intensity of the Mughals' struggle with numerous contenders in India could have led to their isolation from their power base in the west and the disruption of their strategic ties with Afghanistan. This was what had happened in the past to the Greco-Bactrians (third–first centuries BC), the Kushans (first–third centuries AD), and the Ephthalites (fifth–sixth centuries AD) in ancient times; and to the Ghaznavids (tenth–twelfth centuries AD) in the medieval ages. Faced with powerful rivals in the west (the Safavids) and in the northwest (the Uzbeks), such a disruption was hardly an option for the Mughal Empire. For the Mughals, maintaining control over the routes linking their Indian dominions to their northwestern strategic border in Kabul and Kandahar was vital. Mughal strategists serving Emperor Jalaluddin Akbar noted that "Kabul and Kandahar are considered two gates of India. The former provides access to Central Asia and the latter to Iran. . . . Both facilitate links to the outside world."[15] Strategic links to Afghanistan passed through the rugged terrain of warlike Afghan tribes between the Sind (Indus) River and Khyber Pass in the northwest and between the Sind River and Bolan Pass in the southwest. The struggle to keep these routes open and to subdue the defiant Afghan tribes who often blocked the passage of Mughal armies was the main feature of the Mughal Empire's Northwestern-Front policy throughout the sixteenth and seventeenth centuries.

During his five attempts to invade India from his strategic base in Kabul, Zahiruddin Babur (his official name) had two major encounters with the Afghan tribes in the region. Although he established kinship with the Afghans by marrying a Yousafzai girl, his struggle to make a breakthrough took years. The first engagements were mostly violent raids for plunder and to open the route to India through the tribal territories between Kabul and the Sind River. The second major encounter was with the ruling Afghan dynasty of Lodi (1451–1526) at the Battle of Panipat in which the army of the Afghan sultan of Delhi, Ibrahim Lodi (r. 1517–1526), was defeated, paving the way for the establishment of Mughal rule in northern India.

During the two centuries of Mughal domination of the region, their experience with the Afghans followed three interconnected trends:

1. Attempts by the defeated Afghan nobility to regain power in India.
2. The growth of an anti-Mughal nationalist-religious movement in the Afghan tribal areas.
3. Tribal resistance to the movements of Mughal armies through their valleys.

The Afghans Strike Back

During his four years of rule, Babur succeeded in establishing his control over a narrow stretch of land in northern India extending from Patna, Sirhind, Sialkot, and Attock in the north to Chanderi, Bayana, and Mewar in the south. He and his successors had to fight their way in all directions to achieve imperial power. Babur's four years of rule in India (1526–1530) were followed by nine years of his son Humayun's reign (1530–1539), which witnessed a fierce challenge by the Afghan nobles to regain power. The struggle eventually forced Humayun to flee India and take refuge with the Safavid court in Persia. The Mughal power base in Afghanistan helped Humayun to reclaim the crown fifteen years later.

The Afghans' challenge to Mughal rule came from the east rather than the west, where the Afghan nobles under the leadership of Sher Khan (1486–1545) of the Suri tribe wielded increasing power. Sher Khan led his followers to avenge the defeat of Ibrahim Lodi, a fellow Ghilzai-Bittani, by overthrowing Babur's successor. Originally named Farid, Sher Khan earned this nom de guerre after killing a fully grown tiger (*sher*) with his bare hands in a jungle of Bihar. He was the grandson of Ibrahim, an immigrant to India from Afghanistan—the Roh[16] country—and the son of Hasan who entered the service of Sultan Sikandar Lodi. The sultan granted him a *jagir* (feudal life estate) in Sahsaram in Bihar. After an eventful career in Bengal, he served Bahar Khan Lohani, who assumed the title Sultan Mohammad and ruled independently after the fall of the Lodi dynasty.

Meanwhile, Sher Khan, through a connection with a Timuri noble, joined the court of Babur. After observing the Mughal administration, Sher Khan concluded that the Afghans could expel the Mughals and regain their lost sultanate in India.

Sher Khan soon realized his dreams during the reign of Babur's successor, Humayun, who was distracted by constant family disputes that affected his leadership and the cohesiveness of the imperial army. By 1537, Sher Khan was in full control of northern and southern Bihar. He built a formidable military force that was inspired by the desire to regain the lost power of the Afghans in Delhi. By the time Humayun realized the enormity of the Afghan threat, it was too late to stop the Afghan leader, who by that time was well entrenched in the east. Responding to the threat, Humayun led his army east to deal with the Afghans. Sher Khan tried to lure the Mughal emperor deep into Bengal and keep him engaged during the rainy season. While the two armies were facing off on the Ganges, Sher Khan duped the enemy by feigning withdrawal, which caused the Mughal army to lower its guard. Then, on June 26, 1539, Sher Khan returned quickly to launch a surprise attack on Humayun's camp at Chausa[17]on the left bank of the Ganges River. Humayun could hardly form his scattered troops into battle lines as the Afghan army launched a flank strike to the rear of the Mughal army along the Ganges River, pushing the enemy forces up against the river. In a panic, the Mughal army rushed to cross the Ganges to the south, but the only bridge broke apart under the weight of the fleeing masses. Nizamuddin Bakhshi (1551–1621) writes that the bridge was destroyed by the Afghans and that they attacked the fleeing Mughals with an assembled fleet of boats.[18] Finding the bridge broken by the throng of his fleeing army, Humayun plunged his horse into the river and was rescued from drowning by a water carrier named Nizam, who helped him return to Agra. Several Mughal generals and 7,000–8,000 of their troops fell in the battle and all their baggage trains were seized by the victors.[19] As Ishwari Prasad states, no stratagem in history had produced such a decisive impact.[20]

Eyewitnesses speak of the remarkably generous treatment of the royal captives by Sher Khan after the defeat of Humayun. "When the Emperor Humayun's queen, with other noble ladies and a crowd of women, came out from behind the *parda*, as soon as Sher Khan's eye fell upon them, he alighted off his horse, and showed them every respect and consoled them . . . after this he sent the heralds to proclaim throughout the army, that no person should make captives of or keep a Mughal woman, child, or female slave."[21] Sher Khan sent the queen honorably to Agra. The treatment was in line with the universal Afghan (Pashtun) code. Sir Olaf Caroe rightfully states that "it is in the tradition of Afghan tribal warfare not to molest the women or children of the enemy."[22] The victory at Chausa marked the beginning of the Suri Empire, founded by Sher Shah,[23] which was completed nearly a year later at the Battle of Kanauj on the left bank of the Ganges. Determined to deal with Sher Shah once and for all, Humayun led his army east along the right bank of the Ganges and attempted to cross the river at the Bhojpur crossing site, 31 miles northwest of Kanauj. He hoped to bring the Afghans to battle while stemming the increasing desertion in his army. The Afghan army was camped across the river and prevented the Mughals' crossing by destroying the bridge. Humayun moved downstream and camped at Kanauj while Sher Shah deployed his army across the river in a fortified encampment. According to Mirza Haidar, who joined Humayun in the campaign, the two armies were facing each other for a month.[24] When Sher Shah's army was fully assembled, he sent a message to Humayun demanding that either he cross the river to fight the Afghans, in which case he would not interfere with his movements, or he should move away from the river bank so that the Afghans could cross to his side unimpeded to face him in battle. This recalls a similar alleged battle situation reported by Herodotus over two thousand years prior when Cyrus the Great led his army against the Massagetae hordes ruled by their queen Tomyris. Tomyris tried to dissuade Cyrus from waging war against her nation and when Cyrus did not concur, she offered to pull back from the Jaxartes River so that Cyrus could cross unchallenged and resume the fight with her forces beyond the river. Cyrus agreed and crossed the river with no interference from the enemy.[25]

Humayun agreed, built a bridge, and crossed the river to the Afghan side without being interfered with by Sher Shah as promised. Ne'matullah says that Sher Shah had withdrawn about 12 miles from the river to accommodate the enemy's unimpeded crossing.[26] During the crossing of the Mughal army, an Afghan noble, Hamid Khan Kakar, tried to persuade Sher Shah to attack the enemy forces but this was rejected by the Afghan leader, saying this time he wanted to face the Mughals in a straight duel with no deceptions and ruses.[27] Mirza Haidar states that the size of the opposing forces was 200,000, while other sources including *Tabaqat-i Akbari* and *Fereshta* put the size of the Mughal army at 100,000 and the Afghans at 50,000. The Mughal army was supported by 21 heavy guns and 700 light artillery pieces.[28]

The battle of Kanauj on May 17, 1540, took place during a sudden change of weather conditions that were unfavorable to the Mughals. After Humayun got his army across, he deployed it inside a fortified encampment covered by the artillery at the front. Sher Shah's camp faced the enemy from higher ground, which had a decisive impact on the course of the battle. In mid-May 1540, heavy rains began. The Mughal camp, which was located on low ground, was flooded by the heavy downpour and had to be relocated to a higher place. Exploiting the situation, Sher Shah decided to attack the enemy forces on May 17 while they were relocating. The Afghan army was divided into six divisions for quick maneuver and was able to turn the flanks of the Mughal forces, plunging them into chaos. The panicked rush of the service personnel and the *ghulams* into the combat ranks added to the chaos of the Mughal formations. They scattered and rushed for the bridge over the Ganges, which soon collapsed. This turned the Mughal army into an uncontrollable mob. Mirza Haidar, who participated in the battle with his cousin Humayun, wrote that the situation became so confused that "the soldiers split from their amirs and the amirs from their higher ups." He adds that the Mughal army was defeated even before the enemy hit them hard and that up to the time that the Mughals rushed to flee, the Afghans had not even launched an arrow.[29] The Mughal army lost 40,000 troops, excluding the *ghulams*, most of whom fell during their rush to escape the battlefield. The four-mile distance from the battlefield to the Ganges bank turned into killing fields and out of one thousand close aides to Humayun, only eight made it safely to the far bank of the Ganges.[30]

The Battle of Kanauj sealed the fate of Humayun's rule. After reaching Delhi, he saw no prospects for another chance to contain the Afghans; he rushed to Lahore, where his treacherous brother Kamran blocked his passage to Kabul and opened secret negotiations with Sher Shah. Broken and mostly abandoned, Humayun followed his brother Hindal to Sind, where grudgingly he was given quarters. Being under severe political and financial pressure, the desperate emperor of Hindustan headed west to Persia. Meanwhile, his brother Askari, who was governor of Kandahar, wrote to the Baluch chiefs to arrest the emperor, but Humayun slipped away to Persia and reached the court of the Safavi shah Tahmasp in Qazvin. The shah promised him assistance to regain his throne after he was forced to accept Shia doctrine.

The Reign of the Suri Dynasty

After his decisive victories in two pitched battles, Sher Khan seized Delhi and assumed the title of Sher Shah Suri. In Delhi, Sher Shah Suri, after consolidating power, advanced to Jhelum to strengthen the western border of India against future incursions from Afghanistan. Sher Shah Suri was well aware of the vulnerability of India against invasions from the west through the Afghan tribal areas. True, he was a nationalist Afghan, but he was also an Indian ruler. He mobilized the Afghan tribes to drive out of India the Mughals, whom he considered to be usurpers coming from outside to overthrow an Indian sultanate ruled by an Afghan monarch, Ibrahim Lodi. Ethnically he was an Afghan belonging to the Lodi-Suri branch, and he believed in the military capability of his fellow Afghans (Pashtuns). He spoke Pashto and honored the standards of the Pashtun traditions.

Sher Shah Suri proved himself not only an exceptional military leader and creative strategist but also a great administrator and builder. He is remembered in history as the greatest Muslim ruler in India, who, during the five years of his reign, not only restored law and order but also set up a new civic and military administration, issued the first *rupee*, and reorganized the postal system of India. He constructed four great roads dotted with caravansaries (inns where merchants and caravans stop for the night) at regular intervals and planted trees on both sides of the road to give shade to travelers and merchants. The Great Trunk Road from Chittagong in today's Bangladesh to Kabul in Afghanistan by way of the Khyber Pass is still used for transportation in present-day India. It was later improved by the British raj, and over the centuries the road served as the major trade route in the region, facilitating military movement as well as travel and postal service.

But the Suri Empire, which was built with so much blood and treasure, lasted only ten years after the death of Sher Shah Suri. The reign of Islam Shah was marked by factional infighting among the Afghan nobles. The empire further fragmented following the death of Islam Shah in 1554. The Delhi throne was then contested by three claimants from the house of Suri, with 'Adil Shah ruling over Agra and Malwa, Sikandar Shah in the west between Delhi and Punjab, and Ibrahim Shah in an area from the Himalayan foothills to Gujarat. The situation enabled Humayun—who had reestablished his control in Kandahar and Kabul following a power struggle with his brothers—to reconquer India and to restore Mughal rule on July 23, 1555.

Humayun did not survive long after recovering his throne and died in an accident on January 26, 1556, while climbing down the steps from a roof. His son Jalaluddin Akbar ascended to the throne in Punjab at age thirteen and, with the help of his father's generals, moved against 'Adil Shah Sur's military leader Himu (the Corn Chandler), who held Delhi and Agra and had assumed royal status for himself as Raja Vikramaditya. Akbar led his 20,000 troops against an army reported as five times stronger led by Himu. They met on the historic field of Panipat. While the Corn Chandler's army outflanked both wings of the Mughal army, Akbar won the day when an arrow pierced Himu's eye and his army fled the battlefield in panic. This second Battle of Panipat reaffirmed the rule of the Mughal Empire for another three hundred years.

Anti-Mughal Movements in the Afghan Tribal Areas

Immediate reaction to the return of the Mughals to India came from Bengal in the east, where Afghan leaders mobilized their followers against Mughal rule. This forced the imperial armies to fight for control over the region throughout the reign of Jalaluddin Akbar (1556–1605).[31] However, the more enduring challenge against the power of Akbar and his successors was launched in the west. It was spearheaded by a religious/political movement led by Bayazid Ansari (1525–1582), known as Pir Roshan (the Enlightened *Pir*). Born in Punjab and growing up in Kaniguram (today's South Waziristan), the poet-warrior *pir* from the Barak/Urmar tribe was propagating a reformist religious-Sofi ideology that became an inspiration to large masses of Pashtun tribes who were fighting Mughal control in their rugged homelands between the Indus River and the Hindu Kush Mountains—a vital strategic domain that linked the Mughals' Indian dominions to their vital strategic borders in Afghanistan.

Pir Roshan launched his insurgency from his base in Kaniguram and gathered a large following among the Pashtun tribes of Tirah, Waziristan, Bangash, Orakzai, Paktia, Logar, and Nangrahar. He mobilized large *lashkars* (militias) to fight against the Mughal emperor Akbar in response to the Mughals' harsh treatment of the Afghans and Akbar's continuous antitribal military campaigns. He also underpinned his struggle with a puritanical religious duty to counter Jalaluddin Akbar's *Din-i Ilahi*, a syncretic creed derived from Islam, Hinduism, Zoroastrianism, and Christianity as a revisionist and religious reformist concept. Seeing the spiritual and religious hold of Pir Roshan over a large portion of Pashtuns, Akbar not only responded militarily to suppress the movement but also brought in a number of religious figures to assist his struggle. The most notable religious figure was Akhund Darweza, who wrote a Pashto book in an attempt to refute Pir Roshan's ideas. Basically, the clash between Pir Roshan and Akhund Darweza was not political but religious, as the former's doctrine was based on *Tariqat* (the esoteric aspect of the religion, or sophism), while the latter stressed the *Sharia* (the exoteric aspect of the religion).[32] Furthermore, the Mughal emperor launched a broad campaign to discredit the Roshani movement as a cult with alleged connection to the Ismailia sect. This turned several Pashtun tribes (including the Yousafzai and the Khattaks) against Pir Roshan. They regarded the *pir* as a heretic due to his revolutionary ideas.

Pir Roshan's ideological motives in his war against the Mughals and his rivals in the Pashtun society have been interpreted in different ways. The progressive-leftist analysts conveniently portray him as the vanguard of progressive reform in the Pashtun society that was ignoring the conservative and militant aspects of his beliefs. Others consider his movement to be a nationalist drive to unify the Pashtuns against Mughal rule.[33]

Nevertheless, Pir Roshan was the first Pashtun to lead a major ideologically based insurgency against the Mughal emperor Jalaluddin Akbar. Known for his thoughts, which were strongly influenced by Sufi ideology and the unconventional reading of Islamic philosophy, Pir Roshan became a controversial leader challenged by both the orthodox religious community and the Mughal government (which saw him as a threat to its power). Pir Roshan advocated learning and equal treatment for women and social equality, which were considered to be revolutionary concepts in the strictly traditional society of the times. The harshest criticism of his thought came from two major personalities of the time: Sayed Ali of Termez (1501–1584), known as Pir Baba and a highly revered spiritual leader of the Pashtuns; and a disciple of the Pir Baba, Akhund Darweza (1533–1615). It was the latter who dubbed Bayazid Ansari (Pir Roshan) as Pir-i Tarik (the Darkness Pir). A century later, the famed Pashtun poet-warrior Khoshal Khan Khattak (1613–1689), who fought for the Pashtuns' cause against the Mughal emperor Aurangzeb, disparaged both the *pir* and the *akhund* for abusing religion for political ends. Because of a family feud between the Roshanis and the house of the Khattak khans, Pir Roshan was not favored by Khoshal Khan, although the former and his descendants waged a much longer anti-Mughal struggle compared to that led by the latter.

Pir Roshan presented his philosophical ideas in his famed Pashto book *Khayr ul-Bayan* (The Useful Discourse) and several other treatises. *Khayr ul-Bayan* discusses the fundamentals and liturgy of mainstream Islamic *fiqh* (Shari'a, or Islamic jurisprudence),[34] expounds on the paths of Sufi spiritual travel, and advises how to purify one's inner self and cleanse one's heart by turning it from all else but God.[35] Pir Roshan's written works in Islamic theology and Sufism do not contrast with the ideas of many leading Islamic jurisprudents and Sufi mystics. Politically, Pir Roshan was an antiestablishment activist living under

Mughal rule. He intensified his struggle after witnessing the brutal torture of a woman in Kandahar by the Mughal functionaries, which produced a flashback to the Mughals' pyramids made of severed Afghan heads during their conquest. Even his ideological archenemy Akhund Darweza acknowledged Pir Roshan's political insight and forward-looking perceptions.[36]

Although Pir Roshan led his army successfully in several skirmishes and battles against Mughal forces, eventually his followers were routed in a major battle in Nangrahar by the Mughal general Mohsin Khan. The *pir* escaped but later was surrounded and wounded by a Yousafzai *lashkar* (militia) near Topi; he was finally killed in 1581 near Tarbela along with all of his sons save one. His youngest son, fourteen-year-old Jalala, was captured but pardoned and freed by Emperor Akbar himself due to his tender age. The young Jalala soon took up arms and became Pir Jalala Khan. The Roshani movement, which he founded and which was perpetuated by his children, grandchildren, and great-grandchildren, inspired anti-Mughal movements in the Pashtun tribal areas from Attock to Kandahar during the sixteenth and seventeenth centuries. It also created political momentum and a spirit of independence in the hills that survived the Roshani era into the nationalist awakening period in Afghanistan during the eighteenth century.[37]

The Roshani challenge coincided with setbacks suffered by the Mughal military operation against the Yousafzais in Swat and Bajaur. Akbar's military expedition to subjugate the northwestern hills dominated by the Yousafzai Afghans in Swat and the plains north of Peshawar ended in a disastrous loss of Mughal troops and prestige. Having made some progress into Bajaur and Swat, the Mughal army under Zain Khan met strong resistance, and he called for help.

Akbar's military operation in the plains of Sama, northeast of Peshawar and north of the Kabul River, established Mughal control over part of the Yousafzai tracts. Loyal Khattak vassals and the construction of several colonies in the area cemented this control. Inspired by their own local interests, the chief of the Khattaks, Malik Akoray, and his son Shahbaz Khan helped the Mughals in beating the Yousafzais. However, their collaboration ended during the reign of Aurangzeb (1658–1707) when Khoshal Khan Khattak, the son of Shahbaz Khan, raised the anti-Mughal standard and fought them with sword and pen—a pen that was sharper than his blade.

Akbar's army did not fare better on the Roshani front. Several attempts between 1586 and 1592 failed to defeat Jalala despite the capture of thousands of his fighters. At the end of the sixteenth century, Jalala expanded his operation to the west and in 1599 captured Ghazni from its Mughal governor. Jalala finally met his end when a stray bullet killed him while leading his men. He was succeeded by his nephew Ahdad, who was married to Jalala's daughter Bibi Allayee, a strong woman who joined her husband and later her son in fighting the Mughals. With their strong following in Tirah, including the Afridis, Orakzai, and Bangash, the couple prevailed in the hills dominating the communication links between Peshawar and Kabul. Their struggle continued throughout the reign of Akbar's successor, Jahangir.

The death of Emperor Jahangir in 1627 led to a general uprising of the Afghans against Mughal domination. In Tirah, a Roshani *lashkar*, including Afridi and Orakzai tribesmen, led by Abdul Qader and his mother, attacked the Mughal army on its way from Peshawar to Kabul. Muzaffar Khan commanded the army and was killed during the battle. Then, Abdul Qader attacked Peshawar, plundered the city, and besieged the citadel. The operation brought most of the Pashtun tribes, except the Mohmands and Khattaks under Shahbaz Khan, the father of the poet-warrior Khushal Khan, to the standard of Abdul Qader. On the eve of a major victory, however, jealousies among certain Afghan leaders alarmed Abdul Qader. He feared being betrayed and raised the siege and returned to his base in Tirah. Finally, Mughal emperor Shah Jahan (r. 1627–1658), the grandson of Emperor Akbar, brokered a truce (through the Mughal commander Said Khan) with Abdul Qader. Shah Jahan treated the descendants of the Roshani house well. Although the armed struggle of the Roshanis all but ended, their message and example continued to inspire the fighters of the Afghan (Pashtun) hills.

The Culmination of Tribal Uprisings during Aurangzeb's Reign

In the second half of the seventeenth century, the frontier war, which began under Emperor Akbar, reached its peak under his great-grandson, the Mughal emperor Aurangzeb. The context of the war became increasingly complicated by the dynamics of internal rivalries among Afghan tribes, their shifting alliances, and the shifting loyalties of the Mughal allies in the region. The Frontier War during the reign of Aurangzeb developed within two geographic spheres with different outcomes. In the northwest, the Yousafzais' revolt was never defeated but was contained by the Mughal emperor. In the west, Afghan tribes, mostly the Afridis and Mohmands, disrupted Delhi's reach into its dominions in Afghanistan, particularly Kabul and Balkh-Badakhshan, through intermittent closures of the Khyber Pass.

Yousafzais of Bajaur, Swat, and the Sama Plains north of Peshawar presented an enduring challenge to Mughal domination. The ruggedness of the terrain and the long-standing feud between the Yousafzais and the Khattaks, who were favored by the Mughals, contributed to the intensity of the Yousafzai challenge. Earlier, the Khattaks took advantage of Jalaluddin Akbar's suppression of the Yousafzais in the Sama region, north of the Kabul River in the neighborhood of the Khattak lands, to occupy tracts of Yousafzai lands opposite their home at Akora. This led to a century-long tribal feud. During this period, while the opposition to the Mughals was predominantly led by the Yousafzais, the pro-Mughal party enlisted the collaboration of the Khattak chieftains, including Malik Akoray and his successors. This pitted the two major tribes against each other in a complex war of familial, tribal, and state dimensions. Malik Akoray and his son Shahbaz Khan both died on the battlefield fighting their Yousafzai rivals. As Khushal Khan Khattak attests, "My father and grandfather went to their graves martyrs. . . . Up to seven generations [of] my ancestors met their death receiving saber and dart strikes."[38]

Having served the empire under Shah Jahan (r. 1627–1658) in a number of imperial expeditions into India and Afghanistan, Khoshal Khan Khattak, the great Pashtun poet-warrior, became the Khattak chief after the death of his father, Shahbaz Khan (January 1641), and took on his clan's struggle against the Yousafzais. He was able to induce Shah Jahan to annex certain Yousafzai villages north of the Kabul River (Landai Sind) to his *jagir* (feudal land). The imperial edict only intensified the tribal animosity, which preceded another major Yousafzai revolt during the reign of Aurangzeb in 1667. Early that year, the Yousafzai chief, Bahaku, mobilized his tribe and, with the spiritual approval of a revered cleric Mullah Chalak, crowned Mohammad Shah as a nominal king. He led his army of 5,000 clansmen across the Indus above Attock and invaded Pakhli (a plain lying east of the Indus River in the Hazara District where the main road to Kashmir runs). This movement brought to the scene more clansmen, who plundered the Mughal forts and outposts on both sides of the Indus.

Aurangzeb used three columns to invade the rebel country: one moving west from Attock, the second approaching eastward from Afghanistan to cross the Kabul River into the Yousafzai territory west of the Indus River, and a third under the imperial grandee Mohammad Amin

Khan to mop up the area after the two columns broke the main resistance. The seven-month-long operation of punishment and destruction temporarily quelled the uprising before a wider revolt along the frontier five years later in 1572.[39]

The second major uprising of the Afghan tribes located between Peshawar and Kabul was of much greater intensity, wider in scope, and longer in its extent. The leaders of three major Pashtun tribes figured prominently throughout the uprising. They included Aimal Khan Mohmand, Darya Khan Afridi, and the celebrated poet-warrior Khushal Khan Khattak. Aimal Khan Mohmand even crowned himself king and had coins struck in his own name. But the real spirit behind the nationalistic drive was Khushal Khan, whose pen was no less piercing than his sword. His patriotic poetry inspired Afghan nationalists long after his death and continues up until today. His tribe, the Khattaks, was a large and warlike clan settled in the southern part of Peshawar Plain and much of Kohat and Banu. They were hereditary enemies of the Yousafzais and thus cooperated with the imperial forces against the Yousafzais, traditional opponents of the Mughal Empire, on the premise that "the enemy of my enemy is my friend." Khushal Khan and his family further served the Mughals by keeping open the Imperial Road between Attock and Peshawar. This granted them the right to collect the toll at the Attock crossing to the tune of 600,000 rupees annually. This relationship, however, changed under Aurangzeb. He abolished the collection of the toll. That decision, orchestrated by court intrigues, did not move Khushal Khan to take overt action, but the event clouded the relationship. Later, in 1664, he was treacherously arrested and kept for two years in the fortress of Ranthambhor. After he was remanded to house arrest, the Khattak khan took a hostile anti-Mughal stance. Once he was freed on the recommendation of the Mughal governor of Kabul, he was not willing to resume the old relationship and soon raised the standard of freeing all Afghans from the Mughal yoke. "I bound on the sword for the honor of the Afghan; I am Khushal Khattak the proud man of this time."[40]

While resentment and anti-Mughal agitation were simmering in the Pashtun tribal areas, a single event involving the misbehavior of a Mughal official in Nangrahar triggered an uprising that soon expanded across the region. In the spring of 1572, soldiers of the Mughal governor Amin Khan allegedly attempted to molest women of the Safi tribe (who were located in what is modern-day Kunar Province). The tribes retaliated by killing three Mughal soldiers, whereupon the local Mughal *faujdar* (official) of Jalalabad called on the Safi chiefs to seize and hand over those responsible. They refused and called on other Afghan tribes to support them. The anti-Mughal sentiments spread like a brushfire throughout the area, leading to a major mobilization of the Mohmand and Afridi tribes. They blocked the Khyber Pass against the Mughal governor, Amin Khan, who was about to move with his army from Peshawar to Kabul. In Jamrud, the governor found out that Afghans had blocked the way ahead and sent area notables to request that the pass be opened. The request was denied, and the governor, as Sarkar puts it, "intoxicated with wealth and power, and despising the Afghans' prowess, rushed blindly into his doom."[41]

As Mohammad Amin Khan and his army entered the defile at Lwargai, he was faced by the tribal combatants arrayed on both sides of the pass and dug in to fighting positions. The Mughal army deployed to force the passage. Once his elephants were in position at the front, the governor launched the attack. Stones and boulders rained down from the heights, killing many Mughal leaders and forcing back the panic-stricken troops, whose losses were great. Then the tribesmen, led by Aimal Khan Mohmand and Darya Khan Afridi, rushed down from the hillsides and wreaked havoc upon the demoralized enemy soldiers. The fighting continued all day. The pass remained blocked. Mohammad Amin Khan took the advice of his commanders and decided to move around the Tahtara Mountains near Landi Kotal, where water was available. The move brought further disaster to the Mughals. The tribesmen entrapped the beleaguered Mughal army by rolling down stones and boulders from the lofty peaks of Tahtara onto the doomed men packed together within the narrow gorge below. This inflicted a heavy toll on the Mughal leaders, and their horses, elephants, and men were all mixed up in a confused crowd. The Afghan fighters then charged down from the hills for a final blow. Reportedly, Mohammad Amin Khan and four other Mughals were the sole escapees.[42] Twenty thousand men and women were captured and sold into slavery.[43] The Mughal army lost everything, including men, treasure, elephants, and the train baggage. The families of Mughal leaders, including those of Mohammad Amin Khan (his wife, mother, son, sister, and daughters), were captured, and only some of them were later ransomed.

The victory increased the authority and resources of the Afghan leaders, who were glorified by a famous war ballad penned by Khoshal Khan, which in turn inspired defiance of the imperial forces among the region's Afghan tribes. The uprising turned into a national movement spreading across Pashtun lands from Attock to Kandahar. The tidings of the revolt sent shock waves through the Mughal court. Emperor Aurangzeb took immediate measures to protect Peshawar against a potential takeover by the marching Afghans. He removed Mohammad Amin Khan and called Mohabat Khan from the Deccan Plateau and reappointed him as governor of Kabul, a post he had earlier served three times with distinction. The new governor, with years of experience in frontier warfare, was too cautious to risk opening the Khyber Pass through a frontal attack against the resolute and well-entrenched Afridis and Mohmands. Instead, in the spring of 1673, he bribed his passage through to Kabul, taking a side valley across the Karapa Pass and leaving the Khyber highway in the hands of the tribes. The move was seen in Delhi as a cowardly action undermining the prestige of the empire and further emboldening the Afghans.

In November 1673, displeased with Mohabat Khan's lack of decisiveness, Aurangzeb dispatched a large independent force under Shuja'at Khan to punish the Afghan tribes and to open the Khyber Pass and the trunk road to Kabul. The operation proved to be another failed attempt to restore imperial control in the Afghan hills. In the absence of unity of command, there was little coordination between Shuja'at Khan's army and other Mughal forces in the region, including those of Mohabat Khan, governor of Kabul, and Maharajah Jaswant Singh, the mighty leader of the Rajput contingent.

Determined to make a difference and outshine his fellow Mughal leaders, Shuja'at Khan acted recklessly by moving in the middle of winter, crossing the Gandab Valley in Mohmand territory, and ascending the Karapa Pass on February 21, 1674. As the column entered the defile, it met a heavy snowstorm that turned to freezing rain during the night, disabling the Indian soldiers, who suffered from extreme cold and wetness. Then the Afghan tribes, positioned on high ground on both sides of the valley, began to harass the benumbed Mughal troops. At dawn, as the imperial army was almost incapacitated within the narrow gorge, the Afghan tribes charged the wretched columns from all sides. Shuja'at Khan died while fighting in the front ranks. Thousands of his soldiers were killed, and his surviving leaderless troops were surrounded by the clansmen. Discipline collapsed in the Mughal force. A contingent of 500 Rajput soldiers, who were dispatched by Jaswant Singh, fought their way to break through the enemy cordon and extracted the remnants of the army back to camp. Three hundred of the Rajputs fell during the rescue. Meanwhile, Khushal Khan Khattak and Aimal Khan staged a joint attack in 1674 on the strategic Nowshehra fort and captured it. Khushal Khan then resigned from the chieftainship of his tribe and fought as a rebel against the Mughals for the rest of his life.

The back-to-back defeats of the Mughal armies in pitched battles caused so much alarm in Delhi that, four months after the Karapa disaster (June 26, 1674), Aurangzeb himself rushed with a huge military force and artillery park to the region and camped at Hasan Abdal, between Rawalpindi and Peshawar. He stayed there for a year and a half, taking direct charge of the frontier war. The emperor shifted to a new carrot-and-stick strategy. On the one hand, by bestowing grants, pensions, *jagirs* (feudal estates), and posts in the Mughal army, he won over many fighting clans. On the other hand, he unleashed a destructive force under his Turkish commander Aghar Khan to clear the Khyber Pass and punish those irreconcilable tribes whose valleys were penetrated by detachments from Peshawar. The Mughal diplomacy to split and fragment the resistance—pitting clan against clan—began to work. By the end of August, the followers of Darya Khan Afridi promised to bring the head of Aimal Khan Mohmand if their past misdeeds were forgiven. Meanwhile, Mughal expeditions were launched to punish the Ghoria Khels, Ghilzais, Shinwaris, Mohmands, and Yousafzais. Aghar Khan foiled a night attack by the Mohmands and their allied clansmen, slaying hundreds of them, taking 2,000 prisoners, and destroying their homes. This operation lasted until the death of Aurangzeb in 1707.

In the meantime, Khushal Khan continued his struggle for many years by making forays against the enemy. Aurangzeb arrayed a number of Afghan clansmen to stop him and even bribed his son Bahram to fight in the Mughal ranks against him. But neither age nor a sense of hopelessness in uniting the tribes could force Khushal to give up the cause. He was moving from place to place, from valley to valley, single-handedly trying to mobilize the tribes. He found only failure and abandonment, standing forsaken on his battlefield flying the flag of Pashtun freedom. His desperation is clearly heard through his poetry, celebrated by his people long after his death in 1689. "When I girded the sword against the Mughals, I raised the name of the Pashtuns to the world. Alas, unity did not come among the Pashtuns; otherwise I would have torn the authority of the Mughals."[44]

The lengthy frontier war kept the best Mughal troops engaged in the northwest, relieving the Mughal pressure on the Marathas of the Deccan Plateau. Taking advantage of the absence of major Mughal forces, Shivaji, the militant leader of the Marathas, extended his influence into the south, sweeping across vast areas from Golconda to Karnataka and from Mysore and Bijapur to Raigarah. Furthermore, the frontier war and its consequences curbed the employment of the Afghan fighters in the Mughal battles against the Rajputs.

Main Features of the Afghan-Mughal Asymmetric War

The struggle of the Afghan tribes against the Mughal Empire in the second half of the sixteenth century and throughout the seventeenth was an asymmetric war pitting a conventional imperial military machine against fragmented tribal militias in rugged, hilly country between the Indus and the Hindu Kush. The tribes were able to inflict heavy losses on imperial armies but never succeeded in cutting the strategic links between Attock and Kabul for an extended period. They leveraged their ability to disrupt the Mughal operations in order to negotiate better local deals with imperial forces. The Mughals never succeeded in establishing firm control over the hilly terrain near Swat, Bajaur, Buner, Tirah, and Waziristan and the mountainous tract east of Kabul, but they were able to exploit internal tribal feuds by making separate deals with the clansmen and enlisting cooperation from the willing against the irreconcilable.

Militarily, the Mughal army was powerful in numbers, discipline, and equipment. It was strong in cavalry and artillery and other technical assets. But it was hampered by a heavy baggage train that made it vulnerable while fighting in remote areas with lengthy lines of communications. The Mughal forces were fighting far inside southern India against the Marathas on the Deccan Plateau, the Afghans in the mountains of Afghanistan, and the Uzbeks across the Hindu Kush in Badakhshan. Their enemies were fighting on their home turf and were better off in terms of sustainability and familiarity with the terrain. Aurangzeb used to call the Maratha leader Shivaji the "mountain rat," while the Afghan leader Khushal Khan considered himself the "eagle of the mountains." Both were not easy to catch by conventional methods. The Mughal army's enormous cavalry forces enabled it to react rapidly and to concentrate sufficient forces at the right place at the right time. However, the action of cavalry in the rugged terrain was impeded by well-entrenched tribal foot soldiers in the Afghan valleys. By contrast, the limited mobility of the clansmen and their small mounted forces limited their capacity to expand any tactical achievements into strategic gains or to face the Mughals' conventional forces in the open. The Afghans relied mostly on a tribal militia, which was mobilized during the war but was hard to keep together for long. Most of the militia forces were composed of foot soldiers. Abul Fazl-i-'Allami in *Ain-i-Akbari* (The Institutes of Akbar) listed the strength of tribal militias during the Akbar reign, recording a predominance of footmen.[45]

The Afghan tribes such as the Maratha warriors on the Deccan Plateau were waging a guerrilla war against conventional imperial armies. Their fight was of a defensive nature with little capacity to expand local victories into strategic achievements. This situation enabled imperial forces to prevail, strategically speaking. During more than two hundred years of the Mughal Empire's domination of Afghanistan, it never faced a permanent shutdown of the trunk road between Attock and Kabul.

The Indian soldiers often panicked when facing the hillmen in mountains or when hit by the bitter-cold weather of the frontier. But the empire had the ability to recruit from the so-called martial races in order to employ them against similarly tough enemy fighters. They used the hardy Rajput fighters against the Afghans and fought the Rajputs using Afghan highlanders recruited in Afghanistan. They used different clans of martial races against one another. For example, they beat the Yousafzais using their Khattak kinsmen and punished the Khattaks using their Bangash rivals. In Rajasthan, they used to fight the Rajputs of Mewar by using their fellow tribesmen from Bikaner and Jodhpur.

What the Mughals failed to achieve on the battlefield was compensated for by political means. The internal feuds and lack of political mobilization in the tribal areas allowed the Mughal court to make separate deals with competing leaders, set tribe against tribe, and pit clan against clan. In the words of Aurangzeb, they were "breaking two bones by knocking them together."[46] It is not surprising that the son of the Yousafzai chieftain Bahaku, whose father fought fiercely against the Mughals, was appointed as a ranking officer in the Mughal army by Emperor Shah Jahan. Khushal Khan's own son Bahram was promoted by Aurangzeb to a high rank and was tasked with fighting against his militant father. In the words of Khushal, "These offices and these awarded gifts . . . are all snoozes and snares for men."[47]

The Mughal soldiers were better armed, and their infantry was equipped with matchlock muskets. The Afghan tribes had limited access to firearms. In the early 1970s, when I was commissioned to help set up the military museum in Afghanistan, I came across a musket among old army stores that once belonged to Khushal Khan Khattak (1613–1689). He had inherited it from his father, Shahbaz Khan. Known as the "Khattak Gun," it is nearly seven feet long and one inch in caliber. It is a crude matchlock, similar to the weapons used by the Mughal army during the sixteenth century. It meets the specifications of what Khushal Khan defined as a "mountain warfare" gun.[48] Only a limited number of notable Afghan clansmen had access to firearms. In a lengthy history of the Afghans, Khushal Khan's grandson Afzal Khan (died 1769), who assumed the Khattak leadership after his grandfather's death, writes that the Mughal court had authorized Khushal to raise just a thousand gunmen to fight on the Mughals' side against the Yousafzais.[49] The Afghan mountaineers were expert bowmen, and in the mountains their arrows were more effective than the Mughal soldiers' matchlock muskets, which required many steps to reload.

The Mughal Empire and the Uzbek Khanate

During this period, northern Afghanistan—particularly Badakhshan and Balkh—was the frontline between the Mughal Empire of India and the Uzbek khanate of Transoxiana. After Babur was driven out of his ancestral home by Ubaidullah Khan (d. 1539), the Mughal princes' authority was confined to the districts south of the Amu Darya. The internal power struggle within the Uzbek khanate after the death of Ubaidullah Khan eased the Uzbek pressure on the south. In 1556, however, with the rise of Abdullah Khan II (considered to be the greatest Uzbek ruler after Shaybani), the khanate's forward policy southward was reactivated. He invaded Badakhshan in 1584 and drove the Timurid prince Suleiman Mirza out of the area. The governor of Kabul, Hakim Mirza, brother of Jalaluddin Akbar, appealed to his brother for help. Akbar promised assistance in case the Uzbeks moved farther south and attacked Kabul. Such an attack never took place.

The northern provinces remained mostly in the hands of the Uzbek khanate until the middle of the eighteenth century, when Ahmad Shah Durrani annexed them to the Durrani Empire (which he founded in Kandahar in 1747). Nevertheless, the area changed hands intermittently as it was captured by Shah Jahan in 1646–1647 and annexed by Nader Afshar of Persia in 1740–1747 after he captured Bukhara and made its amir a vassal of Persia.

The geopolitics of the region in the middle of the seventeenth century convinced Emperor Jalaluddin Akbar that the key to the defense of India against rival powers in the region was Mughal control over Kabul and Kandahar. With the rise of Uzbek power in Transoxiana, coupled with geographic and topographic realities, Akbar saw his grip on Badakh-shan and Balkh as barely tenable. Furthermore, he believed that the cavalry-dominated Uzbek army was not suitable for making inroads into the Afghan mountains and most likely would continue projecting power across the plains of Khorasan to the west and southwest. He also considered the Hindu Kush Mountains to be a natural barrier against any Uzbek incursion to the south. On the basis of such geopolitical analysis, the Mughal emperor negotiated a treaty with the Uzbek ruler Abdullah Khan in 1588. He ceded Badakhshan and Balkh to permanent Uzbek control on the condition that the Uzbeks would refrain from at-tacking Kabul and its dependencies. Therefore, in spite of his emotional connection to his ancestral homeland, Akbar adopted a realistic policy to set the Hindu Kush as the northern border of his empire and fight the Safavids over control of Kandahar, which was located on the southern access route to India.

More than half a century later, Emperor Shah Jahan (r. 1627–1658) saw internal troubles in Bukhara as an opportunity to reconquer the north and led an army from Kabul across the Hindu Kush in 1646. He easily succeeded in defeating the Uzbek army and capturing Badakh-shan and Balkh. However, the Mughals soon realized that retention of the area in the face of Uzbek harassments was more difficult than its capture and restored Balkh and Badakhshan to the Uzbek khanate in 1647.

The Safavid-Mughal Competition for Control of Kandahar

The struggle for control over Kandahar became a main feature of the relationship between the Mughal Empire of India and the Safavid dy-nasty of Persia. Located at an important strategic point between Kho-rasan and India, Kandahar was a key border buffer for both states. The Timurid princes had ruled Kandahar since the end of the fourteenth century, when it was conquered by Amir Timur (Tamerlane). The rise of the Safavids of Persia in the beginning of the sixteenth century thwarted the power of the Timurids in western Afghanistan, but Kandahar still re-mained under their control. Babur captured Kandahar in 1522 from the Arghuns, a Turko-Mongol dynasty and the vassal of the Timurids. After that, until Kandahar's independence was won by the Ghilzai Afghans in the early eighteenth century, the province changed hands six times between the Mughals and the Safavids.

Although Humayun was defeated and driven out of India in 1540 by the Afghan leader Sher Shah Suri, Afghanistan remained under the rule of Timurid princes. Humayun's brother Kamran ruled in Kabul, and his brother Askari ruled in Kandahar. During his exile in Persia, Humayun won the support of the Safavid monarch Shah Tahmasp, who provided him with a Persian army to regain his throne in India. Humayun was able to capture Kandahar and Kabul from his rebellious brothers between 1545 and 1549. He then launched a military campaign leading to his restoration in India after defeating the last Suri rulers in 1555. Three years later, after the death of Humayun, his young son Jalaluddin Akbar was struggling to consolidate his rule. Shah Tahmasp Safavi seized the opportunity to capture Kandahar and besieged the city in 1558. The failure of the Mughals to send requested reinforcements resulted in the fall of Kandahar to the Safavids.

Jalaluddin Akbar considered Kandahar to be a key citadel against any invasion of India from the west. But it was more than three decades before he was able to attend to affairs in the west following his consolidation of power and establishment of control over Kashmir, Orissa, Sind, Gujarat, and Baluchistan, including the coastal region of Makran. In this way, he achieved strategic encirclement of the southern route to India where Kandahar was located. The rest went smoothly. The Safavid governor, Muzaffar Hussein Mirza, who held the province nominally as a fiefdom of Persia and was on poor terms with the Safavid court, surrendered the city to the Mughals in 1595. It remained under their control until Shah Abbas Safavi captured Kandahar in 1622. By that time, Akbar was dead and Shah Abbas was no longer under Ottoman pressure following the death of Sultan Ahmad in 1617. Shah Abbas decided to recapture Kandahar. As part of his plan, he plotted with the rulers of the Deccan Plateau to distract the attention of the Mughal army away from Kandahar. When the Persian army moved against Kandahar, Jahangir failed to support his governor in the province, however, and the city fell to the Safavids in 1622.

Persian control over Kandahar did not last long. After the death of Shah Abbas in 1629, his successor, Shah Safi, moved against the nobles and murdered most of his relatives and his grandfather's trusted generals and advisers. The governor of Kandahar, Ali Mardan Khan, was summoned to the court of Shah Safi. Fearing for his life, he surrendered the city to an army dispatched by Shah Jahan in 1637. The Mughal army then defeated the Safavi forces sent to recapture the city.

The final round of the Safavi-Mughal fight over Kandahar took place in 1649. The Safavi king, Shah Abbas II (who ascended the throne after the death of his father, Shah Safi, in 1642), launched another campaign to take Kandahar. He was encouraged in his plan by Shah Jahan's preoccupation in the north, where the Mughal army was locked in a drawn-out war with the Uzbeks over control of Balkh and Badakhshan. The Persian monarch actually backed the Uzbek khan of Bukhara with troops for his war against Shah Jahan. About a year after the Mughals' failure in their incursion into the north, Shah Abbas II saw an opportunity to move against Kandahar while the Mughal forces were weak and the prestige of the empire was low. To stave off Shah Jahan's rapid reaction, the Persian monarch launched his attack during wintertime, when the passes between India and Kandahar were blocked by cold and snow. Shah Jahan's failure to reinforce the town led to the fall of Kandahar in February 1649. Superior Persian artillery fired 75-pound cannonballs from the high ground of Chel Zena. Despite three Mughal sieges of Kandahar between 1649 and 1653, the Mughals failed to dislodge the Persians, and consequently the Mughals never regained control over Kandahar. Paradoxically, the province remained in the Safavids' hands until the Afghans of Kandahar not only freed themselves from the Safavid domination but also overthrew the dynasty and occupied their capital of Isfahan in 1722.

10   The Rise of Local Afghan States and Their Invasion of Persia, 1709–1747

During the two hundred years of Safavid-Mughal competition over control of Kandahar, the Persians prevailed in the province more than half the time. However, the Persian domination was intermittent, and the province changed hands several times. Kandahar Province at the time extended from the border of the Mughal *subah* (province) of Kabul (between the Indus River and the town of Muqur southwest of Ghazni) to the plains of Helmand and Farah. Cooperation of the Afghan tribes— or the lack thereof—with the imperial forces played a key part in the victory or defeat of the contending powers. The major Afghan tribes in the region consisted of Ghilzais, who in previous centuries moved from the mountains around Ghazni to Kandahar and settled in Qalat and the Arghandab Valley. The other major tribal confederation was the Abdalis, who also settled in the area after migrating to Kandahar.

The Afghan tribes in Kandahar Province had been under the domination of Turko-Mongol rulers since Chinggis Khan's invasion in the thirteenth century. However, as mentioned in chapter 7, the Afghan tribes maintained their internal autonomy in areas out of reach of the Turko-Mongol ruling powers, which were centered in major cities. The tribes established multichannel rapport with the ruling dynasties. Meanwhile, the Afghan tribes of the eastern plains (west of the Indus River) were oriented toward the Indian dynasties and at times ruled India, while the tribes of the western plains (Kandahar, Helmand, and Farah) were mostly tied to the politics of greater Khorasan and Persia. Naturally, the Afghans of the east became involved in Indian politics and military conquests in India (Lodi, Suri, Khalji, Bittani, etc.), and the tribes in the west became enmeshed in Khorasani and Persian political and military developments. Among them, the Ghilzais, who followed the Ghorids and their successors in the conquest of India, became major players on the Indian political scene for more than three centuries (1192–1526). The Ghilzais of the western plains, by contrast, interacted with the ruling powers in the west, which included the Safavids of Persia after the establishment of the Safavid Empire in the early sixteenth century.

Persia's official adherence to Shi'ism under the Safavid dynasty marked a cultural divide between the Persians and the dominantly Sunni inhabitants living in Afghanistan and Central Asia. State-sanctioned crackdowns on Sunnis during the early years of the Safavid rule forced many non-Shi'a intellectuals to emigrate to Central Asia and India, while Shi'a theologians from Arab lands streamed into Persia.[1] During the following two centuries—when Afghanistan was divided between the Mughal Empire of India and the Safavids of Persia—the sectarian schism left an enduring impact on relations among social communities in the region. Two factors, however, enabled the Safavid rulers to manage the affairs of the Afghan tribes despite the sectarian rift. First, they often left Afghan leaders alone to deal independently with their internal affairs. When Shah Abbas (r. 1587–1629) wrested control of Kandahar from the Mughals, the new local rulers started treating the Afghan tribes as a conquered people. A tribal delegation went to Isfahan to complain to the Safavid monarch of the mistreatment of his officials in Kandahar. Shah Abbas accommodated the tribes by appointing a *kalantar* (administrator) from among the tribesmen to deal with their internal affairs. Second, the Safavid rulers often relaxed religious persecution of the Sunni population of Kandahar.

The Mughals of India (who also intermittently ruled Kandahar) were Sunni Muslims, sharing the same Islamic religious orientation with the Afghan tribes. However, the driver of the Mughal Empire's control of Kandahar was security-based and aimed at blocking an invasion of India from the west through the Kandahar–Sind southern strategic axis extending to the Punjab. In their competition with the Safavids, they often invoked coreligiosity to win cooperation of the Afghan tribes. The policy worked only when the Afghans were suppressed by the Safavid rulers and failed when the Mughal officials controlled Kandahar heavy-handedly. The shifting loyalty of the Kandahar governors was also a factor in the see-saw domination of Kandahar by rival empires. Twice (in 1595 and 1637), the Safavid rulers of Kandahar collaborated with the Mughal emperors to seize control of Kandahar.

In 1694, Shah Suleiman Safavi was succeeded by a mild-mannered son, Shah Sultan Hussein, who devoted his time to his harem and proved to have little influence over his competing ministers and court nobles. The shah was a devoted Shia Muslim and ordered the strict observance of religious tenets across the state. The Safavid religious persecution, which had been relaxed for some time, resumed in a more stringent and violent form during the reign of Shah Sultan Hussein (d. 1726). The shah was greatly influenced by the renowned Shi'a theologian Shaikh-ul-Islam Mohammad Baqer Majlisi, who was a strong supporter of Shia proselytization within the Sunni communities. The uprising of the Hotaks and Abdalis of western Afghanistan in the early eighteenth century, which led to the invasion and occupation of Persia by the Afghans (1722–1729), was partly motivated by sectarian disputes.[2]

During the reign of Shah Sultan Hussein, the Ghilzais were the most powerful tribal confederation in Kandahar. Their main rivals, the Abdalis, were forced to move and settle in Herat Province by Shah Abbas Safavi in the early seventeenth century. This move was in response to their rebellious nature. The Ghilzai leader, Mir Wais Khan of the Hotak clan, also served as the *kalantar* of Kandahar and was the most influential figure among the Afghans. He was held in high esteem by both the Ghilzais and the Abdalis in the province. Doubling as a merchant with business activities in India, Mir Wais Khan was a wealthy man. With the ascension of Shah Hussein Safavi, his ministers reported to him that the Afghans in Kandahar were intriguing with Delhi or preparing for a rebellion. This led to a new policy of cracking down on the inhabitants of Kandahar to stave off rebellion or collaboration with India.

Renewed Persian Repression

Among the contemporary sources are the accounts of the Polish Jesuit priest Tadeusz Jan Krusinski (1675–1751)[3] and the biography of Shaykh Mohammad Ali Hazin (b. December 1691 in Isfahan),[4] both of whom lived in Isfahan during the last years of the Safavid dynasty and the invasion of Persia by the Afghans. Both speak of the increasing repression of the Kandahar tribes by the Safavid rulers. Jonas Hanway (1712–1786), an English traveler and philanthropist, visited Persia some years later (1743) and wrote extensively on the affairs of this period.[5] Three main factors contributed to the increased suppression of the Afghans by the Safavids, which eventually led to a revolt ending the Safavid dynasty and causing the capitulation of the Persian monarch to the triumphant Afghan conqueror. First, the Sunni-Shia split, which was intensified by the Isfahan court's policy to enforce the Shia jurisprudence across its dominions, antagonized the Sunni population and instigated popular resentment in Kandahar. The situation was worsened when the Safavids reached out to the Hazara population of Afghanistan who inhabited the provinces north of Kandahar and practiced Shi'ism. The Hazaras never challenged Persian authority or showed support for the Mughals' efforts to capture Kandahar.[6] Second, the Mughals of India renewed their attempts to regain control of Kandahar and sent an embassy mission to Isfahan to negotiate the return of the province that they had lost to the Persians half a century back. The Mughals' demand caused the Safavi court to strengthen their position in Kandahar both politically and militarily. As the court of Isfahan kept the Delhi ambassador waiting in Isfahan for a response, the Persians took measures to strengthen the defenses of Kandahar—a city that had withstood three attempts by the Mughals during the reign of Shah Jahan. Politically, the Safavid court discouraged the Afghan tribes from collaborating with the Indians and kept them under pressure, as the Safavid ministers believed that Afghan leaders were plotting with the Mughal rulers against Isfahan. Afghan reaction to the Safavids' repression disclosed signs of a simmering revolt, which prompted even more Persian repression.

In 1704, three years before the death of the Mughal emperor Aurangzeb, the Safavid shah Hussein appointed George XI, known by Persians as Gurgin Khan, the governor of Kandahar. Gurgin Khan had led an unsuccessful revolt in his native Georgia and was pardoned by the shah after he rejoined the service of the court. He is believed to have converted to Islam and was known for his strictness and harsh style of administration. On arrival in Kandahar, Gurgin Khan, supported by a large contingent of Georgian soldiers, began intimidating and coercing powerful chieftains while his soldiers acted excessively amid the strongly conservative Afghan society. The Persian governor imprisoned and executed many Afghans suspected of organizing rebellion. Gurgin Khan finally targeted Mir Wais Khan, the most influential Afghan leader. He sent Mir Wais ostensibly on an official mission to Isfahan but secretly recommended his detention there, describing the Afghan chieftain as the spirit behind rebellion in Kandahar.

In Isfahan, Mir Wais Khan realized that the court of the feckless shah was divided and plagued by internal rivalry, intrigues, and pretentiousness, like something out of *King Lear*. The nobles, instead of working together, were plotting to undermine one another. The military leaders, in the words of Shaykh Hazin, had been so much immersed in ease and comfort that they had "hardly drawn a sword in one hundred years."[7] The chaotic political atmosphere in the Safavid court did not escape the sharp mind of Mir Wais Khan, who intended to exploit it in achieving his goals. Despite being under close surveillance in Isfahan, Mir Wais charmed the vying court nobles with words and gifts and soon became a casual visitor to the court, where occasionally his advice on state matters was requested. He won the trust of the Isfahan court to the extent that he could return to Kandahar to watch the activities of Gurgin Khan.

Independence of Kandahar

The Afghan chief Mir Wais, who a few years earlier had been sent to Isfahan as a prisoner, returned to his hometown with the full support of the court. He carried official letters of recommendation admonishing the Kandahar governor Gurgin Khan to restore Mir Wais to his former rank, to treat him as superior to the rest of his nation, and to confer every honor upon him. Mir Wais reached Kandahar and, in a secret tribal *jirga* (assembly) of Afghan and Baluch elders at his estate outside Kandahar, won the support of the tribes for his plan to overthrow the Persian suzerainty. His plan was for the Baluch and Kakar tribes to revolt and refuse to pay taxes after they returned to their districts. This would lure the bulk of Gurgin Khan's Georgian troops out of Kandahar, enabling the Afghan tribes to attack and defeat the reduced numbers of the Persian garrison in the city.

The scheme worked as planned. When the majority of the Georgian troops left Kandahar to punish the Baluch and Kakar rebels, the Afghan chief lured Gurgin Khan to a meeting, where his supporters overwhelmed and killed the Georgian and his small escort.[8] Then Mir Wais and his followers proceeded to Kandahar, surprised the small garrison there, and seized control of the city. Days later, the Afghans also successfully dealt with the main body of Persian forces sent to quell the revolt of the Baluch and Kakar tribes on their return to take Kandahar.

Expecting a strong reaction from the Safavid Empire, Mir Wais Khan strengthened his defenses and mobilized his people to secure their hardwon freedom from the Persian despots. He called on his tribe to show that they were worthy of independence through valor and determination. Using the Mecca fatwa, he denounced Safavid Persians as "heretics" and incited the people to fight them. He asked noncompliant residents to leave the province and "seek the tyranny to which they were devoted."[9] Furthermore, he took measures to protect the rest of Kandahar Province, organized the army, set up an ordnance service, created an artillery park, and established a gunpowder factory. In order to gain time for organizing his administration and defenses, the artful Mir Wais Khan made diplomatic overtures to the Safavi court, explaining the event in Kandahar as a popular insurrection in response to tyrannies committed by Gurgin Khan and his soldiers. He assured the court that he had taken charge of the affairs in the name of the shah and was vigilant against any attempts by the Mughals of Delhi to take advantage of the situation and march on Kandahar. At the same time, the Afghan leader tried to win the trust and support of the Mughal emperor Bahadur Shah (r. 1707–1712). In letters his envoy took to the court of Delhi, Mir Wais stressed the religious commonality between Afghans and Mughals and informed Delhi about his ongoing conflict with the Shi'as of Persia. He indicated allegiance to the Mughal emperor and asked for his support. He advised, however, not to send an army unless asked by the Afghans so that it would not lead to a major confrontation between the two empires, as the Afghans on their own were able to deal with the Persians. This way, Mir Wais forestalled a possible intervention by the Mughals and delayed any military response from the Safavids.[10]

The Isfahan ministers' reaction to the revolt in Kandahar was late and indecisive. Instead of taking military action, they sent an embassy mission to Mir Wais Khan to bring him and his tribe back in line. But the revolt in the province was developing into a movement for independence and was too serious and widespread to be resolved by a limited act of diplomacy. In one case, the Isfahan envoy, Mohammad Ghani Khan, was not given much time to present his message and was stopped short in his harangue by the Afghan leader. "Dost though imagine," asked Mir Wais, "that wisdom dwells only in effeminacy, and has never passed the rugged mountains with which this kingdom is surrounded? Let thy king raise or let fall his arm as he pleases; were he as formidable as thou sayest, it would be with deeds, not empty words that he would oppose our just design."[11]

Persia Strikes Back

When Isfahan finally decided to launch a military campaign to regain control of Kandahar, the Afghans were strongly entrenched. In the next four years (1709–1713), the Afghan tribes held their own and were able to defeat several smaller Safavid military expeditions launched by provincial forces from Khorasan. This not only emboldened the Afghan nationalists but also caused much delay in the Safavids' effort to regain Kandahar. Knowing that the reconquest of Kandahar required a much broader military action, the shah appointed Khusrau Khan, a nephew of Gurgin Khan, to be commander in chief and governor of Kandahar and put him in command of an army of 30,000 Georgian, Arab, and Abdali Afghan troops, of which 6,000 were Persians under Abbas Quli Khan, to reconquer Kandahar and avenge the assassination of his uncle. The number of Georgian troops seems to be highly inflated. Considering the availability of troops and logistic considerations for an expeditionary army, the real number may have been around 10,000.

Mir Wais Khan's strategy to counter the Safavid army used a combination of defensive and offensive actions, a form of "mobile defense" tactics in today's jargon. The "ways and means" of the strategy included three elements. The first element was a defense from behind the walls of the Kandahar fortress to withstand the enemy siege and fight attempts to scale the walls. The second element was supplying Kandahar and other mountain forts with provisions to survive long sieges. The Afghan chief ordered all the harvest along an eleven-day distance on the route by which the Persians were to march reaped and brought into the fortress. He also ordered that after the harvest was collected the country should be laid waste along the enemy's approach routes. He moved the inhabitants of towns and villages on the plains to mountain forts with sufficient supplies for their protection and sustenance. The third element of the strategy was the deployment of a mobile strike force behind the enemy lines on the Helmand River to harass the besieging enemy and cut its lines of communication and disrupt supply routes.

The Persian army left for Kandahar in the autumn of 1713 and was able to break through the Afghan screening force in Farah and Helmand and marched across the barren fields and plains devastated of supplies. The Persian army laid siege to Kandahar and kept battering the ramparts for days. After the Persian commander rejected a peace deal and demanded unconditional surrender, the population of Kandahar saw no option but to fight to the last, making the defenders even more forceful and determined. As the siege continued for nearly a year, there were no signs of cracks seen in the resistance of the defenders of the Kandahar fortress. In the meantime, the besiegers became increasingly vulnerable to incessant attacks by Afghan horsemen operating behind enemy lines, forcing the Persians to detail part of their force for flank and rear-area protection. Furthermore, the strain of supplying a large army in a hostile country presented the Persian commander with an increasingly difficult situation. To make matters even worse, the approach of winter added to the hardships and increased the risk of mutiny among the frustrated and worn-out Persian troops. The situation threatened the Persian army with its very survival. Staying in the area or retiring seemed equally disastrous.

Finally, the Persian command decided to raise the siege and retire to Persia. This was the prelude to a major disaster that befell the invading forces. The Jesuit priest Krusinski's accounts indicate that, when the Persian army decided to raise the siege, the Persian troops marched in one direction to save themselves whereas the Georgians took another route. Receiving the news of the split in the retiring Persian army, the Afghan chief ordered 800 camels mounted with light artillery pieces (Zanbourak swivel cannons) and a cavalry force to get ready for action. Personally leading this combined force, Mir Wais Khan attacked the retiring enemy columns and decisively defeated the Persian army. Khusrau Khan was killed, and only 500 Georgians escaped. The rest were put to the sword.

The victory confirmed the independence of Kandahar. Citing Persian sources, Joseph Ferrier states that the main battle between the retreating Khusrau Khan army and the Afghan forces under Mir Wais Khan took place on October 5, 1714, and that the Persian army was annihilated. An extremely frustrated Khusrau Khan hastened into the thickest of the melee and met his death while fighting alongside his men. Only 100 out of 30,000 troops escaped with their lives.[12] Isfahan made a last, failed attempt to recapture Kandahar when the Persian army under Rustam Khan was defeated by the Afghan leader before it reached Kandahar.

Mir Wais Khan united the Afghan tribes in the province, and they acknowledged him as the supreme leader of the nation. He established governmental institutions and organized a national army and its support elements. Uninterested in royal titles, he served as the top national figure until his death in November 1715. He was succeeded by his brother Mir Abdullah (or Mir Abdul Aziz), who soon lost legitimacy for advocating the unpopular policy of making peace with Persia. The peace deal he advocated would have made Kandahar a dominion of the Safavi king again. The policy was an affront to the Afghan tribes who cherished the achievements of the late Mir Wais Khan and the hard-won independence of their homeland. During the war against the Persian armies, the Afghans proved that the degraded Safavid military was not a match for Afghan fighters. The corrupt and badly administered Persian court proved incapable of forcing the tribes into submission. With growing dissension among the tribes against Mir Abdullah, Mir Wais Khan's eldest son, eighteen-year-old Mir Mahmud, murdered his uncle at the

Narenj Palace of Kandahar in 1717 and was crowned as Shah Mahmud. Mir Mahmud had accompanied his father during most of his battles and was strongly committed to his father's legacy.

Independence of Herat

One year after the death of Mir Wais Khan, the Abdali tribes of Herat, inspired by the Ghilzai revolt in Kandahar, rose up in arms against Safavid rule. The Herati Abdalis called Abdullah Khan the son of Hayat Sultan, the chief of Sadozais, from Multan and proclaimed him their leader in Herat. The Afghans seized control of the districts around Herat, including Sabzevar (today's Shin-dand). The Safavids dispatched an army to reestablish control over Herat that was defeated in a battle about four miles from Herat. Then the Abdalis laid siege to the city of Herat. They scaled the walls at the Feel-Khanah tower and captured the city with collaboration from inside and declared independence. Although the Abdali tribal confederation expanded their rule into Badghis in the northeast, to Farah to the south, and to Mashhad in the northwest over the years, the infighting among different clans and tribal figures weakened their reach beyond the province. Between 1718 and 1729, the governorship of Herat changed hands several times, in some cases violently. The family feud eventually cost the Abdalis their grip on Herat as the Persian military leader Nader Afshar (1688–1747) defeated them in a series of battles and conquered Herat.

The Afghans Conquer Persia

In Kandahar, the Ghilzai Afghans rushed to expand into Persia before consolidating their political and military base inside Afghanistan. When Mir Wais Hotak's young son, Mir Mahmud Hotak, became king of Kandahar Province in 1717, the Safavid court made another attempt to bring Kandahar under its control. It failed decisively after the renowned Persian commander Hussein Quli Khan and his son were killed in the battle. This seriously damaged the prestige of the Safavid state and encouraged local rulers elsewhere to challenge the authority of Isfahan. These events played out against the backdrop of a long period of national resentment against the Safavids' treatment of the Afghans in Kandahar. The Afghans' victories against the Safavid armies on the battlefield, coupled with a deep-seated thirst for vengeance, created a great deal of overconfidence and a passion for revenge. The Hotak monarch decided to invade Persia before putting his own home in order. The Safavids were weakened by maladministration, corruption, and infighting among the court nobles. It was vulnerable to invasion by resolute Afghan forces. But the real challenge was maintaining control of the conquered lands given the weak political and military base at home. Kandahar and Herat were in the hands of rival Afghan powers who were competing for dominance. To the east, the Afghan tribes who had not recovered from the crackdown by the Mughal emperor Aurangzeb (r. 1658–1707) were divided, and many of them were co-opted by the Mughal Empire and its Kabul governor, whose jurisdiction extended from Attock to Ghazni.

In such a politically divided country, Shah Mahmud Hotak decided to invade Persia and capture Isfahan, the center of an empire that had enslaved the Afghans intermittently over the previous one and a half centuries. The drive behind the project was more emotional than cool-headed strategic calculation. It was the deathbed wish of Mir Wais Khan, who advised his descendants to be "no longer subject to the Persians; strain every nerve and repel by every effort the evils they would inflict on you, for their ruin is hastening on through the dissentions of the court, and the wickedness of the people; fear not their spacious numbers, for you being united, and relying on God may conquer them, and occupy Isfahan itself."[13] Conquering the Safavids and occupying Isfahan may have been the easy part, particularly as Persia was on the path of major political and military decline and suffered from sociopolitical decadence. The hard part, however, was holding the conquered lands in the face of a hostile population and limited access to manpower and other resources so far away from the home base. Furthermore, the Hotaks of Kandahar had yet to raise sufficient funds to organize and equip an effective army and its support elements.

The Afghan Army

The Hotak army was composed of Pashtun tribal contingents, the Hazaras, Baluchs, and other Pashtuns and non-Pashtuns from Kabul and eastern Afghan highlands as well as the Zoroastrians known as *guebers*. A high-ranking general, Nasrullah Khan, was Zoroastrian, and another top military leader, Amanullah Khan, was from Kabul and possibly a non-Pashtun, as in one of his letters recorded by Krusinski he confirms that he was of different ethnicity. The personal guard of Shah Mahmud was composed of Hazara soldiers. These different contingents were brought under a hierarchical system. It included infantry musketeers and archers, cavalry, and light artillery. It was at this time that the Afghans in Kandahar undertook an innovative design, transforming the light Zanbourak swivel cannons into mobile, camel-mounted artillery that combined fire and mobility for effective maneuver on the battlefield. They mounted the light gun on a camel saddle with a revolving pivot. In addition to the gun, the camel carried two gunners, 40 two-pound rounds, and a sufficient supply of gunpowder.[14] This innovation, which played a key role in the Afghan victory over the Safavid army at Gulnabad in 1722, was adopted and replicated in later years by the Qajar dynasty of Persia (1785–1925). Tadeusz Krusinski, who witnessed the Afghan army in action near Isfahan in 1722, describes the Afghan force as accustomed to "roving warfare" and skilled in running battle, easily controlled and commanded by their officers.

Krusinski gives high marks to the Afghan horsemen, who could pick up anything that might have fallen to the ground while at full speed and were good marksmen.[15] This expertise is still visible among the Ghilzai Afghans of Ghazni and elsewhere in the races of tent-pegging sports. Hotak fighters were also credited with being extremely dexterous in the use of sword and spear. What impressed outside spectators during the conquest of Persia was the quick response of the Afghan fighters to the call of their leaders. "They are so much under the control of their leaders," writes Krusinski, "that no royal army was to be compared to them; and it was often remarked, that whether they were wandering about on their own private affairs, or taking their meals, they would instantly assemble on the orders being issued, and every man would be found at his post." The Afghan army was rarely reliant on heavy baggage trains. Their simple and Spartan lifestyle had freed them from much of the luxury that the Persian army was accustomed to. This had freed them from encumbering baggage, allowing the army to move lightly while facilitating fast marches over long distances. In 1722, Shah Mahmud Hotak marched on Isfahan through the barren plains and desert to Yazd and then to Isfahan without relying on a heavy logistic tail. The emergency and survival rations of the soldiers during long marches consisted of wheat parched in a pan, which sufficed them, including their officers and their king, in all their marches. The nutrient (*ninay* in Pashto and *gandum-beryan* in Persian/Dari) is still consumed as snacks by Afghan villagers. For water in the field, the Afghan soldiers used "bound intestine, filled with water, round their loins, for use in time of need. . . . They eat wherever they be, without any ceremony, seated on the ground, without table or cloth, placing their meat, cheese or other provisions on their bread and drink nothing but water."[16]

Krusinski notes that the commanders enforced a strict discipline, not allowing the fighters to turn back from the enemy; those who did so were cut down by their officers, who watched from behind. He speaks of an established Afghan custom: those who fall in the battle are buried on the spot where they died, while those who turned their backs on the foe are left unburied as a warning to others. "During the siege of Isfahan, of which I was a witness, in the battle between the Afghans and Persians, near the bridge Abbasabad, they would have killed a soldier who was retiring, after his right arm had been struck off, and ordering him to tear the enemy with his teeth if he lost his left, rather than fly. Inflamed him afresh for the battle with the desire of fame and acquiring a great booty for himself." He adds that "the Afghans are averse to the sale of their captives and after assigning them for some time to their own service they give them their liberty and are wont to adopt the children of the slain. Adultery and the unnatural offence are uncommon among them and when committed are severely punished."

By 1720, the army that Shah Mahmud Hotak had organized, equipped, and trained hardly exceeded 12,000 in number—a force capable of ensuring internal security but inadequate for waging war in foreign lands. And yet, the Afghan leader marched through Sistan and laid siege to Kirman. Although the Afghan army captured the town, it failed to withstand the Persian counterattack led by the Safavids' most capable general, Lutf Ali Khan. Shah Mahmud retired to Kandahar but did not give up his plan to invade Persia. In the next two years, the Afghan leader made efforts to reorganize and expand his military forces and get ready to renew his offensive campaign in Persia.

The Persian Campaign

In early January 1722, Shah Mahmud Hotak led a strong army to Kirman. Krusinski, who had watched the Afghan army at different locations during the siege of Isfahan and had spoken with Afghan military commanders, quotes one Afghan officer as saying that "we left Kandahar with 90,000 men, fit and unfit for war; but after a month's march, 8,000 of them returned, 2,000 others were either ill or dead; in short when Isfahan was sieged, we had 14,000 of Mir Wais's veterans, 8,000 Hazaras, and 4,000 Baluch; the rest of the army consisted of Indians [eastern Pashtuns], and the fire worshippers [Zoroastrians]."[17] From this crowd, many Afghan fighters had returned home with their booty after the Battle of Gulnabad, and most of the Hazaras followed them after the capture of Julfa. In fact, the size of the Afghan army before the fall of Isfahan never exceeded 40,000, of which many were killed, deserted, or died of natural causes. Krusinski concludes that Mahmud had about 40,000 troops before Isfahan, excluding the 14,000 troops he lost to attrition along the way. Therefore, Mahmud must have left Kandahar with 54,000–55,000 troops. There were also service troops handling some 60,000 camels that carried the baggage.[18]

After establishing his operation base in Kerman, Mahmud led his army by a shorter northwestern desert road to Yazd over barren and uncultivated tracts. As it was winter, the Afghan leader picked the desert shortcut to Yazd to shorten the travel time (twenty-four days' journey for mounted forces) and to surprise the Persian command. The Afghan army was estimated at 20,000–40,000. It had suffered attrition on the way due to its battle in Kirman and its unsuccessful assault on Yazd, but large numbers of local Zoroastrians (*guebers*) from Kirman and Yazd, who had been systematically persecuted by the Persians, joined the invading army. The *guebers* hoped that Mahmud's victory might bring them relief from the oppression they had endured.

Within four days' journey to Isfahan, Mahmud was met by two envoys of the Safavid shah who unsuccessfully tried to dissuade Mahmud from marching on in exchange for a payment of 15,000 *tumens*. Mahmud took this offer as a sign of weakness and fear by the Persian monarch. It encouraged him to push on. He moved to Gulnabad, a village only nine miles from Isfahan, and deployed his army in a fortified camp.

The Battle of Gulnabad

What stands out in the saga of the Afghans' invasion of Persia and the Persian counterinvasion sixteen years later is the military distinction of the Battle of Gulnabad (March 8, 1722), where a lightly armed and poorly equipped Afghan army decisively defeated a strongly armed but unmotivated Safavid army more than twice its size. In weapons and equipment, the odds were far more striking. On the one hand, the Persian soldiers looked fresh and splendid with their battle dress, equipment, tents, and sleek horses; on the other hand, the rugged Afghans were clothed in tatters and simply armed, camped in the open with hardly a tent to cover them. Their horses were lean, and their camels were scattered and grazing. Eyewitnesses observed that throughout their camp

Battle of Gulnabad, 1722

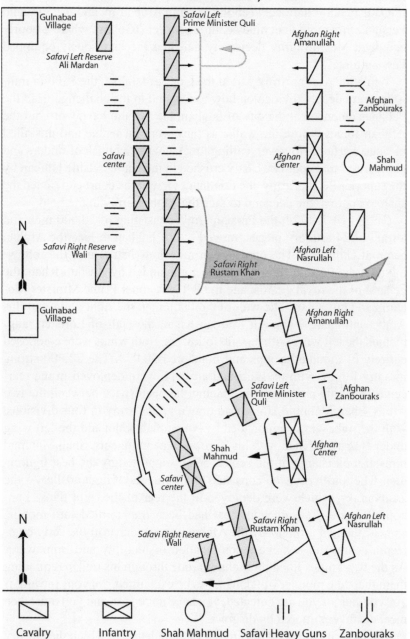

Gulnabad
Village

Safavi Left
Prime Minister Quli

Afghan Right
Amanullah

Safavi Left Reserve
Ali Mardan

Afghan
Zanbouraks

Safavi
center

Afghan
Center

Shah
Mahmud

N

Safavi Right Reserve
Wali

Afghan Left
Nasrullah

Safavi Right
Rustam Khan

Gulnabad
Village

Afghan Right
Amanullah

Safavi Left
Prime Minister
Quli

Afghan
Zanbouraks

Shah
Mahmud

Afghan
Center

Safavi
center

N

Afghan Left
Nasrullah

Safavi Right
Rustam Khan

Safavi Right Reserve
Wali

| Cavalry | Infantry | Shah Mahmud | Safavi Heavy Guns | Zanbouraks |

nothing glittered "but their swords and lances."[19] A renowned Iranian historian, Abdullah Razi Hamadani, compared the scene to the Battle of Qadisiyyah fought between the Muslim Arab army and the Sassanid Persian army more than nine centuries earlier (636 AD), where a poorly equipped Muslim army decisively defeated the luxuriously equipped Persian forces.[20]

While the Afghan army was at the gates of Isfahan, the Safavid ministers were deeply divided on how to respond to the challenge. Had the Persians defended at the city of Isfahan, they would have worn out the Afghan forces before the walls, as they were incapable and unskilled in siege warfare. However, calling the Afghans "a bunch of raiders and plunderers" that could be easily crushed in the battle outside Isfahan by the superior Persian army, the dominant view at the court convinced the shah to approve the decision to face the Afghan army in the field.

On March 7, 1722, the Persian army, consisting of 50,000 men and a train of 24 artillery pieces, moved out of Isfahan to face the Afghan camp at Gulnabad. The opposing armies drew battle lines the following day; the Persian right wing was commanded by Rustam Khan, the general of the royal guards, and the left was under Prime Minister Mohammad Quli Khan. The wali of Arabia joined the right wing with his Arab contingent, while Ali Mardan Khan, the wali of Loristan, augmented the left wing with his 500 followers. Both wings were composed entirely of mounted troops and numbered 30,000. The 20,000-strong infantry forces, with muskets and artillery, were deployed in the rear-center, forming a separate line facing the open space between the two wings. Shah Mahmud Hotak had drawn up his army in four divisions, with the right wing commanded by Amanullah Khan and the left wing under Nasrullah Khan with his Zoroastrian contingents. Shah Mahmud himself took charge of the center, being supported by the best fighting men. The fourth division consisted of 100 pieces of light artillery—the Zanbouraks, which were deployed in the rear of the right flank. Zanbouraks were the light guns that had been transformed into mobile, camel-mounted artillery by the Afghans of Kandahar in the early eighteenth century to achieve a combination of mobility and firepower.[21] As the two armies lined up Mahmud rode through his ranks, reminding them that "the plunder of Isfahan," as he exclaimed, "is your reward, if you conquer; if you are defeated, you have no retreat, and you must then meet death, embittered by disgrace."[22]

The fight at Gulnabad began as a running battle in which the cavalry of both sides played key roles by outmaneuvering the opposing forces and knocking them off balance with flanking movements. The Persian heavy artillery failed notably, while the Afghans' camel-mounted Zanbouraks proved to be the decisive weapons that sealed the fate of the day. The battle opened at noon with a cavalry charge by the Persian right wing against the Afghan left. The Persians drove the Afghans back. Simultaneously, the forces under the wali exploited the breakthrough by turning around the Afghan left wing and falling on its camp and plundering it. Busy with looting, the Arabs failed to hold the ground that they had just secured. By shifting forces from the center, the Afghans contained any further breakup of the left wing.

Meanwhile, the Persian left wing, under the prime minister, charged the Afghan right, led by the veteran Afghan commander Amanullah Khan. Facing the galloping enemy horsemen, the Afghan forces—instructed by Mahmud—conducted a clever maneuver by opening their lines to allow the Persian riders to pass through, thereby exposing them to the 100 camel-mounted Zanbouraks lined up in the rear. A barrage of swivel fire caused great havoc within the ranks of the Persian horsemen and turned them into a disorganized mob fleeing the field.[23] Seeing the enemy columns in disarray, the Afghan right wing launched its deadly assault and charged the reeling enemy columns. As the Persian cavalry fled, the pursuing Afghans wheeled to the rear of the Persian artillery, which had no escort and whose guns had not discharged even once.[24] The gunners were cut to pieces and the guns turned on the Persian infantry, which also broke up and fled. At that point, the Persian army had lost only 2,000 men, but it turned around and fled ignominiously. In the words of Sir Percy Sykes, "The Persian nation had ceased to be virile, and the verdict of history is that when it fell, it fell deservedly through its own cowardice."[25] The Afghan forces failed to pursue the retreating enemy forces, which would have completed their defeat. The victors instead busied themselves with plundering the Persian camp.

After the Battle of Gulnabad, the Afghan king Mahmud faced the enormous challenge of forcing the capitulation of Persia. This did not seem achievable without reducing its capital, Isfahan. Despite a lack of skills and technology for a long siege, Mahmud deployed his army to blockade the capital and force it to submit through starvation. The reported population of 600,000 of Isfahan endured increasing hardships and saw little action by the shah and his ministers. They poured into the streets, calling on the king and the wali of Arabia (the khan of Ahwaz, who was appointed commander in chief) to lead them into battle against the besiegers. Continued inaction by the court drove the people to riot, forcing the shah to come out from the comfort of his palace to quiet the angry mob. Frustrated and under increasing pressure, Shah Sultan Hussein sent envoys to Shah Mahmud offering to accept the terms he had earlier rejected. Now the situation had drastically changed. "The monarch of Persia," said the proud Afghan leader, "offers me nothing that is his. Himself and all his family are within my power. He is not now master of the three provinces he so generously desires to bestow upon me, but if he were, the question now at issue between us concerns not them, but his whole kingdom."[26] As the negotiations were proceeding, Malik Mahmud, the governor of Sistan, with a 10,000-strong army, marched to relieve the capital, but before he reached the city Malik Mahmud and Shah Mahmud came to an agreement whereby Malik Mahmud was confirmed as the ruler of Sistan. He returned home to take charge of his possessions. The Afghan king knew that he was getting into a stronger and stronger position as the blockade continued. He prolonged the negotiations for the city's surrender, as he did not want to lose more men while storming the town.

The plight of more than 600,000 citizens inside the blockade was dramatized in the accounts of Krusinski and Shaykh Hazin, both of whom were in Isfahan during the siege. As supplies to the city stopped, the inhabitants who had not stocked up on stores faced a deepening famine that took a heavy toll on the population. People were eventually forced to feed on dead animals, including dogs and cats, on the leaves and bark of trees, and on leather, which they softened by boiling. Some resorted to cannibalism.[27] Krusinski estimates that about 20,000 persons perished in the battle and another 100,000 citizens died of famine.[28]

Finally, the fateful day arrived. On October 22, 1722, Shah Sultan Hussein abdicated and surrendered his throne to the Afghan monarch. On the following day, the Safavid shah left Isfahan, attended by some of his nobles and 300 of his troops. He moved to the Afghan camp in Farahabad. There, the vanquished monarch addressed Shah Mahmud: "Son, since the great Sovereign of the Universe does not will that I should reign any longer, and the moment has come which he has appointed for thy ascending the throne of Persia, I resign the empire to thee. May thy reign be prosperous."[29] He took the tiara, or royal plume of feathers, from his turban and placed it in Mahmud's turban, exclaiming, "Reign in peace." The next day, Shah Mahmud entered Isfahan as the new shah of Persia. He now faced the enormous challenge of ruling an empire being threatened internally and externally.

The Road to Glory and the Path to Disaster

The real challenge facing the Afghans was how to rule and govern a vast country while detached from their divided power base in Afghanistan. Even though the Afghans won an easy victory against all odds in the Battle of Gulnabad, translating their tactical achievement into strategic gains was an enormous challenge and not easy to undertake. They were in a hostile land with little access to local elements of power. Their enemies had the potential to mobilize enormous political, financial, military, and public sources of power against them over time. Their power base back home had not been fully consolidated to support long-term conquests in a foreign country. True, the Safavids were losing control over far-flung provinces and were less capable of a massive mobilization of the people against the Afghans. But this was a temporary condition. In a country so vast, rich, and socially close-knit as Persia, winning single battles or capturing the capital did not guarantee the enduring rule of a foreign conqueror merely through the limited use of arms. Resort to arms to establish control entailed violence that led to growing counterviolence that in turn led to anticonqueror popular mobilization. This was what the Hotaks eventually faced in Persia.

During nearly eight years of occupation, Shah Mahmud Hotak and his successor, Shah Ashraf (r. 1725–1729), faced dwindling resources and increasing public resentment against the Afghans' domination. Frustrated by increasing revolts and decreasing numbers in the occupation army, the Afghan leaders resorted to sheer force, brutality, and escalating violence. The systematic application of this policy contributed to the mobilization of other forces in Persia against the Afghans' domination and to its violent termination in less than a decade. After the fall of Isfahan, the existing Afghan troops were adequate for the conquest of a fragmented Persia under a corrupt and weak leadership but clearly insufficient for administering the kingdom they had won so easily. Shah Mahmud ordered a head count of military forces after the fall of Isfahan. The Afghan army numbered about 25,000 troops, excluding the wounded. Such a small army lacked the ability to control the conquered land, particularly when the attrition rate—due to desertion, casualties, and expatriation—was high and replacements by Afghan recruits were extremely limited. The Afghans were usurpers and alien conquerors in Persia, and there were few prospects for local recruitment. Further, the Afghan rulers doubted the loyalty of the non-Afghan troops. After the fall of Isfahan, Mahmud ordered immigrating Afghans to settle with their families in Persia and to support the government. Except for those who held high offices in the country, few people, including the military, were eager to relocate permanently. Thus, the Afghans constituted a mobile population in occupied Persia. They acted in variance with previous conquerors, such as the Mongols and Tatars, who settled in great numbers in the occupied country, which helped perpetuate their rule. Throughout their presence in Persia, the Afghans remained a small community of foreigners amid a sea of hostile locals.

The situation forced the Afghan rulers to recruit from Kandahar and other parts of Afghanistan. This was not always easy because of the long distances, unsafe routes, and reluctance of many Afghans to stay long in foreign lands. Mahmud's successor, Shah Ashraf, faced tougher recruiting problems, as his cousin Shah Hussein in Kandahar broke ties with Isfahan and the flow of men trickled to a halt. In the face of these challenges, the Afghan rulers in Persia resorted to local recruiting among fellow Sunni populations such as the Kurds and Tatars. In 1729, when Shah Ashraf moved against the combined army of Tahmasp and Nader Afshar, more than half of his 30,000 troops were non-Afghan soldiers.

Prince Tahmasp Mirza, the son of the deposed Safavid monarch, had escaped the Isfahan blockade; he was crowned as the new shah and mobilized the Persian army for driving out the Afghans. In 1726, Nader Quli Afshar, who formerly led the life of a brigand, adventurer, and soldier of fortune, joined Tahmasp with his 2,000 followers. Soon, the Tahmasp–Nader coalition made significant inroads south into Khorasan and established a base for much larger campaigns. From that base the coalition reestablished Persian influence in Herat and then moved against Shah Ashraf in Isfahan.[30] Nader saw the reestablishment of Persian rule in Herat as essential to dealing with the Afghan leader in Isfahan. Three contemporary accounts of Nader Afshar (later Nader Shah)—written by Mohammad Kazim and Mirza Mehdi Asterabadi—describe Nader's tactics in his battles with the Afghans around Herat and elsewhere in great detail.[31] Nader consistently avoided frontal attacks on Afghan positions but made every effort to lure the Afghan infantry out of their positions to subject them to withering artillery and musket fire. Following the defeat of the Herati forces in successive battles, Nader reconfirmed Allahyar Khan Abdali as the governor of Herat. Nader's most important achievement in the campaign, as Laurence Lockhart suggests, was dispelling the notion that the Afghans were not as invincible as his Persian soldiers had believed.[32]

Although Shah Ashraf adopted a far gentler policy by treating the population with kindness, justice, and generosity, the shock caused by Mahmud's reign of terror cast a long shadow over Ashraf's efforts to restore Persian confidence in Afghan rule. Ashraf ordered that a highly attended funeral be held for the slain Safavid princes, murdered earlier by Mahmud, who were then buried with much pomp and honor at the sacred shrine of Qum in the royal Safavids' mausoleum. He even offered his resignation so that Shah Hussein could be restored to the throne. All these niceties notwithstanding, the legitimacy of the Afghan government had been undermined by its shaky control of the country as well as by the suppressive rule of Shah Mahmud and his commanders.

The Afghans' legitimacy was further impaired by their lack of capacity to take immediate action against the incursions by neighbors of Persia who had started annexing Persian territories. Following the capitulation of Isfahan to the Afghans, Turks and Russians, taking advantage of the distracted state of Persia, seized Armenia, Georgia, Gilan, and Kurdistan. The Afghan army in 1727 did confront the Ottoman incursions in an inconclusive war against the Turkish army, albeit with some initial success.[33] But, in fact, it was Tahmasp—not the Afghans in Isfahan—who negotiated with Russia and Turkey concerning their relations with Persia. He also sought their assistance in expelling the Afghans from Persia. It took the Afghans five years to act against the Turkish encroachment.

As the coalition force under Tahmasp and Nader gained momentum, it challenged the authority of the Afghan leader in Isfahan in a series of military confrontations. In less than two years (1729–1730), that combined force defeated the Afghan army in four major battles and drove Ashraf out of Isfahan.[34] The Persian army rapidly pursued the remnants of the Afghan army to the south, giving it no respite to regroup for an organized stand in Shiraz. While the Afghan rearguard covered Ashraf's escape, the remaining Afghan contingents scattered in different directions, and the war was over. Ashraf retired to Lar and then Sistan with a small party, where he was interdicted southwest of Kandahar by agents of Shah Hussein of Kandahar or elements of a Baluch tribe who brutally murdered him.

Such was the end of Afghan rule in Persia, which had lasted more than seven years. The Afghans had achieved a remarkable victory with extremely limited means but failed miserably to rule a fragmented country. Their poor administrative ability and lack of statecraft were apparent. They failed to unite their fellow tribesmen into building strong and numerous armies capable of enduring the occupation of a foreign land. Their nascent military organization and rudimentary administrative setup was sufficient for conquering a country under a weak, corrupt, and divided polity, but it was incapable of governing the state they had won so easily. In contrast to earlier conquerors of Persia, the Afghans did not have a strong government in a unified country of their own, with a formidable army, before launching an ambitious venture to conquer a foreign land. Once they occupied Persia, they received little support from home to fill the ranks of the dwindling army, beset by combat losses, deaths, and desertions. Throughout their rule in Persia, they remained an alien power with a small army among a population that they antagonized by harsh means of control, including massacre, destruction, and population displacements.

Persian Reconquest

The defeat of Shah Ashraf in Shiraz terminated Afghan rule in Persia but did not end the hostility between Persia and Afghan rulers in Afghanistan. In the space of five years after capturing Herat in 1732, Nader Afshar, who was appointed commander in chief of the Persian army, reunited Persia and recovered the provinces annexed by the Ottoman Turks and Russia. He besieged Baghdad in the west and reduced Ganja in the north. In March 1735, he signed a treaty with the Russians in Ganja in which the latter agreed to withdraw all their troops from Persian territory. During these years, the former shepherd Afshar wielded so much power that in 1736 he deposed the last members of the Safavid dynasty and ascended to the throne as Nader Shah.

A few months after his coronation, Nader Shah made preparations to invade Afghanistan and conquer Kandahar—the place from which the Afghan army had launched the conquest of Persia sixteen years earlier. Nader left Isfahan in November 1736 with a large army of 80,000–100,000,[35] consisting mainly of cavalry, on a campaign that lasted nearly a year and a half. Kandahar was under the rule of Shah Hussein Hotak, the brother of Shah Mahmud, the victor of Isfahan, who had ruled independently since his brother's death in Isfahan in 1725. Shah Hussein assembled more than 30,000 (likely less than 20,000) troops and supplied large quantities of provisions to Kandahar to sustain the city during an awfully long siege. After some initial battles west of Kandahar, the massive Persian army, with its enormous baggage convoy and contingent of camp followers, laid siege to the Afghan capital, which lasted about a year. During this period, the Persian army was under constant attack from within and without the city, forcing Nader to build walls and defensive towers around his camp.

The Persian army besieging Kandahar had to protect itself against attacks from the Afghans' mobile columns in the countryside, as well as sorties from within the walls that sallied out throughout the siege. During this period, the garrison conducted many sallies that spilled much blood on both sides. In the beginning of August 1737, a great number of Afghan troops swooped down on the Persians with such zeal that the Persians were barely able to withstand the shock. In several additional sallies, the Afghans captured a great number of horses belonging to the Persians and drove them back into the city. Such actions prolonged the siege to an extraordinary length. As the siege lengthened, Nader constructed a ring of forts with towers at intervals of a hundred yards around the city and built a walled town for his army two miles southeast of Kandahar. He ordered several houses to be built in the walled town, as he had done during his siege of Baghdad, signaling to the Kandaharis that he would not decamp until he had taken the place.

Finally, the Persian army surprised the defenders on Friday, March 24, 1738, by scaling a lightly held tower and pouring into the city.[36] Once the walls were overcome, Nader pushed large bodies of his troops into the city. Shah Hussein was forced to move into the citadel, which was bombarded with heavy cannon fire. The next day, the Afghan leader made terms with Nader, who gave him quarter upon condition that "he would surrender the town, and that his army might be recruited with those soldiers who had behaved so gallantly in the defense of the place."[37] Nader exiled Shah Hussein, the last Hotak ruler, and his followers to Mazenderan. In Kandahar, Nader found his old enemy, Zulfiqar Khan, and his younger brother, Ahmad Khan (later Ahmad Shah Durrani), in Hussein's jail. He treated them gently and sent them to Mazenderan. Ahmad Khan later joined Nader Shah's personal guard unit and served until the death of the Persian monarch. Impressed by the valor and toughness of the Afghan fighters, Nader raised a 16,000-strong Afghan cavalry force using 12,000 Abdalis and 4,000 Ghilzais. They were commanded by ten commanders, eight of whom were Abdali officers and two Ghilzai. These troops became the most trusted and favored units of Nader Shah, and they served with him in all his military conquests.

The campaign in Kandahar cost Nader enormous resources, time, and effort. In military terms, it hardly added to his professional reputation. As a soldier, he failed to reduce a town defended by a force three times smaller than his army. His blockade of the city for more than a year failed to break the will of the besieged population, and he was eventually forced to launch scaling operations. The capture of Kandahar did send a psychological message that the Persians had finally got even with the Afghans by avenging the disaster at Isfahan sixteen years earlier.

Following the conquest of Kandahar, Nader Shah launched his planned invasion of India, matching the feat of his Turkic hero, Tamerlane. The Persian army defeated the Mughal army at the monumental Battle of Karnal, and Nader Shah entered Delhi, which his soldiers looted. The Indian conquest and the expedition into Central Asia represented the peak of Nader Shah's military achievements, providing him with enormous power and causing him to become an increasingly despotic ruler. Influenced by a growing paranoia, he even blinded his own son, Reza Quli, on suspicion of conspiracy against him. During his last years, Nader Shah acted with excessive brutality, sparking numerous revolts that he crushed ruthlessly. He even built towers with his victims' skulls in imitation of his hero Timur. Finally, he met his violent death on June 20, 1747, in Khorasan. He was killed by his own officers, who feared Nader was about to execute them. They decided instead to undertake the bloody preemption.[38]

Nader took his place in history as the last great Asian conqueror after Tamerlane. Some named him the "Napoleon of Asia"; others viewed him as a powerful plunderer whose rapidly built empire unraveled instantly after his death. He was a creative military leader and a ruthless monarch. The countries he conquered regained their freedom after his death, while his own country was torn apart by several contenders. He accumulated enormous wealth from his conquests of India and Central Asia. These made him powerful and extremely tyrannical during the last years of his rule. He freed the Persians from the harsh rule of the Ghilzai Afghans, but he himself turned into an absolute and despotic sovereign. Even his family and close aides did not feel secure—a situation that led to his assassination by his own army in 1747.

11   The Durrani Empire and the Emergence of Modern Afghanistan, 1747–1834

In the first half of the eighteenth century, the nascent national Afghan governments in Kandahar and Herat failed to survive the blitz of resurging military might in Persia. Persia not only terminated the Afghan domination of Iran but also invaded Afghanistan, ending the rule of the native dynasties in Kandahar and Herat. The brief but eventful experience of state-building in Afghanistan, however, inspired a national revival and a political momentum a few years later that became a driving force behind a far wider campaign to establish a united and sustainable national state. The fall of the Ghilzai government in Kandahar and that of the Durranis in Herat were followed by tectonic political shifts and momentous changes in the region caused by a sudden unraveling of the Afsharid Persian Empire after the death of Nader Shah Afshar in 1747. The post-Nader political and security turbulence ushered in a period of new opportunities for Afghans to restore authority at home and expand outward, filling power vacuums created by decaying regional states.

Following the assassination of Nader Afshar in Khorasan by his own troops, his empire was reduced into a free-for-all competition for power that lasted more than a decade. Nader was succeeded by his nephew Ali Quli Khan (renamed Adil Shah), who was suspected of involvement in Nader's assassination plot. He was deposed a year later amid a three-way power struggle among him, his brother Ibrahim Khan, and Nader's grandson Shah Rukh. The first two were killed in the struggle; Shah Rukh escaped death but lost his eyesight in the violence. Meanwhile, nearly all the provincial governors declared independence, plunging the entire empire into anarchy. In Azerbaijan, Azad Khan, a Ghilzai Afghan leader, took over the province with the help of 15,000 troops. Hasan Khan, the Qajar chief, ruled in Asterabad (Gorgan), and Karim Khan Zand ruled in southern and central Persia. Finally, by 1760, Karim Khan defeated most of his rivals and founded the Zand dynasty (1750–1796), which controlled all of Persia except Khorasan in the northeast. This was Shah Rukh's territory. He continued to rule under the suzerainty of

Ahmad Shah Durrani, the former commander of Nader Shah's personal guard. Durrani had already proclaimed independence in the east, marking the foundation of modern Afghanistan.

Following the assassination of Nader, Ahmad Khan and his fellow Abdali and Ghilzai troops, who constituted Nader's trusted elite corps, fought their way out of the Persian camp. After helping Nader's harem to safety, the Afghan guard was rewarded with the famous *Koh-e Noor* diamond for its service; they decided to return home and chart out the future of their people. The Afghans, with a 16,000-strong contingent under the overall command of Noor Muhammad Khan Alizai, headed to Kandahar, where they called on the Afghan tribesmen to decide the future of their country. The Afghan chiefs assembled at the mausoleum of a widely revered saint, Sher Surkh, in the suburbs of Kandahar to decide on the formation of a national government for an independent state. After eight tumultuous meetings, during which Ahmad Khan quietly listened, the chieftains failed to reach a consensus on choosing a leader. With the meeting deadlocked, Faqir Saber Shah, the highly respected guardian of the shrine, rose and recommended Ahmad Khan as the most suitable king. He reached out and crowned him with a wreath of straw and proclaimed "may this serve you as a diadem." With this ceremony, the Afghan chiefs consented to elect Ahmad Khan as their king. He assumed the title of Ahmad Shah Durrani.[1] The Afghan contingent that accompanied him from Persia was the core of his army, which he augmented with tribal levies drawn by the promise of conquest and plunder of other lands. At the time, the Afghan king urgently needed funds for raising an army and building state institutions. Luckily, he intercepted and seized a convoy laden with more than a million British pounds' worth of taxes and customs, dues from Kabul, Peshawar, and Punjab, that was moving through Kandahar under Mohammad Taqi Shirazi. Ahmad Shah shared the wealth with the Afghan chieftains, an act that consolidated his position among the people.

Ahmad Shah, son of Zaman Khan Abdali, belonged to the Sadozai clan of the Popalzai tribe. His father had joined other Abdali chieftains in the struggle to free Herat from the Persian yoke in 1716. Zaman Khan and his eldest son, Zulfiqar Khan, governed Herat at different times between 1718 and 1731. Ahmad Shah was born in Herat in 1722 shortly after the death of his father, and he was raised by his brother Zulfiqar. Both Abdali nobles left Herat for Farah in 1731 and thence to Kandahar after the fall of Farah to Nader Afshar's army in 1732. In Kandahar, Shah Hussein Hotak placed the two brothers in jail due to tribal feuds. As noted in chapter 10, Nader Shah Afshar freed them after capturing Kandahar and by one account took Ahmad Shah with him in his conquest of India. Later, Nader put the young Afghan in command of a trusted elite guard.

Thus, at the time he ascended to the throne, Ahmad Shah was an experienced military leader and a polished administrator. The major task ahead was to build an independent polity dominated by the Afghans and expand its territory to incorporate secure borders. Ahmad Shah considered himself the chosen leader of the Afghans and other ethnicities living in common lands. In a 1761 correspondence with the Ottoman sultan Mustafa III, Ahmad Shah stated that he was given the mandate to rule over the Afghan (Pashtun) tribes (population 2.4 million), as well as other tribes and ethnicities that numbered 2.2 million. He added that a million people lived in Kandahar, while the others had settled in Kabul, Ghazni, Peshawar, and other provinces.[2] In the letter, the Afghan monarch condemned Nader Shah's cruelties toward the Afghans and his hubris and viciousness against other nations, including the Ottoman Caliphate. Ahmad Shah also detailed his empire-building experience and his military feats in India and Persia. He stressed that, in the regional chaos created by the death of Nader Shah, he refrained from invading neighboring countries before building his home base and then launched conquests to punish those forces that were bent on creating instability and injustice or on prosecuting the Muslim *umma* in the region.[3]

Having learned from the Ghilzais' hollow state-building experience and their poorly supported conquest of Persia, Ahmad Shah intended to move steadily and surely to build the state and expand it in a way that, instead of overextending his forces, augmented his power base. The chaotic situation on Afghanistan's borders offered the temptation of easy conquests into Persia or across the weakly defended borders of India. While Ahmad Shah saw these opportunities, he was also concerned with building a solid basis at home before embarking on major foreign adventures.

To enlist the support of the Afghan tribes, Ahmad Shah set up a council of major Abdali tribal chiefs, with whom he consulted on all important matters. This inclusiveness ensured wide support of his decisions about state matters. Further, as military conquests underpinned his policy of building the Afghan state, the stakeholders at the top were often in agreement with his decisions. The military expeditions not only provided tribes with the opportunity to loot and plunder but also served as a unifying factor in bringing together the turbulent factions into a nation of conquerors. His centralized system was supplemented by the internal autonomy of the chiefs within their tribes. The tribal chiefs in return provided military contingents under the king's standards, for which they were compensated in cash, tax allotments, or land grants. The army thus reflected the pure and simple feudal system that prevailed throughout the rule of the Durrani dynasty.

Ahmad Shah was presented with a unique opportunity to help establish a national state at home after nearly six centuries during which the states and empires in Afghanistan were built by outside powers. During this period, the Afghan tribes, in their rugged country and hard-to-reach valleys, resisted long-lasting imperial encroachments and preserved some level of practical autonomy. Paradoxically, while the Afghans failed to form their own state within their own country, they did succeed in ruling over empires in foreign lands. Between the fourteenth and early sixteenth centuries, three Afghan dynasties (the Khalji, Suri, and Lodi) ruled over northern India with an Afghan (Pashtun) king sitting on the Delhi throne, while their homeland between the Indus and Hindu Kush was under the domination of Turko-Mongol kings and emperors. True, the Ghilzai Hotaks founded an Afghan state in Kandahar at the turn of the eighteenth century, but their conquest of Persia distracted their power and energy from the consolidation of their government at home, which collapsed in a relatively short period after a foreign invasion.

Ahmad Shah was elected king by the Pashtun tribes, mostly by the Abdalis of Kandahar. Many other Pashtuns between Kandahar and the Indus River, as well as other non-Pashtun people of the country, were not involved in the decision. The first issue of legitimacy facing the young king was to get the mandate of the other tribes and communities that he considered to be citizens of the state he intended to build. Traditionally, legitimacy stems from dynastic rights or is based on military power. Further, governments often invoked Islam and potential threats by "infidel" foreign powers to motivate their people to serve the Muslim ruler and his government. Although Ahmad Shah claimed to be a descendant of a ruling Afghan house (and made the assertion in his correspondence with foreign powers), in the eyes of his fellow Afghans he lacked royal blood. He therefore needed to base his legitimacy on power that was achievable only through military conquest, with promises of plunder for the people who were willing to join him.

But what made Ahmad Shah distinct from the previous conquerors was that he intended to conquer other lands to build his own state rather than follow the examples of past Afghan rulers of India or the Hotaks, who chose to preside over empires in foreign lands. Alexander Dow (1735–1779), a British orientalist and a contemporary of Ahmad Shah, wrote that the Afghan monarch was the only leader at that time who could restore imperial power to Delhi if he would assume sovereignty in India and rule as king from Delhi.[4] It was a tempting proposition, but the situation in India was changing and the balance of power was rapidly shifting. Ahmad Shah did try to legitimize his claim to the throne of Delhi as the heir of previous Afghan kings there who "ruled the vast land with honor, leaving good names, until the invasion of Amir Timur *Saheb Qiran*." He specifically named the Lodi and Suri monarchs as the Afghan ruling predecessors.[5] But as Ahmad Shah's real actions indicated, he knew that getting tied up in India would undermine his plans to build an Afghan state between the Indus and Amu Darya Rivers. During twenty-six years of rule, he never compromised any part of this territory to expand to northern India or into the depths of Persia in the west. In one of the poems attributed to him, he states that "I forget the throne of Delhi when I remember the mountain tops of my Afghan land. If I must choose between the world and you, I shall not hesitate to claim your barren deserts as my own."[6]

The changes in the balance of power in India hardly supported a permanent Afghan occupation of the territory so long as the center of the Ahmad Shah's kingdom was in Afghanistan. Several competing powers arose in the subcontinent and hindered any foreign power's attempt to establish an enduring rule there. While the Mughal Empire was weakened significantly and had lost influence in the south and east, the Marathas of Deccan, the Sikhs of Punjab, the Europeans in general, and other large and small groups were rising to prominence.

In the south, the resurgence of Maratha power, after the death of Aurangzeb in 1707, led to the formation of the mighty Maratha confederacy, which expanded north and made major military gains outside their original territory. Just after Ahmad Shah ascended the throne in Kandahar, the Marathas extended their conquest to northern and central India and became more independent and difficult to control. Although their control in the north ended after a great defeat at the historic Battle of Panipat by the Afghan army led by Ahmad Shah, their state continued to exist as the political endowment of a highly disciplined community that combined spiritual purpose and goals with political and military ambitions. In its later years (the second half of the eighteenth century), the Maratha Empire was headed by a confederacy of five chiefs at Pune in western India that challenged the growing power of the British in India.

In Punjab, the Sikhs had become militarized after their leader, Guru Gobind Singh (r. 1666–1708), formed the Khalsa in 1666 as the faith's temporal authority. The Khalsa was a disciplined community inspired by a spiritual purpose and political goals. Its martial wing, the Dal Khalsa, grew into a formidable organization of highly motivated fighters who controlled the main roads between the Indus and Sutlej Rivers and could disrupt the lines of communication between Afghanistan and northern India. The Sikhs had freed themselves from Mughal control and were not ready to accept Afghan domination.

The commercial rivalry that brought several European powers to India in the seventeenth century turned into a race for domination using proxy Indian rulers. It took another fifty years before British power expanded rapidly throughout the greater part of the subcontinent. Following the defeat of the French-backed Mysore king Tipu Sultan (1750–1799) in 1799, Britain became a serious actor on the Indian political scene, with a growing military capacity.

West of Afghanistan, the disintegration of the Afsharid Empire and the continuing power struggle among several contenders made Persia vulnerable to outside intervention. Ahmad Shah could exploit the situation by leading his disciplined and experienced army (supported by the Afghan tribes) to make major gains in Persia. However, he was unwilling to repeat the mistake of the preceding Afghan dynasty by winning an easy victory but failing to rule the empire. The limits of Ahmad Shah's expansion to the west were defined by the vital security considerations of Afghanistan. He did not advance beyond Mashhad and Nishapur. Sir John Malcolm (1769–1833) wrote that

Ahmad Khan was now in a condition to attempt the reduction of all Persia, but the prospect was not inviting. Every province was exhausted. The Afghans were still deemed the original authors of the misery which the nation endured; and the unsuccessful attempt to alter their religion of the country, had revived, in all their vigor, those sentiment of the hatred which the Persians entertained from that race as Sunnis. In addition to these obstacles, the example of usurpation which Nader Shah had given had inspired every governor of a province and every chief of a tribe with the desire of rule, and Persia abounds with pretenders to regal power. Under such circumstances, we must admire that wisdom which led the Afghan prince to withdraw from this scene of turbulence, that he might exclusively direct his future exertions to the nobler and more legitimate object of establishing a power in his native country, which while it gave a crown to his descendants, raised his nation to a rank and consideration far beyond what they have ever enjoyed.[7]

Based on a similar argument, Ahmad Shah considered the Amu Darya River to be the practical border of the Afghan state in the north. Despite the vulnerability of the Uzbek khanate caused by continued power struggles among the Khiva, Bukhara, and Khoqand khanates, Ahmad Shah did not want to be drawn beyond the Amu Darya deep into Central Asia.

But expansion through attacks on surrounding states became a requirement for the Afghan state, not merely to build a "raiding polity" and find a better distraction for his feuding and turbulent subjects; it was also a means to wield power in a competitive environment. Realistically, moving east was more advantageous to Ahmad Shah than venturing west into the unsettled vastness of Persia. To the east, down to the Indus River basin, the land was inhabited by fellow Afghan (Pashtun) tribes who could add to the influence and legitimacy of the Afghan state and provide a rich source of recruits for his army of conquest. Farther east, there were large pockets of Afghan tribes in India who had migrated into the subcontinent in the wake of victorious armies from Afghanistan. Over the centuries they had established numerous spheres of political influence by sharing power with the several Afghan dynasties that ruled India at different periods. They served as natural allies of the Afghan expeditionary armies. Finally, the political confusion that befell India following Nader Afshar's invasion and the plunder of Delhi made India an attractive target of conquest—a land poorly protected and temptingly rich.

The Durrani State

During more than five centuries of rule by various Turko-Mongol dynasties in Afghanistan (thirteenth–eighteenth centuries), absolute sovereigns governed their dominions through proxies, particularly in the peripheries and remote tribal areas. Their failure to integrate the populations through wider networks of political and economic institutions left most of Afghanistan tribalized and occasionally "atomized." The Durranis faced this sociopolitical environment when they chose to build a modern state.

The state structure adopted by the Durrani Empire, paradoxically, was based on central control over decentralized tribal and communal military, administrative, and economic institutions. Historically, such a system worked in the country only under powerful and charismatic leaders who mobilized the nation in a spirit of common cause such as undertaking foreign conquest, fighting off foreign invasion, or waging ideological war. Ahmad Shah Durrani achieved such a mobilization by tapping into the *assabiyya* (social solidarity) of the Afghans, encouraging them to build a vast empire that would permanently secure the homeland of some 4.6 million Pashtuns and other tribes living between the Indus and Oxus (Amu Darya) Rivers. Further, he invoked the Islamic duty of Afghan Muslims to protect the oppressed Muslim population of India[8] and claimed the Afghans' hereditary right to the throne in Delhi.[9] The Afghan ruler mobilized and maintained the unity of the tribes and offered them the opportunity to secure their homeland and conquer prosperous foreign lands. But failure to consolidate this unification by integrating national institutions, plus the perpetuation of the militarized Afghan state, accentuated the tribal fault lines once the drive to conquest slowed down and internal competition for power intensified. Thus, the empire of Ahmad Shah began to dissolve within two generations of the founder's death as the loosely united structures gradually fragmented. However, despite the long periods of internal strife and foreign invasions that dismembered part of the country in the nineteenth century, the state founded by Ahmad Shah endured along with the identity of the country as Afghanistan.

The Durrani state was organized into twenty-seven provinces, eighteen[10] of which were administered by a *hakim* (governor), who collected the revenue and commanded the militia, and a *sardar* (noble), who commanded the regular army forces and maintained law and order in the province. If the *sardar* was a Durrani, he also doubled as the *hakim*.

The central governmental institutions that Ahmad Shah Durrani set up and his descendants preserved were in line with the formal institutions of Safavid and Afsharid Persia. In later years, certain institutional elements of India were adopted as the empire extended into the subcontinent. The king had absolute power bolstered by the alliance of a strong Durrani aristocracy—the *sardars*—who constituted a state council with a loose institutional structure and advised the king on important issues. The government had always shown a good deal of moderation toward its own subjects, its dependent states, and even its enemies. According to Mounstuart Elphinstone (1779–1859), it was mild in its punishments, and "its lenity was more conspicuous, from a comparison with the severity of the Persians."[11]

The Afghan Military Establishment

The military forces of the Durrani Empire were structured in line with the political makeup of the state. The army developed incrementally as Afghan rulers expanded the limits of the state and brought more and more people under their domination. There was a close relationship between the growth of the army and the extent of imperial expansion. Expansion required large armies, and maintaining such armies required funds, which were often unavailable locally and had to be acquired from other areas—usually through the military invasion and conquest of resource-rich countries. Thus, the quest for power through expansion led to a need to form larger military forces. Further, control of conquered lands required more military forces and the need for more funds. Therefore, the empire that Ahmad Shah Durrani founded was based mostly on military power manifested in maintaining large armies.

The development of the Afghan army began with the forces at hand, mostly the 16,000 Afghan troops that had served under Nader Shah in Persia and returned home after his death. In terms of professional training and discipline, they were the elite units. In the words of Elphinstone, they had good reason to consider themselves the best troops in Asia.[12] This force was augmented with contingents provided by tribal levies commanded by their tribal chiefs. For more than a century and a half, with occasional adjustments, this system created a corporate military establishment that became the model for future Afghan armies. Thus, the central military establishment was not the only military institution within a social system imbued with tribal military pluralism. The advantage of the model was its low maintenance cost and the opportunity it provided for national integration. It worked well if the government was in firm control of the tribal chiefs and involved them in the governing bodies. The system, however, became a problem rather than the solution in the nineteenth century when, in the absence of a strong central government, competing contenders to the throne employed the fragmented tribal military contingents to advance their personal claims to royal power, plunging the country into unrelenting civil wars and opening the door to neighboring states that encroached on Afghanistan's territories from all directions.

The Durrani army was composed of a regular professional component (*Fauj-e Nizam*) plus a wider pool of irregular forces (*Fauj-e Gu-shada*) provided by the tribal and community leaders when needed in exchange for cash payments, tax collection rights, or allotment of fief estates proportionate to the size of the contingent each feudal chief pro-vided. The regular army constituted nearly one-third of the entire army, nearly three-fourths of which was cavalry. The troops were mostly dressed in uniforms, while in combat they were outfitted in mail-shirts or buff leather jackets, with a helmet or chain-twisted turban as head-gear. A French Captain Jean Law (1719–1797), who observed Ahamad Shah Abdali's army in Delhi in 1757 wrote: "Their main strength is in cavalry, of which many corps are armed with muskets and pistols of the Tartar style. Their infantry is perhaps the best in India. . . . What give the Pathans the special edge over others is their discipline and subordination which is very closely enforced in armies of Abdali. One does not see here, as one does in most Mohammadan armies—as well as the Gentiles—those grandiose contraptions which are designed only to dazzle the beholder but are actually good for nothing."[13]

The regular army permanently served the throne and included spe-cial royal regiments known by different names such as *ghulaman-e saf-shekan*, *resala-e shahi*, and *ghulam-khana*, and *ghulam-e shah*. Like their medieval counterparts, these "slave troops" were made up of non-tribal servicemen who were not attached to any other leader but the king. This corps was first formed by Ahmad Shah from foreigners who had settled on Afghan territory and from the troops of Nader Shah and other Persians who joined the Durrani government. Later, they were also recruited from Tajiks in Kabul and the surrounding districts. In the early nineteenth century, the Shia Qizil-bash, who had settled in Kabul, formed a third of the corps and were enlisted for perpetual ser-vice. The corps was divided into 8–10 *dastahs* (regiments) with varying strengths. These troops numbered 12,000 during the reign of Ahmad Shah and were maintained at that level by his immediate successors.[14] They constituted a third of the regular forces and were commanded by the *Qular-Aqasi* (the head of the slave soldiers), who usually was one of the high-ranking nobles. They were all mounted soldiers who were pro-vided with horses by the government. They were armed with flintlock and matchlock muskets as well as pistols, swords, and lances.[15] Their role was comparable with Napoleon Bonaparte's Imperial Guard that acted as his bodyguard and the tactical reserve in battle.

According to Jean Law, in contrast to the pompous Indian armies, everything in the Abdali army is real: the men, as well as the horses and weapons. The army is divided into squadrons of a thousand cavaliers. Each squadron is distinguished by its bonnets or *kullahs* (hat) and is led by a commander who reports to Abdali twice a day. This chief has some subordinate officers charged with maintaining discipline. The troops are reviewed every month and those who merit attention are punished there and then while others may be complemented for their fine turnout. . . . While the troops of Abdali are generally good, there are some corps which are superior to others. These are those whose bravery has been more often tested. As soon as the prince sets out on a campaign, 12 or 15 of these squadrons are separated from the others to constitute his reserve, and these are the ones chosen to deliver the decisive blows and whose weight the Marathas have so often felt.[16]

Another military formation, the royal guard, provided security at court and for the royal camp. Additionally, during the reign of Shah Shuja (r. 1803–1809), several hundred Indian troops dressed in European-style uniforms were part of the court's guard units. Other units, including the camel-mounted cavalry from Baluchistan and the regular infantry troops, together represented a quarter of the regular army. The infantry forces were divided into musketeers and Jazairchis (light guns) and an elite unit of foot soldiers from Kohistan north of Kabul. The military police (*nasaqchian*) and signal and postal units were also part of the regular force. Service units numbering 7,000 men were responsible for transportation, stable management, and other services.[17]

Artillery troops were also an important component of the regular army, as were the war-elephant units. Nearly two-thirds of the artillery consisted of heavy guns while the remaining one-third were light guns. The light swivels, differently called *Zanbouraks*, *Shahins*, and *Ushturnals* (camel-mounted guns), were carried singly or in twos and threes on the backs of camels. Easily maneuverable, some 2,000 of these camel-mounted swivels played a decisive role at Panipat in mowing down the Marathas. The artillery gunners numbered 1,200 under Zaman Shah (r. 1793–1801), the grandson of Ahmad Shah, and included the crew and commanders of guns and light swivels. Engineers, sappers, and miners were also included in the regular forces. In the provinces, a smaller replica of the central regular army served while additional troops were raised to garrison main towns and fortresses.[18]

As Afghans traditionally were in favor of mobile light artillery, the regular army maintained 700–800 camel-mounted *shahinchis* (gunners) who operated the light guns, including the Zanbouraks.

The irregular army consisted of a variety of part-time and emergency reserve components that served under the royal standards at times of national need. They constituted the wartime army that joined the regular forces collectively or in separate contingents at different places. They included the *Khawanin Sawaran, Kara Nokar, Eilajari, Dawatalab* (volunteers), and *Wolossi*. A collection of all these components was labeled *Fauj-i Ghushada* (open or public army).

Tribal chieftains were obliged to furnish a specific number of troops defined by their contract with the state in exchange for holding their rent-free land (*tiyul*). The Durranis also received three months' pay during the year while on active service. When the need arose, the leaders assembled the specified number of men at the time and place ordered by the king; after being registered, they were subdivided into clan-based corps called *dastahs* (regiments) commanded by traditional chieftains and maliks. The closer the military operation was conducted to the tribes' home turf, the larger their contribution became. The tribes in the east contributed larger contingents to the Indian conquests, while the western tribes contributed larger contingents to operations waged in Khorasan.

The troops maintained by governors of provinces were rarely employed except in wars carried out in that province or in its neighborhood. The irregular infantry also included garrison troops at forts who were paid with revenue from their home provinces. There were only 150 troops at most in the strategic fort of Attock.

The *Kara Nokar* was an emergency draft militia furnished by landowners in predetermined numbers. Their expenses were defrayed by remission of revenue at the first settlement. The numbers varied. The rule of thumb was drafting one horseman per plough (*qolbah*), but the actual number of draftees depended on the level of government control in any specific area.[19] The more powerful and the more remote tribes supplied much smaller bodies than the inhabitants around major cities, or none at all. The Tajiks contributed more horsemen than the Pashtun tribes. The militia was organized into *dastahs* commanded by Durrani *sardars* or the governors of the respective provinces, who shared command with the militia's local or tribal elders. The draftees had the choice to serve personally or to pay for a substitute (*ewaz*), the amount depending on the duration of service. It was not difficult for wealthier men to find a substitute among poorer people who were readily available. Sometimes a tribe paid a collective sum in lieu of providing the militia. *Kara Nokar* recruits were obliged to serve until dismissed without any allowance from the government, but their families were supplied with grain (*ghalah*). The *Kara Nokar* were all horsemen except for a corps of foot soldiers numbering up to 2,000 men, which was called up from Kohistan north of Kabul.

The *Eilajari* was a public militia called out on extraordinary occasions and theoretically could amount to 10 percent of the adult male population, but that number was never raised. The number of *Eilajari*, drawn from the poorest section of the population, that was called up by the king depended on the need. They were paid a nominal wage during the time they served. The village chiefs paid the wage and defrayed this expense with a tax levied on all the inhabitants of the village. There were few volunteers for such service, and *Eilajari* were raised mostly in areas under strong government control. These men could not always be moved away from their neighborhoods or kept for long. The *Eilajari* were almost all infantry and received no pay from the king unless they were kept for more than three months in the field.

Dawatalab were fighters who joined in wars of conquest or in defense of their homes and villages against threats. They were raised only for expeditions and paid enough for one campaign. They were always most numerous in expeditions to India in the hope of plunder, and many served even without pay. The *Wolossi* was a public uprising by the Afghans against foreign invasions in the affected areas. The uprising was often spontaneous, with no direct regulation by the state.

The number of troops in the Durrani army varied at different times. The size of the force increased with the expansion of the empire and the need to respond to security threats and rival powers across its vast territories. At its greatest extent, under Ahmad Shah (r. 1747–1772) and his son Timur Shah (r. 1772–1793), the territory of the empire extended from Nishapur in the west to Sarhind in the east and from the Amu Darya River in the north to the Sea of Oman in the south—a total area of 2.1 million square kilometers—an area larger than the combined size of France, Britain, Italy, and Spain today. The control of such a vast area required massive military forces that had to be augmented while waging major wars against rival powers. Ahmad Shah led an army of 18,000–25,000 troops in his initial conquest of Punjab in 1747. Fourteen years later, the strength of his army in his Indian expedition was reported at 60,000–85,000 men. Obviously, these field forces included the regular and irregular contingents and excluded the provincial security forces and the garrisons deployed across the empire. The standing regular army rarely exceeded 30,000 troops. The size of the Durrani expeditionary forces under Zaman Shah (r. 1793–1801) was estimated at 100,000.

Contemporary Afghan accounts list the composition of the Durrani army at the end of the eighteenth century as follows:[20] 12,000 horsemen of the *Ghulaman-i Saf Shekan* royal guard; 30,000 Durrani and Ghilzai irregular cavalry; 2,300 tribal troops provided by the chiefs of Peshawar, Khattak, Bangash, Mohmand, and Yousafzai; 5,000–6,000 men of Baluch regiments provided by the amir of Baluchistan; 18,000 cavalry contributed by the tribes of Wardak, Suleiman Khel, Khogyani, Shinwari, Afridi, Kohati, and Chach Hazara; 12,000 royal security units (*keshikchis*); 7,000 court and household details; 2,000 Khybari and Afridi troops; 12,000 horsemen from Khorasan; and 15,000 troops from Sind, Multan, Dera Ismail Khan, and Dera Ghazi Khan. All this adds up to 115,000–116,000 troops.

Given the type of military operations conducted in distant lands, the overwhelming majority of the Durrani army was cavalry. They were organized in units of different sizes. The smallest unit was a section of five or ten horse commanded by a *panj bashi* (leader of five) or *dah bashi* (leader of ten); several sections formed a platoon of 20–50 horsemen led by an officer (*bist-bashi* or *pinjah- bashi*). Two to five platoons grouped together into a company were commanded by a *yuz-bashi*. A regiment (*dastah*) was composed of several companies under the command of a *ming-bashi*. The guard contingents were organized in *dastahs* of up to 1,200 horses each. In the irregular forces, a group of 100 troopers constituted a company designated as a *bairaq* (banner) led by an officer known as *bairaqdar*. *Dastah* was the next higher formation consisting of several *bairaqs*. Smaller *dastahs* were commanded by a *sar-karda*, while larger *dastahs* were led by an officer titled *khan-i sawari*.

Military Conquests

Ahmad Shah's military conquest to the east was aimed at establishing the political limits of the Afghan kingdom based on the geographic and cultural boundaries of the Afghan tribes. These borders had not been independently defined by any ruler in the past. There were also Afghans settled in the west, but the largest tribal concentration was in the east down to the Indus (Sind) River. Once the Durrani armies reached the banks of the Indus and asserted their authority, Ahmad Shah turned west and annexed the Afghan provinces of Herat and Farah and secured them by establishing control over Mashhad and Nishapur in Khorasan. No border, however, could have been secured unless the lands beyond it were stable and not threatening. With the weakening of the Mughal Empire in India and the emergence of rival contenders in the subcontinent, the edges of the Durrani state became insecure, forcing Ahmad Shah to extend his conquests far beyond the natural geography of his kingdom. In fact, rising empires are like fast-moving torrents that overflow the decaying banks of a stream.

Expansion of the Durrani Empire to the east featured two sets of military campaigns, both with monumental consequences. The first consisted of military actions to establish Afghan control over Punjab and lasted until the first quarter of the nineteenth century. The second series comprised Ahmad Shah's wars to defend the eastern imperial boundaries against the rising power of the Hindu dynasty of the Marathas and their allies in India. The out-and-out defeat and destruction of the mighty Maratha army by the Afghans at the Battle of Panipat in 1761 decisively weakened the indigenous military power in India and facilitated British occupation of the subcontinent.

The Expansion to Punjab

As a result of four military conquest in India (1747–1756), the Durrani Empire established control over large territories stretching from Punjab to Delhi. In military terms, Ahmad Shah's first campaign to the east was marked by several major military exploits by the Afghan army. When the Afghan army crossed the Indus and advanced unopposed to the Ravi River, they were faced by Shah Nawaz Khan's provincial army, which was entrenched across the river at the gates of Lahore. As the river was swollen and hard to cross, the opposing armies had to wait until the river fell to a crossable level. But Ahmad Shah wanted to deal with the governor before he could be reinforced by the Delhi army, which was reported to be on its way. So at early dawn on the third day of his arrival at the river, following a thorough survey of the area and the situation, Ahmad Shah left his infantry on the river face to face with the enemy and led his 10,000 elite cavalry forces several kilometers upstream, where he crossed the river. He suddenly descended from the north on Lahore, placing his army between the camp of Shah Nawaz Khan and the city of Lahore. The enemy never recovered from the stratagem; finally, on January 12, 1748, Lahore surrendered to the Durrani monarch.[21]

Ahmad Shah repeated such a flanking maneuver once again during the same operation while confronting the imperial Mughal army sent from Delhi to repulse the Afghan invasion of Punjab. The imperial army, led by Delhi vizier Qamaruddin Khan, numbered 100,000 troops[22] and departed Delhi on January 8, 1748, the same day Ahmad Shah reached the Ravi River in Punjab. The Mughal army had hardly moved 16 miles from Delhi when news of Lahore's surrender reached the relief army. This loss alarmed the Mughal emperor, Mohammad Shah, who dispatched his son, Ahmad Shah, to represent him as commander in chief of the imperial army. The Mughal force reached Sarhind on February 25 and left its baggage trains, treasures, and surplus stores at that location guarded by only 1,000 security troops. There were two main crossing sites on the river: the Machhiwara and the Lodhiana. The Mughal army crossed at the former site, leaving the latter open. Ahmad Shah seized the opportunity to outflank the imperial army by moving north and crossing through Lodhiana on March 1. After crossing the river and covering 40 miles at night, the Afghan army descended on Sarhind, attacking the rear of the Mughal army on March 2.[23] The Afghans seized the Mughal's huge baggage trains and treasures.[24] Shocked by the surprise attack by the Afghan leader, the Mughal army had to turn around to face the Afghans, which were one day's march to the east. After sending his booty and heavy baggage to Lahore, Ahmad Shah sought out the imperial army, which had entrenched at the nearby village of Manipur.

The Battle at Manipur proved inconclusive, and it took another military campaign a year later for the Afghans to restore their position in Punjab. However, full domination of Punjab by the Durranis came only in 1751 following two more Afghan incursions into the province. It was at this time that Ahmad Shah's archenemy, the tough Mughal governor of Punjab, Mir Manu, surrendered to the victor. In an interesting conversation with the defeated governor, Ahmad Shah asked him what he would have done if instead he had captured the Durrani king? Mir Manu replied he would have cut off his head and sent it to his master at Delhi. Then, the Afghan monarch asked the vanquished chief, "What should I do to you?" The straight-speaking governor replied: "If you are a shopkeeper, sell me for a ransom; if you are a butcher, kill me; but if you are a monarch, pardon me."[25] Ahmad Shah liked the answer and treated him with honor. He finally reappointed Mir Manu as the governor of Punjab while the badly shaken Mughal emperor formally ceded the Punjab as far as Sirhind and Multan to the Afghan monarch. Before returning to Kandahar, Ahmad Shah also conquered Kashmir.

The Afghan conquest came against the backdrop of rapid expansion by the Marathas, who rose to imperial power in central and southern India in the seventeenth century and made fast inroads into northern India as the Mughal Empire declined. A confederacy of the Hindu warrior caste, the Marathas covered vast parts of the Deccan Plateau. It encompassed predominantly the modern Indian states of Maharashtra, Madhya Pradesh, Gujarat, and Karnataka. The empire was founded and consolidated in 1674 under Shivaji, who made Fort Raigad, located 175 kilometers south of Mumbai (Bombay), its capital and successfully defended his territory against the Mughal Empire during a twenty-seven-year war until the death of Aurangzeb in 1707. Aurangzeb's successors presided over a rapid disintegration of the empire, and finally the Maratha chief Baji Rao defeated the Mughal army near Delhi in 1737 and established control over much of the former Mughal territory south of Delhi. The Marathas were inspired by the aspirations of the Hindu communities who were frustrated with the domination of the Muslims across the subcontinent. A renowned Indian historian writes that the Mughals, Afghans, and Rohillas who were living in India did not consider themselves Indians since they recruited thousands of Central Asian people in their armies and in civil services in preference to Indians, both Hindus and Muslims. Further, they invited foreign hordes to crush every Indian nationalist movement irrespective of any consideration for caste, creed, or religion. He takes note that even the celebrated scholar and theologian of Delhi, Shah Waliullah, used all his power and influence to persuade Ahmad Shah Durrani to destroy the Marathas, the Jats, and the Sikhs.[26] Despite the admirable military prowess of the Marathas against the Muslim rulers of India, they did not win over the common public because of their arrogance, excesses, and oppression.[27] Besides, as Verma notes, in the eighteenth century, India was completely dominated by the caste system, where "Hinduism provided no foundation for the brotherhood." Consequently, in the prevailing social and economic system of Hindu society there was no basis for unity. He also notes that politically the relations of one Hindu state with another Hindu power were governed by competition rather than cooperation.[28] In fact, some Indian Hindu Rajahs, including Madho Singh of Jaipur and Bijay Singh of Marwar had invited Ahmad Shah for "protection of their territories from the inroads of the Daccanies."[29]

Nevertheless, the Marathas raised the standard of freeing the Hindus from the yoke of the Muslim rulers who had dominated the subcontinent for more than six centuries. The sources of the Maratha power were its highly motivated and disciplined military forces and its skill in waging effective guerrilla war against enemies' conventional forces. However, when they branched out from their home turf and organized their fighters in a heavy conventional army, they lost much of their advantage.

The capture of Delhi by Ahmad Shah in 1756 brought the Marathas into direct confrontation with the Durrani Empire on the edges of their claimed territories. Before returning home in 1757, Ahmad Shah reconfirmed the weak Mughal emperor Alamgir II on the throne in Delhi (appointing Indian-based Afghan leader Najib ud-Daulah his viceroy and military commander in Delhi) and placed his son Prince Timur in charge of the provinces east of the Indus assisted by Sardar Jahan Khan.[30]

The Khorasan Campaign

The immediate strategic objective of Ahmad Shah was to recover Afghan territories in the west and to secure them by establishing control over Mashhad and Nishapur. In 1751, he led a strong army to Herat, which was held by Shah Rukh Mirza, the grandson of Nader Shah. The city surrendered after a siege. As the province of Khorasan was in a state of anarchy following the death of Nader, Ahmad Shah marched on Mashhad, where he confirmed Shah Rukh on the throne under his suzerainty. Ahmad Shah then advanced on Nishapur but failed to reduce it and was forced to retreat, losing thousands of his men and abandoning his artillery in the process. The next year, in command of a fresh army, he marched on Nishapur again. As he could not transport the heavy siege guns required to reduce the city, he took his engineer to the site and had him cast a very heavy gun that fired a 500-pound projectile. During the siege of Nishapur, on the first discharge of the gun, the defenders were so terrified that they surrendered without being aware that the gun had burst from its first and only discharge. The surrender of Nishapur resulted in a treaty between the Afghan monarch and Shah Rukh Mirza whereby several districts bordering Herat Province were ceded to the Durrani Empire and the official currency would be coined in Ahmad Shah's name. During this campaign, the Afghan monarch dispatched an army from Herat to annex northern Afghanistan. The army secured the submission of Balkh, Badakhshan, and other provinces between the Hindu Kush Mountains and the Amu Darya River. Thus, the boundaries of the new kingdom between the Indus and Oxus were established.

The Maratha War

During the absence of the Afghan monarch, the Maratha armies poured into Delhi and drove out Ahmad Shah's appointed officials. Assisted by their local allies, the Maratha forces pushed farther north into Punjab, forcing Prince Timur out of the province in 1758. Seeing the Marathas on the doorsteps of his kingdom, Ahmad Shah returned to India at the head of a large army in 1759 and made several gains against separate Maratha garrisons in Punjab and around Delhi. The successive defeats of the Marathas in those two places frustrated the arrogant Maratha nobles and their allies in northern India. They urged the *peshwa* (prime minister) to send a larger army to drive out the Afghans and permit the Hindus to overthrow the Muslim domination of India. In the spring of 1760, the *peshwa*, Balaji Bajirao, mobilized a huge army under the nominal command of his young son Viswasrao but with actual command exercised by Sadashiv Rao Bhau (1730–1761), accompanied by a large contingent of up to 300,000 noncombatants and camp followers. An eyewitness, Mohammad Ja'far Shamlu, who was serving under a senior Afghan commander Shah Pesand Khan and was accompanying the Abdali army, claims that the Maratha army numbered 350,000 cavalry and infantry troops.[31] One modern Indian historian explains that the "fighting strength of the Maratha army was around 25,000. Nearly four times that number also accompanied as followers. women, children, old age people, clerk, personal servants and shopkeepers who joined to perform pilgrimage in North India. The Maratha Sardars employed a large number of servants known as *khidmatgars* for doing petty jobs."[32]

The slow-moving army headed north, reaching Delhi on August 1, 1760; from there it moved farther north to encounter the Durrani army five months later in the fateful Battle of Panipat. Bhau soon felt the difficulty of supplying his large army and its much larger hordes of camp followers. So as the rainy season was ending, Bhau moved north to Sirhind in early October 1760 to cut Ahmad Shah's lines of communications. He stormed the strong fort of Kunjpura, 75 miles north of Delhi. There he put its 10,000-strong Rohilla garrison to the sword and plundered the supplies and treasure that he desperately needed. Further, by seizing control of Kunjpura, he secured the crossing site over the Jumna River to attack Ahmad Shah. But the river was still swollen by heavy rains, and Bhau did not expect Ahmad Shah to cross to the right bank and move against the Maratha army. Still, Bhau made the main crossing at Sonipat, 12 miles north of Delhi, with a detachment of 1,000 troopers.

In order to face the main Maratha army, the Afghan leader formed a broad coalition with his Indian allies, including the Rohilla Afghans of the Gangetic Doab and the *nawab* (ruler) of Oudh, Shuja u-Dawlah.[33] With the news of the fall of Kunjpura, Ahmad Shah moved from his rainy season camp at Anupshahr, located across the Jumna River northeast of Delhi, to face the Maratha forces. Although the river was still remarkably high, the Afghan monarch led his army to Baghpat, 28 miles north of Delhi, and camped there for a few days while looking for a crossing site. On the third day, he identified a relatively favorable ford. While the Maratha forces were celebrating the Hindu *Dussehra* festival in the captured city of Kunjpura, Ahmad Shah avoided their detection and began crossing the Jumna River on October 23, two weeks after the fall of Kunjpura. It took his army two days to cross; the king crossed as soon as half of his army was on the far bank. Although the operation took a toll in drowned soldiers and horses, and the marshy ground on the far side hindered movement of the troops and the guns, the crossing went unopposed by the Marathas,[34] who could have created major impediments. According to some accounts, Ahmad Shah ordered Shah Pesand Khan and his detachment of 4,000 troopers to attack the Maratha covering party, located 12 miles downstream at Sonipat. The detachment made a surprise attack on the Maratha troops, killing them to the last man, and then rejoined the main body.[35] On October 25, 1760, Ahmad Shah crossed the Jumna and headed to Panipat, where the Maratha army had set up camp northwest and southwest of there. The old Mughal road, the *Shah Rah*, passed directly through the town.

Having surprised the enemy, Ahmad Shah rapidly moved north to meet the main body of Maratha forces, which had retraced its steps south and was now encamped at Panipat. The Afghan advance guard under Shah Pesand Khan contacted the enemy's forward detachment at Sarai Samalkha, about 12 miles south of Panipat, and fended it off with losses to the enemy estimated at 2,000 troops. The main body of the Afghan army camped at Ganaur (October 28–30); after three days of rest it advanced to Panipat and camped five miles from the enemy's dispositions. The Maratha army had moved from the north with Lahore at its back while the Afghan force had advanced from the south with Delhi at its back, and thus the two sides confronted one another at Panipat, with each party sitting on the communication lines of the other.

The Third Battle of Panipat

The two armies faced each other for more than two months at Panipat, an ancient historic city in India nearly 60 miles north of Delhi. During this time, each side made attempts to cut the supply lines of the other to choke its logistics lifelines. Each side was trying to bait the enemy into a battle under conditions unfavorable to him. Having entrenched in their encampment, the Marathas would have liked the Afghans to attack their camp and be pounded by their heavy guns, firmly positioned on the ramparts. The entrenchment stretched over the plain 10 kilometers in length from west to east and four kilometers in depth southwards of Panipat. But Ahmad Shah was not in hurry. He resisted his Indian Afghan allies' constant demand for immediate action, advising them to wait until he shaped the tactical situation into a favorable opportunity that would lead to a successful conclusion of the conflict.[36] The Maratha command tried to force the Afghans to attack by cutting off their supplies. Ahmad Shah, however, was in a better position to choke the enemy camp, as the Durrani army was sitting on the supply routes of the enemy and had easy access to resources from its Afghan allies across the Jumna.

The Maratha army, with its heavy baggage trains, artillery equipment, and large hordes of families and camp followers, was more vulnerable. Eyewitness accounts indicate that the camp was populated by a half-million souls.[37] Bhau supplied his forces from Delhi, which was serving as his forward logistic base. That base was replenished daily by large convoys of stores moving through a long supply route that stretched from Pune to Delhi. Other sources of procurement were the districts around Delhi. The Durrani army was sitting on a key position that enabled it to disrupt both of these enemy supply routes. The Maratha camp was also fed by Sikh leaders from Punjab and the raja of Patiala through the Sirhind–Patiala supply route. Ahmad Shah eventually disrupted that route, too, when the Afghans recaptured Kunjpura behind the Maratha camp. Thus, the Afghans targeted the enemy's supply lines within a large circle; its diameter extended from Delhi to Sirhind. Ahmad Shah wrote that the width of the inner circle of interception was 30 miles.[38]

For their part, the Maratha commanders were overconfident due to their large numbers and the strength of their forces, which included hundreds of artillery pieces. They were further encouraged by their successive military victories in northern India over the past year. Bhau hoped to wait out Ahmad Shah and believed that his Sikh allies, sitting in key locations in Punjab, would cut off the Afghans from their bases in the west and force their Rohilla allies and the *nawab* of Oudh to abandon the isolated Afghan forces. According to Mahmud al-Husseini (the official historiographer of Ahmad Shah Durrani who completed his work in 1773–1774, immediately after the death of the Afghan monarch), the Afghan king moved parts of his camp several times during the stalemate to place his forces in positions suitable for cutting the enemy communication lines and intercepting its supply convoys.[39] Contemporary sources indicate that the Afghan army initially encamped southwest of the Maratha camp about seven miles south of Panipat at the Passina Kalan–Dimana line two miles south of Siwa across the Delhi road. On the first day of December, he shifted his camp six to seven miles to the east, close to the Jumna River, to escape from the pollution of air and water of the place rendered foul by such a vast mass of men and animals. Finally, on December 30, Ahmad Shah returned to the south of Panipat and sat astride the Delhi road a mile or so north of his old camp.

Meanwhile, Ahmad Shah kept the enemy camp under pressure by continuing cavalry attacks on its flanks and rear. Accordingly, every night a detachment of 5,000 horsemen would advance to the Maratha camp and keep it under surveillance until dawn. In the meantime, as an eyewitness (Shamlu) wrote, Ahmad Shah directed Sardar Jahan Khan Popalzai, along with 3,000–4,000 special troops (*Qizil-bash*) as well as Hají Nawab Khan Alkozai, to mount every day and patrol around the Mahratta camp at a distance of two *kos* (four miles) from their entrenchments, one from the northern side, and the other from the southern and to cut off every provision convoy that attempted to sneak into the Maratha camp and every party of camp followers that left under cover of darkness to gather firewood and fodder in the neighboring woods.

Sitting on the main Delhi route, the Afghan forces succeeded in closing the southern route and continued their efforts to cut the other supply line reaching the enemy camp from the north. The Marathas made a similar effort to cut Ahmad Shah's lines of communication. Bhau ordered one of his commanders, Gobind Pundit, to raid the Rohilla Afghans' territories in Doab (the land between the rivers Jumna and Ganges) and cut off the supply of all provisions in the rear of Ahmad Shah's army. Gobind moved with 10,000–12,000 horsemen and ravaged the area as far as Meerut. The operation caused supply problems in the Afghan camp. Ahmad Shah ordered Attai Khan, a nephew of Vizier Shah Wali Khan, and Haji Karim-dad Khan at the head of 5,000 horse-

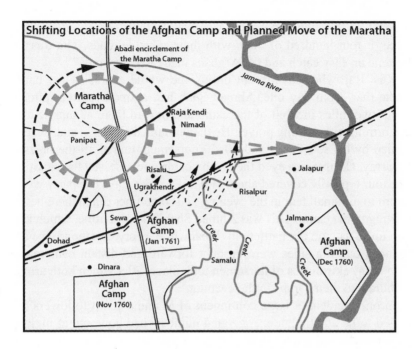

Shifting Locations of the Afghan Camp and Planned Move of the Maratha

men to march day and night and attack the Maratha force in Doab. The Afghan detachment moved rapidly, crossed the Jumna at Baghpat on December 16, 1760, and covered a hundred miles in one day and night. At daybreak, the Afghans fell like lightning on the unprepared camp of the Maratha force. Taken by surprise, the Marathas fled wildly and were cut down by the raiding Afghans. Gobind Pundit was captured as he was trying to flee and was beheaded by the pursuers. The Afghan detachment returned to its camp on the fourth day with the head of Gobind Pundit in tow.[40]

Soon after the defeat of Gobind Pundit, the Maratha commander Bhau dispatched a body of 1,000 horsemen to Delhi to receive and escort the transfer of some treasure to pay for his rising expenses. The troops were ordered to march secretly at night over unfrequented roads, with each man carrying a bag of 2,000 rupees on the return trip. The troops reached Delhi uninterrupted, but during the return, purely due to bad luck, they missed the designated road in the darkness and stumbled into the Durrani camp instead of taking the road to their own forces. The Afghans seized one of them and his money bag. Working on information extracted from the strayed enemy rider, the Abdali troops chased the rest of the money-carrying Marathas to their camp and captured three or four hundred of them with their valuable loads. The treasure became an easy catch and the Afghans made it a "pay day."[41]

Kasi Raj, who was present during the whole course of the battle, wrote that, from day one, Ahmad Shah had a small red tent pitched about two miles in front of the camp and moved there at sunrise after performing his morning prayer. He then mounted his horse and, accompanied by his son Timur and 40–50 horsemen, toured all the posts of his army. He also surveyed the enemy camp and assessed the situation. The tour typically covered about 100 miles every day. The party would return to the small tent in the evening and sometimes dined there before moving to the camp. This was Ahmad Shah's daily routine, which kept him up to date on the battlefield. Meanwhile, every day the troops and cannons on both sides were brought forward and distant cannonades with many skirmishes of horsemen took place, after which both armies withdrew to their camps in the evening.[42]

In one incident, a large contingent of Maratha camp followers (reported to be 20,000, an exaggerated number) had gone out at night to gather wood and fodder in the jungle. Some distance from camp, they were intercepted by a routine roving body of 5,000 Afghan horsemen under Shah Pesand Khan. They were surrounded. Although no rescue troops were sent from the Maratha camp, all the camp followers were put to the sword. The psychological impact of the massacre was enormous and terrified the Maratha camp. Even the bravehearted Bhau began to "give way to fear and despondence."[43]

The large concentration of Maratha military forces and camp followers in the limited space of the camps (10 kilometers long and four kilometers wide) was causing an acute problem with lodging and hygiene, with adverse impacts on army morale. The longer the standoff continued, the greater the anxiety and discomfort. The Durrani army eased the adverse conditions of the long encampment by moving in the last week of November to a location about four miles southeast; they crossed a water channel and set up a new camp near the village of Bapauli close to the Jumna River. This took the Afghan forces out of enemy artillery range and eased the obtainment of supplies from across the Jumna from Najib ud-Daulah territory, as the river water went down in the winter. Further, the new location offered fresh water. The move was perceived by the Marathas as one of weakness, also reflecting the success of its artillery. Bhau wrote on December 6, 1760, that "Abdali has no strength to attack us. Our firing hurt him and killed men and horses in his camp.

Out of fear he moved away two *kos* (four miles) and has taken his guns. This is his courage, which is reducing each day. We will soon defeat him."[44]

The increasing shortage of supplies and the interdiction of the supply lines plunged the Maratha camp into growing confusion. The local *Banjara* (Indian nomadic people) vendors in Panipat were charging high prices for the limited amount of provisions that they supplied under difficult conditions. By the end of December, the distress in the Maratha camp became so serious that the troops plundered the town of Panipat for grain. Faced with increasing pressure from the troops, Bhau appealed to Shuja ud-Daulah to mediate a peace agreement with the Durrani vizier. He showed readiness "to submit to any conditions if he could but preserve himself and his army and would by every means manifest his gratitude to the mediators." While the vizier and all other chiefs, including the Rohillas, were not opposed to peace, Najib ud-Daulah was against it, arguing that the Marathas should not be trusted, as their overture for peace was due to weakness, which should be exploited. The Marathas, he stressed, should be dealt with once and for all. He suggested to Ahmad Shah that the Marathas were "the thorn of Hindustan; and if they were out of the way, this empire might be your Majesty's whenever you should please." Ahmad Shah approved his counsel and overruled the party of peace in his camp.

By the first week of January 1761, the growing famine pushed the Maratha camp to the brink. The army chiefs appealed to Bhau to let the army go to battle instead of perishing through starvation and misery. They wanted to move immediately against the Afghans and face their destiny honorably.[45] According to contemporary original Afghan and Indian sources, including Marathi accounts, when the lack of supplies and famine "cast a shadow of death on the Maratha camp," their leaders decided on January 13, 1761, to march toward Delhi, where supplies could be found and the army would be in a much stronger position to fight the Afghans.[46] Marathi sources painted a bleak picture of the Bhau camp on the eve of the Panipat Battle:

> The strength of Abdali was growing while the Maratha army was growing weak without supplies. Horses were dying and even army chiefs had to move on foot. It was best to leave this camp, but thick forests all around meant the army could only move along the road toward Delhi. The *gilcha* [Ahmad Shah][47] was blocking the road, so it was best to move toward the Jumna five *kos* [ten miles] away and putting the river at

one's back and the guns toward the *gilcha* in the front . . . move to Delhi,
get supplies, rejuvenate the army, make our camp by the Jumna. . . .
Holker felt when the *gilcha* is blocking the road, how will you make
a path through his army? So it was decided, everybody including the
banagas fighting their way would proceed forwards.[48]

Most accounts indicate that, on the eve of the battle, the dispute over
fighting tactics dominated heated discussions among the top Maratha
military leaders. The old guard wanted to employ the traditional Maratha
mode of warfare, known as *Ganimi Kava*, or guerrilla-style hit-and-run
tactics. Others, led by Ibrahim Gardi, head of Maratha's artillery and
foot musketeers, and supported by Sadashivrao Bhau, argued that the
battlefield situation was hardly suited for adopting such a method of
fighting. Instead, the latter advocated the use of the well-drilled infantry
equipped with muskets and matchlocks, backed by heavy artillery, to
lead the way while wedded to the hollow-square formation.

The plan was to fight their way to Delhi through potential obstruc-
tion by the Afghan forces. In order to be ready for battle from the line
of march, the Maratha forces were formed into what in military terms
is called the "infantry square" or "hollow square." Known from ancient
times, this form of combat order was used by infantry threatened by an
enemy's cavalry charge. This close-order formation was utilized by the
Roman legions at the Battle of Carrhae in 53 BC against Parthia's cavalry
attack. The Maratha hollow square was a wide square formed by combat
troops with noncombatants moving within the square protected by the
troops around them. The Marathas put infantry with guns and muskets
on the outside and moved the noncombatants, supplies, and families
inside the square. With such a clumsy formation, the Marathas intended
to march southeast across the field toward the Jumna River, about 10
miles away, and then follow the right bank of the river to Delhi.

The political significance of the Battle of Panipat for both sides of the
conflict, and the Marathas' massive losses of life and property following
their disastrous defeat, have prompted exaggerated estimates of the size
of the forces that fought on that fateful January day. Ahmad Shah Durrani put the number of the Maratha troops at more than a million, supported by a thousand cannons and light guns and half a million rockets
(*ban*).[49] Obviously, these are extremely inflated figures. The real numbers may have been ten times lower. Given the size of the camps and
the battlefield expanse, plus the constraints of command and control and

logistical limitations, each of the opposing armies may have deployed between 60,000 and 85,000 cavalry and infantry troops on the battlefield, excluding the baggage trains and camp followers, which were estimated at over half a million in the Maratha camp. Kasi Raj Pundit, who participated in the battle and recorded the event as secretary of Nawab Shuja ud-Daulah, the ally of Ahmad Shah, visited the Maratha camp in Panipat as the *nawab*'s envoy. He recorded the breakdown of the opposing forces using the accounts of Maratha military *daftars* (offices of musters) and his interviews with officials there. He listed the Afghan army at 41,800 horsemen and 38,000 foot soldiers with 70–80 cannons. Kasi Raj's estimate puts the number of irregulars who accompanied the troops at four times that of the army. These irregulars usually moved in the wake of a successful charge by the regulars to fall on the broken enemy with swords in hand to complete the rout.[50] The Maratha army contingents included 55,000 horsemen, 15,000 foot soldiers, and 15,000 Pindaries (auxiliaries) plus 2,000–3,000 mounted troops from local allies.[51] The number of accompanying family members and camp followers was estimated at more than half a million. There were also around 20,000 females. Most of these were slaves of their masters, who served in various capacities and also as concubines.[52]

Moving to Battle

As the two armies took the field, their professional military capacities were mostly uneven. In his late thirties, the Afghan king Ahmad Shah Abdali was a battle-hardened soldier. The core of his army was a well-structured, harmonized, and highly disciplined force operated under a hierarchical command system. In contrast, the thirty-year-old Sadashivrao Bhau commanded an assortment of a diverse Maratha fighting force. It consisted of four different classes of troops of unequal professional status. The most privileged and best-armed class was the Peshwa's private cavalry, or *kasagi paga*. The second in status were the *silhedars* belonging to other Maratha chiefs, paid by their respective *sardars*, who were assigned Jagirs to maintain their troops. The self-sustained volunteer *ekandas* and the freebooter *pindaharis* ranked third and fourth in fighting effectiveness. Furthermore, the Maratha commanders and soldiers were said to have not been easily amenable to discipline and were "strangers to team-work so essential for a fighting force on or off the battlefield."[53]

An hour before daybreak on January 14, the Maratha forces started moving out of their trenches and marched several hours to join the battle at nine o'clock. As the huge sea of men and animals, with their enormous maintenance and service gear, streamed out in a circular formation, the columns advanced slowly with "every symptom of hopeless despair rather than of steady resolution. The ends of their turbans were let loose, their hands and faces anointed with a preparation of turmeric," signifying that they were coming forth to die.[54] Continued starvation took a heavy toll on the physical strength of the usually small-framed Maratha fighters, and their horses became too weak to display the required combat stamina.[55] Their garments were very light, more suited for the warm weather of their home in the South. On that cold day in January, the common soldiers were often clad with nothing more than a loose trouser (*dhoti*) wrapped around the waist. In reference to their poor clothing, Ahmad Shah often scornfully called them *berahana kun* (in Persian) or *lots kwani* (in Pashto) meaning bare backed.[56]

Alerted by the spies about the Maratha plan, the Afghan army was ordered early on January 14 to line up and block the enemy, which had broken camp and was moving as a sea of men, animals, guns, trains of carriages, and camp followers on foot. Given the sequence of the combat and the description of primary sources, the battle took place in modern terms as a "meeting engagement" or "moving to contact," as the Maratha columns set out southeast and hit the right flank of the Afghan line, which was seven miles long and two miles in depth and was drawn up obliquely to the Maratha line of march. Maratha sources indicate that the Maratha army had to wheel to its right to face the onslaught. Consequently, "the last night's plan of a square was given up."[57]

According to Shamlu, the center of the Afghan line was covered by 2,000 camel swivels (*Zanbouraks*) backed by 20,000 infantry musketeers (*jazailchis*). The domestics of the royal *darbar* and the music band were deployed behind them just ahead of Ahmad Shah's command post, which was supported by the 10,000 special guard (Qizil-bash) cavalry deployed behind the supreme headquarters and ready to reinforce any division as needed. Communication between several divisions, stretched along a seven-mile front, was facilitated by couriers who were constantly moving and running around.

The Maratha movement to content faced several tactical flaws. The march order suffered breaks caused by the heaviness of the Maratha guns which, due to their long range, overshot the targets with rounds landing at the back of the enemy. This way ammunition was wasted without gaining the desired effect of breaking the Afghan line and creating a gap in it for the troops to advance. One Indian historian writes that "even the whole plan of marching to Jamuna under the cover of artillery was almost impossible due to the heaviness of the Maratha guns which always lagged behind the main army and whose range could not be altered easily."[58]

The eight-hour battle on January 14, 1761, opened with a barrage by Maratha cannons, musketry, and rockets as they advanced southeast across the field toward the Jumna River. After the opposing forces covered the few kilometers that separated the two camps, the Maratha forward columns advanced against the Afghan right. In the ensuing close combat, the Marathas pushed back the Afghans' right flank but failed to penetrate the lines. As the Afghan right was heavily engaged in fighting off the disciplined Maratha regular infantry under Ibrahim Gardi, the Maratha center under Bhau and Viswasrao charged the Afghan divisions in the center under Shah Wali Khan and broke through a line of 10,000 horsemen, 7,000 Persian musketeers, and 1,000 camel-mounted Zanbouraks. Meanwhile, on the Afghans' left flank, Najib ud-Daulah's 8,000 foot troopers and 6,000 horsemen advanced steadily against the Maratha right under Jankoji Sindhia, which was 4–5 miles distant from the Afghan left. The Afghan column advanced in bounds. When the wings reached the effective range of muskets and rockets, the *najib*'s division unleashed a barrage of musket fire and rockets, discharging 2,000 volleys at a time, which by their dreadful noise not only terrified the enemy horses but also caused so much terror that the enemy could not advance.

The Maratha guns were too heavy and were difficult to handle whereas the smaller artillery of the Afghans included better and lighter field guns and mobile swivels (Zanbouraks and shuturnals). There was also imparity in light arms. Marathas mostly fought with swords and spears; only few musketeers were employed in Ibrahim Khan Gardi's regiment; but the Afghans and Rohillas had many trained musketeers in their army. The few muskets used by the Marathas were of inferior quality compared to those of the Afghans.

Around noon, Ahmad Shah decided to commit his reserves in order to stabilize the center and the right flank, which were under Maratha pressure, and push the left wing forward to outflank the enemy with a sweeping attack to the enemy rear. He assembled every possible body of troops and his slave guard troops for a final decisive effort. He moved 4,000 troops to cover the right flank and dispatched 10,000 horsemen to

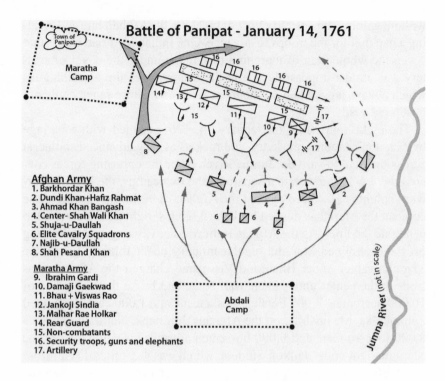

Battle of Panipat - January 14, 1761

Afghan Army
1. Barkhordar Khan
2. Dundi Khan+Hafiz Rahmat
3. Ahmad Khan Bangash
4. Center- Shah Wali Khan
5. Shuja-u-Daullah
6. Elite Cavalry Squadrons
7. Najib-u-Daullah
8. Shah Pesand Khan

Maratha Army
9. Ibrahim Gardi
10. Damaji Gaekwad
11. Bhau + Viswas Rao
12. Jankoji Sindia
13. Malhar Rae Holkar
14. Rear Guard
15. Non-combatants
16. Security troops, guns and elephants
17. Artillery

the center to Vizier Shah Wali Khan with instructions to charge the enemy in close order at full gallop. He ordered Najib ud-Daulah and Shah Pesand Khan on the left flank to launch a simultaneous attack on the enemy's flank. At about one o'clock, the reserve joined the battle. The vizier charged the Maratha army where Bhau commanded in person. In support, three regiments of mounted slave troops used their usual fire and maneuver drill—firing their muskets and galloping off to reload and then returning to repeat the attack. Jean Law (1719–1797) rated these squadrons as the elite forces of the Afghan army for their tested bravery and effectiveness; they constituted the king's reserve. He wrote that "these are the ones chosen to deliver the decisive blows and whose weight the Marathas have so often felt."[59] The enemy was now massed together and falling under the withering fire and cavalry charges. Meanwhile, Najib ud-Daulah and Shah Pesand Khan charged the Maratha flank with a decisive impact. The combat in the center lasted for an hour, during which both sides fought with spears, swords, battle axes, and even daggers.

Shortly after two o'clock, Viswasrao was killed by a musket ball, and the Marathas—who for religious reasons were fighting on empty stomachs—lost all hope and were on the verge of collapse. Half an hour later, Bhau, under whom three horses had been killed, fell while fighting. At around three o'clock, the fate of the battle became obvious when all at once the entire Maratha army turned their backs and fled at full speed, leaving the field of battle covered with heaps of the dead. According to Maratha sources, because of differences of opinion within the Maratha command regarding the kind of warfare that should be waged, the old guard, including senior commanders such as Malhar Raw Holker, Damaji Gaikwad, and some others, suddenly deciding that "their own skin was soon to be pulled into the fire," found the opportunity in the afternoon and "sneaked out of the battlefield with their troops and turned the heads of their horses south."[60]

As Kasi Raj relates, the moment the Marathas gave way, the victors pursued them with utmost fury, giving no quarter. Consequently, the slaughter was "scarcely to be conceived" as the pursuit continued for 25–30 miles in every direction the wretched victims fled. Reportedly, 500,000 men, women, and children of the Maratha camp were killed or taken prisoner.[61] This sounds greatly exaggerated, but the number of Marathas killed in battle and during their attempted escape was not less than 100,000. A renowned Urdu poet and the head of a Chishti Sufi family, who lived in his sanctuary in Panipat on the day of the battle (January 14), wrote that in the evening "it was announced that the Shah had granted amnesty and that nobody should worry. But immediately after nightfall these freebooters (Rohillas) commenced committing atrocities. The city was set on fire. Houses were destroyed. They carried off everything. The following morning was the doomsday."[62] The hatred caused by the lengthy war was so deep that a large part of 40,000 prisoners were murdered by the Abdalis in cold blood. Among the senior Maratha commanders, Jankoji Sindhia and Ibrahim Khan Gardi were taken prisoner and executed at the Afghan camp.

The plunder taken from the Maratha camp was enormous. Reportedly, in addition to millions of rupees and treasures of every kind, 50,000 horses, 200,000 oxen, many thousands of camels, and 500 elephants were taken.[63] One of the Afghan horsemen was said to have driven off eight or ten camels loaded with valuables. Captured horses were driven away in herds like cattle. An assortment of 300 heavy and light guns (artillery pieces) and some 25,000 matchblocks and muskets fell into the

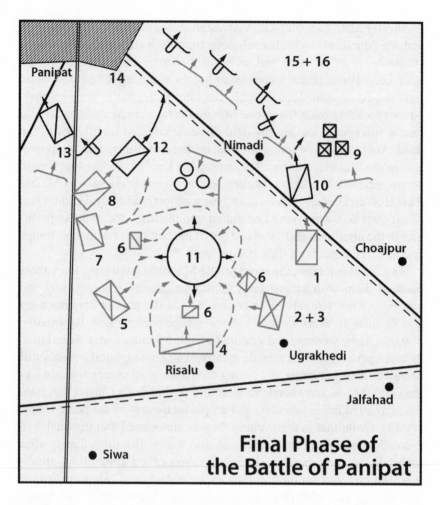

Final Phase of the Battle of Panipat

hands of the Afghans. Shamlu too reports a quantity of 100,000 swords, shields, and spears in the possession of both combatants and noncombatants must have been looted by the victors.

The news of the Maratha defeat sent shock waves across India. The *Peshwa* Balaji Baji Rao, who was unaware of the destruction of his army while he was crossing the Narmada River with reinforcements, received this cryptic message from a tired runner: "Two pearls (his son Viswasrao and Bhau) have been dissolved, 27 gold coins (senior leaders) have been lost and of the silver and copper the total cannot be cast up." The *Peshwa* never recovered from the shock of the total debacle at Panipat. He returned to Pune and died a broken man in a temple atop the nearby Paravati Hill.[64]

On the fifth day, Ahmad Shah returned to Delhi. Shuja ud-Daulah had sent all the Maratha fugitives who had taken refuge with him under guard to the safety of the Jats dominion. Contrary to all expectations, Ahmad Shah refused to occupy India and ascend the throne of Delhi. He was more interested in ruling his own homeland and avoiding getting caught up in the complex affairs of India. He kept the Mughal state as a vassal of his kingdom and put Prince Ali Gauhar, son of the murdered Alamgir II, as emperor under the title of Shah Alam. He appointed Shuja ud-Daulah the vizier and Najib ud-Daulah the commander in chief of the army. On March 20, 1761, Ahmad Shah left Delhi with the treasures of Hindustan and returned home.

This battle, known as the Third Battle of Panipat, is widely considered to be one of the most decisive battles in world history. The Afghans stopped the Marathas' expansion and defeated the most formidable indigenous power on the subcontinent, which changed the history of India forever. This battle was so fatal to the Marathas' power that they immediately abandoned their designs on northern India, and it took them many years before they resumed their enterprise under a new leader and with new tactics. Despite their partial recovery after a generation, they never regained any unity; infighting broke out within the weakened empire, facilitating the conquest of India by the British some fifty years later. In military terms, the battle demonstrated the dominance of light forces with strategic mobility and tactical agility over a heavy and slow-moving force fighting in traditional rank tactics.

Panipat was a source of inspiration for Rudyard Kipling's poem "With Scindia to Delhi":

Our hands and scarfs were saffron-dyed for signal of despair,
When we went forth to Paniput [*sic*] to battle with the Mlecha [alien],
Ere we came back from Paniput and left a kingdom there

For Ahmad Shah, the battle became an epic feat of military accomplishment. His exploits raised the image of the Durrani Empire far beyond the borders of India and Persia. The Afghan military prowess inspired hope among many orthodox Muslims and Mughal royalists and caused fear among the British. However, it did not secure the eastern borders of the Durrani state, which was one of the main purposes of the campaign. The security threat to the Durrani dominions in Punjab was posed mainly by the Sikhs who lived there, while the Marathas' power center was 1,500 miles to the south. The destruction of the Maratha

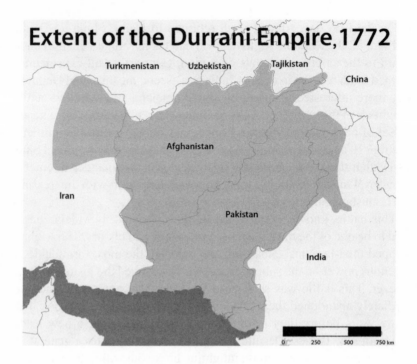

Extent of the Durrani Empire, 1772

Turkmenistan   Uzbekistan   Tajikistan

China

Afghanistan

Iran

Pakistan

India

0   250   500   750 km

army left the Sikhs mostly untouched. The Sikhs' *Dal Khalsa* army soon retook Lahore, forcing Ahmad Shah to launch three successive campaigns to quell the Sikh rebellions temporarily.

Ahmad Shah and the Sikhs

After Ahmad Shah's victory at Panipat, the whole of India appeared to be at the mercy of the Afghan monarch. However, he committed to his original plan of remaining content with the dominions ceded to him in Punjab, enjoying the glory of having Delhi as a vassal of Kandahar, and putting his Indian Afghan nobles, who had assisted him, in charge of provinces in northern India. The wisdom of the policy was confirmed over the next decade, when the rising power of the Sikhs in Punjab created a politico-strategic barrier between Delhi and the Afghan homeland.

Ahmad Shah's homeward journey following the Third Battle of Panipat was harassed by roving armed bands of Sikhs, who harried some Durrani columns during their passage through Punjab. Less than a year later, in early 1762, Ahmad Shah returned to Punjab and drove all the Sikhs from the plains into the mountains and other remote areas in a series of campaigns throughout the province. The Sikhs often avoided decisive engagement with large Afghan forces, only to hit back when and where the enemy was vulnerable. Ahmad Shah's three military campaigns between 1762 and 1767 inflicted heavy losses on the Sikhs, including destruction of their Golden Temple and several other buildings in Amritsar; but they failed to break the spirit of Sikh militancy. Each time, the Sikhs evaded major battles but made it difficult for Ahmad Shah to root out all the militant Sikhs. They continued their struggle for years during the reign of Ahmad Shah's descendants in the eighteenth and early nineteenth centuries. This struggle led to the establishment of the Sikh state in Punjab and its peripheries.

Decline of the Empire

Ahmad Shah died in June 1773 at the age of fifty from a lingering serious illness. During his twenty-six years of rule, he founded a vast empire that stretched from Delhi in the east to Nishapur in the west and from the Oxus River (Amu Darya) in the north to the Arabian Sea in the south. He was succeeded by his son Timur Shah, who faced a region undergoing political and military changes. Domestically, he was faced with the difficult task of keeping the tribal chiefs happy and united without having them engage in lucrative foreign conquests. Externally, he faced the challenge of holding the extended empire together and putting down rebellions. All his life, he struggled to assert his rule over the empire. In 1776, Timur Shah moved the capital from Kandahar to Kabul and used Peshawar as his winter capital. Kabul at that time was a modest city in comparison to Kandahar. A British traveler, George Forster, who visited Kabul during Timur Shah's reign, describes Kabul as a walled city of about a mile and a half in circumference, where the houses built of rough stones, clay, and unburned bricks "exhibit a mean appearance and are ill suited to the grandeur which I expected to see in the capital of a great empire."[65] Although Timur Shah lacked the charisma of his father, he managed to maintain the integrity of the imperial dominions despite difficulty in certain cases.

Timur Shah left 36 children from ten mothers of different tribes. When he died in 1793, several of the princes were governors of provinces and maintained personal followings and ambitions for the throne. A long period of power struggle ensued, with the Durrani throne changing hands four times in less than two decades. The long fraternal strife degenerated into dynastical shift as the powerful Barakzai house of Abdali challenged the authority of the last Durrani monarch, Shah Mahmud, and seized control of the country beginning in 1816. By 1826, the Barakzai prince Dost Mohammad became the acknowledged ruler of Kabul, Ghazni, and later Jalalabad,[66] while Kandahar remained in the hands of his half-brother Kohendil Khan and Kohendil Khan's full brothers. Herat was governed by Shah Mahmud and then his son until 1842, while Balkh, Kholm, Kunduz, and Badakhshan became independent petty states.

The long period of civil war and regime change split the army and polarized the tribes. The situation encouraged foreign states to chip away at the Durrani Empire's dominions. The rise of the Sikh state in Punjab to the east and the growth of the Persian power under the Qajar dynasty in the west strongly influenced the military history of Afghanistan at the turn of the nineteenth century. Motivated by the aspirations to establish an independent state in Punjab, the Sikh military effort took a major turn at the end of the eighteenth century, when the power of the Marathas was weakened and divided and the Durrani Empire was inhibited by domestic power struggles and palace revolutions.

The British authorities in India—who were not directly involved in the affairs of Afghanistan until the closing years of the eighteenth century—became major actors in Afghan politics due to several factors that emerged over time. In the early years of the nineteenth century, Britain extended its sphere of influence in the northwest to the Sutlej River bordering the Sikh state in Punjab under Maharaja Ranjit Singh. Early British meddling in Afghan affairs, with significant strategic implications, began in the closing years of the eighteenth century during the reign of Zaman Shah, the son of Timur Shah (r. 1793–1801), who was inspired by calls from Indian Muslims, including the Mughal emperor of Delhi and several Muslim Indian rulers, to help them against the Hindu Marathas. The Marathas were raiding Muslim principalities and Mughal dominions as the British were advancing west. Still in command of a large army and with the support of unified tribes, Zaman Shah was about to invade northern India, following the example set by his grandfather. As William Kaye wrote, "For many years Zaman Shah's descent on Hindustan [northern India] kept the British Indian Empire in a chronic state of unrest." This fear was somewhat exaggerated, as Zaman Shah never advanced farther than Lahore, and each time he moved toward Punjab, he was compelled to hurry back to deal with domestic troubles. What made the Afghan venture a formidable threat was that Zaman Shah could turn into "the willing agent of a hostile confederacy" and thus become a more serious opponent and a more successful one. Because the threat of a Napoleonic invasion of British India through Persia and Afghanistan was possible, an offensive alliance of France, Persia, and Afghanistan could become a real and imminent threat.

Alarmed by this threat, the British authorities took actions to serve two objectives: first, winning an alliance with Persia against a potential French invasion through Persian territory; and second, distracting the Durrani monarch from pursuing his Indian project. Securing the friendship of Persia was the key to achieving both objectives. The British believed that, if Afghanistan was threatened with an invasion from the west by the Persian army, Zaman Shah could never conduct a successful expedition against Hindustan. Further, if Persia remained true to Great Britain, there was nothing that French intrigues could accomplish in Central Asia. Persia's encouragement and support of Zaman Shah's rival brother, Shah Mahmud, in fact distracted Zaman Shah from moving into India on more than one occasion.

The threat to the British dominions in India temporarily disappeared with the fall of Zaman Shah and continuing civil strife in Afghanistan. Soon, however, another threat from far beyond the subcontinent alarmed the British government regarding the security of their Indian possessions. Napoleon, who had failed to advance through Egypt, chose to make an alliance with Persia for a land advance to India through Persia and Afghanistan. A potential invasion of India by Napoleon loomed large on the minds of English officials during this time, and the British decided to negotiate a defensive alliance with the Sikhs and the Afghans to serve as an outer line of defense to India. The Sikh maharaja Ranjit Singh and the Afghan Durrani monarch Shah Shuja signed defensive treaties with the British authorities in 1809. The treaty with Shah Shuja was an instrument used to form an alliance to defend Afghanistan against invasion by France and Russia.[67]

Briefly after the treaty of 1809, Shah Shuja was dethroned by Shah Mahmud, who had presided over the fall of the Sadozai dynasty in 1818, which had led to the fragmentation of the Afghan state through civil war. For British India, both the Afghan threat and the fleeting menace of a French invasion of India had long since disappeared. This was replaced by a long-term threat of Russian expansion, which influenced political and military developments in the region throughout the nineteenth century. This became known as the "Great Game."

Epilogue

The sequel to this volume, by the same author, is *A Military History of Afghanistan: From the Great Game to the Global War on Terror*, which was published in 2017 by the University Press of Kansas.

After the death of Ahmad Shah Durrani in 1773, the next four decades saw the gradual decline of the Afghan Empire. Internal competition for power by the descendants of Ahmad Shah weakened the authority of the state as it faced challenges from outside. In the nineteenth century, the empire came under threat first by the Persians in the west and the Sikhs in the east and later by the European imperial powers.

As the century wore on, Afghanistan was drawn further and further into the "Great Game" prompted by British and Russian rivalry for influence in central Asia. This led to two Anglo-Afghan wars (1939–1942 and 1978–1980) in which the British armies unsuccessfully tried to occupy Afghanistan to check Soviet expansion in Central Asia. However, in the second half of the nineteenth century, Great Game politics forced Afghanistan to embrace the state system under British suzerainty as a buffer against Russia. After World War I, Afghanistan won full independence following another Anglo-Afghan war in 1919.

Mostly untouched by the two world wars, Afghanistan became a peaceful battlefield of the Cold War in the second half of the twentieth century, with the United States and the Soviet Union vying for influence through economic assistance. This focus coincided with democratic changes in Afghanistan between 1963 and 1973. The top-down democratic changes paved the way for the expansion of civil society and the emergence of a new, urban-based, educated elite as the core of political opposition to the government. Although liberalization produced few lasting reforms or viable democratic institutions, it gave rise to differing political movements that featured a pro-Soviet communist block, embodied by the People's Democratic Party of Afghanistan, and a revolutionary Islamist movement, represented by activists clustered

around several religious figures, some of whom later formed the Mujahedin political parties. The alignments later became agents of enormous
violence and destruction to the nation during the closing decades of the
twentieth century.

The military coup of 1978 brought to power pro-Moscow leftists who
faced growing resistance from the nation. Less than two years later,
the Soviet military intervention in Afghanistan to prop up the falling
communist regime became Moscow's longest foreign war of the century. Assistance to the Islamic-led Afghan resistance (the Mujahedin)
turned into the largest covert US operation after World War II. Neither the end of more than nine years of Soviet military occupation in
1989 nor the collapse of the communist regime in 1992 brought peace
to the country. Once the Mujahedin forces drove out the common enemy, they turned their guns against each other in a power struggle that
fragmented the multiethnic country. The chaos opened the door to the
rise of a traditional, antimodernist clerical movement. Schooled in religious institutions (madrasas), thousands of Afghan refugee students in
Pakistan, mullahs, and their supporters coalesced in 1994 into a major
political movement known as the Taliban, which drove the fractured
Mujahedin government from Kabul and established the Islamic Emirate
of Afghanistan.

The populist support that helped the Taliban to explode into power
and dominate about 90 percent of Afghanistan's territory in about five
years took a downturn as the militia failed to live up to the expectations of those who supported them. The Taliban won public support for
their pledge to end fighting, disarm the people, and establish the rule of
law based on Islamic Sharia. As their rule elapsed, other factors made
them unpopular even among their own Pashtun constituencies. These
included harsh treatment of non-Pashtun ethnicities, particularly Tajiks
and Hazaras; rigid and extremist interpretations of Islam in running
the government, in variance with the mainstream Islamic norms of the
Afghan society; dependence on Pakistan intelligence and the al-Qaeda
terrorist network; economic failure; and driving Afghanistan toward international isolation.

Then came 9/11. The suicide attackers who crashed hijacked passen-
ger planes into the World Trade Center in New York, the Pentagon in
Washington, and a field in Pennsylvania on September 11, 2001, were
linked to Osama bin Laden's worldwide terrorist network, al-Qaeda,
which was centered in Taliban-controlled Afghanistan. However, none
of those who committed the dreadful crime were Afghan nationals, and

the violence was not inspired by Afghan politics. The tragic event that cost more than 3,000 innocent lives and enormous material damage marked a new turn in an international war on terrorism and ushered in a new phase in the drawn-out civil strife within Afghanistan.

For the United States and its international partners, the main purpose for which they went to war in Afghanistan was achieved in less than three months: The al-Qaeda network was disrupted, and the Taliban regime was overthrown. It was an accidental short war for the allies but became a long process to achieve their responsible exit—a process that would take nearly another two decades and may take longer. The challenge was how to prevent Afghanistan from again becoming a source of terrorist threats to the United States and its allies in the West.

Notes

Introduction

1. H. G. Rawlinson, *Bactria: The History of a Forgotten Empire* (Probsthain: London, 1912), 28, 32, 85.

2. Sir Aurel Stein, *On Alexander's Track to Indus* (London: Macmillan, 1929), 41.

3. Minhaj-u-Seraj Jawzjani, *Tabaqat-i Nasiri*, ed. Abdul Hai Habibi, vol. 2 (Tehran: Dunaya-e-Kitab, 1984), 104.

4. G. Jailani Jalali, ed., *Nama-ye Ahmad Shah Baba Banam-e Sultan Mustafa Thales Osmani* (Ahmad Shah's Letter to the Ottoman Sultan Mustafa III) (Kabul: Afghanistan History Society, 1967), 55–56.

Chapter 1. A Geographic Overview

1. Thomas H. Holdich, *The Gates of India, Being an Historical Narrative* (London: Macmillan, 1910), 1–2.

2. Abul Fazl-i-'Allami, *Ain-i-Akbari* (The Institutes of Akbar), vol. 2 (Nolakshor, India: 1310 H, 1899), 192.

3. Horace Hayman Wilson, *Aryana Antiqua: A Descriptive Account of the Antiquities and Coins of Afghanistan* (London: East India Company, 1841), 168–188; Sir Aurel Stein, *On Alexander's Track to Indus* (London: Macmillan, 1929), 42–45.

4. Eratosthenes assumed a mountain range extended from the western seas all the way to India in a straight line dividing Asia lengthwise into two parts, making one the northern part and the other the southern.

5. *Eratosthenes' Geographica: Fragments Collected and Translated with Commentary and Additional Material*, by Duane W. Roller (Princeton: Princeton University Press, 2010), 42–43, 96, 100–101.

6. *Eratosthenes'* Geographica, 85.

7. *Dictionary of Greek and Roman Geography*, ed. William Smith, vol. 1 (Boston: Little, Brown and Company, 1870), 210–211.

8. Strabo, *Geography*, trans. Horace Leonard Jones (London: Harvard University Press, 1930), Book XV.2.1–2.

9. Strabo, Book XV.2.8–9. Also see Wilson, *Aryana Antiqua*, 120–122.

10. Aruzi-i-Samarqandi, a Persian poet and prose writer of the twelfth century who spent most of his time in Khorasan and Transoxiana, locates Laghman (east of Kabul) as part of Sind (India) and a district of Ghazna. See Nizami-i Aruzi-i Samarqandi, *Chahar Maqalah* (Four Discourses), ed. Mohammad Qazwini, 12th ed. (Tehran: Sada-i-Ma'asir, 2003), 29. Estakhri too included Kabul in India.

11. *Babur-Nama*, trans. Annette S. Beveridge (Lahore: Sange Meel, 1987), 202.

12. Abu Ishak Ibrahim Estakhri, *Al Masalik al Mamalik* (Traditions of Countries) (Leiden: Brill, 1927), 240–265.

13. Parmanand Gupta, *Geography from Ancient Indian Coins and Seals* (New Delhi: Concept Publishing Company, 1989), 17–18.

14. This word is *asp* in Persian and *aas* in Pashto, meaning "horse."

15. Herodotus, Book VII, 64–68.

16. *Archeological Recollections*, vol. 4 (Shiraz, 1959), cited in Abdul Hay Habibi, unpublished notes on Afghan and Afghanistan, and author's conversation with him in 1960s. Abdul Hai Habibi, *Afghan and Afghanistan*.

17. Vahara Mihtra, *Brihat Samita*, trans. N. Chindambaram (Matura: South Indian Press, 1884), 75, 96–97.

18. Thomas Watters et al., eds., *On Yuan Chwang's Travels in India*, vol. 2 (London: Royal Asiatic Society, 1906), 298–303.

19. *Memoires sur les Contrees Occidentales*, translated from Sanskrit to Chinese in 648 by Hioun-Thsang and from Chinese to French by M. Stanislas Julien, vol. 2 (Paris, 1858), 198–200.

20. Anonymous Author from Jawzjan (983 AD), *Hudud Al-'Alam, "The Regions of the World," A Persian Geography 982 A.D.* (2nd ed.), by unknown author from Jawzjan, translated and explained by V. Minorsky, ed. C. E. Bosworth (E. J. W. Gibb Memorial Trust, 1970), 91.

21. Abu Rayhan Al-Biruni, *Albiruni's India*, translated and edited by Edward Sachau, vol. 1 (Delhi: Rupa, 2005), 279.

22. Ibn Battuta, *The Adventures of ibn Battuta*, ed. Ross E. Dunn (Berkeley: University of California Press, 1989), 175, 178, 184, 186.

23. Saifi Herawi (Saif ibn Mohammad ibn Ya'qub al-Herawi), *Tarikh Nama-i-Herat*, ed. M. Zubair Siddiqi (Calcutta: Gulshan, 1943), 111, 188–192, 201–207, 213–221.

24. Henry Walter Bellew, *An Inquiry into the Ethnography of Afghanistan: Prepared and Presented to the Ninth International Congress of Orientalists* (Karachi: Indus, 1977 [London, 1891]), 3–4.

Chapter 2. The Early History of Afghanistan

1. Ali Ahmad Jalali, *Mutale'a-i Tarikh-i Afghanistan az Negah-i Askari* (The Study of Afghanistan History from a Military Perspective), vol. 1 (Kabul: Military Press, 1964), 38–40.

2. H. G. Rawlinson, *Bactria: The History of a Forgotten Empire* (London: Probsthain, 1912), 19–20.

3. Bactria is the Grecized form of the Persian name of Bakhtri, Its earlier form, mentioned in Zend Avesta, is Bakhdi, which is glorified in Avesta as *Bakhdhim sriram erdhvo drafsham* (Bakhdi the beautiful. Crowned with banners). This ancient Avestan appellation later transformed into Balkh.

4. Thomas H. Holdich, *The Gates of India, Being an Historical Narrative* (London: Macmillan, 1910), 73.

5. Wilhelm Geiger, *Civilization of the Eastern Iranians in Ancient Times with an Introduction on the Avesta Religion*, vol. 2 (London: Henry Frowde, 1886), 85–110.

6. Geiger, *Civilization*, vol. 2, 90.

7. Strabo, Book XI.11.1. Also see Rawlinson, *Bactria*, 2.

8. Romesh Chunder Dutt, *History of India from the Earliest Times to the Sixth Century B.C.*, vol. 1 (London: Grolier Society, 1906), 34–42.

9. Rigveda, I. 130, 8, All Rigveda references are cited in Romesh Chunder Dutt, *Ancient India 200 B.C.–800 A.D.* (London: Longmans, Green, 1893), 13–14.

10. Geiger, *Civilization*, vol. 1, 19–20.

11. Rigveda, I. 174, 7, 8.

12. Geiger, *Civilization*, vol. 1, 18.

13. E. J. Rapson, *The Cambridge History of India*, vol. 1, *Ancient India* (Cambridge: Cambridge University Press, 2011), 95.

14. Abdul Qasim Firdausi, *Shah-Nama* (The Book of Kings), "The Combat of Rustam and Esfandyar," folio from The Book of Kings, 4th ed. (Tehran: Qatra, 1999), 21, 1025, www.worldcat.org/title/the-combat-of-rustam-and-ashkabus-folio-from-the-book-of-kings/oclc/8686685857&referer=brief_results.

اگر جنگ خواهی و خون ریختن بدین گونه سختی بر آویختن

بگو تاسوار آورم زابلی که باشند با خنجر کابلی

تو ایرانیان را بفرمای نیز که تاگوهر اید پدید از پشیز

15. Rigveda, VI. 75.

16. *Avesta*, Yisht V.131, Geiger, *Civilization*, vol. 2, 22.

17. *Avesta*, Yisht XIII. 89, vol. 2, 22.

18. Romesh Chunder Dutt, *History of India from the Earliest Times to the Sixth Century B.C.*, vol. 1 (New York: Cosimo, 1906), 17.

19. Geiger, *Civilization*, vol. 1, 28–29.

20. Horace Hayman Wilson, *Aryana Antiqua: A Descriptive Account of the Antiquities and Coins of Afghanistan* (London: East India Company, 1841), 126.

21. Rawlinson, *Bactria*, 25.

22. Wilson, *Aryana Antiqua*, 127.

23. Geiger, *Civilization*, vol. 1, 45.

24. Wilson, *Aryana Antiqua*, 127.

25. Herodotus, *The History of Herodotus*, trans. George Rawlinson, Book III (New York, 1958), 89–94.

26. Herodotus, Book III, 61.

27. Herodotus, Book III, 205–215.

28. Herodotus, Book IV, 44.

29. Josef Wiesehofer, *Ancient Persia from 550 B.C. to 650 A.D.*, trans. Azizeh Azodi (London: I. B. Tauris, 1996), 89.

30. Herodotus, Book VII, 83.

31. Mark, Drury. "The Early Achaemenid Persian Army: Arms and Equipment." *Achaemenid Persia: A History Resource*. Web. September 10, 2011.

32. Herodotus, Book VII, 64–68.

33. Herodotus, Book VII, 81.

34. Drury, *Achaemenid Persia*.

35. Herodotus, Book VII, 41.

36. Harold Lamb, *Cyrus the Great* (New York: Doubleday, 1960), 295.

37. Rawlinson, *Bactria*, 34–35.

Chapter 3. The Passage of Alexander the Great, 330–323 BC

1. Quran (18:83–94). Some Western and traditional Muslim scholars identify Alexander the Great as the figure mentioned in the Quran as *Dhul-Qarnayn*, although some early Muslim scholars believed it to be a reference to a pre-Islamic monarch Cyrus the Great. The Quran describes Dhul-Qarnayn (or Zulqarnain) as a monotheist, kind-hearted, and just ruler; Alexander as historical figure is known as a polytheist who destroyed cities and massacred many inhabitants of the conquered lands.

2. حکم لري د یوه لنیکر محبوبا

دا دیدبه دی دسلطان سکند ر محبوبا

3. Benjamin Ide Wheeler, *Alexander the Great—The Emerging of the East and West in Universal History* (New York: G. P. Putnam's Sons, 1900), 397.

4. Henry Smith Williams, ed., *The Historian's History of the World*, vol. 4, *Greece to Roman Conquest* (New York: Outlook, 1904), 279.

5. Hans Delbruck, *History of the Art of War*, vol. 1, *Warfare in Antiquity*, trans. Walter J. Renfroe Jr. (Lincoln: University of Nebraska Press, 1990 [1900]), 447.

6. The exact number is said to be 42,864 infantry and 6,580 cavalry. See Donald W. Engels, *Alexander the Great and the Logistics of the Macedonian Army* (Berkeley: University of California Press, 1980), 148.

7. Quintus Rufus Curtius, *The History of Alexander*, trans. John Yardley (New York: Penguin Books, 1984), Book VIII.5.4.

8. Engels, *Alexander the Great*, 18, 143–154.

9. Engels, 83.

10. Engels, 12.

11. Curtius, Book VI.6.14–15.

12. Plutarch, *The Life of Alexander the Great*, trans. John Dryden and Arthur Hugh Clough (New York: Modern Library, 2004), 55.

13. Engels, *Alexander the Great*.

14. C. Neumann, "A Note on Alexander's March-Rates." *Historia: Zeitschrift Für Alte Geschichte*, 20, no. 2/3 (1971): 196–198. *JSTOR*, www.jstor.org/stable/4435191.

15. Ali Ahmad Jalali, *A Military History of Afghanistan from the Great Game to the Global War on Terror* (Lawrence: University Press of Kansas, 2017), 116.

16. Delbruck, *History of the Art of War*, vol. 1, 35.

17. Williams, *Historian's History of the World*, vol. 4, 276.

18. Plutarch, *Life of Alexander the Great*, 15.

19. Strabo, *Geography*, trans. Horace Leonard Jones (London: Harvard University Press, 1930), Book XV.9.

20. Arrian, Book III, 18.

21. Arrian, Book IV, 24.

22. Curtius, Book V.9.3–8.

23. Williams, *The Historian's History of the World*, vol. 4, 338–340.

24. Alexander like many ancient Greeks believed that there is a great outer sea beyond India where the world ends.

25. Curtius, Book VI.3.9–12.

26. Curtius, Book VI.4.1.

27. Strabo, Book XI.8.9.

28. Engels (*Alexander the Great and the Logistics of the Macedonian Army*, 90–91)

suggests the Kalat-e Naderi, over 500 kilometers northwest of the current location of Herat, was the Greeks' Artacoana. Although the topographical description of Artacoana by Curtius matches the Kalat-e Naderi's physical features, its distance to Herat and its position on Alexander's intended route to Bactria does not.

29. Thomas H. Holdich, *The Gates of India, Being an Historical Narrative* (London: Macmillan, 1910), 77.

30. The detachment included Companions, the mounted javelin-men, the archers, the Agrianes, and the Amyntas' and Coenus battalions.

31. Curtius, Book VI.6.27–35.

32. Sayf ibn Muhammad al-Herawi, *Tarikh Nama-i Herat* (The History of Herat), ed. Muhammad Zubayr As-Siddiqi, professor of Calcutta University, 2nd ed. (Tehran: Khaiam Library, 1352 H 1973).

33. Curtius, Book VIII.13.3–4.

34. Arrian, Book III, 28; Curtius, Book VII.3.2.

35. Curtius, Book VII.4.33–37.

36. Ptolemy, *The Geography*, translated and edited by Edward Luther Stevenson (New York: Dover, 1991), 147–148.

37. Curtius, Book VII.3.5.

38. Curtius, Book VII.3.11–14.

39. Ptolemy, 147. Horace Hayman Wilson, *Ariana Antiqua: A Descriptive Account of the Antiquities and Coins of Afghanistan* (London: East India Company, 1841), 176. Wilson believes that it's very possible that Ortospana or Orthospana is nothing more than the Sanskrit Urddhasthana, or "high place," an allusion to the elevated plain on which Kabul is situated.

40. Wilson, 176. Also Ahmad Ali Kuhzad, *The History of Afghanistan*, vol. 1 (Kabul: History Society) (rpt. Kabul: Amiri Press, 2018), 380.

41. Strabo, Book XV.2.10.

42. Curtius, Book VII.3.19.

43. Tarn suggests that Alexandria on the Caucasus and Alexandria-Kapisa may have been double cities located at the confluence of the Panjsher and Ghorband Rivers that dominate three routes going east to India and north to Bactria and west to Arachosia. Alexandria-Kapisa later became the capital of the Paropamisadae and served as a major base for the Greco-Bactrian and Kushanid dynasties. See William W. Tarn, *The Greeks in Bactria and India* (Cambridge: Cambridge University Press, 1966), 460–462.

44. Engels, *Alexander the Great*, 18, 95–96.

45. Curtius, Book VII.3.22–25.

46. Bessus made these comments in Bactra as he received the news of Alexander's approach. See Curtius, Book VII.4.1–5.

47. These proverbs are still in use in Afghanistan.

48. Bactra was also called Zariaspa. Zariaspa is either another name for Bactra or part of a Bactra-Zariaspa twin city.

49. Arrian, Book III, 29.

50. Holdich, *The Gates of India*, 89.

51. Henry Lansdell, *Russian Central Asia Including Kuldja, Bokhara, Khiva and Merv*, vol. 1 (London: Sampson Low and Co., 1885), 196.

52. Strabo, Book XI.7.4.

53. Strabo, Book XI.88.4.

54. H. G. Rawlinson, *Bactria: The History of a Forgotten Empire* (London: Probst-hain, 1912), 42.

55. Nau or Nov is a town in Tajikistan's Sughd Province located southwest of Khu-jand. It is the center of the Spitamenes District with a population of nearly 15,000.

56. Ura-Tuba or Urateppe is the ancient city of Istaravshan now located in Sughd Province in Tajikistan with a population of about 200,000. Located in the northern foothills of the Turkistan mountain range, about 45 miles southwest of Khujand, Istara-vshan is one of the oldest cities in Tajikistan, having existed for more than 2,500 years. Before 2000, it was known as Ура-Тюбе (Ura-Tyube) in Russian, Уротеппа (Uroteppa) in Tajik, and Uratepe in Turkish. The ancient city of Cyropolis is believed to be a very close approximation to that of modern day Istaravshan.

57. Curtius, Book VII.6.22–23.

58. Curtius, Book VII.7.31–39.

59. Arrian, Book IV, 6.

60. Arrian, Book IV, 7.

61. Curtius, Book VII.40.

62. Curtius, Book VII.10.11–13.

63. Curtius, Book VIII.3. 8–16.

64. Arrian, Book IV, 18–19.

65. Arrian, Book IV, 19–20; Curtius, Book VIII.4.23–26.

66. Agnes Savill, *Alexander the Great and His Time* (New York: Dorset Press, 1990), 91.

67. John Watson et al., *The Invasion of India by Alexander the Great as Described by Arrian, Q. Curtius, Diodorus, Plutarch and Justin*, 2nd ed. (London: Westminster, 1896), preface at xv.

68. Watson et al., *The Invasion of India.*

69. Arrian, Book IV, 22.

70. Curtius, Book VIII.5.4–5. Given the logistics of supporting such an army in dif-ficult territory ahead, the number seems exaggerated unless noncombatant service ele-ments are also counted in the mix.

71. This word is *asp* in Persian and *aas* in Pashto, meaning "horse."

72. The foot Companions were another distinguished corps of guards.

73. Agrianians were crack javelin-throwers and an elite unit of Alexander the Great's light infantry, who fought under the command of General Attalus, and made excellent lightly armed troops.

74. Diodorus in Janos Harmatta et al., *History of Civilizations of Central Asia*, vol. 2, *The Development of Sedentary and Nomadic Civilizations, 700 B.C. to A.D. 250* (Paris: Unesco Publishing, August 1, 1994), 5.

75. Plutarch, *The Life of Alexander the Great*, 12–13.

76. Strabo and Curtius call it the Choaspes, which the best authorities identify with the Kaniah or Kunar, a river that rivals the Kophen itself in the volume of its waters and the length of its course.

77. The mountains to which the inhabitants fled for refuge may perhaps, as V. de Saint-Martin suggests, be those that Justin (XII. 7) calls Daedali, whereto he says Alex-ander led his troops after the Bacchanalian revelry with which they had been indulged at Nysa.

78. These numbers seem inflated unless they include the local population, who normally picked up arms to face the invaders.

79. The Mughals built a fort here in 1586, occupied in 1895 by the British, who built the current fort in 1896 and were forced to defend it during the Siege of Malakand in 1897.

80. Sir Olaf Caroe, *The Pathans* (Oxford: Oxford University Press, 1958), 51–53.

81. Wilson, *Aryana Antiqua*, 189.

82. Curtius writes that the chief had died before the arrival of Alexander.

83. Arrian, *Anabasis* Book IV, 27; Diodorus XVII, 84, Curtius, Book VIII, 10, cited in Vincent Smith, *The Early History of India from 600 B.C. to the Mohammadan Conquest* (Oxford: Clarendon Press, 1904), 48.

84. Curtius, Book VIII.10.22.

85. Ramesh C. Majumdar, *Ancient India* (New Delhi: Sheri Jainendra Press, 1960), 98–99.

86. Harmatta et al., *History of Civilizations*, 75.

87. Arrian, Book IV, 26–27.

88. Holdich, *The Gates of India*, 106.

89. Sir Aurel Stein, *On Alexander's Track to the Indus: Personal Narrative of Explorations on the North-West Frontier of India* (London: Macmillan, 1929), 42–45.

90. Stein, *On Alexander's Track*, 128–148.

91. Arrian, Book IV, 18.

92. Smith, *Early History of India*, 52.

93. Pamela Mensch and James Romm, eds., *Alexander the Great: Selections from Arrian, Diodorus, Plutarch, and Quintus Curtius* (Indianapolis: Hackett Publishing Company, 2005), 149.

94. Rawlinson, *Bactria*, 51.

95. Wheeler, *Alexander the Great*, 495–496.

96. A. B. Bosworth, *Alexander and the East—The Tragedy of Triumph* (New York: Oxford University Press, 1996), preface.

97. Wheeler, *Alexander the Great*, 500–501, n. 89.

Chapter 4. Disintegration of Greek Power in the East and the Rise of New Empires

1. Quintus Curtius Rufus, *The History of Alexander*, trans. John Yardley (New York: Penguin, 1984), Book X.5.4.

2. H. G. Rawlinson, *The Sixth Great Oriental Monarchy or the Geography, History and Antiquities of Parthia* (New York: Belford Clarke, 1887), 60–62.

3. Justin, *History of Justin (Justini, Hiitorias Phillippicae)*, English translation by John Clarke, Book XLI (Glocester: R. Raixes, 1790), 4.

4. Strabo, *Geography*, trans. Horace Leonard Jones (London: Harvard University Press, 1930), Book XI.11.1.

5. For example, the Achaemenids (sixth–fourth centuries BC), Parthians (third century BC–third century AD), Sassanids (third–seventh centuries AD), Buyids (tenth–eleventh centuries AD), and Saljuqs (eleventh–thirteenth centuries AD) were mostly engaged in the Near Eastern and the Gulf region's political and military developments. On the

other hand, the Greco-Bactrians (third–first centuries BC), the Kushans (first–third centuries AD), Ephthalites (fifth–sixth centuries AD), Ghaznavids (tenth–twelfth centuries AD), Ghorids (twelfth–thirteenth centuries AD), and Babur and his dynasty (sixteenth–eighteenth centuries AD) were mostly drawn to the events of Central and South Asia.

6. Strabo, Book XI.11.1.

7. Polybius, *The Histories of Polybius*, English translation by Evelyn S. Shuckburgh, vol. 2 (London: Macmillan, 1889), Book XI.84.

8. Justin, Book XLI, 6.

9. W. W. Tarn, *The Greeks in Bactria and India* (New York: Cambridge University Press, 1966), 322–323.

10. Ephthalites are mentioned as Ye-ti-i-li-do. It is Khion for a Hun in Middle Persian, while Arabic and Persian sources referred to them as Haytal or Hayatila (plural).

11. H. G. Rawlinson, *The Seventh Great Oriental Monarchy or the Geography, History and Antiquities of the Sassanian or New Persian Empire*, vol. 1 (New York: Belford Clarke, 1887), 330–334.

12. Herodotus, Book III, 205–215.

13. Tarn, *Greeks in Bactria and India*, 116–118.

14. Strabo, Book XI.5.11.

15. Tarn, *Greeks in Bactria and India*, 122.

16. Justin, Book XLI, 4.

17. The ancient country between the Oxus River and the Hindu Kush Mountains.

18. W. [V. V.] Barthold, *The History of Turks in Central Asia*, Persian translation by Ghafar Hosseini (Tehran: Tous Publisher, 1997/1376), 52–53.

19. The *cataphract* was a form of armored heavy cavalry utilized in ancient warfare by a number of peoples in Western Eurasia and the Eurasian Steppe.

20. J. B. Bury, *A History of Greece to the Death of Alexander the Great* (London: Macmillan, 1900), 819–820.

21. Arrian, Book VII, 6.

22. Herodotus, Book IV, 46.

23. Rawlinson, *The Sixth Great Oriental Monarchy*, 404.

24. Rawlinson, 159–166.

25. The text purports to record a dialogue in which the Indo-Greek king Menander I (Milinda in Pali) of Bactria, who reigned in the second century BC, poses questions on Buddhism to the sage Nāgasena.

26. *Milindapanha—The Questions of King Milinda*, translated from Pali by T. W. Rhys Davids (Oxford: Oxford University Press, 1890), 54, 60–62.

27. Hans Delbruck, *History of the Art of War*, vol. 1, *Warfare in Antiquity* (Lincoln: University of Nebraska Press, 1990 [1900]), 561.

28. Arthur Christensen, *Sassanid Persia*, 2nd ed. (Tehran: unknown publisher, 1965), 237.

Chapter 5. The Arab Conquest and Islamization of Afghanistan, 642–921 AD

1. Edward Gibbon, *History of the Decline and Fall of the Roman Empire*, vol. 5, and chapter LI, part IX.

2. *Ghazwa* meant "military expeditions" or "raiding," with a new connotation of religious warfare, often led by the Prophet Mohammad.

3. Mohammad ibn Jarir Tabari, *Tarikh al-Rusul wa al-Muluk*, trans. Abul Qasim Payendah, 6th ed., vol. 4 (Tehran: Asateer, 2004), 1654–1655.

4. Montgomery Watt, *The Majesty That Was Islam* (London: Sidgwick and Jackson, 1974), 36.

5. Ibn Athir, Ali 'Izz al-Din al-Jazari, *Al-Kamil fi al-Tarikh*, translated from Arabic into Persian by Dr. Slayed Hosseini Rohani, 2nd ed., vol. 3 (1995), 1309–1310.

6. Georgie Zeidan, *Ta'rikh al-Tamaddun al-Islamii*, Persian translation, vol. 1 (Tehran: Government Press, 1919), 165–167.

7. For the Muslim Arab military system I draw mainly on Hugh Kennedy's *The Armies of the Caliphs: Military and Society in the Early Islamic State* (London: Routledge, 2001); and Zeidan, *Ta'rikh al-Tamaddun al-Islamii.*

8. Zeidan, *Ta'rikh al-Tamaddun al-Islamii*, 155.

9. Zeidan, 166–167.

10. Mohammad ibn Mansur Mubarakshah Fakhr-e Modabber, *Adab al Harb wa-Shja'a*, ed. Ahmad Sohaili Khwansari (Tehran: Eqbal, 1967), 240–241.

11. Hugh Kennedy, *The Great Arab Conquests: How the Spread of Islam Changed the World We Live In* (Boston: Da Capo Press, 2007), 60.

12. Kennedy, *Armies of the Caliphs*, 107, 110, 113.

13. Kennedy, *Great Arab Conquests*, 61.

14. *Chach-Nama*, 104–106.

15. Tabari, vol. 4, 1353; Ibn Athir, vol. 3, 1211–1212.

16. Robert Payne, *The History of Islam* (Barnes and Noble Books, 1995), 104.

17. Payne, *History of Islam.*

18. Ibn Athir, 2753–2754; Tabari, vol. 9, 3810–3813.

19. H. A. R. Gibb, *The Arab Conquest in Central Asia* (London: Royal Asiatic Society, 1923), 40–42.

20. Abul Qasem Obaidullah Ibn Khordadbeh, *Kitab al-Masalik wa Mamalik* (Book of Roads and Kingdoms), a ninth-century geography in Arabic (870 AD) (Leiden: Brill, 1889), 39–40.

21. Abu Rayhan Biruni, *Tarikh-al-Hind*, trans. E. C. Sachau (Delhi: Rupa, 2010), 414–416.

22. Abul Hai Habibi, *The Temple of Zoor or Zoon in Zamindawar*, 1969. alamahabibi.net/English_Articles/Zoor_or_zoon_temple.htm.

23. Clifford Edmund Bosworth, *Encyclopedia of Islam* (Leiden: Brill, 2002); Zamindawar, 439.

24. Tabari, vol. 5, 2015.

25. Estakhri, *Al-Masalik al-mamalik*, 239–241.

26. Tabari, vol. 5., 2015–2016.

27. Anonymous (circa 1062 AD), *Tarikh-i Sistan*, ed. Mohammad Taqi Bahar (Tehran, 1930), 80–83.

28. Ibn Athir, vol. 4, 1661–1662.

29. Remnants of the walls have survived since and are visible today as they snake around the surrounding hills.

30. Anonymous, *Tarikh-i Sistan*, 88.

31. Tabari, vol. 8, 3664.

32. Tabari, vol. 8, 3664–3666.

33. Ibn Athir, vol. 6, 2672–2675.

34. Al-Muqaddasi, *Ahsan al-Taqasim fi Ma'rifat al-Aqalim* (The Best Division for Knowledge of the Regions), trans. Basir Collins (Reading, UK: Garnet, 1994), 239.

35. Gibb, *Arab Conquest in Central Asia*, 1.

36. W. Barthold, *Turkestan down to The Mongol Invasion*, ed. C. E. Bosworth, 3rd ed. (London: Luzac, 1968), 66–68.

37. Gibb, *Arab Conquest in Central Asia*, 8.

38. Gibb, 9.

39. Ibn Athir, vol. 6, 2556–2558.

40. Gibb, *Arab Conquest in Central Asia*, 15–88; Kennedy, *Great Arab Conquests*, 215–216.

41. Al-Baladhuri, *Kitab Futuh al-Buldan*, 490–492.

42. Tabari, vol. 5, 2167–2169.

43. *Proceedings Geographical Society and Monthly Record of Geography, New Monthly Series*, vol. 7 (London, 1885), 283.

44. According to Gardizi, Abdullah ibn Aamir later built the "Qasr-I Ahnaf," which Ibn Khordadbeh places at a point 20 miles from Marv-ar-Rud. (Gardizi, Abu Sa'id Abdul-Hay Dhahhak, *Zayn al-Akhbar*, ed. Abdul Hay Habibi [Tehran: Armaghan, 1884], 228). The ruins in modern Maruchaq are considered to be the ruins of Qasr-i Ahnaf, one of the Marv-ar-Rud settlements. See Bosworth, *The Encyclopedia of Islam*, 2nd ed., vol. 6, 617.

45. He was one of the leaders of the army during the Battle of Karbala in 680 (10th Muharram—'ashura'—61 H), where the Umayyad army faced the defiant Hussein ibn Ali, the grandson of the Prophet Mohammad, who had refused to recognize the legitimacy of the rule of Mu'awiya's son Yazid as the caliph. In the encounter, a large detachment of the Umayyad army massacred Hussein and a small group of his supporters. The Battle of Karbala is commemorated during an annual ten-day period held every Muharram by the Shia as well as many Sunnis, culminating on its tenth day, known as 'ashura.

46. Gardizi, *Zayn al-Akhbar*, 238.

47. Narshakhi, *Tarikh-i Bukhara* (The History of Bukhara), trans. Richard Frye (Princeton: Markus Wiener, 2007), 55–56.

48. Narshakhi, 57–58.

49. Gibb, *Arab Conquest in Central Asia*, 22.

50. Narshakhi, *Tarikh-i Bukhara*, 65–66.

51. Narshakhi, 63–74.

52. Tabari, vol. 9, 3810–3813.

53. Gibb, *Arab Conquest in Central Asia*, 52–53.

54. Ibn Athir, vol. 6, 2831–2837.

55. Ibn Athir, vol. 7, 2962–2964.

56. Arab external expeditions ended with the end of the Umayyad Caliphate.

57. Watt, *The Majesty That Was Islam*, 37.

58. W. Barthold, *Turkistan down to the Mongol Invasion*, translated into English by Minorsky, 3rd ed., 195–196.

59. M. A. Shaban, *The Abbasid Revolution* (Cambridge University Press, 1970), 65.

60. Tabari, vol. 9, 4094.

61. Tabari, vol. 7, 2880–2881.

62. Tabari, vol. 7, 2779.

63. Ibn Khaldun, *Muqaddimah* (Prolegomena, or an Introduction on History), Translated from the Arabic by Franz, 246–247.

64. Payne, *The History of Islam*, 146.

65. Watt, *The Majesty That Was Islam*, 99.

66. Al-Baladhuri, *Kitab Futuh al-Buldan*, 151, 205, 261, 292–293, 297.

67. Tabari, vol. 11, 4692, 4706–4709.

68. Narshakhi, *Tarikh-i Bukhara*, 87–94.

69. Tarikh-i Sistan, 268.

70. Abu Hasan Ali Mas'udi, *Muruj adh-dhahab wa ma'adin al-jawhar* (The Meadows of Gold and Mines of Gems), ed. Charles Horne (Whitefish, MT: Kessinger Publishing's Rare Reprints, 2010), 65.

71. Tabari, vol. 12, 5308–5310.

72. Mas'udi, 79; Tabari, vol. 13, 5686–5688.

73. Tabari, vol. 13, 5707–5708.

Chapter 6. Decline of the Abbasid Caliphate and the Rise of Local Muslim Dynasties, 921–1215 AD

1. Al-Muqaddasi, *Ahsan al-Taqasim fi Ma'rifat al-Aqalim* (The Best Division for Knowledge of the regions), translated by Basir Collins (Reading, UK: Garnet, 1994), 273.

2. Guillain Denoeux, *Urban Unrest in the Middle East: A Comparative Study of Informal Networks in Egypt, Iran, and Lebanon* (Albany: State University of New York, 1993), 42.

3. Denoeux, 42.

4. Clifford Edmund Bosworth, *The Ghaznavids, Their Empire in Afghanistan and Eastern Iran*, First Indian Edition, 1992, Munshiram Manoharlal Publishers, 167.

5. Such characterization of *'ayyaran* abounds in Persian folk tales. For example in Sadiduddin Mohammed 'Awfi's *Jawami'-al-Hekayat wa Lawami'-al-Rawayat*, ed. Ja'far Sh'ar, Tehran 1984, 259, 359–361.

6. Kazim Kazimini, *'Ayyaran: ba Wizhagi ha-ye Pahlawani az Tarikh-i-Ejtema'i wa Qawmi Iran* ('Ayarran—their specialized feats in the national and social history of Iran) (Tehran: Maihan Publisher, 1970), 307–317.

7. Bosworth, *The Ghaznavids*, 98.

8. Ibn Athir, Ali 'Izz al-Din al-Jazari, *Al-Kamil fi al-Tarikh*, translated from Arabic into Persian by Dr. Slayed Hosseini Rohani, 2nd ed., 1995, vol. 10, 4383.

9. Anonymous (circa 1062 AD), *Tarikh-i Sistan*, ed. Mohammad Taqi Bahar (Tehran, 1930), 29.

10. Abu Sa'id Abdul-Hay Dhahhak Gardizi, *Zayn al-Akhbar*, ed. Abdul Hay Habibi (Tehran: Armaghan, 1884), 305.

11. C. E. Bosworth, *The Tahirids and Saffarids, the Cambridge History of Iran, from the Arab Invasion to the Seljuqs*, ed. Richard Nelson Frye, William Bayne Fisher, and John Andrew Boyle, vol. 4 (Cambridge: Cambridge University Press, 1975), 111.

12. Gardizi, *Zayn al-Akhbar*, 309.

13. Anonymous, *Tarikh-i Sistan*, 267–268.

14. Tabari, vol. 15, 6451.

15. Ibn Athir, vol. 10, 4382–4383.

340 Notes to Pages 134-148

16. Tabari, vol. 15, 6627; Ibn Athir, vol. 10, 4459–4460.

17. Tabari, vol. 15, 6635.

18. Narshakhi, *Tarikh-i Bukhara* (The History of Bukhara), trans. Richard Frye (Princeton: Markus Wiener, 2007), 105.

19. Narshakhi, *Tarikh-i Bukhara*, 114–119.

20. W. Barthold, *Turkestan down to the Mongol Invasion*, ed. C. E. Bosworth, 3rd ed. (London: Luzac, 1968), 218–219; C. E. Bosworth, *The Cambridge History of Iran*, vol. 4, *From the Arab Invasion to the Saljuqs* (Cambridge: Cambridge University Press, 1975), chapter 3, "The Tahirids and Saffarids," 125.

21. Ghiasuddin ibn Humamuddin al-Hosseini Khwandmir, *Habib-us-Siar*, ed. Mohammad Dabir Saiyaqi, vol. 2 (Tehran: Khayyam, 1974), 346.

22. Daniel Pipes, *Slave Soldiers and Islam: The Genesis of a Military System* (Yale University Press, 1981), 140–151.

23. Nizam ul-Mulk, *Siyasat-nama* (Book of Government), ed. M. Qazwini and Mohammad Chahardehi (Tehran, 1956), 53.

24. Bosworth, *Cambridge History of Iran*, vol. 4, chapter 3, "The Tahirids and Saffarids," 126–127.

25. Gardizi, *Zayn al-Akhbar*, 314–315.

26. Bosworth, *The Ghaznavids*, 122.

27. Mohammad ibn Mansur Mubarakshah Fakhr-e Modabber, *Adab al Harb wa-Shja'a*, ed. Ahmad Sohaili Khwansari (Tehran: Eqbal, 1967), 276–277.

28. Tabari, vol. 14, 6276–6278; Ibn Athir, vol. 7, 75.

29. Narshakhi, *Tarikh-i Bukhara*, 103–104 and 112–113.

30. Al-Muqaddasi, *Ahsan al-Taqasim fi Ma'rifat al-Aqalim*, 275.

31. Bosworth, *The Ghaznavids*, 27.

32. Barthold, *Turkestan down to the Mongol Invasion*, 225–226.

33. Narshakhi, *Tarikh-i Bukhara*, 24.

34. Al-Muqaddasi, *Ahsan al-Taqasim fi Ma'rifat al-Aqalim*, 274.

35. Nizam ul-Mulk, *Siyasat-nama*, 95.

36. Narshakhi, *Tarikh-i Bukhara*, 112.

37. Al-Muqaddasi, *Ahsan al-Taqasim fi Ma'rifat al-Aqalim*, 225–226.

38. Bosworth, *The Ghaznavids*, 271.

39. Al-Muqaddasi, *Ahsan al-Taqasim fi Ma'rifat al-Aqalim*, 239.

40. Stanley Lane-Poole, *History of India*, vol. 3, *Mediaeval India from the Mohammadan Conquest to the Reign of Akbar the Great* (London: Grolier Society, 1907), 12.

41. Abu Nasr Muhammad Al-Utbi, b. Abdul Jabar, *Kitab-i-Yamini*, trans. James Reynolds (London: Oriental Translation Fund, 1858), 244–245.

42. Abul-Fadl Bayhaqi, *Tarikh-I Mas'udi*, ed. Dr. Ghani (Tehran, 1928), 328, 409, 429.

43. Minhaj-u-Seraj Jawzjani, *Tabaqat-i Nasiri*, ed. Abdul Hai Habibi (Tehran: Dunaya-e-Kitab, 1984), 230.

44. Bayhaqi, *Tarikh-I Mas'udi*, 374.

45. Nizam ul-Mulk, *Siyasat-nama*, 110–111.

46. Nizam ul-Mulk, 111.

47. Utbi, *Kitab-i-Yamini*, 33–43.

48. Mohammad ibn Mansur Mubarakshah Fakhr-i-Modabber, *Adab al Harb wa-Shja'a*, ed. Sohaili Khwansari (Tehran: Eqbal Publisher, 1967), 260.

49. Bayhaqi, *Tarikh-I Mas'udi*, 477.

50. 'Utbi, Mohammad ibn Mohammad Abu Nasr al-Jabbar, *Kitab-i-Yamini*, trans. Rev. James Reynolds (London: Harrison and Sons, 1858), 337–338.

51. Muhammad Nazim, *The Life and Times of Sultan Mahmud of Ghazna*, 2nd ed. (Delhi: Munshiram Manoharlal, 1971), 141–142.

52. Bayhaqi, *Tarikh-I Mas'udi*, 228, 275, 374, 414, 451, 597–598 et seq.

53. Nazim, *Life and Times of Sultan Mahmud of Ghazna*, 140.

54. Jawzjani, *Tabaqat-i Nasiri*, 119–120.

55. Nazim, *Life and Times of Sultan Mahmud of Ghazna*, 115.

56. Nazim, 209–224.

57. Jaywant D. Joglekar, *Decisive Battles India Lost (326 B.C. to 1083 A.D.)*, 1st Marathi ed., English version (Lexington, KY: Somaiya, 2012), 7.

58. K. M. Panikar, *Problems of Indian Defense*, cited in Joglekar, *Decisive Battles*, 12.

59. Vincent A. Smith, *The Oxford History of India from the Earliest Times to the End of 1911* (Oxford: Oxford University Press, 1919), 220.

60. C. E. Bosworth, *Ghaznavids*, Encyclopedia Iranica, online edition, 2012.

61. Nazim, *Life and Times of Sultan Mahmud of Ghazna*, 155.

62. Stanley Lane-Poole, *History of India*, vol. 3, *Mediaeval India from the Mohammadan Conquest to the Reign of Akbar the Greet* (London: Grolier Society, 1907), 31.

63. Bayhaqi, *Tarikh-I Mas'udi*, 834–838.

64. Utbi, *Kitab-i-Yamini*, 362–365.

65. C. E. Bosworth, *Ghurids*, Encyclopedia Iranica, 2012.

66. Mounstuart Elphinstone, *The History of India*, vol. 1 (London: J. Maurray, 1841), 598–599; Stanley Lane-Poole, *History of India*, vol. 3, *Mediaeval India from the Mohammadan Conquest to the Reign of Akbar the Great* (London: Grolier Society, 1907), 51.

67. Major H. G. Raverty, *Ghaznin and Its Environs: Geographical, Ethnographical and Historical*, ed. Ahmad Nabi Khan (Lahore: Sang-e-Meel, 1995), 161; Sir Olaf Caroe, *The Pathans*, 7th impression (Oxford: Oxford University Press, 1990), 122; Bosworth, *Ghurids*, Encyclopedia Iranica.

68. Mohammad Hotak, *Patta Khazana*, in Pashto, ed. Abdul Hai Habibi, 2nd ed. (Kabul, 1958), 30–38.

69. The most intensive critical occupation with the manuscript among Pashto scholars was published by the Pakistani Pashtun scholar Qalandar Mohmand in 1988.

70. Bayhaqi, *Tarikh-I Mas'udi*, 140.

71. Jawzjani, *Tabaqat-i Nasiri*, 344.

جهان داند که من شاه جهانم
چراغ دودهٔ عباسيانم
بران بودم که از اوباش غزنين
چو رود نيل جوى خون برانم
وليكن گنده پيرانند و طفلان
شفاعت ميكند بخت جوانم

72. Jawzjani, *Tabaqat-i Nasiri* (Calcutta, 1864), 169–170.

73. Jawzjani, *Tabakat-i Nasiri*, trans. Major Raverty, vol. 1 (London: Gilbert and Rivington, 1881), 370.

74. Stanley Lane-Pool, *History of India*, 55.

75. Joglekar, *Decisive Battles*, 40.

76. Joglekar, 12–13.

77. Jawzjani, Minhaj-u-Seraj, *Tabaqat-i Nasiri*, 115–119.

78. Joglekar, *Decisive Battles*, 46.

79. Mohammad Qasim Hindu Shah, *Tarikh-i Fereshta* (Calcutta: Newalkishore Press, 1874), 57–58.

80. Jawzjani, Minhaj-u-Seraj, *Tabaqat-i Nasiri*, 119–120.

81. Vincent A. Smith, *The Oxford History of India from the Earliest Times to the End of 1911* (Oxford: Oxford University Press, 1919), 220.

Chapter 7. The Mongol Cataclysm, 1220–1370

1. 'Alauddin 'Ata Malik Juwayni, *Tarikh-i, Jahan-Gusha*, ed. M. M. Qazwini (Leiden: E. J. Brill, 1912), vol. 1, 82.

آمدند و کندند و کُشتند و بُردند و رفتند

2. *The Secret History of the Mongols*, adaptation by Paul Kahn (Boston: Cheng & Tsui, 1998), 114–115.

3. Carl Fredrik Sverdrup, *Mongol Conquests: The Military Operation of Genghis Khan and Subbe'etei* (England: Helion, 2016), 148.

4. W. Barthold, *Turkestan down to The Mongol Invasion*, ed. C. E. Bosworth, 3rd ed. (London: Luzac, 1968), 376–377.

5. Charles Holcombe, *A History of East Asia from the Origins of Civilization to the Twenty First Century* (Cambridge: Cambridge University Press, 2011), 136.

6. Minhaj-u-Seraj Jawzjani, *Tabaqat-i Nasiri*, ed. Abdul Hai Habibi, vol. 2 (Tehran: Dunaya-e-Kitab, 1984), 102–103; Barthold, *Turkestan down to The Mongol Invasion*, 394.

7. Sir Henry Hoyle Howorth, *History of the Mongols from 9th to the 19th Century*, part 1 (London: Longmans, 1876), 74.

8. David Morgan, *The Mongols* (Cambridge, MA: Blackwell, 1986), 84.

9. Timothy May, *The Mongol Art of War* (South Yorkshire: Pen & Sword Military, 2007), 28–30.

10. Paul D. Buell, *Historical Dictionary of the Mongol World Empire* (Lanham, MD: Scarecrow Press, 2003), 113.

11. *The Secret History of the Mongols*, 128.

12. 'Alauddin 'Ata Malik Juwayni, *Tarikh-i, Jahan-Gusha*, ed. M. M. Qazwini (Leiden: E. J. Brill, 1912), vol. 1, 23.

13. Larry Moses, "Legends by the Numbers: The Symbols of Numbers in *The Secret History of the Mongols*," *Asian Folklore Studies* 55, no. 1 (1996): 95–96.

14. Sverdrup, *Mongol Conquests*, 167.

15. Sverdrup, *Mongol Conquests*, 24.

16. Buell, *Historical Dictionary of the Mongol World Empire*, 109–111.

17. Sverdrup, *Mongol Conquests*, 23–24.

18. Juwayni, *Tarikh-i*, vol. 1, 19–20.

19. Jawzjani/Habibi, *Tabaqat-i Nasiri*, vol. 2, 104–105.

20. Marco Polo, *The Travels*, trans. Ronald Latham (London: Penguin, 1958), 100–101.

21. Juwayni, *Tarikh-i Jahan Gusha*, vol. 1, 21–23. Also see Ata-Malik Juwayni, *Tarikh-i, Jahan-Gusha*, translated and edited by A. A. Boyle (Manchester: Manchester University Press, 1958), 30–32.

22. Howorth, *History of the Mongols*, vol. 1, 154.

23. Yusuf Khass Hajib, *Wisdom of Royal Glory (Qutadghu Bilig): A Turko-Islamic Mirror for Princes*, translated and with an introduction and notes by Robert Dankoff (Chicago and London: Chicago University Press, 1983), 116.

24. Jawzjani, *Tarikh-i Jahan Gusha*, vol. 2, 104.

25. Barthold, *Turkestan down to The Mongol Invasion*, 404; C.C. Walker, *Jenghiz Khan* (London: Luzac, 1939), 82.

26. B. H. Liddell Hart, *Great Captains Unveiled, from Genghis Khan to General Wolfe* (London: Greenhill, 1990), 11–17.

27. John Mann, *Genghis Khan, Life, Death and Resurrection* (New York: Thomas Dunn, 2007), 150–151.

28. *The Secret History of the Mongols*, 157.

29. Barthold, *Turkestan down to the Mongol Invasion*, 405.

30. Hart, *Great Captains*, 11–15.

31. Rashiduddin Fazlullah, *Jami'u-Tawarikh*, ed. M. Roshan Mustafa Mousavi, vol. 1 (Tehran: Alburz, 1994), 489.

32. Juwayni/Boyle, 104.

33. Howorth, *History of the Mongols*, 78.

34. Juwayni, *Tarikh-i*, vol. 1, 82.

35. Jawzjani/Habibi, vol. 2, 107.

36. Ashura Day falls on the tenth of Muharram, the first month in the Islamic lunar calendar and is commemorated by the Muslims as the day of mourning for the martyrdom of Hussein ibn Ali, the grandson of Prophet Mohammad at the Battle of Karbala on the tenth of Muharram in the year 61 H. (October 10, 680 AD).

37. Nakhshab, mentioned as "Nasaf" by medieval Muslim geographers, is a fertile oasis used as a military staging area and resting place throughout history. Alexander the Great wintered there in 328 BC when the major city there was known as Nautaka near modern Qarshi. In recent times, Qarshi (Karshi) temporarily served as a US air force base in support of mission in Afghanistan between 2001 and 2005.

38. Juwayni, *Tarikh-i*, vol. 1, 102.

39. Howorth, *History of the Mongols*, 121.

40. Percy Sykes, *A History of Afghanistan*, vol. 1 (New Delhi: Munshiram Manoharlal, 2002), 222–223.

41. Hamdullah Mustawfi, *The Geographic Part of the Nuzhat al-Qulub*, trans. G. Le Strange (Cambridge: Cambridge University Press, 1919), chapter XIV, 146–159.

42. Mustawfi, *Geographic Part*.

43. Mustawfi.

44. Saif ibn Mohammad ibn Ya'qub al-Herawi, *Tarikh Nama-i-Herat*, ed. M. Zubair Siddiqi (Calcutta: Gulshan, 1943), 67.

45. al-Herawi, *Tarikh Nama-i-Herat*, 60–63; Jawzjani/Habibi, vol. 2, 121.

46. C. E. Bosworth, *The Ghaznavids: Their Empire in Afghanistan and Eastern Iran*, 1st Indian ed. (New Delhi: Mushaira Manoharlal, 1992), 162.

47. Mustawfi, *Geographic Part of the Nuzhat al-Qulub*, 146–159.

48. Tertius Chandler and Gerald Fox, *3000 Years of Urban Growth*, 232–246. https://en.wikipedia.org/wiki/Mongol_conquest_of_the_Khwarazmian_Empire#cite_note-36.

49. Mann, *Genghis Khan*, 172–176.

50. Mann, *Genghis Khan*, 180. The population of roughly the same area (Persia and

Central Asia) plus some others (Caucasia and northeast Anatolia) is estimated at 5–6 million nearly four hundred years later under the rule of the Safavid dynasty. "Mongol Conquest of the Khwarazmian Empire," Wikipedia, Stephen Frederic Dale (August 15, 2002), *Indian Merchants and Eurasian Trade, 1600–1750,* 19.

51. Hudud Al-'Alam, *"The Regions of the World," A Persian Geography, 982 A.D.,* 2nd ed., by unknown author from Jawzjan, translated and explained by V. Minorsky, ed. C. E. Bosworth (Cambridge: E. J. W. Gibb Memorial Trust, 1970), 107, 109.

52. Muhammad Abol Qasim Ibn Hawqal, *Surat al-Ard,* also published as *Ibn Hawqal's Kitab Masalik wa mamalik (مسالک و مالک تصنیف ابن حوقل),* Arabian traveler of the tenth century, ed. Sir William Ousley (London: Oriental Press by Wilson and Co., 1800), 220–221.

53. Jawzjani, *Tabakat-i Nasiri,* vol. 2, trans. Major Raverty (London: Gilbert and Rivington), 188, fn., 1009.

54. Muqaddasi, the tenth-century Arab traveler/geographer in his map of Khorasan distinguishes between the Taleqan of Marv ar-Rud and the Taleqan of Tokharistan. The former is located in the Murghab Valley west of Sheberghan, the latter east of Balkh and west of Badakhshan (in its current location). Al-Muqaddasi, 416.

55. Jawzjani, *Tabakat-i Nasiri,* vol. 2, 1012.

56. Ibn Athir says it lasted ten months.

57. Jawzjani/Raverty, vol. 2, 1013.

58. Mohammad ibn Ahmad Nesawi, *Sirat-i Jalaluddin Mungaberti* (Tehran, 1987), 107.

59. The 30,000–45,000 recorded by some sources looks highly exaggerated. The nature of the mission and operational mode of the Mongols' military make it improbable to field such a large force for the purpose.

60. Juwayni, *Tarikh-i,* 105.

61. Barthold, *Turkestan down to the Mongol Invasion,* 445–446.

62. John Wood, *A Personal Narrative of a Journey to the Source of the River by the Route of the Indus, Kabul and Badakhshan* (London: Government of India, 1841), 141, 124.

63. Nesawi, *Sirat-i Jalaluddin Mungaberti,* 117.

64. Jeremiah Curtin, *The Mongols: A History* (Conshohocken, PA: Combine Books, 1996), 127.

65. Juwayni, *Tarikh-i,* vol. 1, 106–107; Nesawi, *Sirat-i Jalaluddin Mungaberti,* 117–118.

66. Jawzjani/Raverty, vol. 2, 1045–1047.

67. Jawzjani/Habibi, vol. 2, 28.

68. Mu'inuddin Mohammad Zamchi Esfazari, *Rauzat al-Jannat fi Auwsaf-i Madint-i Herat,* ed. Saiyed M. Kazem Imam (Tehran: Tehran University Press, 1959), 361.

69. Walker, *Jenghiz Khan,* 148.

70. Jawzjani/Raverty, vol. 2, 1049–1051.

71. Walker, *Jenghiz Khan,* 148.

72. Minhaj-u-Seraj, Jawzjani, *Tabaqat-i Nasiri,* ed. Abdul Hai Habibi, vol. 2 (Tehran, 1984), 129.

73. According to Jawzjani, the Kaliun fortress was located about 40 miles from the fortress of Fiwar in the Qadis District. Since the Qadis District is situated in today's Badghis Province of Afghanistan, bordering the province of Ghor, the Kaliun must have

stood in the mountains that straddle the southwest corner of Badghis and northwest confines of Ghor.

74. Curtin, *The Mongols: A History*, 128.

75. There are several places in central mountainous districts of Afghanistan ending with "tau," from the Mongolian root meaning "mountain." Examples are Jagha-tau, Shemir-tau, Jerma-tau, etc.

76. Jawzjani/ Habibi, vol. 2, 131.

77. Mann, *Genghis Khan*, 180.

78. Harold Lamb, *Genghis Khan, Emperor of All Men* (Garden City Publishing Company, New York, 1927), 18.

79. Lamb, *Tamerlane, Conqueror of the Earth* (Bantam Books, New York, 1955), 193.

80. Rashiduddin Fazlullah, *Jami'u-Tawarikh*, ed. Mohammad Roshan Mustafa Mousavi, vol. 1 (Tehran: Alburz, 1994), 591–592.

81. Herawi, *Tarikh Nama-i-Herat*, 198, 205.

82. Henry Howorth, *History of the Mongols*, vol. 3 (London, 1888), 590–591.

83. Herawi, *Tarikh Nama-i-Herat*, 107–111.

84. Rashiduddin Fazlullah, *Jami'u-Tawarikh*, ed. Mohammad Roshan Mustafa Mousavi, Alburz Publisher, Tehran 1994.

85. Nizamuddin Shami, *Zafarnama*, Persian text, ed. Felix Tauer, vol. 1 (Praha [Prague]: Oriental Institute, 1937), 94.

86. Mohammad Ishaq Akhlaqi, *Hazara dar Jarayan-i Tarrikh*, vol. 1 (Qom, Iran: Sharaye', 2001), 30; Sayed Askar Mousavi, *The Hazaras of Afghanistan- an Historical, Economic and Political Study*, translated into Persian by Assadullah Shefayee, Tehran, 2000, 50–61.

87. Faiz Mohammad Kateb, *Nezhad-Namah-e Afghan* (Afghan Ethnography), ed. Kazim Yazdani (Qom, Iran: Shahid Publishers, 1993), 141.

88. Mousavi, *Hazaras*, 51.

89. Akhlaqi, *Hazara dar Jarayan-i Tarrikh*, 37.

90. Akhlaqi, 33.

91. Elizabeth Bacon, "The Inquiry into the History of the Hazara Mongols of Afghanistan," *Southwestern Journal of Anthropology* 7, no. 3 (Autumn 1951): 230–247.

Chapter 8. Timur and the Timurids, 1335–1526

1. Beatrice Forbes Manz, *The Rise and Rule of Tamerlane* (Cambridge: Cambridge University Press, 1989), 12.

2. Manz, *Rise and Rule*, 21.

3. Percy Sykes, *A History of Afghanistan*, vol. 1 (New Delhi: Munshiram Manoharlal, 2002), 266.

4. Harold Lamb, *Tamerlane, Conqueror of the Earth* (New York: Bantam Books, 1955), 193.

5. *Tuzukat-e Timuri, Institutes, Political and Military, written originally in the Mongol Language by the Great Timur*, translated into Persian by Abu Taulib al-Hisseini and thence into English by Major Davy, Oxford, 1783, 162.

6. These included Barlas, Jalayir, Arlat, and Selduz.

7. Ghiasuddin ibn Humamuddin al-Hosseini Khwandmir, *Habib-us-Siar*, ed. Mohammad Dabir Saiyaqi, vol. 3 (Tehran: Khayyam, 1974), 392. Timur's alleged autobi-

ography claims that Qarachar was Chaghatay's son-in-law (Gurgan), from which the title "Gurgan" derives.

8. W. Barthold, *Turkestan down to the Mongol Invasion*, ed. C. E. Bosworth, 3rd ed. (London: Luzac, 1968), 239–240.

9. Nizamuddin Shami, *Zafarnama*, vol. 1, Persian text, ed. Felix Tauer (Praha [Prague]: Oriental Institute, 1937), 16–17; Yazdi, *Zafarnama*, 35; *Timur-nama*, MS, Library of Congress, 26.

10. Manz, *Rise and Rule*, 47.

11. Shami, *Zafarnama*, 18–19; Yazdi, *Zafarnama*, 44–45; *Timur-nama*, MS, Library of Congress, 32.

12. Khwandmir, *Habib-us-Siar*, vol. 3, 394, Shami, *Zafarnama*, 24, *Timur-nama*, 15.

13. Timur revered Sayyid Baraka to the point that before his death he ordered that he be buried at the feet of Sayyid, who was interred at a place of honor in Samarqand.

14. *Tuzukat-e Timuri*, 268.

15. Lucien Bouvat, *L'Empire Mongol (2emePhase)* (Paris: Bibliothecaire de la Société Asiatique, 1927), 700.

16. *Tuzukat-e Timuri*, 269–273.

17. *Tuzukat-e Timuri*, 271.

18. Lamb, *Tamerlane*, 42.

19. Shami, *Zafarnama*, vol. 1, 142–144.

20. *Tuzukat-e Timuri*, 233–237.

21. *Tuzukat-e Timuri*, 372–408.

22. Lamb, *Tamerlane*, 270.

23. Shami, *Zafarnama*, vol. 1, 82.

24. Ahmad Ibn 'Arabshah, *'Aja'ib al-Maqdur fi Nawa'ib al-Taymur* (Life of Tamerlane) (Lahore, 1868), 35–36.

25. Khwandmir, *Habib-us-Siar*, vol. 3, 431.

26. Khwandmir, 435.

27. Shami, *Zafarnama*, 91–94.

28. Shami, 94.

29. Shami, 105.

30. Shami, 62.

31. The Golden Horde khanate was established by the descendant of Juji, the eldest son of Chinggis Khan. The khanate at its peak included most of European Russia from the Urals to the Carpathian Mountains and extended deep into Siberia and spread south to the Black Sea and the borders of the Ilkhanids of Persia.

32. K. M. Munshi et al., eds., *The Delhi Sultanate* (Bombay: S. Ramaakrishnan, 1967), 120.

33. Lord Kinross, *The Ottoman Centuries—The Rise and Fall of the Turkish Empire* (New York: Morrow Quill, 1977), 75.

34. Sykes, *History of Afghanistan*, vol. 1, 262.

35. Berthold Spuler, *The Muslim World*, Part 2, *The Mongol Period*, trans. F. R. C. Bagley (Leiden: E. J. Brill, 1969), 66.

36. Barthold, *Turkestan*, 249–250.

37. Manz, *Rise and Rule*, 153.

38. Rene Grousset, *The Empire of the Steppes: A History of Central Asia* (New Brunswick, NJ: Rutgers University Press, 1999), 414–415.

39. Of all known original sources the best are *Mehman-Nama-ye Bokhara* by Fazlullah Ibn Ruzbehan Khonji (1455–1522), *Badaye' al-Waqaye'* of Wassefi Herawi (early sixteenth century), *Babur-Nama* (Memoirs of Babur) of Zahiruddin Babur, *Shaybani-Nama* of Mohammad Salih (1455–1506), *Tarikh-e Habib-u-Siyar* by Ghiasuddin Ben Humam-al-Hosseini, known as Khawand-Mir (finished in 1525), and Haidar Mirza's *Dughlat's Tarikh-e Rashidi* (finished in 1547).

40. Fazlullah Ibn Ruzbehan Khonji, *Mehman-Name-ye Bokhara*, ed. Manochehr Sotoodeh (Tehran, 1962).

41. Khonji, *Mehman-Name-ye Bokhara*, 356.

42. Khonji, 22–28, 29–31, 32–40, 48–53, 78–84, 95–99.

43. Khonji, 44, 57, 104–106, 346.

44. Fazlullah's anti-Shi'ite prejudice traces back to the time when he wrote *Tarikh-e Alamaray-e Amini* recording events under the *Aq-Qoyunlu* ruler Uzun Hasan. In that book he vilified Ismail Safavi's ancestors. When Ismail conquered Iran, Fazlullah felt unsafe and moved to the court of the Safavids' enemy Mohammad Shaybani.

45. Although Fazlullah admits that the Kazaks embraced Islam at the same time that the Uzbeks did, he claims that the Kazaks later went astray because they worship idols (Sanam). Therefore he calls them apostate and states that they deserve to be fought. Fazlullah, *Mehman-Name-ye Bokhara*, 42–43.

46. Fazlullah, *Mehman-Name-ye Bokhara*, 1, 41, 89.

47. In a separate treatise, *Hadiss-e Haris*, Fazlullah cites a prophecy by the Prophet Mohammad referring to the appearance of a savior of the faith in *Ma Wara u-Nahr*. The *hadis* calls on all Muslims to support that savior. In a detailed argument, Fazlullah suggests that that person is Mohammad Shaybani. Fazlullah, *Mehman-Name-ye Bokhara*, 95–99.

48. Ismail Safavi turned Mohammad Shaybani's skull, set in gold, into a drinking cup for himself; he sent the straw-stuffed skin of Shaybani's head to the Ottoman sultan Bayazid II and his arm to the governor of Azerbaijan.

49. *Babur-Nama* (Memoirs of Babur), translated from the original Turki text by Annette S. Beveridge (Lahore: Sange Meel, 1987), 353–357. Also see Grousset, *Empire of the Steppes*, 483–484.

50. *Babur-Nama*, 124–185.

51. Grousset, *Empire of the Steppes*, 483.

Chapter 9. Afghan Tribes and the Gunpowder Empires, 1500–1709

1. V. D. Mahajan, *The Sultanate of Delhi* (Delhi: S. Chand, 1963), 83.

2. Edward Thomas, *The Chronicles of the Pathan Kings of Delhi* (Delhi: Trubner, 1871), 203.

3. حکم خداوند عالم از دهلی تا پالم.

4. Ishwari Prasad, *History of Mediaeval India from 647 A.D. to the Mughal Conquest* (Allahabad: Indian Press, 1925), 486.

5. Abbas Khan Sarwani (1580), *Tarikh-i Sher Shahi*, also known as *Tuhfata-yi Akbar Shahi* (Persian Literature in Translation), trans. E. C. Bayley, chapter 1, "Account of the Reign of the Sher Shah Suri," trans. by Sir H. M. Elliot (London: Packard Humanities Institute, n.d.), 301–433; Sir Olaf Caroe, *The Pathans* (Oxford: Oxford University Press, 1958), 137–138.

6. *Babur-Nama*, trans. Annette S. Beveridge (New Delhi: Munshiram Manoharlal, 1979), 382, 440, 443, 453, 456.

7. Jaywant D. Joglekar, *Decisive Battles India Lost (326 B.C. to 1083 A.D.)*, 1st Marathi ed., English version (Lexington, KY: Somaiya, 2012), 69–70.

8. Dr. Krishnaswami Lynagar, cited in Joglekar, *Decisive Battles*, 69.

9. These included the Nizamshahi of Ahmednagar, Qutubshahi of Golconda (Hydrabad), Baridshahi of Bidar, Imadshahi of Berar, and Adilshahi of Bijapur. They are collectively known as the "Deccan sultanates."

10. Joglekar, *Decisive Battles*, 70.

11. N. Venkatramanayya, *Studies in the History of the Third Dynasty of Vijayanagara*, cited in Joglekar, *Decisive Battles*, 71.

12. Wolseley Haig, ed., *The Cambridge History of India*, vol. 3, *Turks and Afghans* (Cambridge: Cambridge University Press, 1929), 40.

13. *Babur-Nama*, 440; Alfred David, *Indian Art of War* (Delhi: Atma Ram & Sons, 1953), 64.

14. *Din-i-Ilahi* was a syncretic creed derived from Islam, Hinduism, Zoroastrianism, and Christianity. A simple, monotheistic cult tolerant in outlook, it centered on Akbar as a revisionist and religious reformist, for which he drew the ire of the Muslim clergy, the *ulema*, and orthodox Muslims.

15. Abul Fazl-i-'Allami, *Ain-i-Akbari* (The Institutes of Akbar), vol. 2 (Nolakshor, India: 1310 H, 1899), 192.

16. The Roh country was known as the hilly area between Hasan Abdal in the east to Kabul in the west, and from Swat and Bajaur in the north to the Sui area at a location where the provinces of Baluchistan, Sindh, and Punjab meet near the Sind River. The immigrants from the Roh were called Rohilla Afghans; Rohilkand, a region of northwestern Uttar Pradesh State, is named after the Rohilla Afghan tribes.

17. Chausa is a village four miles west of the Buxer District in Bihar located on the Eastern Railway of India.

18. *Ṭabaqāt-i-Akbarī* (Calcutta, 1927), 1973, vol. 2, 101–110.

19. Mohammad Qasim Hindu Shah, *Tarikh-i Fereshta* (Calcutta: Newalkishore Press, 1874), 217–230; Ne'matullah Herawi, *Makhzan-i Afghani*, MS, Afghan Academy Library, Kabul.

20. Ishwari Prasad, *The Life and Times of Humayun* (Calcutta, 1955), 135–136.

21. Abbas Khan Sarwani, *Tarikh-i Sher Shahi* (Persian Literature in Translation), trans. E. C. Bayley, chapter 1.

22. Sir Olaf Caroe, *The Pathans* (Oxford: Oxford University Press, 1958), 144.

23. Elevation to the throne changed Sher Khan's designation to Sher Shah.

24. Mirza Mohammad Haidar Dughlat, *Tarikh-i Rashidi*, ed. Abbasquli Ghaffari Fard (Tehran: Miras-i Maktub Publisher, 2004), 68.

25. Herodotus, Book III, 205–215.

26. Ne'matullah Herawi, *Makhzan-i Afghani*, MS, Afghan Academy Library, Kabul.

27. Prasad, *The Life and Times of Humayun*, 143.

28. Mirza Mohammad Haidar Dughlat, *Tarikh-I Rashidi*, 680.

29. Dughlat, 683.

30. Dughlat, 684.

31. Beni Prasad, *History of Jahangir* (Delhi: Indian Press, 1940), 184–185.

32. Qabil Khan Afridi, *Literary Heritage of Khyber, Past and Present*, a UGC research Project, University of Peshawar, April 25, 1998.

33. Himayatullah Yaqubi, "Bayazid Ansari and Roshaniya Movement, a Conservative Cult or a Nationalist Endeavor?" J.R.S.P. (Journal of the Research Society of Pakistan) 50, no. 1 (2013).

34. Bayazid Roshan, *Khayr ul-Bayan*, ed. Abdul Hay Habibi et al. (Kabul: Kabul University Press, 1975), 58–108.

35. Roshan, *Khayr ul-Bayan*, 109–136.

36. Akhund Darweza, *Makhzan-ul-Islam*, 13, cited in Habibi's introduction to *Khayr ul-Bayan* (Kabul, 1975).

37. *Hal-Nama*, 399–404.

38. *Kulliyat*, Khoshal Khan Poetry Collection, ed. Dost Mohammad Kamil (Peshawar: University Book Agency, 1960), 220.

پلار نیکه می شهیدان وگور ته تللی

پشتاپشت می هنر دادی حال په حال

تر اوو پیریو پوری

واړه مړه په تیغ او تیر

39. Sir Jadunath Sarkar, *A Short History of Aurangzeb, 1618–1707* (Calcutta: Oriental Longmans, 1979), 116–117.

40. *Kulliyat*, Khoshal Khan Poetry Collection.

د افغان په ننگ می وټرله توره

ننگیالی د زمانی خوشحال خټک یم

41. Sarkar, *A Short History of Aurangzeb*, 117.

42. Sir Olaf Caroe, *The Pathans*, 235.

43. E. J. Rapson et al., *The Cambridge History of India*, vol. 4, *The Mughal Period* (Delhi: S. Chand Publisher, 1963), 238.

44. چی مغلو ته می وټرله توره

درست پښتون می و عالم و ته ښکاره کړ

اتفاق په پښتانه کی پیدا نه شو

کنه ما به د مغل گریوان پاره کړ

45. The list shows the tribal militias as follows: Khalil 500 horse and 6,500 foot; Khattak 200 horse, 4,000 foot; Daudzai 3,000 horse 37,000 foot; Safi 100 horse 1,400 foot; Afridi 500 horse 10,500 foot.

46. Sarkar, *A Short History of Aurangzeb*, 122.

47. دا منصبونه دا انعامونه

واړه زندیه دی واړه دامونه

48. Khoshal Khan Khattak, *Dastarnama* (Kabul, 1966), 27.

49. Afzal Khan Khattak, *Tarikh-i Murassa*, ed. Dost Mohammad Kamel (Peshawar, 1974), 262.

Chapter 10. The Rise of Local Afghan States and Their Invasion of Persia, 1709–1747

1. See E. G. Brown, *A Literary History of Persia* (Cambridge: Cambridge University Press, 1928), vol. 4, 50–55; and Said Amir Arjomand, *The Turban for the Crown* (Oxford: Oxford University Press, 1988), 11–13.

2. Rustam-ul-Hokama, *Rustam-u-Tawarikh*, ed. Mohammad Moshiri (Tehran: Sher-

kat-e-Sahami Kitab ha-i-Jibi, 1965), 115–118; see Said Amir Arjomand, *The Shadow of God and the Hidden Imam* (Chicago: Chicago University Press, 1984), 190–191; and Ralph Magnus and Eden Naby, *Afghanistan: Mullah, Marx, and Mujahid* (Boulder: Westview Press, 1998), 28–29.

3. Tadeusz Jan Krusinski, *The Chronicles of a Traveler or a History of the Afghan Wars with Persia in the Beginning of the Last Century from Their Commencement to the Accession of Sultan Ashraf*, translated into English by George Mitford, Esq. (London: James Ridgway, 1840).

4. Shaykh Mohammad Ali Hazin, *Tarikh-i Ahwal wa Tazkerah-i Mawlana Moham-mad Ali Hazin*, ed. Abd-Jani Ardakani (Bombay: Shahabi Press, 1905).

5. Jonas Hanway, *An Historical Account of the British Trade over the Caspian Sea with a Journal of Travels from London through Russia into Russia*, 4 vols. (London, 1753).

6. Krusinski, *Chronicles*, 30.

7. Hazin, *Tarikh-i Ahwal*, 49.

8. Hazin, 48.

9. Major General Sir John Malcolm, *The History of Persia from the Most Early Period Containing an Account of the Religion, Government and Character of the Inhabit-ants of that Kingdom* (London: John Murray, 1829), 410.

10. Krusinski, *Chronicles*, 50–53.

11. Hanway, *An Historical Account*, vol. 3, 33–34.

12. Joseph Ferrier, *History of the Afghans*, translated into English by William Jesse (London: John Murray, 1858), 32.

13. Krusinski, *Chronicles*, 58.

14. Colonel Colombari, *Les Zemboureks—Artillerie de Campagne a Dromedaire* (Paris: Spectateur Militare, 1853), 294–295.

15. Krusinski, *Chronicles*, 24.

16. Krusinski, 26.

17. Krusinski, 160.

18. *The History of Revolution in Persia, Taken from the Memoirs of Father Krusinski*, ed. Father Du Cerceau, vol. 2 (London, 1728), 10–12.

19. Sir John Malcolm, *History of Persia*, 421.

20. Abdullah Razi Hamadani, *Comprehensive History of Iran*, 4th ed. (Tehran: Iqbal Publisher, 1969), 432–433. Percy Sykes writes: "Many years ago, when camped on the site of this battle I read how the Persians sumptuously armed and splendidly horsed with saddles and stirups mounted with gold laughed to scorn the ragged sun-scorched Afghans. My thoughts went back to the battles fought by the last Sasanian monarchs against the Arabs and I was stuck by the similarity of the circumstances and conditions." Sir Percy Sykes, *A History of Persia*, vol. 2 (London: Macmillan, 1915), 314–315.

21. Colombari, *Les Zemboureks*, 294–295.

22. Hanway, *An Historical Account*, vol. 2, 153.

23. Sayed Jamaluddin Afghani, *Tatmat ul-Bayan fi Tarikh al-Afghan*, trans. Moham-mad Amin Khogiani (Kabul, 1839), 30.

24. Krusinski, *Chronicles*, 95.

25. Sir Percy Sykes, *History of Persia*, vol. 2, 316.

26. Sir John Malcolm, *History of Persia*, vol. 1, 434.

27. Hazin, *Tarikh-i Ahwal*, 51–52; Krusinski, *Chronicles*, 121–123.

28. Krusinski, *Chronicles*, 125.

29. Hanway, *An Historical Account*, vol. 3, 92.

30. Mirza Medi, *Jahangosha-e Naderi*, ed. S. A. Anwar (Tehran, 1962), 57.

31. Mohammad Kazim, *Namay-e Alamara-ye Naderi*, vol. 1; Mirza Mehdi, *Jahangosha-e Naderi*, ed. S. A. Anwar (Tehran, 1962); and Mirza Mehdi, *Durra-ye Nadera*, ed. Shahidi (Tehran, 1962).

32. Laurence Lockhart, *Nader Shah: A Critical Study Based Mainly upon Contemporary Sources* (London: Luzac, 1938), 34.

33. William Floor, *Ashraf-i-Afghan bar Takhtgah-i-Isfahan* (Ashraf the Afghan on the Throne of Isfahan) based on Dutch witness accounts, translated from English by Abul-Qasem Siri (Tehran: Tous, 1988), 19.

34. Muhammad Kazim, *Namay-e Alamara-ye Naderi*, vol. 1, 84; Lockhart, *Nader Shah*, 38.

35. Hanway, vol. 4, 94. Hanway traveled to Persia at that time and visited Nader's camp in 1743. Also see Joseph Ferrier, *The History of the Afghans*, translated into English by William Jesse and John Murray (London: n.p., 1858), 95.

36. Muhammad Kazim, *Namay-e Alamara-ye Naderi*, vol. 1, 73–76.

37. Hanway, *An Historical Account*, vol. 4, 95.

38. Hanway, 168–169.

Chapter 11. The Durrani Empire and the Emergence of Modern Afghanistan, 1747–1834

1. Mahmud al-Husseini al-Munshi, *Tarikh-I Ahmad Shahi* (1753), rotograph of the manuscript, ed. Sayed Muradov (Moscow: Nauka Press, 1974), vol. 1, 51–52.

2. *Nama-ye Ahmad Shah Baba Banam-e Sultan Mustafa Thales Osmani* (Ahmad Shah's Letter to the Ottoman Sultan Mustafa III), ed. G. Jailani Jalali (Kabul: Afghanistan History Society, 1967), 11.

3. *Nama-ye Ahmad Shah*, 14–15.

4. Alexander Dow, Esq., *The History of Hindustan*, 3 vols., 3rd ed., vol. 2 (London: John Murray, 1792), 409. Also see Ganda Singh, *Ahmad Shah Durrani: Father of Modern Afghanistan* (London: Asia Publishing House, 1959), 344.

5. *Nama-ye Ahmad Shah*, 15.

6. Ahmad Shah, *Diwan-i Ahmad Shah Abdali* (Collection of Ahmad Shah Abdali Pashto Poetry) (Kabul, 1963).

ددیلی تخت هیرومه چی را یاد کړم

زما د ښکلی پښتونخوا د غرو سرونه

که هر څو می ددنیا ملکونه ډیر سی

زما خوښ دی ستا خالی تش ډگرونه

7. Sir John Malcolm, *The History of Persia from the Most Early Period Containing an Account of the Religion, Government and Character of the Inhabitants of that Kingdom*, vol. 2 (London: John Murray, 1829), 56–57.

8. *Nama-ye Ahmad Shah*, 42–43, 52–55.

9. *Nama-ye Ahmad Shah*, 15–16.

10. The eighteen provinces, excluding Baluchistan, Mashhad, and Nishapur and Indian dominions, included Herat, Farah, Kandahar, Ghazni, Kabul, Bamian and Ghorband, Jalalabad, Laghman, Peshawar, Dera Ismail Khan, Dera Ghazi Khan, Shikarpur, Sui Sind, Kashmir, Chach Hazara, Lia, and Multan.

11. Mounstuart Elphinstone, *An Account of the Kingdom of Kabul and its dependencies in Persia, Tartary and India*, vol. 2 (London: Richard Bentley, 1842), 284.

12. Elphinstone, *Account of the Kingdom of Kabul.*

13. Jean Law de Lauriston, *A Memoir of the Mughal Empire, Events of 1757–1761*, translated from the original French by G. S. Cheema (Delhi: Manohar Publishers, 2014), 134.

14. Faiz Mohammad Kateb, *Seraj u-Tawarikh*, vol. 1 (Kabul: Government Press, 1911), 56; Mir Imamuddin Husseini, *Tarikh-e Hussein Shahi*, MS copy, Afghanistan Academy of Sciences.

15. Elphinstone, *Account of the Kingdom of Kabul*, vol. 2, 268.

16. de Lauriston, *A Memoir of the Mughal Empire*, 136.

17. *Tarikh-e Hussein Shahi*, MS copy, Afghanistan Academy of Sciences.

18. U. V. Gankovsky, ed., *Istoriya Vorozhoniekh Sil Afganistana, 1747–1977* (The History of Armed Forces of Afghanistan, 1747–1977) (Moscow: Oriental Studies Institute, 1985).

19. The plough, or carucate, is an ancient British measurement of area and is the area that can be tilled by a plough team of eight oxen during an annual tilling season. It is roughly 120 acres.

20. Faiz Mohammad Kateb, *Seraj u-Tawarikh*, vol. 1, 56; Mir Imamuddin Husseini, *Tarikh-e Hussein Shahi*, MS copy.

21. Ganda Singh, *Ahmad Shah Durrani*, 55; Ferrier, *History of the Afghans*, 72; Tarikh-e Hussein Shahi MS; Faiz Mohammad Kateb, *Seraj u-Tawarikh*, vol. 1, 12.

22. Singh, *Ahmad Shah Durrani*, 55.

23. al-Munshi, *Tarikh-I Ahmad Shahi* (1753), vol. 1, 109–110.

24. Mir Ghulam Ali Azad Bilgrami (1704–1786), *Khizanah-i-'Amirah*, Indian publication (Kabul: Kabul Public Library).

25. Abdul Karim Alavi, *Tarikh-i Ahmad* (Lucknow: Mustafai Press, 1850), 8; Imamuddin Husseini, *Tarikh-e Hussein Shahi* (1798), MS, Afghanistan Academy of Science, 32–33.

26. P. N. Verma, *Maratha and Panipat*, ed. Heri Ram Gupta (Chandigarh: Punjab University, 1961), preface, xi–xii.

27. James Grant Duff, *A History of the Mahrattas*, vol. 1 (London: Longman, Rees. Orme, Brown and Green, 1826), 357–358; vol. 3, 427–428.

28. Verma, *Maratha and Panipat*, xiii.

29. Singh, *Ahmad Shah Durrani*, 225.

30. Duff, *History of the Mahrattas*, 12.

31. M. Ja'far Shamlu, *Tarikh-I Manazilu-l Futuh of Mohammad Ja'far Shamlu*, Sir H. M. Elliot (London: Packard Humanities Institute), section ciii.

32. Abhhas Verma, *The Third Battle of Panipat* (India: Baharatia Prakashan Publisher, 2013), 97.

33. Rohilkand was a region in the northwestern Indian state of Uttar Pradesh that was named after Afghan highlanders, known as Rohilla (mountaineers) who had settled in the area during the reign of Shah Jahan (1628–1658) and later. The area included the cities of Bareily, Moradabad, Rampur, Bijore, Farahabad, Shahjahanpur, and others. Their major leaders in the middle of the eighteenth century were Najib ud-Daulah, the governor of Saharanpur, Hafiz Rahmat Khan, Dundi Khan, and Ahmad Khan Bangash.

34. *Nama-ye Ahmad Shah*, 60–63.

35. Sayed Nuruddin Hussein, *An Account of Najib ud-Daulah*, English translation by Abdul Rashid (India), 34–40.

36. Kasi Raj Pundit, *An Account of the Last Battle of Panipat and of the Events Leading to It*, English translation by James Brown; edited by George Rawlinson (London: Oxford University Press, 1926), 26.

37. Pundit, *Account of the Last Battle of Panipat*, 40.

38. *Nama-ye Ahmad Shah*, 64.

39. al-Munshi, *Tarikh-I Ahmad Shahi* (1753), vol. 2, 938, 940, 942, 952, 958.

40. Ganda Singh, *Ahmad Shah Durrani*, 235; Kasi Raj, *Account of the Last Battle of Panipat*, 23; Faiz Mohammad, *Seraj u-Tawarikh*, vol. 1, 24.

41. Shamlu, *Tarikh-I Manazilu-l Futuh*. Also see Kasi Raj, 24. Sultan Muhammad Barakzai, *Tarikh-i Sultani*, 140.

42. Pundit, *Account of the Last Battle of Panipat*, 24–25.

43. Jaywant D. Joglekar, *Decisive Battles India Lost (326 B.C. to 1083 A.D.)*, 1st Marathi ed., English version (Lexington, KY: Somaiya, 2012), 90–91.

44. G. S. Sardesai, *Selections of the Peshwa dater* (accounts), cited in Uday S. Kalkarani, *Solstice at Panipat 14 January 1761* (Pune, India: Mula Mutba, 2011), 185.

45. Duff, *History of the Mahrattas*.

46. Joglekar, *Decisive Battles*, 65–76. al-Munshi, *Tarikh-I Ahmad Shahi* (1753), vol. 2, 965–966.

47. *Gilcha* is seemingly a local pronunciation of Ghilzai Pashtuns who were among the major players in medieval Indian history. They were instrumental in founding and ruling several Muslim dynasties in India, including in the southern provinces. The Marathas referred to all Afghans (Pashtuns) including the Abdalis as *gilcha* or the Ghilzais (Ghiljais). Apparently for this reason they called Ahmad Shah and his tribes the *gilcha*. Grant Duff wrote that a native of Maharashtra only knows the Afghans by the name of *Gilija*, while Afghans, generally, are merely distinguished as *Pathans* (Duff, vol. 2, 27).

48. *Bhausaheb-arch Kaifiyat*, p. 33, Hervadkar Rv, 1990, cited in Uday S. Kulkarni, 195.

49. *Nama-ye Ahmad Shah*, 55–56.

50. Pundit, *Account of the Last Battle of Panipat*, 17–19.

51. Pundit, 19–20.

52. Verma, *Third Battle of Panipat*, 98.

53. Verma, 193.

54. Duff, *A History of Mahrattas*, vol. 2, 149.

55. Verma, *Third Battle of Panipat*, 237.

56. Sir Jadunath Sarkar, *The Fall of the Mughal Empire*, vol. 2, 233. Also see Verma, *Maratha and Panipat*, 790.

57. Uday S. Kalkarani, *Solstice at Panipat 14 January 1761* (Pune, India: Mula Mutba, 2011), 201, cited in *Bhau saheb Bakhar* (memoir).

58. Verma, *Third Battle of Panipat*, 173.

59. de Lauriston, *A Memoir of the Mughal Empire*, 136.

60. Vishwas, *Panipat*, translated from Marathi by Nadeem Khan. First published in Marathi in 1988, English edition (India: Eka Publisher, 2019), xviii.

61. Pundit, *Account of the Last Battle of Panipat*, 40.

62. P. N. Verma, *Maratha and Panipat* (Chandigarh: Punjab University, 1961), ed. Heri Ram Gupta, 329.

63. Azad Bilgrami, *Khizanah-i-'Amirah*, 109; *Seraj u-Tawarikh*, vol. 1, 25.

64. Vishwas, *Panipat*, 429.

65. George Forster, *A Journey from Bengal to England through the North Part of India, Kashmir, Afghanistan and Persia and into Russia by the Caspian Sea*, vol. 2 (London: East India Company, 1798), 70.

66. Mohan Lal, *Life of Amir Dost Mohammad Khan of Kabul*, vol. 1 (New Delhi: Asian Educational Services, 2004), 144–145.

67. Faiz Mohammad Kateb, *Seraj u-Tawarikh*, vol. 1, 143.

Selected Bibliography

Ancient Period (Second Millennium BC–650 AD)

Arrian. *Anabasis—The Campaigns of Alexander*. Translated by Aubrey de Selincourt. Harmondsworth, UK: Penguin Books, 1971.

Avesta, the Religious Book of the Persees. Translated by Arthur Henry Bleeck. 3 vols. Hartford: Printed for Muncherjee Hormusjee Cama by Stephen Austin, 1864. This is a translation from the German translation by Professor Spiegel.

Brihat Samita of Vahara Mihtra. Translated by N. Chindambaram. Matura: South Indian Press, 1884.

Bury, J. B. *A History of Greece to the Death of Alexander the Great*. London: Macmillan, 1900.

Chandler, Tertius, and Gerald Fox. *3000 Years of Urban Growth*. https://en.wikipedia.org/wiki/Mongol_conquest_of_the_Khwarazmian_Empire#cite_note-36.

Christensen, Arthur. *Sassanid Persia* (iran dar Zaman-e Sassanian). 2nd ed. Tehran: unknown publisher, 1965.

Chunder Dutt, Romesh. *Ancient India 200 B.C.–800 A.D.* London: Longmans, Green, 1893.

———. *History of India from the Earliest Times to the Sixth Century B.C.* New York: Cosimo Books, 1906.

Curtius, Quintus Rufus. *The History of Alexander*. Translated by John Yardley. London: Penguin Books, 1984.

Delbruck, Hans. *History of the Art of War*. Vol. 1, *Warfare in Antiquity*. Translated by Walter J. Renfroe Jr. Lincoln: University of Nebraska Press, [1900] 1990.

———. *History of the Art of War*. Vol. 3, *Medieval Warfare*. Lincoln: University of Nebraska Press, [1900] 1990.

Drury, Mark. "The Early Achaemenid Persian Army: Arms and Equipment." *Achaemenid Persia: A History Resource*. September 2011. Cf. "The Achemenid (Achaemenid) Persian Armies under FoG." www.madaxeman.com.

Engels, Donald W. *Alexander the Great and the Logistics of the Macedonian Army*. Berkeley: University of California Press, 1980.

Eratosthenes' Geographica: Fragments Collected and Translated with Commentary and Additional Material. By Duane W. Roller. Princeton: Princeton University Press, 2010.

Firdausi, Abul Qasim. *Shah-Nama*. Full Text. Tehran: Qatra, 1999.

Geiger, Wilhelm. *Civilization of the Eastern Iranians in Ancient Times with an Intro-duction on the Avesta Religion.* Vols. 1 and 2. London: Henry Frowde, 1885–1886.

Gibbon, Edward. *History of the Decline and Fall of the Roman Empire.* Vol. 5. Edited by B. Bury. London: Methuen, 1909–1914. Rpt. New York: AMS Press, 1974.

Gupta, Parmanand. *Geography from Ancient Indian Coins and Seals.* New Delhi: Concept Publishing Company, 1989.

Harmatta, Janos, et al. *History of Civilizations of Central Asia.* Vol. 2, *The Development of Sedentary and Nomadic Civilizations, 700 B.C. to A.D. 250.* Paris: Unesco Publishing, August 1, 1994.

Herodotus. *The History of Herodotus.* Books III, IV, and VII. Translated by George Rawlinson. Edited by Manuel Komroff. New York: Tudor, 1958.

Hioun-Thsang. *Memoires sur les Contrees Occidentales.* Translated by M. Stanislas Julien. 2nd vol. Paris, 1858. This French translation of the Chinese translation was made by Hioun-Thsang.

Holdich, Thomas H. *The Gates of India, Being an Historical Narrative.* London: MacMillan, 1910.

The Holy Vedas; Rig Veda, Yajur Veda, Sama Veda, Atharva Veda. 7th ed. Mumbai, India: Bahavan's Book University, Sudakshina, 2006.

Justin. *History of Justin (Justini, Hiitorias Phillippicae).* Translated by John Clarke. Glocester: R. Raixes, 1790.

Kuhzad, Ahmad Ali. *The History of Afghanistan.* Vol. 1. Kabul: History Society; rpt. Kabul: Amiri Press, 2018.

Lamb, Harold. *Alexander of Macedon.* 5th ed. New York: Bantam, 1953.

———. *Cyrus the Great.* New York: Doubleday, 1960.

———. *Hannibal, One Man against Rome.* New York: Doubleday, 1958.

Majumdar, Ramesh C. *Ancient India.* New Delhi: Sheri Jainendra Press, 1960.

Mensch, Pamela, and James Romm, eds. *Alexander the Great: Selections from Arrian, Diodorus, Plutarch, and Quintus Curtius.* Indianapolis: Hackett Publishing Company, 2005.

Milindapanha—The Questions of King Milinda. Translated from Pali by T. W. Rhys Davids. Oxford: Oxford University Press, 1890.

Neumann, C. "A Note on Alexander's March-Rates." *Historia: Zeitschrift Für Alte Geschichte* 20, no. 2/3, 1971, 196–198. *JSTOR*, www.jstor.org/stable/4435191.

Paret, Peter, et al. *Makers of Modern Strategy.* Rev. ed. Princeton: Princeton University Press, 1986.

Plutarch. *The Life of Alexander the Great.* Translated by John Dryden. Paperback ed. New York: Modern Library, 2004.

Polybius. *The Histories of Polybius.* Vol. 2. Translated by Evelyn S. Shuckburgh. London and New York: Macmillan, 1889.

Ptolemy. *The Geography.* Translated and edited by Edward Luther Stevenson. New York: Dover, 1991.

Rapson, E. J. *The Cambridge History of India.* Vol. 1, *Ancient India.* Cambridge: Cambridge University Press, 2011.

Rawlinson, H. G. *Bactria: The History of a Forgotten Empire.* London: Probsthain, 1912.

———. *The Seventh Great Oriental Monarchy or the Geography, History and Antiquities of the Sassanian or New Persian Empire.* New York: Belford Clarke, 1887.

————. *The Sixth Great Oriental Monarchy or the Geography, History and Antiquities of Parthia*. New York: Belford Clarke, 1887.

Savill, Agnes. *Alexander the Great and His Time*. New York: Dorset Press, 1990.

Shamlu, M. Ja'far. *Tarikh-I Manazilu-l Futuh of Mohammad Ja'far Shamlu*. Sir H. M. Elliot. London: Packard Humanities Institute, n.d.

Smith, Vincent. *The Early History of India from 600 B.C. to the Mohammadan Conquest*. Oxford: Clarendon Press, 1904.

Smith, William, ed. *Dictionary of Greek and Roman Geography*. Vol. 1. Boston: Little, Brown and Company, 1870.

Stein, Sir Aurel. *On Alexander's Track to Indus*. London: Macmillan, 1929.

Strabo. *Geography*. Books 11 and Book 15. Translated by Horace Leonard Jones. London: Harvard University Press, 1930.

Tarn, William W. *The Greeks in Bactria and India*. Cambridge: Cambridge University Press, 1966.

Thucydides. *The History of the Peloponnesian War*. Translated by Richard Crawley. Digireas.com Publishing, 2004.

Toynbee, Arnold J. *Between Oxus and Jumna*. London: Oxford University Press, 1961.

Watson, John, et al. *The Invasion of India by Alexander the Great as Described by Arrian, Q. Curtius, Diodorus, Plutarch and Justin*. 2nd ed. London: Westminster, 1896.

Watters, Thomas, et al., eds. *On Yuan Chwang's Travels in India*. Vol. 2. London: Royal Asiatic Society, 1906.

Wheeler, Benjamin Ide. *Alexander the Great—The Emerging of the East and West in Universal History*. New York: G. P. Putnam's Sons, 1900.

Wiesehofer, Josef. *Ancient Persia from 550 B.C. to 650 A.D.* Translated by Azizeh Azodi. London: I. B. Tauris, 1996.

Williams, Henry Smith, ed. *The Historian's History of the World*. Vol. 4, *Greece to Roman Conquest*. New York: Outlook, 1904.

Wilson, Horace Hayman. *Aryana Antiqua: A Descriptive Account of the Antiquities and Coins of Afghanistan*. London: East India Company, 1841.

Early Islamic Period (650–1218)

Al-Baladhuri, Abul Abbas Ahmad ibn Jabir. *Kitab Futuh al-Buldan*. Translated by Philip Khuri Hitai. Piscataway, NJ: Gorgias Press, 2002.

Al-Biruni, Abu Rayhan. *Albiruni's India*. Vol. 1. Translated and edited by Edward Sachau. Delhi: Rupa, 2005.

Al-Muqaddasi. *Ahsan al-Taqasim fi Ma'rifat al-Aqalim* (The Best Division for Knowledge of the Regions). Translated by Basir Collins. Reading, UK: Garnet, 1994.

Al-Utbi, Abu Nasr Muhammad b. Abdul Jabar. *Kitab-i yamini*. Translated by James Reynolds. London: Oriental Translation Fund, 1858.

Anonymous (circa 1062 AD). *Tarikh-i Sistan*. Edited by Mohammad Taqi Bahar. Tehran: Kitābkhānah-i Zavvā, 1930.

Anonymous author from Jawzjan. *Hudud Al-'Alam, "The Regions of the World," A Persian Geography 982 A.D.* Translated and explained by V. Minorsky. Edited by C. E. Bosworth. E. J. W. Gibb Memorial Trust, 1970.

Anonymous author from Jawzjan (982 AD). *Hudud al Alam* (حدودالعالم من المشرق والمغرب). Edited by Manoucher Sotoudeh. Tehran: Tehran University Press, 1961.

'Awfi, Sadiduddin Mohammed. *Jawami'-al-Hekayat wa Lawami'-al-Rawayat*. Edited by Ja'far Sh'ar. Published by فرهنگی و علمی انتشارات شرکت. Tehran: Scientific and Cultural Publications Company, 1984.

Bartold, W. [V. V.] *The History of Turks in Central Asia*. Persian translation by Ghafar Hosseini Tehran: Tous Publisher, 1997 [1376].

———. *Turkistan*. 3rd ed. English translation by Mrs. T Minorsky. Edited by C. E. Bosworth. London: Luzac & Co. Ltd., 1968.

Battuta, Ibn. *The Adventures of ibn Battuta*. Edited by Ross E. Dunn. Berkeley: University of California Press, 1989.

Bayhaqi, Abul Fadl. *Tarikh-i Mas'udi*. Edited by Dr. Ghani. Tehran: State Press, 1945.

Bosworth, A. B. *Alexander and the East-the Tragedy of Triumph*. New York: Oxford University Press, 1996.

Bosworth, Clifford Edmund. *The Ghaznavids: Their Empire in Afghanistan and Eastern Iran*. 1st Indian ed. New Delhi: Mushaira Manoharlal, 1992.

———. *The Tahirids and Saffarids, the Cambridge History of Iran, from the Arab Invasion to the Seljuqs*. Vol. 4. Edited by Richard Nelson Frye, William Bayne Fisher, and John Andrew Boyle. Cambridge: Cambridge University Press, 1975.

Browne, E. G. *A Literary History of Persia*. Vol. 4. Cambridge: Cambridge University Press, 1928.

Denoeux, Guillain. *Urban Unrest in the Middle East: A Comparative Study of Informal Networks in Egypt, Iran, and Lebanon* (Albany: State University of New York, 1993).

Estakhri, Abu Ishak Ibrahim. *Al-Masalik al-mamalik* (Traditions of Countries). Leiden: Brill, 1927.

———. *Masalik wa Mamalik*, anonymous Persian translation of twelfth–thirteenth century. 3rd ed. Edited by Iraj Afshar. Tehran Scientific and Cultural Publications Company, 1989.

Fakhr-i-Modabber, Mohammad ibn Mansur Mubarakshah. *Adab al Harb wa-Shja'a*. Edited by Sohaili Khwansari. Tehran: Eqbal, 1967.

Gardizi, Abu Sa'id Abdul-Hay Dhahhak. *Zayn al-Akhbar*. Edited by Abdul Hay Habibi. Tehran: Armaghan, 1884.

Habibi, Abul Hai. *The Temple of Zoor or Zoon in Zamindawar*. 1969. alamahabibi.net/English_Articles/Zoor_or_zoon_temple.htm.

Hotak, Mohammad. *Patta Khazana*, in Pashto. 2nd ed. Edited by Abdul Hai Habibi. Kabul: Ministry of Education, 1960.

Ibn Athir, Ali 'Izz al-Din al-Jazari. *Al-Kamil fi al-Tarikh*. 12 vols. Translated from Arabic into Persian by Dr. Slayed Hosseini Rohani. 2nd ed. Tehran, Iran: Asatir Publisher, 1995.

Ibn Hawqal, Muhammad Abol Qasim. *Surat al-Ard* (الارض صورة). Also published as *Ibn Hawqal's Kitab Masalik wa mamalik* (حوقل ابن تصنیف مالک و مسالک). Arabian traveler of tenth century. Edited by Sir William Ousley. London: Oriental Press by Wilson and Co., 1800.

Ibn Khaldun, Abdurrahman. *Al-Muqaddimah*. Translated from the Persian by Muhammad Parvin Gunabadi. Tehran: Scientific and Cultural Publication Company, 1996.

Ibn Khordadbeh, Abul Qasem Obaidullah. *Kitab al-Masalik wa Mamalik* (Book of Roads and Kingdoms). A ninth-century geography in Arabic (870 AD). Leiden: Brill, 1889.

Jawzjani, Minhaj-u-Seraj. *Tabaqat-i Nasiri*. Calcutta: Unknown publisher, 1864.

———. *Tabakat-i Nasiri*. Translated by Major Raverty. London: Gilbert and Rivington, 1881.

———. *Tabaqat-i Nasiri*. Edited by Abdul Hai Habibi. Tehran: Dunaya-e-Kitab, 1984.

Joglekar, Jaywant D. *Decisive Battles India Lost (326 B.C. to 1083 A.D.)*. 1st Marathi ed. English ed. Lexington, KY: Somaiya, 2012.

Kazimini, Kazim. *'Ayyaran: ba Wizhagi ha-ye Pahlawani Az Tarikh-i-Ejtema'i WA Qawmi Iran* ('Ayarran—Their Specialized Feats in the National and Social History of Iran). Tehran: Maihan, 1970.

Kennedy, Hugh. *The Armies of the Caliphs: Military and Society in the Early Islamic State*. Rutledge: London, 2001.

———. *The Great Arab Conquests: How the Spread of Islam Changed the World We Live In*. Boston: Da Capo Press, 2007.

Lane-Poole, Stanley. *History of India*. Vol. 3, *Mediaeval India from the Mohammadan Conquest to the Reign of Akbar the Great*. London: Grolier Society, 1907.

Mas'udi, Abu Hasan Ali. *The Meadows of Gold—Abbasids*. Translated by Paul Lunde and Caroline Stone. New York: Routledge, 2010.

———. *Muruj adh-dhahab wa ma'adin al-jawhar* (The Meadows of Gold and Mines of Gems). Edited by Charles Horne. Whitefish, MT: Kessinger Publishing's Rare Reprints, 2010.

Narshakhi. *Tarikh-i Bukhara* (The History of Bukhara). Translated by Richard Frye. Princeton: Markus Wiener, 2007.

Nizam ul-Mulk. *Siyasat-nama* (Book of Government). Edited by M. Qazwini and Mohammad Chahardehi. Tehran: Government Press, 1956.

Nizami-i Aruzi-i Samarqandi. *Chahar Maqalah* (Four Discourses). Edited by Mohammad Qazwini. 12th ed. Tehran: Sada-i-Ma'asir, 2003.

Payne, Robert. *The History of Islam*. Barnes and Noble Books, 1995.

Pipes, Daniel. *Slave Soldiers, and Islam—The Genesis of a Military System*. New Haven: Yale University Press, 1981.

Qadhi Ismail (seventh century). *Chach-Nama also known as the Fateh nama Sindh*. Translated into Persian by Muhammad Ali bin Hamid bin Abu Bakr Kufi in 1216, in India. N.p. n.d.

Tabari, Mohammad ibn Jarir. *Tarikh al-Rusul wa al-Muluk*. 6th ed. 16 vols. Translated into Persian by Abul Qasim Payendah. Tehran: Asateer, 2004.

Watt, Montgomery. *The Majesty That Was Islam*. London: Sedgwick and Jackson, 1974.

Yaqub, Ahmad bin Abi Yaqub. *Tarikh al-Yaqubi*. Edited by M. Houtsma. 2 vols. Leiden: Brill, 1883.

Zeidan, Georgie. *Ta'rikh al-Tamaddun al-Islamii*, Persian translation. Tehran: Government Press, 1919.

Turks, Mongols, and Afghans (1211–1707)

Abdullah. *Tarikh-i Daudi*. Persian Literature in Translation. Extract. Translated by Sir H. M. Elliot. London: Packard Humanities Institute, n.d. PHI Persian Literature in Translation—The History of India. Vol. 4. packhum.org.

Abul Fazl-i-'Allami. *Ain-i-Akbari* (The Institutes of Akbar). Nolakshor, India: 1310H 1899.

Amir Timur. *Tarikh-i- Sultan-e Mabrour Mosama beh Tuzuk-e Timur*. Bombay: Unknown publisher, 1879.

————. *Tuzukat-e Timuri, Institutes, Political and Military, written originally in the Mongol Language by the Great Timur, translated into Persian by Abu Taulib al-Hisseini and thence into English by Major Davy*. Oxford edition of 1783, reprinted by Asadi Books, Tehran, 1963.

Babur-Nama. Translated by Annette S. Beveridge. New Delhi: Munshiram Manoharlal, 1979.

Babur-Nama. Translated by Annette S. Beveridge. Lahore: Sange Meel, 1987.

Bacon, Elizabeth. "The Inquiry into the History of the Hazara Mongols of Afghanistan." *Southwestern Journal of Anthropology* 7, no. 3 (Autumn 1951): 230–247.

Barthold, W. [V. V.]. *Turkestan down to the Mongol Invasion*. Edited by C. E. Bosworth. 3rd ed. London: Luzac, 1968.

Bouvat, Lucien. *L'Empire Mongol (2emePhase)*. Paris: Bibliothecaire de la Société Asiatique, 1927.

Clavijo, Ruy Gonzales de. *Narrative of the Spanish Embassy to the Court of Timur at Samarqand in the Years 1403–1406*. Translated by Guy Le Strange. London: Routledge, 1928.

Curtin, Jeremiah. *The Mongols: A History*. Conshohocken, PA: Combine Books, 1996. Originally published by Little, Brown in Boston, 1908.

Dale, Stephen Frederic. *Indian Merchants and Eurasian Trade, 1600–1750*. Cambridge: Cambridge University Press, 1994 (online publication September 2009).

Dughlat, Mirza Mohammad Haidar. *Tarikh-i Rashidi*. Edited by Abbasquli Ghaffari Fard. Tehran: Miras-I Maktub, 2004.

Esfazari, Mu'inuddin Mohammad Zamchi. *Rauzat al-Jannat fi Auwsaf-i Madint-i Herat*. Edited by Saiyed M. Kazem Imam. Tehran: Tehran University Press, 1959.

Grousset, Rene. *The Empire of the Steppes: A History of Central Asia*. New Brunswick, NJ: Rutgers University Press, 1999.

Gulbadan Begum (daughter of Babur). *Humayun-nama*. Edited by Iraj Afshar. Tehran: Thoraya, 1994.

Hart, Liddell. *Great Captains Unveiled*. London: Blackwood & Son, 1927. Reprint B. H. Liddell Hart, *Great Captains Unveiled, from Genghis Khan to General Wolfe*. London: Greenhill Books, 1990.

Herawi, Ne'matullah. *Makhzan-i Afghani*. MS, Afghan Academy Library, Kabul.

Herawi, Saifi (Saif ibn Mohammad ibn Ya'qub al-Herawi). *Tarikh Nama-i-Herat*. Edited by M. Zubair Siddiqi. Calcutta: Gulshan, 1943.

Herawi, Sayf ibn Muhammad al-Herawi. *Tarikh Nama-i Herat* (The History of Herat). 2nd ed. Edited by Muhammad Zubayr As-Siddiqi, professor of Calcutta University. Tehran: Khaiam Library, 1352 H [1973].

Himayatullah Yaqubi. "Bayazid Ansari and Roshaniya Movement, a Conservative Cult, or a Nationalist Endeavor?" *J.R.S.P.* (Journal of the Research Society of Pakistan) 50, no. 1 (2013).

Hindu Shah, Mohammad Qasim. *Tarikh-i Fereshta*. Calcutta: Newalkishore Press, 1874.

Holcomb, Charles E. *A History of East Asia from the Origins of Civilization to the Twenty First Century*. Cambridge: Cambridge University Press, 2011.

Holt, Frank L. *Into the Land of Bones: Alexander the Great in Afghanistan*. Berkeley: University of California Press, 2006.

Howorth, Sir Henry Hoyle. *History of the Mongols from 9th to the 19th Century*. Part 1. London: Longmans, 1876.

Ibn 'Arabshah, Ahmad. *'Aja'ib al-Maqdur fi Nawa'ib al-Taymur* (Life of Tamerlane). Lahore: Sang-e-Meel, 1868.

———. *Tamerlane or Timur the Great Amir*. Translated by J. H. Sanders. London: Luzac, 1936.

Juwayni, 'Alauddin 'Ata Malik. *Tarikh-i, Jahan-Gusha*. Edited by M. M. Qazwini. 3 vols. Leiden: E. J. Brill, 1911. Rpt. Tehran: Afrasiab Publisher, 2003.

Juwayni, Ata-Malik. *Tarikh-i, Jahan-Gusha*. Translated and edited by A. A. Boyle. Manchester: Manchester University Press, 1958.

Khara-Davan. *Erenzhen, Chinggis Khanka Polkovodets i yivo Nasledei* (Chinggis Khan as Military Leader and His Feats). Alma-Ata: KRAMDC—Ahmad Yassawi, 1992.

Khattak, Afzal Khan. *Tarikh-i Murassa*. Edited by Dost Mohammad Kamel. Peshawar: University Book Agency, 1974.

Khattak, Khoshal Khan. *Dastarnama*. Kabul: Afghan Government Press, 1967. This classic treatise on norms and practice of leadership is in Pashto.

———. *Kulliyat*. Poetry collection. Edited by Dost Mohammad Kamil. Peshawar: University Book Agency, 1960.

Khonji, Fazlullah Ibn Ruzbehan. *Mehman-Name-ye Bokhara*. Edited by Manochehr Sotoodeh. (بنگاه ترجمه ونشر کتاب) Tehran: Foundation of Translation and Publication of Books, 1962.

Khwandmir, Ghiyath al-Din b. Humam al-Din. *Dastur al-Wuzara*. Edited by Sa'id Nafisi. Tehran: Government Press, 1317H 1938.

———. *Habib-us-Siar*. 3rd ed. Tehran: Khayyam, 1883.

Kinross, Lord. *The Ottoman Centuries— The Rise and Fall of the Turkish Empire*. New York: Morrow Quill, 1977.

Lamb, Harold. *Genghis Khan, Emperor of All Men*. Garden City, NY: Garden City Publishing, 1927.

———. *Tamerlane, Conqueror of the Earth*. New York: Bantam, 1955.

Listner, R. P. *Genghis Khan*. New York: Dorset Press, 1969.

Mahajan, V. D. *The Sultanate of Delhi*. Delhi: S. Chand, 1963.

Mann, John. *Genghis Khan: Life, Death and Resurrection*. New York: Thomas Dunn, 2007.

Mansouri, Zabihullah. *Khaterat-e Ousqof-e Sultaniya Raje' beh Timur-e Leng* (The Memoirs of the Archbishop of Sultaniya). Copy in Paris National Library. Translated by Zabihullah Mansouri. Tehran: Unknown publisher, 1372/1993.

Manz, Beatrice Forbes. *The Rise and Rule of Tamerlane*. Cambridge: Cambridge University Press, 1989.

Marco Polo. *The Travels*. Translated by Ronald Latham, London: Penguin, 1958.

May, Timothy. *The Mongol Art of War*. South Yorkshire: Pen & Sword Military, 2007.

Mir Khwand, Muhammad ibn Khawand Shah. *Rawdatu's Safa*. Calcutta: Newalkishore Press, 1883.

Morgan, David. *The Mongols*. Oxford: Blackwell, 1986.

Munshi, K. M., et al., eds. *The Delhi Sultanate*. Bombay: S. Ramaakrishnan, 1967.

Mustaid Khan, Mohammad Saqui. *Maasr-i-Alamgiri*. Edited by Mawlawi Agha Ahmad Ali. Calcutta: Lewis British Mission Press, 1871.

Mustawfi, Hamdullah. *The Geographic Part of the Nuzhat al-Qulub*. Translated by G. Le Strange. Cambridge: Cambridge University Press, 1919.

Nasawi, Shahabuddin Muhammad. *Sirat-e Jalaluddin*. Edited by Mujtaba Minawi. Tehran: Foundation of Translation and Publication of Books (بنگاه ترجمه ونشر کتاب), 1965.

Ne'matullah Herawi. *Makhzan-i Afghani*. MS. Kabul: Afghan Academy Library.

Nesawi, Mohammad ibn Ahmad. *Sirat-i Jalaluddin Mungaberti*. Edited by Ḥ. A. Ḥamdi. Cairo: 1953.

Nizamuddin, Ahmad Bakhshi. *Ṭabaqāt-i-Akbarī*. 3 vols. Calcutta: Sang-e-Meel, 1927, 1973.

Prasad, Beni. *History of Jahangir*. Delhi: Indian Press, 1940.

Prasad, Ishwari. *History of Mediaeval India from 647 A.D. to the Mughal Conquest*. Allahabad: Indian Press, 1925.

———. *The Life and Times of Humayun*. Calcutta: 1955.

Qabil Khan Afridi. *Literary Heritage of Khyber, Past and Present*. A UGC Research Project. University of Peshawar, April 25, 1998.

Rahmanalieva, P., and P. Vlasova, eds. *Tamirlan—Epokha, Lichnost, Deyniya* (Tamerlane—His Era, His Personality, and His Feats). Moscow: GURASH, 1992.

Rapson, E. J., et al. *The Cambridge History of India*. Vol. 4, *The Mughal Period*. Delhi: S. Chand, 1963.

Rashiduddin, Fazlullah. *Jami'u-Tawarikh*. Edited by Mohammad Roshan Mustafa Mousavi. 4 vols. Tehran: Alburz, 1994.

Roshan, Bayazid. *Khayr ul-Bayan*. Edited by Abdul Hay Habibi et al. Kabul: Kabul University Press, 1975.

Roshan, Bayazid, and Mohammad Ali Mukhlis Kandahari. *Hal-Nama*. Edited by Ali Mohammad Mukhlis Kandahari. Kabul: Ministry of Information and Culture, 2009. The first part of the book was written by Pir Roshan during his life, and it was completed by his disciple Mohammad Ali Mukhlis Kandahari Shinwari to include the life of his descendants in the seventeenth century.

Sarkar, Sir Jadunath. *Fall of the Mughal Empire*. 4 vols. 3rd ed. Bombay: Orient Longman, 1964.

———. *History of Aurangzeb*. Calcutta: Sang-e-Meel, 1925.

———. *A Short History of Aurangzeb, 1618–1707*. Calcutta: Oriental Longmans, 1979.

Sarwani, Abbas Khan. *Tarikh-i Sher Shahi* also known as *Tuhfata-yi Akbar Shahi*. Translated by E. C. Bayley and Sir H. M. Elliot. London: Packard Humanities Institute, n.d. PHI Persian Literature in Translation—The History of India. Vol. 4. packhum.org.

The Secret History of the Mongols. Adaptation by Paul Kahn. Boston: Cheng & Tsui, 1998.

Shah, Zahid. "Dogmas and Doctrines of the Roshanites and the Dispute of Pantheism." *Research Journal of South Asian Studies* 28, no. 1 (January–June 2013): 151–164.

———. "Religio-Political Movement in the Pashtun Belt—The Roshanites." *Journal of Political Studies* 18, no. 2 (2011): 119–132

Shami, Nizamuddin. *Zafarnama*. Persian text. Edited by Felix Tauer. Praha (Prague): Oriental Institute, 1937.

Spuler, Berthold. *The Muslim World*, Part 2, *The Mongol Period*. Translated by F. R. C. Bagley. Leiden: E. J. Brill, 1969.

Sverdrup, Carl Fredrik. *The Mongol Conquests: The Military Operation of Genghis Khan and Subbe'etei*. West Midland, UK: Helion, 2016.

Thomas, Edward. *The Chronicles of the Pathan Kings of Delhi*. London: Trubner, 1871.

Tuzuk-i Jahangiri (Memoirs of Jahangir). Delhi: Munshiram Manoharlal, 1968.

Walker, C. C. *Jenghiz Khan*. London: Luzac, 1939.

Weatherford, Jack. *Genghis Khan*. New York: Crown, 2004.

———. *The Secret History of the Mongol Queens*. New York: Broadway, 2010.

Wolseley, Haig, ed. *The Cambridge History of India*. Vol. 3, *Turks and Afghans*. Cambridge: Cambridge University Press, 1929.

Wood, John. *A Personal Narrative of a Journey to the Source of the River by the Route of the Indus, Kabul and Badakhshan*. London: Government of India, 1841.

Yaqut Hamawi, Abu Abdullah ar-Rumi. *Mu'jam al-buldan*. 6 vols. Edited by Ferdinand Wustenfeld. Leipzig, 1866–1873.

Yazdi, Sharafuddin Ali. *Zafarnama*. 2 vols. 1st ed. Edited by Mohammad 'Abbasi. Tehran: Amir Kabir Publisher, 1336/1957.

———. *Timur-nama*. MS. Library of Congress.

Yusuf Khass Hajib. *Wisdom of Royal Glory (Qutadghu Bilig): A Turko-Islamic Mirror for Princes*. Translated and with an introduction and notes by Robert Dankoff. Chicago and London: Chicago University Press, 1983.

The Emergence of Modern Afghanistan (1707–1809)

Abdul Karim Alavi. *Tarikh-i Ahmad*. Lucknow: Mustafai Press, 1850.

Adamac, Ludwig. *Dictionary of the Afghan Wars, Revolutions, and Insurgencies*. Lanham, MD: Scarecrow Press, 1996.

Afghani, Sayed Jamaluddin. *Tatmat ul-Bayan fi Tarikh al-Afghan*. Translated by Mohammad Amin Khogiani. Kabul: Government Press, 1839.

Ahmad Shah. *Diwan-i Ahmad Shah Abdali* (Collection of Ahmad Shah Abdali Pashto Poetry). Kabul: Government Press, 1963.

Akhlaqi, Mohammad Ishaq. *Hazara dar Jarayan-i Tarrikh*. Qom, Iran: Sharaye', 2001.

Allen, Rev. *Diary of a March Through Sinde and Afghanistan with the Troops under Command of General Sir William Nott*. London: J. Hatchard and Son, 1843.

Archeological Recollections. Vol. 4. Printed in Shiraz in 1959. Cited in Habibi, *Afghan and Afghanistan*.

Arjomand, Said Amir. *The Shadow of God and the Hidden Imam*. Chicago: University of Chicago Press, 1984.

———. *The Turban for the Crown*. Oxford: Oxford University Press, 1988.

Azad Bilgrami, Mir Ghulam Ali (1704–1786). *Khizanah-i-'Amirah*. Indian publication. Kabul: Kabul Public Library.

Bellew, H. W. *An Inquiry into the Ethnography of Afghanistan*. Karachi: Indus, 1977. Originally published in London in 1891.

Caroe, Sir Olaf. *The Pathans*. Oxford: Oxford University Press, 1958.

Colombari, Colonel. *Les Zemboureks—Artillerie de Campagne a Dromedaire*. Paris: Spectateur Militaire, 1853.

Cunningham, Joseph Davey. *A History of the Sikhs from the Origin of the Nation to the Battles of Sutlej.* 2nd ed. London: John Murray, 1853.

David, Alfred. *Indian Art of War.* Delhi: Atma Ram & Sons, 1953.

Dow, Alexander, Esq. *The History of Hindustan.* Vol. 2 (of 3). 3rd ed. London: John Murray, 1792.

Duff, James Grant. *A History of Mahrattas.* Vol. 2. 1826; Cambridge University Press, 2011.

Elphinstone, Mounstuart. *An Account of the Kingdom of Kabul and Its dependencies in Persia, Tartary and India.* London: Richard Bentley, 1842.

Faiz, Mohammad Kateb. *Nezhad-Namah-e Afghan* (Afghan Ethnography). Edited by Kazim Yazdani. Qom, Iran: Shahid, 1993.

———. *Seraj u-Tawarikh.* Vols. 1 and 2. Kabul: Government Press, 1911.

Ferrier, J. P. *Caravan Journeys and Wanderings in Persia, Afghanistan, Turkistan and Beloochistan.* Translated from an unpublished manuscript by William Jesse. London: John Murray, 1856.

———. *The History of the Afghans.* Translated into English by William Jesse. London: John Murray, 1858.

Floor, Willem. *The Afghan Occupation of Safavid Persia, 1721–1729.* Louvain: Peeters, 1998.

———. *Ashraf-i-Afghan bar Takhtgah-i-Isfahan* (Ashraf the Afghan on the Throne of Isfahan). Translated from English by Abul-Qasem Siri. Tehran: Tous, 1988. Based on Persian-based Dutch Trade Company's accounts.

Forster, George. *A Journey from Bengal to England through the North Part of India, Kashmir, Afghanistan and Persia and into Russia by the Caspian Sea.* Vol. 2. London: East India Company, 1798.

Gankovsky, U. V., ed. *Istoriya Vorozhoniekh Sil Afganistana 1747–1977* (The History of Armed Forces of Afghanistan, 1747–1977). Moscow: Oriental Studies Institute, 1985.

Hanway, Jonas. *An Historical Account of the British Trade over the Caspian Sea with a Journal of Travels from London through Russia into Russia.* London: 1753. Sold by Mr. Dodsley, in Pall-mall; Mr. Nourse, Mr. Millar, Mr. Vaillant, and Mr. Patterson, in the Stran; Mr. Waugh, in Lombard-Street; and Mr. Willock, in Cornhill.

Hazin, Shaykh Mohammad Ali. *Tarikh-i Ahwal wa Tazkerah-i Mawlana Mohammad Ali Hazin.* Edited by Abd-Jani Ardakani. Bombay: Shahabi Press, 1905.

The History of Revolution in Persia, Taken from the Memoirs of Father Krusinski. Vol. 2. Edited by Father Du Cerceau. London: 1729.

Imamuddin Husseini. *Tarikh-e Hussein Shahi.* MS. Afghanistan Academy of Sciences, 1798.

Jalali, Ali A. *Da Khoshal khan da 'Asr aw Chaperial Poudzi Tserana* (Military Study of Khoshal Khan Time and Strategic Environment). Kabul: Afghanistan Pen Association, 2011.

———. *A Military History of Afghanistan from the Great Game to the Global War on Terror.* Lawrence: University Press of Kansas, 2017.

———. *Mutale'a-i Tarikh-i Afghanistan az Negah-i Askari* (The Study of Afghanistan History from a Military Perspective). Vols. 1 and 2. Kabul: Military Press, 1964, 1967.

Jalali, G. Jailani, ed. *Nama-ye Ahmad Shah Baba Banam-e Sultan Mustafa Thales Os-*

mani (Ahmad Shah's Letter to the Ottoman Sultan Mustafa III). Kabul: Afghanistan History Society, 1967.

Kalkarani, Uday S. *Solstice at Panipat 14 January 1761*. Pune, India: Mula Mutba, 2011.

Kasi Raj Pundit. *An Account of the Last Battle of Panipat and of the Events Leading to It*. Translated by James Brown. Edited by George Rawlinson. London: Oxford University Press, 1926.

Krusinski, Tadeusz Jan. *The Chronicles of a Traveler or a History of the Afghan Wars with Persia in the Beginning of the Last Century from Their Commencement to the Accession of Sultan Ashraf*. Translated by into English by George Mitford, Esq. London: James Ridgway, 1840.

Lansdell, Henry. *Russian Central Asia Including Kuldja, Bokhara, Khiva and Merv*. Vol. 1. London: Sampson Low and Co., 1885.

Law de Lauriston, Jean. *A Memoir of the Mughal Empire, Events of 1757–1761*. Translated from the original French by G. S. Cheema. Delhi: Manohar Publishers, 2014.

Lee, Jonathan. *Afghanistan and the Battle for Balkh, 1731–1901*. Leiden: E. J. Brill, 1996.

Lockhart, Laurence. *Nader Shah: A Critical Study Based Mainly upon Contemporary Sources*. London: Luzac, 1938.

Mahmud al-Husseini al-Munshi. *Tarikh-iAhmad Shah*i (1753). Rotograph of the manuscript. 2 vols. Edited by Sayed Muradov. Moscow: Nauka Press, 1974.

Matthee, Rudi. *Persia in Crisis—Safavid Decline and the Fall of Isfahan*. New York: I. B. Tauris & Co. in association with the Iran Heritage Foundation, 2012.

Mehdi, Mirza. *Asterabadi, Durra-ye Nadera* (The Life of Nader Shah Afshar). Edited by Shahidi. Tehran: 1962.

———. *Jahangosha-e Naderi*. Edited by S. A. Anwar. Tehran: 1962.

Mohammad Kazim. *Namay-e Alamara-ye Naderi*. 2 vols. Rotograph of the manuscript by the Oriental Studies of the Russian Academy of Sciences.

Mohan, Lal. *Life of Amir Dost Mohammad Khan of Kabu*. Vol. 1. New Delhi: Asian Educational Services, 2004.

Mousavi, Sayed Askar. *The Hazaras of Afghanistan—An Historical, Economic and Political Study*. Translated into Persian by Assadullah Shefayee. Tehran: Naqsh-e-Simorgh, 2000.

Ralph, Magnus, and Eden Naby. *Afghanistan: Mullah, Marx, and Mujahid*. Boulder: Westview Press, 1998.

Raverty, Major H. C. G. *Ghaznin and Its Environs: Geographical, Ethnographical and Historical*. Edited by Ahmad Nabi Khan. Lahore: Sang-e-Meel, 1995.

Razi Hamadani, Abdullah. *Comprehensive History of Iran,* 4th ed. Iqbal Publisher, 1347/ 1968.

Rostam-ul-Hokama. *Rustam-u-Tawarikh*. Edited by Mohammad Moshiri. Tehran: Sherkat-e-Sahami Kitab ha-i-Jibi, 1965.

Rudy, Matthee. *Persia in Crisis: Safavids Decline and the Fall of Isfahan*. London: I. B. Tauris, 2012.

Sardesai, G. S. *Selections of the Peshwa dater* (accounts), cited in Kulkarni, *Solstice at Panipat 14 January 1761*.

Sayed Nuruddin Hussein. *An Account of Najib ud-Daulah*. Translated from Persian to English and edited by S. H. Abdul Rashid. Aligarh, India: Aligarh University, August 1932.

Singh, Ganda. *Ahmad Shah Durrani: Father of Modern Afghanistan*. London: Asia Publishing House, 1959.

Smith, Vincent A. *The Oxford History of India from the Earliest Times to the End of 1911*. Oxford: Oxford University Press, 1919.

Sykes, Sir Percy. *A History of Afghanistan*. New Delhi: Munshiram Manoharlal, 2002.

———. *A History of Persia*. London: Macmillan, 1915.

Verma, Abhhas. *The Third Battle of Panipat*. India: Baharatia Prakashan Publisher, 2018.

Verma, P. N. *Maratha and Panipat*. Edited by Heri Ram Gupta. Chandigarh: Punjab University, 1961.

Vishwas, Patil. *Panipat*. Translated from Marathi by Nadeem Khan. First published in Marathi in 1988. English edition, India: Eka Publisher, 2019.

Index

Abagan, 17
Abaqa Khan, 207
Abbas, 122
Abbas II, Shah, 264–265
Abbasid Caliphate, 98, 119, 127, 133, 135, 139; campaign against, 124; dissolution of, 145
Abbasid Empire, 121, 144
Abbasid Revolution, 122, 123
Abbasids, 119, 122, 123, 124
Abbas Khan Sarwani, 347n5
Abbas Quli Khan, 272
Abbas Safavi, Shah, 264, 267, 268
Abbas Sarwani, 240–241
Abbassa, 125
Abdalis, 16, 266, 272, 287, 290, 291, 292, 298, 299, 307, 312, 313, 319, 324; Herat and, 274; uprising of, 268, 274
Abdul Jabar 'Utbi, 144–145
Abdullah ibn Khazim, 113
Abdullah Khan, 263, 274
Abdullah Khan II, 262
Abdul Latif, 230
Abdul Malik, Amir, 107, 142, 143
Abdul Qader, attack by, 254
Abdur Rahman ibn Sumra, 106, 107, 108
Abdur Rahman ibn Ziyad, 121, 122
Abhisara kingdom, 77
Abi Khalid, 126
Abiward, 129
Abu Bakr, *Rashidun* army and, 101
Abu Bakr Lawik, 143
Abu Hanifa, 129
Abul Abbas Abdullah, 122
Abul Fazl-i-'Allami, 10, 261
Abul-Khayr, 233
Abul-Khayr Khan Shaybani, 233

Abu-Muslim, 122, 123–124, 133
Abu Rayhan al-Biruni, 17
Abu Sa'id, 207, 208–209, 230, 231
Abu-Salama, 133
Achaemenid army, 6, 32, 33, 36, 78
Achaemenid Empire, 29, 30, 55, 44, 89
Achaemenid period, 29, 31, 34, 92
Achaemenids, 2, 9, 27, 28, 29, 32, 78, 87, 149, 335n5
'Adil Shah, 250, 289
Afghan army, 249, 275–277, 280, 281, 297–302, 308–309, 312, 316; development of, 297, 298–299; elite forces of, 318; exploits of, 303; lifestyle of, 276; Ottomans and, 285; Panipat and, 293; strength of, 283
Afghan camp, 280, 282, 310, 319; locations of, 311 (map)
Afghan Empire, 3, 18, 236, 238, 326
Afghanistan: boundaries for, 18; as geographic name, 17–18; map of, 10, 186; naming of, 18
Afghans, 17, 148, 154, 162, 170, 238, 250, 251, 305, 317; counterattack by, 246–249; defense by, 325; Persians and, 277
Afghan tribes, 224, 238, 257, 292, 295; anti-Mughal movements in, 251–254; Mughal Empire and, 243–246
Afridis, 254, 257, 258, 302, 349n45
Afsharid Empire, 289, 294, 296
Afzal Khan, 262
Aghar Khan, 259
Agra, 244, 247, 250
Agrianians, 38, 67, 69, 70, 75, 334n73
Ahdad, 254
Ahmad, Sultan, 225, 231, 264
Ahmad ibn Ismail, 137, 138, 140, 146
Ahmad Inaltigin, 146

367